THE GUINNESS BOOK OF
WEATHER FACTS AND FEATS

THE GUINNESS BOOK OF WEATHER FACTS & FEATS

Ingrid Holford

SECOND EDITION

Editor: Beatrice Frei
Design and layout: Jean Whitcombe
Artwork: Eddie Botchway, Diana Davies, Peter Milne and Keith Shone

Published in Great Britain by Guinness Superlatives Ltd,
2 Cecil Court, London Road, Enfield, Middlesex

Composition in Photina by Filmtype Services Limited,
Scarborough, North Yorkshire
Printed and bound in Singapore by Times Printers
Sdn. Bhd.

British Library Cataloguing in Publication Data
Holford, Ingrid
Guinness book of weather facts and feats.—
2nd ed.
1. Meteorology
I. Title
551.5 QC861.2

ISBN 0—85112—243—4

Title page picture: Orographic cloud on Mt Sefton, New Zealand, as the light wind ascends the ice face. (M.J. Hammersley)

GUINNESS SUPERLATIVES LIMITED
2 Cecil Court, London Road, Enfield, Middlesex

Contents

ACKNOWLEDGEMENTS

This book could not have been written without the co-operation of weather enthusiasts all over the world.

I should like to thank the many professional bodies in Britain whose members have spared valuable time to provide me with information.

The UK Meteorological Office, at Bracknell, Easthampstead, London, and Southampton, as well as the Radar Research Laboratory at Malvern and the weather station at Braemar. The staff of the National Meteorological Library at Bracknell have been tireless in helping me find references and statistics.

The European Centre for Medium Range Weather Forecasts at Shinfield, The National Maritime Institute at Feltham, and the Institute of Oceanographic Sciences at Wormley.

Staff at the maritime and meteorological departments at the University of Edinburgh, Heriot-Watt University at Edinburgh, the University of Dundee, the University of Wales at Cardiff, and Plymouth Polytechnic have been most helpful.

In the United States, several branches of the National Oceanographic and Atmospheric Administration (NOAA) have contributed information:

The Hurricane Center at Coral Gables, the Flood Information Center at Silver Spring and the Environment Data Service at Asheville. I also gratefully acknowledge documents from scientists at Texas Technical University at Lubbock and the State University of New York at Albany, as well as from the National Aeronautics and Space Administration (NASA) and the National Science Foundation, both in Washington.

Members of the Commonwealth Scientific and Industrial Research Organisation (CSIRO) in Australia, the Canadian Climate Centre, and the European Space Agency in West Germany, have also given me assistance.

Photographers all over the world have contributed to this book and are acknowledged individually. The diagrams have been drawn by E. Botchway, D. Davies, P. Milne, K. Shone and S. Burt and I thank them all for interpreting my ideas so well. R. Tyssen-Gee kindly searched my script for technical errors.

My thanks also to Jean Whitcombe for the attractive design of this book.

My particular gratitude goes to authors, too numerous to mention, who have contributed to my fund of knowledge over many years through *Weather*, *Weatherwise* and the *Journal of Meteorology*. I should like to thank them all, through their Editors, and some of the more specialised articles are listed in the bibliography.

The difficulties in writing this book have been considerable, and I owe a great deal to Colin Smith and Beatrice Frei of Guinness Superlatives Ltd for their unfailing help and advice, and for guiding my script through to publication.

Introduction

Weather rules our lives and has accordingly interested people throughout history. Our ancestors described their experiences with the weather, and after instruments were invented they kept meticulous diaries with measurements of pressure, temperature and wind. Their efforts were the foundation upon which scientists later built.

Today, meteorology is so full of difficult concepts that there may seem to be no room left for contributions from the amateur. Nothing could be further from the truth. Details of unusual occurrences are still invaluable to the meteorologist, and a basic understanding of weather is essential to the recipient of a forecast in order to interpret it to advantage. *The Guinness Book of Weather Facts and Feats* is written for everyone who has an interest in the weather.

This new edition contains up-dated records and further examples of weather which overstep average conditions, called climate, in which we live. There is a new selection of photographs and some revised diagrams. The topics of Weather Charts, as well as Wind on Sea and Sand, have been allotted separate chapters and the new subject of Microclimate has been introduced. The text has also been re-written and re-arranged in order to improve clarity and continuity.

The premier units for measuring temperature and wind remain Fahrenheit and miles per hour, because most English speaking people still think in these terms. Celsius and metric conversions are added. However, we have taken advice on the need for a separate nomenclature for intervals of temperature, to avoid confusion about the two different formulae used in converting from one scale to another. Temperatures are written according to international convention, °F and °C, but intervals of temperature are designated F degrees and C degrees. A full explanation is given at the end of chapter 3.

1. The radiating sun

Weather is the state of the atmosphere at a particular place and moment. It can be described precisely in terms of cloud type and amount, wind speed and direction, precipitation, air temperature, atmospheric pressure and visibility.

Climate is the average weather condition of a particular part of the world. It can be described broadly in terms of seasonal mean temperatures, mean rainfall, mean wind speeds and directions and mean cloud amounts. At any one time the weather may be very different from the normal given by climatic description.

Nicholas Copernicus. (Mary Evans Picture Library)

The function of weather is to balance, throughout Earth's atmosphere, the heat which is bestowed by the Sun.

The Sun has been revered throughout history as the source of light, warmth and life itself, and has brought about the most complex mythologies. Until rational explanations evolved the Sun was usually personified as a god, whose routine appearances and disappearances were foibles of his personality. Some of the better known names for the Sun god were *Helios* (Greek), *Sol* (Roman), *Mithras* (Iranian), *Shamash* (Assyrian), *Surya* (Indian), and *Tezcatlipoca* (Mexican).

However, there were races which symbolised and worshipped objects instead; the Egyptian reverence of the scarab beetle was probably an allusion to the way the god *Ra* rolled the Sun around the sky in the same way as the beetle rolls its ball of dung ahead of itself. Even the orientation of Christian churches according to the position of the Sun is a remnant of sunworship.

Preoccupation with the Sun and its benefits led to extraordinarily accurate observations of its behaviour long before scientific explanations evolved. All over the world apparently useless megaliths turn out to be accurate instruments for measuring the time of year according to the position of the Sun.

Claudius Ptolemaeus, said to have been born in Ptolemais Hermii, Egypt, was a Greek astronomer at Alexandria between AD 127 and AD 151. He was the first to propound an explanation of observed facts about the Sun. Ptolemy, as he became known, thought the Earth was stationary and that the Sun, Moon and planets revolved around it. On this basic assumption, astronomers of succeeding centuries built an elaborate concept of the paths of the heavenly bodies, a theory in fundamental sympathy with Christian belief in God's preoccupation with man and Earth.

Nicholas Copernicus (1473–1543), was born in Prussia, studied medicine at Padua, Italy, became doctor of canon law at Ferrara in 1503 and then devoted himself to astronomy. He was the first to dare to contradict Ptolemy's theory and thought the Earth and planets revolved round the Sun—a revolutionary idea which was considered subversive and banned by the Church. However, scientists such as the Danish astronomer Tycho Brahe (1546–1601), the German astronomer Johann Kepler (1571–1630) and the Italian astronomer and physicist Galileo Galilei (1564–1642) defied disapproval and even persecution, to develop the Copernican theory and lay down the principles of modern astronomy.

The Sun is a radiant globe composed mainly of gases which whirl in a vortex around an axis. It has a mean diameter of 865 000 miles (1 392 000 km) and provides a luminosity of 3×10^{27} candlepower.

The Earth traces an elliptical path round the Sun, so the distance between the two varies, but is on average 93 million miles (150 million km).

Sun spots are flaring vortices, seen as dark spots, on the face of the Sun. They vary in frequency over approximately eleven-year cycles. Periods of great sunspot activity are accompanied by magnetic disturbances which disrupt radio communications on Earth. Meteorologists are investigating a possible connection between weather cycles and sunspot activity.

The Perihelion is that position in the Earth's orbit at which it is nearest to the Sun, 91·4 million miles (147·1 million km) occurring in early January.

The Aphelion is the occasion when the Earth is furthest from the Sun, 94·5 million miles (152·1 million km), in early July.

Seasons exist because the Earth's axis is tilted at 66½° to the plane in which it travels round the Sun, and each hemisphere alternately leans towards or away from the Sun.

Day and night occur because the Earth rotates about its own axis once in 24 hours, and everywhere alternately faces and turns away from the Sun. However, the relative movement between Sun and Earth does not always take exactly 24 hours, and for the purposes of consistent timekeeping a theoretical Mean Sun has been invented.

The Mean Sun is a fictitious sun which moves uniformly along the path of the true Sun so that each day and night measures exactly 24 hours.

Greenwich Mean Time is the time measured according to the Mean Sun on the 0° longitude through Greenwich, London. To simplify time schedules, world clock times remain the same within each 15° belt of longitude. Time is one hour later each 15° longitude eastward of the Greenwich meridian, and one hour earlier each 15° longitude westward of Greenwich. The date changes on the 180° meridian, which passes almost entirely over uninhabited Pacific Ocean. Greenwich Mean Time was adopted throughout the whole British Isles in 1880.

Day glow, or day sky, are terms for the very pale glow in the sky which lingers after sunset, indicating that 'just round the corner' the atmosphere is still fully illuminated by the Sun. One of the first people to draw attention to this was Erasmus Darwin (1731–1802) grandfather of Charles Darwin. Erasmus was a country doctor and keen weather observer, and his frequent journeys outdoors at night, in an era when there was little street lighting to confuse the eye, enabled him to detect day glow. The duration of day glow varies with latitude. Jersey, in the Channel Isles, experiences a pale light in the sky towards the north west for a few hours between May and August. The Shetland Isles, however, have a semblance of almost continual day between 26 April and 22 August, which the inhabitants call 'simmer dim' (*simmer* being a Scottish form of the word summer). In suitable weather there is enough light at midnight on 21 June to take a photograph.

Equinox means equality of day and night and happens when the Sun is vertical over the Equator, on 21 March and 22 September. After the first occasion, the southern hemisphere starts to tilt away from the Sun and the South Pole experiences twilight followed by 180 continuous days of darkness. After 22 September, the northern hemisphere tilts away from the Sun, and it is the turn of the North Pole to begin its long half-year of night.

Solstices are the two occasions, occurring about 21 June and 21 December, when the Earth's equator is

Right: Daylight spreading across the Atlantic, 0950 GMT on 17 February 1978. Only the tops of the highest clouds over the Atlantic are discernible on this picture, taken on visible wave length. Compare with the identical view in Chapter 2, taken on infra-red wave length, when the whole Atlantic cloud system is discernible despite darkness. (University of Dundee)

furthest from the Sun, so that there is maximum or minimum daylight in the two hemispheres. The Sun then appears to be stationary while the Earth swings back again into the opposite side of its elliptical track.

The Tropics of Cancer and Capricorn, 23° 27′ north and south of the equator respectively, encompass the only regions of the Earth on which the Sun shines directly overhead at some time of the year.

A sun-dial measures the time of day by the position on a graduated surface of a shadow cast by the Sun behind a projecting rod or obstruction. The most popular variety for gardens consists of a horizontal flat plate with an inclined arm set in the centre, but curved or angled dials have been used throughout history.

Rays of sunshine, passing through a solid glass sphere, or sphere containing water, bend and focus to a point. Athanasius Kircher, professor of mathematics and Hebrew in Rome, first suggested in 1646 that this concentration of rays might be used to burn a mark on wood or paper and record the duration of sunshine.

The Campbell Stokes sunshine recorder is a practical adaptation of Kircher's idea and is attributed to two men. In 1853 John Francis Campbell (1821–85), better known as 'Campbell of Islay' and a collector of Gaelic ballads, mounted a spherical bowl of water in

Campbell Stokes sunshine recorder. A paper chart fixes into the curved back plate. (Casella, London)

Left: Sundial on a house wall at Salisbury, Wiltshire. (R. G. Holford)

Right: A sunshine recorder, proposed by Athanasius Kircher in 1646. In addition to a visible scorch mark inside the bowl, he suggested fuses in the small holes around the side of the bowl, which would give a sound signal at each hour. (Photo. Science Museum, London)

a round wooden frame and placed it where it received unimpeded sunlight. The Sun's rays penetrated the bowl which was left in place for 6 months at a stretch and focused on the wood, making a scorch trace, thus measuring the length of time that the surface received sunshine. In 1875 Campbell started to place paper behind the bowl in order to get a daily record of sunshine. A year later, the Irish physicist Sir George Stokes (1819–1903), improved the instrument by using a solid glass sphere and supporting it between clamps on a curved metal mounting, holding a paper chart. Kew Observatory was one of the first to be equipped with the instrument in 1880 where sunshine records were maintained for 100 years, until closure in 1980.

The sunniest place in the world is the eastern Sahara desert with a mean annual sunshine of 4300 hours, 97 per cent of the possible total.

Seaside resorts usually have more sunshine than places inland, where convection clouds develop more readily. In the British Isles, all monthly sunshine records have been registered along the southern coasts.

Cloud obscures sunshine, in the British Isles frequently but intermittently. No sunshine was recorded at

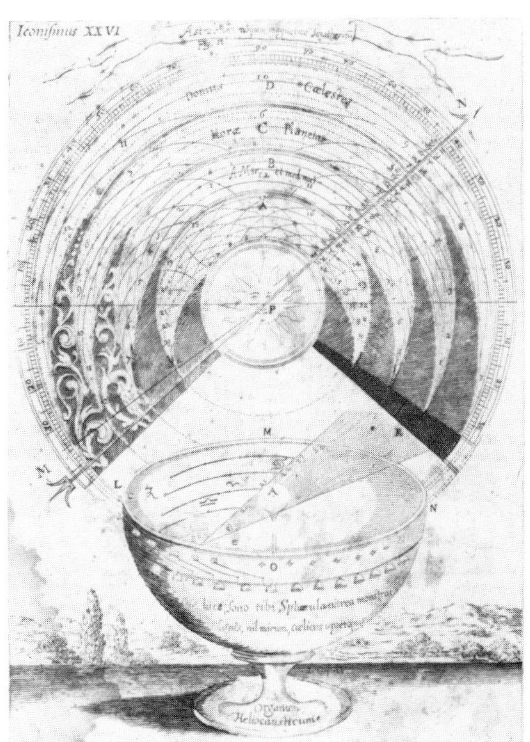

Westminster, London during the whole of December 1890. Neither was sunshine reported from any of 50 reporting stations in Great Britain on 10 January 1965. Again, no sunshine was recorded at Kew, London on 17–21 June 1977, the longest sunless spell for June since records started there in 1881. In 1981, the first seven months were the dullest in London since 1937; but the first eight months were the sunniest in Aberdeen since 1955.

Mountains may block sunshine at certain regular times of the year. Lochranza, a village on the Isle of Arran, off the west coast of Scotland, stretches for $1\frac{1}{4}$ miles (2 km) along a NW-SE axis, and has three hills rising steeply between 750 ft and 1600 ft high (229 m–488 m). These block the sight of the Sun from the landward part of the village between 18 November and 8 February each year.

Volcanic ash obscures the Sun during an eruption and dims it afterwards, for a period depending upon the winds prevailing at the time.

Tiny particles from the eruption of Krakatoa, East Indies, in 1883 remained in the atmosphere for two years and resulted in widespread brilliant sunsets in the following six months.

Mt St Helens, Washington State, USA, erupted on 18 May 1980, and strong upper winds carried the ash eastwards across the country in about three days. Ash above 30 000 ft (9 km) circled the Earth in 17 days. The subsequent summer in the USA was very hot.

The volcano Tambora in Indonesia erupted in 1815 and ejected 80 times as much ash and pumice as did Mt St Helens in 1980. Many countries had cold summers in the following year and this was blamed upon the eruption. So far there is no proven connection between the very slight fall in temperature caused by ash in the atmosphere and weather.

The Sun provides heat, and it used to be thought that the atmosphere must get warmer further from the Earth and therefore nearer the Sun. Galileo was the first person to realise that the opposite might be the case. He wrote in 1640 to Prince Leopold of Tuscany that he thought the Sun's rays were only transformed into heat when they encountered obstructions to their passage, and so it has been proved. In general, the atmosphere is warmer near the Earth than at higher altitudes.

The Sun's energy is transmitted by electro-magnetic waves of various wave-lengths. Approximately 12 per cent are short-wave ultra-violet rays, 37 per cent are visible light rays and the remaining 51 per cent are still longer infra-red rays. About 40 per cent of all this radiation is reflected by the atmosphere surrounding the Earth, without benefit to man, 15 per cent is absorbed directly by the atmosphere en route to Earth and the remaining 45 per cent reaches the lower levels in which weather forms. There, the rays may be further reflected or absorbed by cloud or smoke, or they may reach the Earth unimpeded. At the surface, absorbed energy is converted to heat, and reflected energy imparts colour to the reflecting body.

The albedo of any substance is its ability to reflect the Sun's radiation. This is usually expressed as a percentage as follows:

Forests and wet earth	5–10%
Rock and dry earth	10–25%
Sand and grass	20–30%
Clouds	50–65%
Old snow	55%
New snow	80%

A water surface acts like a mirror when the Sun's rays strike it obliquely and it may reflect as much as 70 per cent of radiant energy. When the Sun is high, as little as five per cent of the energy may be reflected, the rest being absorbed.

Approximate hours of daylight, sunrise to sunset, at different latitudes on the solstice dates

Latitude°	Place (*Northern Hemisphere*)	21 June (N) / 21 December (S)	21 December (N) / 21 June (S)	Place (*Southern Hemisphere*)
70	Jan Mayen I., N. Atlantic	24	nil	Cape Adare, Antarctica
65	Murmansk, USSR	22½	3½	Hope Bay, Falkland Islands
60	Bergen, Norway Shetland Is, Scotland	18¾	5¼	Elephant I., S. Atlantic
55	Newcastle-upon-Tyne, England Smolensk, USSR	17¼	7¼	Cape Horn, Chile
50	Land's End, England Winnipeg, Canada	16¼	8	Santa Cruz, Argentina
45	Ottawa, Canada Bordeaux, France	15¾	8¾	Queenstown, New Zealand
40	Madrid, Spain Peking, China	15	9¼	Bahia Blanca, Argentina Wanganui, New Zealand
35	Memphis, USA Nicosia, Cyprus	14½	9¾	Sydney, Australia Montevideo, Uruguay
30	New Orleans, USA Cairo, Egypt	14	10¼	Durban, S. Africa Kalgoorlie, W. Australia
20	Bombay, India Mexico City, Mexico	13¼	10¾	Bulawayo, Zimbabwe Hilo, Hawaii
10	Saigon, S. Vietnam Panama Canal, Panama	12¾	11½	Port Moresby, Papua New Guinea Lima, Peru
0	Singapore, Malaysia	12	12	Quito, Ecuador

The setting Sun, whose radiation is the basic cause of weather in Earth's atmosphere. (M. J. Hammersley)

People walking over a clean snow surface absorb radiant energy from the Sun and also reflected rays from the snow. Hence skin can get sunburnt even though snow itself absorbs too little energy to cause melting.

The amount of reflection from the colour bands of the light spectrum varies according to the substance. Those which reflect all the colours appear white, those which reflect one or several colours acquire the colour of the light reflected, and substances which absorb all the visible rays appear black.

Smooth substances reflect more radiant energy than rough ones, which trap the energy between adjacent faces of the uneven contours. A polished metal surface can reflect 94 per cent of radiant energy falling upon it.

A black body is a term used to describe a surface which absorbs all radiant energy falling upon it. A perfect black body exists in theory only, since everything reflects some energy, but a surface coated with lampblack may absorb as much as 97 per cent.

Absorbed rays are converted to heat and raise the temperature of a substance according to its composition. A given mass of water requires more heat than the same mass of rock to raise its temperature by the same amount. Moreover, the Sun's rays penetrate to a considerable depth in clear water, spreading the heat throughout. Hence large stretches of water heat up only imperceptibly from one day to another, reaching maximum temperature in late summer.

Soil, which is made up of tiny rock particles, heats quickly in the sunshine. When soil is, dry, the insulating air pockets prevent heat being conducted downwards. The heat is all used to raise the temperature of the surface. When soil is wet, heat is conducted more easily downward and the temperature of the surface does not rise in such a disproportionate way.

Glass is almost transparent to the Sun's rays. Consequently, the material itself does not warm much in the sunshine, but anything enclosed by glass does.

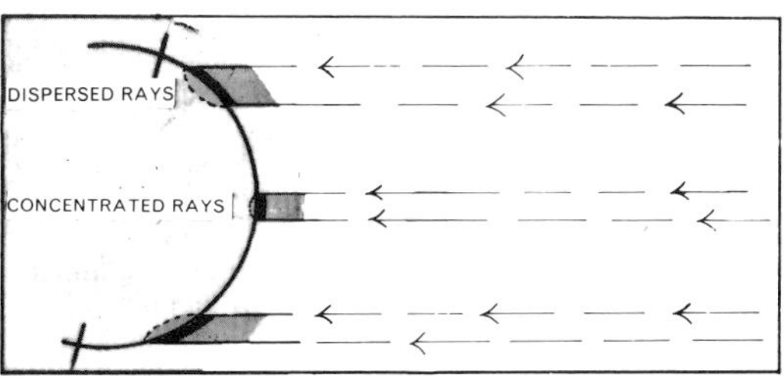

Right: Radiant energy, reaching unit area of the Earth's surface, is greatest at the Equator when the Sun is overhead, and least at the Poles when the Sun just skirts the horizon. (Diana Davies)

Concentration of radiant energy reaching a unit area of the Earth's surface is greatest at the equator when the Sun is vertically overhead and the radiant waves travel through the smallest depth of atmosphere. Radiant energy over a unit area is least at the poles when the Sun just skirts the horizon, and the rays travel obliquely through a long distance of atmosphere, to spread out over a large surface area on arrival.

Some small increase in heat can be engineered by presenting a sloping surface to a low altitude Sun so that the rays impinge more nearly to the perpendicular. South facing terraced vineyards in mountainous areas of Europe or south facing slopes of the Jersey potato fields therefore make the most of available sunshine.

Distribution of absorbed heat is achieved in three ways:

CONDUCTION through a material, and then on to any other material with which it is in contact. Heat always moves from the warmer surface to the colder.

Air is a poor conductor of heat, water a good one. Hence heat acquired by the top layer of dry sand or soil is conducted very slowly downwards because of the insulating air pockets between the particles. Wet soil, however, conducts heat much more quickly from the surface downwards.

RE-RADIATION (on long wave-length) to anything nearby which is colder. A person sitting on a sunny terrace, for instance, receives direct radiation from the Sun and also re-radiation from the terrace.

Once the Sun sets, the Earth cannot benefit from incoming radiation from that source. The Earth itself and everything upon it become the only effective radiators of heat. When there is no cloud cover to trap the Earth's long-wave emissions of energy then all temperatures fall considerably. Cloud, however, acts like a protective blanket, reflecting back again much of the radiant energy from the ground and preventing excessive falls in temperature.

CONVECTION A heat distribution method only available to fluids such as air and water. Air in immediate contact with a surface warmer than itself warms by conduction. This causes it to become less dense so that it acquires buoyancy and rises. Colder air from above or alongside moves in to take its place and after warming on the heating agent, rises in turn. Thus an air circulation forms, either in the horizontal plane or in the vertical but always with

Right: Kew Observatory, London, built for George III in order to make observations of the transit of Venus on 3 June 1769. Meteorological observations started in 1773 and after 1842 the Observatory concentrated entirely upon meteorological and geophysical affairs. It was closed down in 1980. (P. Defries)

Summer sunshine in United Kingdom for the record year 1976 and three subsequent years

	Percentage of mean hours of sunshine, June–August			
District	1976	1977	1978	1979
N. Scotland	123	112	76	78
E. Scotland	130	118	93	98
E. and N.E. England	149	91	78	101
East Anglia	142	81	80	91
Midlands	140	91	86	95
S.E. and Central S. England	141	82	86	89
W. Scotland	128	132	88	87
N.W. England and N. Wales	133	107	81	92
S.W. England and S. Wales	131	93	88	94
N. Ireland	125	123	77	85

A century of sunshine at Kew Observatory

Month	*Mean monthly sunshine* hours	% of possible	*Sunniest* hours	year	*Dullest* hours	year
Jan	48	19	82	1952	15	1885
Feb	61	24	110	1970	19	1947
Mar	110	32	183	1907	57	1888[1]
Apr	151	39	239	1909	79	1920
May	201	44	315	1909	114	1932[2]
June	205	44	302	1975	105	1909
July	198	42	334	1911	103	1888
Aug	186	44	279	1947	109	1912
Sept	145	41	224	1911	64	1945
Oct	99	33	159	1959	51	1894
Nov	56	23	103	1971	22	1897
Dec	40	19	72	1886	0	1890
Year	1 496	36	1 852	1959	1 129	1888

[1] *March 1981 dullest in London since records began, with 58 per cent of mean sunshine.*

[2] *10–16 May 1980, sunshine at Kew 97 hours, 90 per cent of possible, and more than twice the mean for that week.*

D. J. Hatch, *Journal of Meteorology*, Apr 1981

heavier and colder air replacing lighter warm air. In this manner warmth circulates in a centrally heated room, warm air gradually spreads to the shady parts of a garden and the major winds of the world circulate warmth from one place to another.

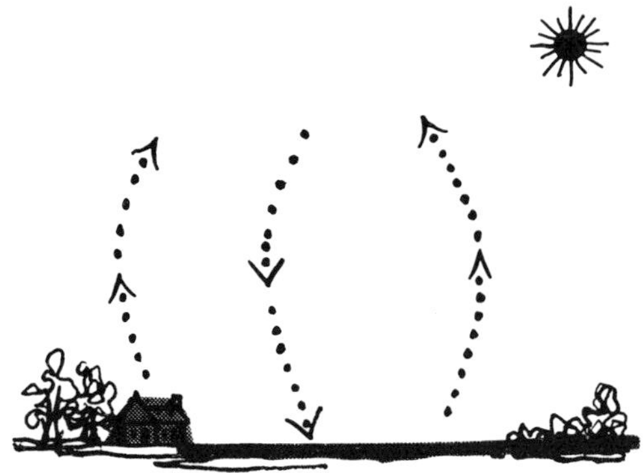

Convection of air over a warming surface. (Diana Davies)

Water uses upside-down-convection to distribute heat within itself. As soon as the top layer of water cools because of re-radiation it becomes heavier than the warmer water below and sinks beneath it. That warmer water then cools in turn and sinks in consequence. The important result as far as weather formation is concerned, is that a river, lake or sea surface cools only very slowly during any one night and only appreciably by the end of winter. It is often warmer than adjacent land during the winter even though it it usually colder than the same land in summer.

Glass is peculiar because it is transparent to short-wave radiation from the Sun, but it is only partly transparent to the long wave re-radiation from substances heated under glass.

The Greenhouse Effect is the name given to the accumulation of heat under closed glass on a sunny day. More short-wave energy passes through the glass than can pass out again when re-radiated as long-wave energy.

Carbon dioxide creates a Greenhouse Effect in the same way as glass. Small quantities of this gas are always present in our atmosphere, which is therefore warmer than it would be if the Earth re-radiated heat as efficiently as it receives it from the Sun. The increased use of fossil fuels and consequent growth of carbon dioxide in the atmosphere is one reason advanced for a possible future warming of the Earth's climate.

Venus has an atmosphere almost entirely composed of carbon dioxide. The Greenhouse Effect causes temperature near the ground to be around 900°F (482°C), high enough to melt lead and twice as hot as the hottest kitchen oven.

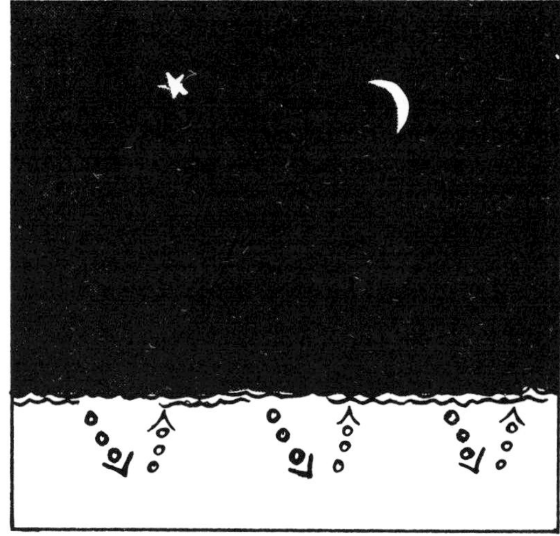

Upside-down convection below a cooling water surface. (Diana Davies)

2. The invention of thermometers

A thermometer measures the temperature of any substance, and this is determined by the internal energy of the molecules; the faster these move the hotter is the substance. Temperature is a difficult abstract concept, but is a familiar and practical measurement nowadays because of the ubiquitous thermometer. It is hard to appreciate the problems of scientists without thermometers who could only measure in terms of comparative warmth, ie—*this* feels hotter than *that*.

By the end of the 16th century scientists knew from observation that substances such as metal, expand when heated and contract when cooled. The search commenced for substances which had a constant temperature under normal conditions, and which could be used as standards for measuring the temperature of other materials.

Philo of Byzantium, physicist and philosopher living in the 2nd century BC, was probably the first person to prove that air expands on heating. He inserted a bent tube into the top of a hollow leaden globe and dipped the open end of the tube into a flask of water. Then he set the apparatus in the Sun. As the air in the lead flask warmed, bubbles were seen coming from the tube and escaping upwards, through the water in the flask. Philo concluded that the air must have expanded on warming. Then he took the apparatus into the shade so that the lead globe cooled, and he noticed that the level of the water in the open flask fell. He deduced that the water must have risen in the tube because of shrinkage of the inside air caused by cooling. Little development of the idea took place for 1500 years.

Galileo Galilei (1564–1642), Italian physicist and astronomer, made a similar instrument in 1593, when trying to measure the temperature of air, calling it a **thermoscope**. It was a tube with a bulb at one end but open at the other, and therefore contained air. Galileo warmed the bulb by holding it in his hand

Galileo Galilei 1564–1642. (Negretti and Zambra Ltd)

and then inverted the tube in a container of coloured water. As the air in the tube cooled again the coloured water moved up the small bore tube for a distance proportional to the amount of cooling. This thermoscope had no scale and its limitation was that it took no account of atmospheric pressure acting on the water in the open container.

Francesco Sagredo, Italian scientist, corresponded with Galileo on the subject of temperature and mentioned his experiments which indicated that a mixture of snow and salt is colder than snow alone.

Santorio Santorio (1561–1636), another contemporary of Galileo and physician at the University of Padua, was particularly interested in body temperature as an indication of fever. He was the first to

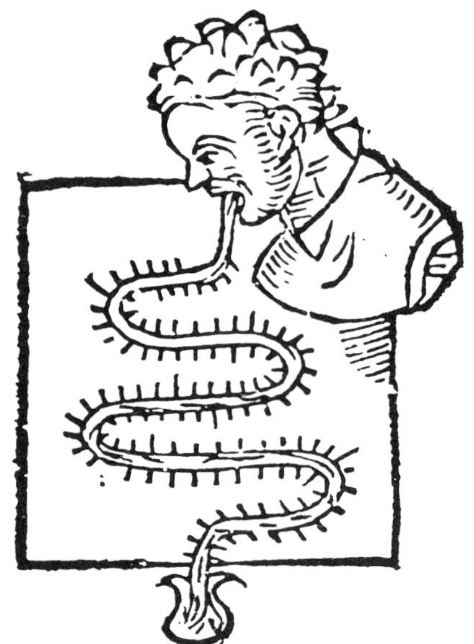

Design for a clinical thermoscope by Santorio Santorio in 1612. The tube contained liquid and air and was graduated with glass beads. The closed tube was held in the mouth and temperature was registered by the distance that the expanding air pushed the liquid down into the open vessel.

appreciate that there is a 'normal' temperature of good health. He made a scale for the thermoscope by dividing into degrees the range between the temperature of snow and the heat of a candle flame.

The first liquid expansion thermometer was made by the French physician Jean Rey in 1631. He filled with water a small round flask with a long slender neck and placed it in the hands of fevered patients. As the water warmed it climbed up the neck of the flask. The upper end of the tube was open to the atmosphere, hence it was not very accurate.

The first sealed thermometer, known as the Florentine thermometer, was made by Ferdinand II, Grand Duke of Tuscany, in 1641. He used alcohol, which we now know has a freezing point of -175°F (-115°C), well below normal air temperature, and he sealed the tip of the glass tube so as to exclude the influence of atmospheric pressure. His scale was divided between the temperature of snow in deepest winter and the blood temperature of animals. Alcohol, however, was discovered to boil at a temperature below that at which water boiled, which made the liquid unsuitable for general use in thermometers.

Mercury thermometers were introduced in 1657 by the Academia del Cimento at Florence. Mercury is a silver-white liquid metal which is a good conductor of heat and therefore expands and contracts quickly when warmed or cooled. (It freezes at -39°F (-38°C) and boils at 673°F (357°C), which is well above the upper limit of air temperature.) There were initial problems with mercury which tended to cling to the side of the glass but, nevertheless, mercury thermometers gained in popularity throughout Europe.

Robert Boyle (1627–91), Irish chemist and natural philosopher, visited Florence and studied the work of Galileo. In 1664 he conducted experiments with

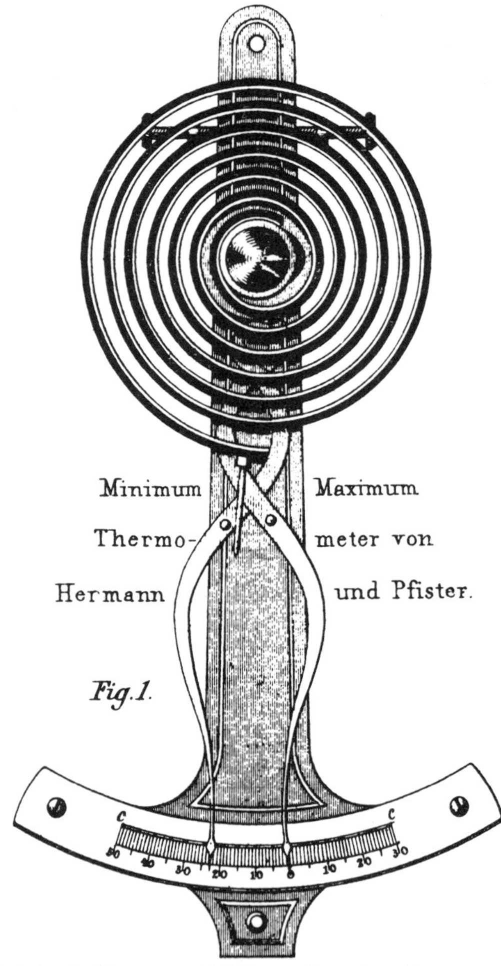

Design by Herman and Pfister, 19th century, for a maximum and minimum thermometer, using differential expansion in a bi-metallic coil.

thermometers at the request of the Royal Society founded four years earlier. He suggested using the freezing point of oil of aniseed as the lower fixed point of the thermometer scale, because he realised there was something not quite consistent about the freezing point of water (See Chapter 9). The first thermometer of English origin based on the expansion of alcohol in a hermetically sealed glass tube was made under Boyle's direction.

Robert Hooke (1635–1703), English physicist and associate of Boyle, developed a thermometer scale in 1665 which used the temperature of freezing water as zero.

Carlo Renaldini of Pisa suggested in 1694 that the upper fixed point of the thermometer scale should be the boiling point of water and the lower fixed point should be the melting point of ice, the whole scale to be divided into twelve degrees.

Sir Isaac Newton (1642–1727), English scientist and mathematician, also favoured the division of the temperature scale into twelve units, and suggested that the lower point be the temperature of freezing salt water and the upper fixed point be the temperature of the normal healthy human body.

Gabriel Daniel Fahrenheit (1686–1736), German physicist who settled in Holland, was the first person to consolidate disjointed ideas into a thermometer scale which was to gain permanent popularity. Fahrenheit decided not to use alcohol as his thermometer liquid because it boiled at too low a temperature to be generally useful; he experimented with a mixture of alcohol and water, but this contracted and expanded at too uneven a rate when temperature altered. In 1714 he settled for mercury, after having invented a cleaning method which prevented the liquid from sticking to the walls of the tube. He approved of the twelve degree scale because of its divisibility into whole numbers, but felt the need for smaller units. Therefore, he multiplied the basic twelve degrees by eight and spread them between zero (the lowest temperature he could reach with a mixture of water and sal ammoniac) and normal blood heat of the human body, which therefore became 96 degrees. Calculations from these fixed points gave 32 degrees for the melting point of ice and 212 degrees for the boiling point of water. The Fahrenheit scale remains popular in many countries. The unit degree is small enough to record air temperature with adequate precision in whole numbers, avoiding the false impression of accuracy given by the decimal point. And with a freezing point of 32°, there is less need for the use of the negative sign, often a source of printing error.

René-Antoine Ferchault de Réaumur (1683–1757), French physicist, was meanwhile working independently on the matter of temperature scale and in 1730 suggested a scale divided into 80 degrees. He chose this figure because he used alcohol in his thermometer stem, and he noted that its volume increased by 8 per cent between measurements taken in melting ice and boiling water. This scale was used for a time but never really established itself.

Anders Celsius (1701–44), Swedish astronomer, published his idea of temperature scale in 1742, namely zero for the boiling point of water and 100 degrees for the melting point of ice. This was a

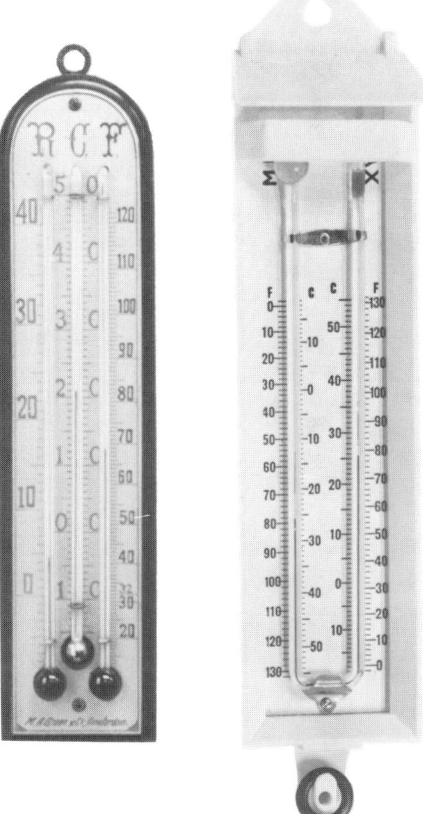

Left: Thermometers, recording separately in Réaumur, Celsius and Fahrenheit degrees, mounted on one board. Made by M. A. Groen of Amsterdam, probably in the early 20th century. (P. Chase)

Right: Six's maximum and minimum thermometer.

curious reversal of the usual instinctive principle of giving the highest numerals to the warmest temperatures, and many people reacted against it. The scale was therefore soon turned upside down. Amongst claimants to have been the first to allocate zero to the melting point of ice and 100 degrees to the boiling point of water were Jean Pierre Christen (1683–1755) of France and Marten Stromer of Sweden in 1743. Some people even think that the Swedish botanist, Carl von Linné (Linnaeus) (1707–78), already had a thermometer graduated in

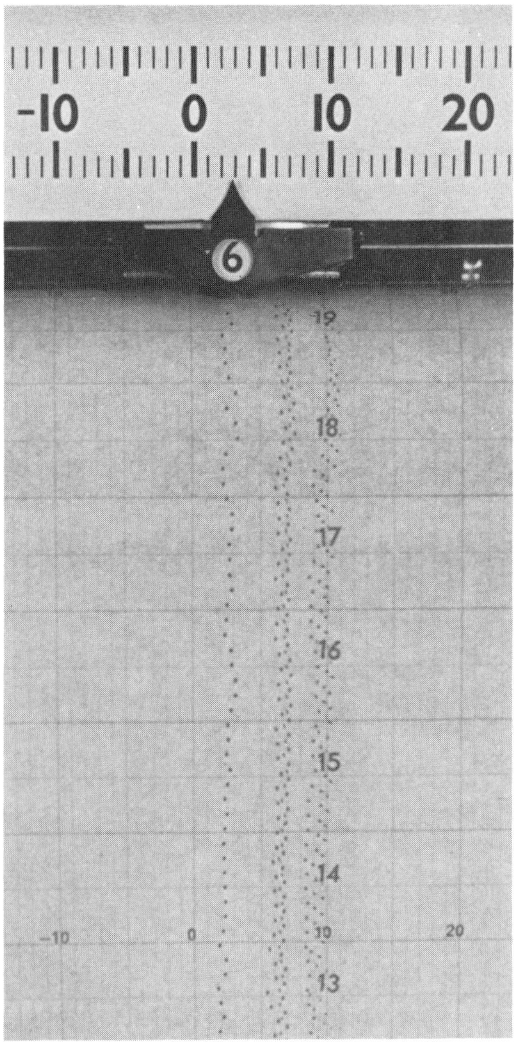

Electrical resistance thermometer records continuously as a series of dots on a rotating roll of graph paper.
(P. Defries)

the present centigrade manner as early as 1737. This reversed Celsius scale was adopted by the scientific world at once because of the simplicity of the metric system for complicated mathematics. Recently it was chosen as the international unit by the World Meteorological Organisation, which then had to decide whether to honour any particular name. It decided that the scale should be attributed to Celsius despite other claimants.

Early thermometers were liable to be inaccurate even after a sensible scale had evolved. There were imperfections in glass manufacture, difficulties in getting a consistent bore in the tubes and problems of applying graduations accurately to the glass. Modern instruments for precision work are graduated directly onto the glass, but cheaper thermometers, adequate for popular use, have graduations marked upon the board on which the thermometer is mounted.

Six's maximum and minimum thermometer was invented by James Six, of Cambridge University, in 1780, and this self-recording instrument is still popular. A U-shaped tube contains mercury in the lower part and a transparent liquid in the upper arms, completely filling one arm but only partially filling the other. A small index with an iron core grips the sides of each upper arm by means of a small spring, but the index can be pulled down by magnet to rest on the surface of the mercury below. When temperature rises, the liquid in the upper arm which is filled right up to the top, expands and pushes the mercury column down so that the index in the other arm is forced upwards, remaining at the highest point reached. When the temperature falls, the liquid in the filled arm contracts, the mercury is forced upwards by the weight of the liquid in the other arm and the index is carried along with the mercury to register the lowest temperature reached. The indices are reset each day by magnet.

The self registering clinical thermometer was patented by Negretti and Zambra of London in 1852. The capillary tube containing mercury has a constriction near the bulb which prevents the flow of mercury back to the bulb except by shaking.

Precision maximum meteorological thermometers also have a constriction near the bulb and require shaking to re-set.

Right: Infra-red satellite view of clouds over Europe and the Atlantic at 0950 GMT on 17 February 1978. Whitest areas are the coldest, and clouds are discernible over the Atlantic where it is still dark. Compare with the identical view, taken on visible wave length, in chapter 1.
(University of Dundee)

Precision minimum meteorological thermometers contain alcohol because of its low freezing point. They contain an index that is able to slide within the liquid but which cannot break through the meniscus of the alcohol. The index is re-set by tilting the tube.

Correct exposure of thermometers is essential if air temperatures read at different places are to be comparable. Thermometers must be screened from direct sunshine and from ground radiation. An acceptable position for a domestic thermometer is 4 ft (1·2 m) high on a north-facing wall.

The Stevenson Screen is a standard meteorological housing for thermometers. It was designed by Thomas Stevenson (1818–87), father of the author Robert Louis and has louvred sides to permit a regulated through-flow of air. It has a double roof as insulation against direct sunshine and stands 4 ft (1·2 m) above ground, well away from any obstruction. Stevenson Screens are frequently mistaken for beehives by the uninitiated!

Grass minimum temperatures are read from a thermometer resting horizontally on supports so that its bulb just touches short cut grass and is freely exposed to the sky.

A black bulb thermometer is a mercury thermometer, encased in an outer sheath evacuated of air and exposed horizontally to the Sun. It attempts to measure direct radiation heat from the Sun, but exposures are difficult to standardise. The black coating to the bulb deteriorates quickly and it is difficult to eliminate the effect of the temperature of the outside air. A pyrheliometer is now usually used instead.

A pyrheliometer is an instrument for measuring the direct radiation from the Sun. A normal incidence pyrheliometer consists of metal plates exposed at right angles to the Sun's rays and a device for converting the energy received into a measurable electric current.

A bent stem soil thermometer measures the temperature of soil, the length of bent stem depending upon the depth of insertion required. The bulb is adequately insulated against the temperature of the outside air and of other layers of soil.

Non-liquid thermometers measure temperature in various ways, such as:

Electrical resistance of a metal wire, varying in known fashion according to temperature.

Amount of curl in a bimetallic strip whose materials have different coefficients of expansion.

Current induced in a closed circuit of dissimilar metals, where one joint remains at standard temperature and the other changes.

A Marine Thermometer Screen, so called because it was first developed for use on Weather Ships, houses electrical thermometers. It looks rather like five inverted soup plates stacked on top of each other!

A thermograph is a thermometer connected to a pen which records temperature on a drum rotating by clockwork. The temperature element is usually a coil of two dissimilar metals with different coefficients of expansion.

The photothermograph is an elaborate thermograph, designed for the Meteorological Office in 1867, using mirrors and beams of light. Two bent stem thermometers are fixed to an outside north-facing wall and are long enough to enter a hole in the wall and bend upwards again to an indoor table. One thermometer has a wet bulb. The mercury in the tubes contains an air gap within their vertical length indoors. A series of lenses and a mirror on the table directs light from a gas lamp between vertical plates in front of the air gaps, and the resulting light beam focuses on to photosensitive paper attached to a rotating drum. A photothermograph, formerly at the Radcliffe Observatory in Oxford, is now in the Science Museum, London, complete with the Stevenson Screen which housed the thermometers on the outside wall. A photothermograph was first installed at Kew Observatory, London, in October 1867. It was in continuous use until the Observatory closed in 1980, apart from a few months at the beginning of 1969 when it was being serviced.

Infra-red thermography uses sensors to detect heat radiated by substances or gases, and computers to convert the results into pictures. Infra-red pictures of the Earth, taken from satellites, grade the surfaces from warmest (black) to coldest (white). The highest cloud tops are the coldest and whitest features on the picture.

Temperature is measured either in degrees Fahrenheit or degrees Celsius, universally abbreviated as °F and °C. 32°F (0°C) is the temperature of a mixture of pure ice and water at an atmospheric pressure of 1013·25 millibars. 212°F (100°C) is the temperature of boiling water at an atmospheric pressure of 1013·25 millibars.

Photothermograph invented by Robert Beckley, assistant at Kew Observatory from 1853 to 1872. Temperatures were registered indoors (left) but the thermometers were housed in a screen on the outside wall (right).
(Crown Copyright. Science Museum, London)

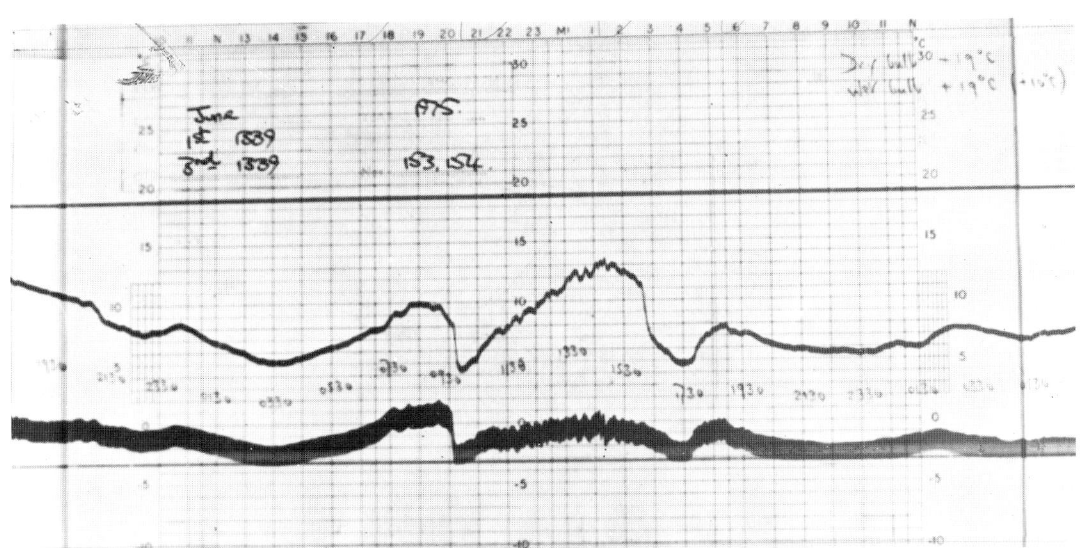

Trace from the photothermograph used at Kew Observatory until 1980. The overlay grid served to determine temperature, which was read at the lower edge of the traces. The wet bulb trace was thicker than the dry bulb trace because the air gap in the mercury, through which light passed, was different in the two thermometers.
(P. Defries)

Centigrade remains a popular name for the Celsius scale, denoting simply that there are 100 degrees between the two fixed points.

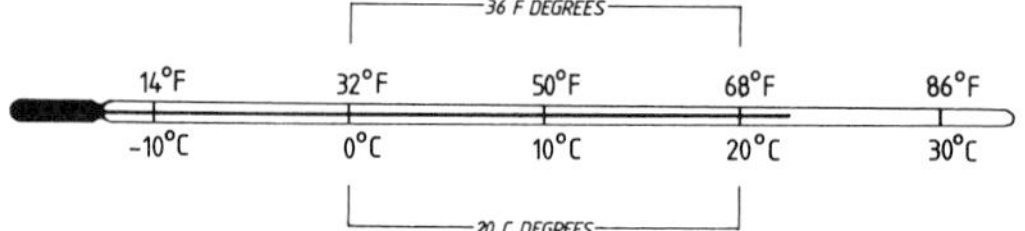

The value of one degree, or a span of several degrees, converts from Fahrenheit to Celsius in the ratio of 5:9.

Each Fahrenheit degree = 5/9 a Celsius degree
Each Celsius degree = 9/5 a Fahrenheit degree

Hence, a rise in temperature from 32°F to 68°F (from 0°C to 20°C) forms an interval of 36 Fahrenheit degrees (20 Celsius degrees). Note the convention of this book to abbreviate such an interval as 36F (20C) degrees, to distinguish it from the temperature 36°F which is equivalent to the temperature 2·2°C and is written as 36°F (2·2°C).

Temperature conversion formulae must take account not only of the different size degree in each scale but also the different zero which each scale has. Convert in the following manner

Celsius to Fahrenheit: Multiply by 9/5, then add 32
Fahrenheit to Celsius: Deduct 32, then multiply by 5/9

There is only one temperature which reads the same on both scales, and that is −40. This provides another conversion formula which many people find easier to remember.

Celsius to Fahrenheit: Add 40, multiply by 9/5, deduct 40
Fahrenheit to Celsius: Add 40, multiply by 5/9, deduct 40

CELSIUS FAHRENHEIT CONVERSION TABLES
Fahrenheit in bold type

FAHRENHEIT	0	1	2	3	4	5	6	7	8	9
−10	−23·3	−23·9	−24·4	−25	−25·6	−26·1	−26·7	−27·2	−27·8	−28·3
−0	−17·8	−18·3	−18·9	−19·4	−20	−20·6	−21·1	−21·7	−22·2	−22·8
0	−17·8	−17·2	−16·7	−16·1	−15·6	−15	−14·4	−13·9	−13·3	−12·8
10	−12·2	−11·7	−11·1	−10·6	−10	−9·4	−8·9	−8·3	−7·8	−7·2
20	−6·7	−6·1	−5·6	−5	−4·4	−3·9	−3·3	−2·8	−2·2	−1·7
30	−1·1	−0·6	0	0·6	1·1	1·7	2·2	2·8	3·3	3·9
40	4·4	5	5·6	6·1	6·7	7·2	7·8	8·3	8·9	9·4
50	10	10·6	11·1	11·7	12·2	12·8	13·3	13·9	14·4	15
60	15·6	16·1	16·7	17·2	17·8	18·3	18·9	19·4	20	20·6
70	21·1	21·7	22·2	22·8	23·3	23·9	24·4	25	25·6	26·1
80	26·7	27·2	27·8	28·3	28·9	29·4	30	30·6	31·1	31·7
90	32·3	32·8	33·3	33·9	34·4	35	35·6	36·1	36·7	37·2

CELSIUS	0	1	2	3	4	5	6	7	8	9
−40·0	**−40.0**	**−41·8**	**−43·6**	**−45·4**	**−47·2**	**−49·0**	**−50·8**	**−52·6**	**−54·4**	**−56·2**
−30·0	**−22·0**	**−23·8**	**−25·6**	**−27·4**	**−29·2**	**−31·0**	**−32·8**	**−34·6**	**−36·4**	**−38·2**
−20·0	**−4·0**	**−5·8**	**−7·6**	**−9·4**	**−11·2**	**−13·0**	**−14·8**	**−16·6**	**−18·4**	**−20·2**
−10·0	**14·0**	**12·2**	**10·4**	**8·6**	**6·8**	**5·0**	**3·2**	**1·4**	**−0·4**	**−2·2**
−0·0	**32·0**	**30·2**	**28·4**	**26·6**	**24·8**	**23·0**	**21·2**	**19·4**	**17·6**	**15·8**
+0·0	**32·0**	**33·8**	**35·6**	**37·4**	**39·2**	**41·0**	**42·8**	**44·6**	**46·4**	**48·2**
+10·0	**50·0**	**51·8**	**53·6**	**55·4**	**57·2**	**59·0**	**60·8**	**62·6**	**64·4**	**66·2**
+20·0	**68·0**	**69·8**	**71·6**	**73·4**	**75·2**	**77·0**	**78·8**	**80·6**	**82·4**	**84·2**
+30·0	**86·0**	**87·8**	**89·6**	**91·4**	**93·2**	**95·0**	**96·8**	**98·6**	**100·4**	**102·2**
+40·0	**104·0**	**105·8**	**107·6**	**109·4**	**111·2**	**113·0**	**114·8**	**116·6**	**118·4**	**120·0**

3. Temperatures near the ground

Surface air temperature is that which is measured at 4 ft above the ground by a thermometer in a Stevenson screen or with other acceptable exposure. It is valid for that place and time only, and temperatures elsewhere in the locality may differ considerably. Therefore a decimal point's difference between two temperatures is useful as a comparative guide but gives a somewhat false impression of the accuracy with which local air temperature can be defined.

Maximum and minimum temperatures can only be the highest and lowest *recorded* under acceptable meteorological conditions. Nobody can disprove any personal conviction that greater extremes have been experienced in some place where there is no thermometer.

A mean, or average, temperature is the sum of several individual readings, divided by the number of readings. The resulting figure gives a good indication of a typical temperature, but it camouflages individual extremes within the series.

Comparable temperature records only go back about 120 years, but earlier weather conditions can be traced by referring to documents.

The earliest known journal about the weather was written by Walter Merle, a Fellow of Merton College Oxford, between 1337 and 1344. It was translated from the original Latin and published under the supervision of G. J. Symons, editor of the *Monthly Meteorological Magazine*. The entries reveal such details as the mildness and absence of severe frost in the last quarters of the years 1340–43, twelve weeks

Extract from Thomas Barker's weather diary, August 1759. (Lancing College)

A very hot dry clear month, very fine haytime, ground burning, toward the end 24?
harvest ripe and begun, very fine crops of all sorts.
31 morns 21 97 | 202 93 | 39 3/4 Mean 29.71 | 65.5 | 1.3
30 evens 21 10 | 204 18 | 70 | 68.8
August 1759
16 45 29 30 383 619 W 2 W 2 } Sunny sometimes hot, and showers.
17 25 33 376 623 — W 1 } Wind betw WSW & WNW 1½.
2 6 35 39 397 609. W 2 W 2 } Windy morning; Sunny showery day
17 25 51 382 622 WNW 1 06 } Wind betw W & NNW 1½
3 6 20 65 408 600 — WNW 1 03 } Sunny and hot, a shower or 2. Wind WNW to W 1.
4 7 0 61 392 613 — SW 2 } Cloudy windy and often rain; clearing up and
17 0 35 375 626 WSW 3 WSW 3 50 } calm after 20. Wind SW to W 2¼
☉ 6 15 53 379 622 — WNW 1 } Some Sunshine.
17 10 57 379 621 W by N 1 W 1 } Wind WNW & W 1.

Infra-red view of the British Isles at 1028 GMT on 20 August 1976, during the hottest summer of the century. The land is the warmest area (black) and there are only a few wisps of very high cloud over the whole country. Sea temperature is considerably less than that of the land, particularly in the Celtic Sea and the English Channel. (University of Dundee)

of freezing weather in the winter 1339 and spells of great heat in 1337, 1339, 1340.

Tycho Brahe's weather journal, covering the years 1582–97, included wind observations. This together with the log books and letters written by Spanish and British naval officers in 1588, has enabled meteorologists at the Climatic Research Unit at Norwich to re-construct the weather situations which defeated the Spanish Armada.

Samuel Pepys wrote in his diary on 21 January

1661 that there had been no cold so far that winter and 'the rose bushes are full of leaves'. His entry for 7 June 1665 was 'the hottest day that ever I felt in my life.'

Weather diaries became a hobby of the intelligentsia soon after thermometers were generally available to the public. The Royal Society, London, founded in 1660 for the exchange and promotion of philosophical and scientific information, gave its seal of approval to the habit of making regular weather observations. As the quality of instruments improved and the value of consistent observations became clear, these isolated diaries improved and have become invaluable for research. Holland probably has the best series, allowing reliable records of weather to be traced back continuously to 1706. France, Italy, Germany and England can trace weather back as far as 1700 or a little earlier, but some gaps have to be filled by estimation. London weather is known for every day since 1668.

Highest recorded maximum air temperatures

		°F	°C	
World	Al'azizyah, Libya	136·4	58·0	13 Sept 1922
N. America	Death Valley, California	134·0	56·7	10 July 1913
Australia	Cloncurry, Queensland	127·5	53·1	13 Jan 1889
Greenland	Fvitgut	86·1	30·1	23 June 1915
Antarctica	Hope Bay	53·0	11·7	23 Mar 1946
Great Britain	Tonbridge, Kent	100·5[1]	38·1[1]	22 July 1868

[1] *Recorded in a screen similar to a Stevenson screen.*

Recent notable maximum temperatures

Antarctica, McMurdo Sound	Jan 1979, 49°F (9·4°C), warmest spell on record
Antarctica, South Pole	Jan 1979, 6·8°F (−14°C)
Australia, Kalgoolie, Western Australia	Jan 1980 highest recorded, 115·5°F (46·4°C)
Greece (central)	June 1981, 105°F (40·6°C)
India (northern)	Apr 1980, 112°F (44·4°C)
Iran (Arabian coast)	June 1978, 117°F (47·2°C)
Turkey (south east)	July 1980, 120°F (48·9°C)
United Kingdom	1975–1976, (p. 32)
United States	1978–1980, (p. 33)
Soviet Union (grain areas)	July 1981, more than 100°C (37·8°C)
Soviet Union, Moscow	June 1981, hottest since 1901, 90°F (32·2°C)

From press reports

Notable long sequences of high maximum temperatures

Place	°F	°C	*Consecutive days*	*Date*
Death Valley, California, USA	120	48·9	43	6 July–17 Aug 1917
Yuma, Arizona, USA	110	43·3	14	1955
Marble Bar, W. Australia	100	37·8	160	31 Oct–7 Apr 1924
Melbourne, Victoria, Australia	100	37·8	3	Dec 1979
Wyndham, W. Australia	90	32·2	333	1946
Melbourne, Victoria, Australia	89·6	32	7	26 June–2 July 1976
Heathrow Airport, London	87·8	31	14	23 June–8 July 1976

Thomas Barker of Rutland kept one of the most valuable series of weather diaries in Great Britain between 1736 and 1798. They were well set out and legibly written in ink.

The Manley records are realistic temperatures for central England traced back to 1659 by the late Professor Gordon Manley. His figures are widely used for comparative purposes.

The summer season, meteorologically speaking, comprises June, July and August in the northern hemisphere. In the southern hemisphere, summer is made up of December, January, February and is dated by the year in which January and February occur.

An isotherm is a line on a map which joins places having equal temperature for the period specified. The quality of summers throughout the world is indicated on maps by mean July isotherms for the northern hemisphere and mean January isotherms for the southern. Only by referring to such mean values can one judge temperature excesses in a particular year.

The hottest place in the world, amongst those having reliable temperature statistics, is Dallol, Ethiopia, which has hardly any seasonal relief from high temperatures.

Weather records were kept there by a prospecting company on the edge of the Danakil Depression, below sea-level and near the southern end of the Red Sea, for the years 1960–66. The mean of the daily maxima was more than 100°F (37·8°C) for every month of the year except two. In December the mean was 98°F (36·7°C) and in January it was 97°F (36·1°C).

The mean of the daily minima for each month varied between 75°F and 89°F (24·2°C–31·7°C).

The mean annual temperature (average of the mean maximum and mean minimum) was 94°F (34·4°C).

By comparison, the highest mean annual temperature, averaged over the years 1931–60, in Great Britain was 52·7°F (11·5°C) at Penzance, Cornwall, and on the Isles of Scilly.

Sunshine buckled this conductor rail on the Upney Line, London, on 1 July 1957. (Syndication International)

NOTABLE TEMPERATURES IN THE BRITISH ISLES

Mean 24-hour temperatures of extreme summers in central England

Hottest Year	°F	°C	*Coolest* Year	°F	°C
1826	63·5	17·6	1725	55·5	13·1
1976	63·5	17·5	1816	56·1	13·4
1846	62·8	17·1	1860	56·3	13·5
1781, 1911, 1933, 1947	62·6	17·0	1823, 1888, 1907	56·5	13·6
1899	62·5	16·9	1879, 1922	56·7	13·7
1868, 1975	62·2	16·8	1909	55·0	13·9

Sequences of hot and cool summers in central England

Mean 24-hour temperature more than 60°F (15·6°C)		*Mean 24-hour temperature less than 59°F (15°C)*	
Consecutive years	Dates	Consecutive years	Dates
4	1726–29, 1772–75, 1778–81, 1932–35	9	1809–17
3	1731–33, 1741–43, 1857–59, 1943–45	4	1907–10
		3	1881–83, 1890–92, 1918–20, 1927–29

Highest monthly maximum temperatures in Great Britain

		°F	°C	
Jan	Aber, Gwynedd	65·0	18·3	10 Jan 1971
Feb	Barnstaple, Devon	67·0	19·4	28 Feb 1891
	Cambridge, Cambs	67·0	19·4	28 Feb 1891
Mar	Wakefield, South Yorks	77·0	25·0	29 Mar 1929
	Cromer, Norfolk	77·0	25·0	29 Mar 1968
	Santon Downham, Norfolk	77·0	25·0	29 Mar 1968
Apr	London (Camden Square)	85·0	29·4	16 Apr 1949
May	Tunbridge Wells, Kent	91·0	32·8	29 May 1944
	Horsham, West Sussex	91·0	32·8	29 May 1944
	London (various)	91·0	32·8	29 May 1944
June	Southampton, Hants	96·0	35·6	28 June 1976
	London (Camden Square)	96·0	35·6	29 June 1957
July	Tonbridge, Kent	100·5	38·1	22 July 1868
Aug	London (Ponders End, Middx)	98·8	37·1	9 Aug 1911
Sept	Barnet, Herts	96·0	35·6	2 Sept 1906
	Epsom, Surrey	96·0	35·6	2 Sept 1906
	Bawtry, West Yorks	96·0	35·6	2 Sept 1906
Oct	London (various)	84·0	28·9	6 Oct 1921
Nov	Prestatyn, Clwyd	71·0	21·7	4 Nov 1946
Dec	Achnashellach, Highland	65·0	18·3	2 Dec 1948

Table by G.T. Meaden, *Journal of Meteorology*, October 1975

In the United Kingdom, which has a maritime climate, summers are only hot when high pressure predominates. Even then temperature never climbs to the maxima experienced on continents.

Mean summer temperatures, June–August, evaluated over the years 1941–70 are:

District	Mean 24-hour temperature °F	°C
N. Scotland	54·5	12·5
E. and W. Scotland	56·5	13·6
N.E. England	58·6	14·8
N. Wales and N.W. England	58·3	14·6
Central England and East Anglia	60·1	15·6
S.E. and central south England	61·0	16·1
S. Wales and S.W. England	60·1	15·6
N. Ireland	57·0	13·9

Summers 1975 and 1976 were particularly hot. In central England the consecutive summers were both within the six hottest since 1725, a feat unparalleled in the history of British meteorological records.

In 1975 the heat wave started at the beginning of August, so that maximum temperatures did not reach the excesses of summer 1976. Central England experienced the hottest August since 1725.

In 1976 June and July were the hottest months and there were some notable long sequences of high maxima. Cheltenham, Gloucestershire, recorded 89·6°F (32°C) on 11 out of 12 days from 26 June to 7 July.

Maximum temperatures in summer 1976 were often more than 6·3F (3.5C) degrees higher than average. There were many reports of temperatures reaching 89·6°F (32°C) or more, notably:

		°F	°C
Cheltenham, Glos.	3 July	98·6	35·9
Rickmansworth, Herts.	26 June	95·2	35·1
Epping, Essex	27 June	96·0	35·6
Newport, Isle of Wight	27 June	94·6	34·8
Kettering, Northants	3 July	93·6	34·2
Liverpool, Merseyside	29 June	90·1	32·3

RECENT NOTABLE SUMMERS IN THE UNITED STATES

Summer 1978

Wilmington, N. Carolina	28 June, 100°F (37·8°C) maximum, very high for a coastal town
Cape Hatteras, N. Carolina	28 June, 95°F (35°C) maximum, only 2°F below the record in 1952
El Paso, Texas	13–27 June, 100°F (37·8°C) or more
Abilene, Texas	July, mean temperature 89°F (31·7°C), hottest on record; 21 days reaching 100°F (37·8°C) or more
Wichita Falls, Texas	15 July, 114°F (45·6°C) maximum
Red Bluff, California	5–9 Aug, 113°F (45°C) maximum or more; 8 Aug, 119°F (48·3°C) maximum
Medford, Oregon	8 Aug, 119°F (48.3°C) maximum

Summer 1979

Californian Valley,	4–10 June, maximum temperatures 9F (5C) degrees higher than usual, Los Angeles 103°F (39·4°C) San Diego 101°F (38·3°C)
Phoenix, Arizona	End June, 115–117°F (46–47°C) maxima on several occasions
Albuquerque, New Mexico	9–15 July, 100°F (37·8°C) or more each day
Washington State	Second week July, 110°F (43·3°C) in several places

Summer 1980

Record temperatures from some of the 48 contiguous states

		°F	°C
Wichita Falls, Texas	27 June	117	47·2
Wichita, Kansas	12 July	112	44·2
Memphis, Tennessee	13 July	108	42·2
Little Rock, Arkansas	13 July	108	42·2
Meridian, Mississippi	14 July	107	41·7
Georgia, Atlanta	10 July	104	40
New York City, New Jersey	20 July	102	38·9
Providence, Rhode Island	20 July	100	37·8
Portland, Oregon	end July	101	38·3
Boise, Idaho	end July	106	41·1

Washington National Airport had an average August temperature of 82·3°F (27·9°C) the hottest in 110 years of records.

Compiled from monthly reports in *Weatherwise*

In the United States summer temperatures vary widely according to latitude and distance from the sea. Heat waves inland can be devastating.

The mean daily maximum temperature for July varies from about 70°F (21°C) in northern coastal states to about 90°F (32°C) in southern coastal and central states. 100°F (38°C) is quite usual in the western desert and maxima higher than 110°F have been recorded frequently.

Death Valley, California, where temperature reached 134 °F (56.7°C) on 10 July 1913. (J. Collins)

The three consecutive summers 1978–80 were notably hot in many states. In 1978 the heat wave started in eastern states in June, and in 1979 in the southwestern states, also in June.

In 1980, northern states already had temperatures up to 8F (4·4C) degrees higher than average in May. The main heat wave started in the south west desert and mid-west about 22 June, and gradually spread to the eastern states. The summer was the hottest since 1954 and many temperature records were broken. It remained hot with a few brief interludes of cooler weather, until the end of September.

The Föhn effect is a marked rise in temperature on the lee side of mountain ranges, when wind blows across the barrier in stable air conditions. Air warms partly due to compression when descending on the lee side, particularly if rain has fallen over the summit. In addition, wind sometimes sucks down warmer air from above the upper temperature inversion.

In the European Alps, valleys can experience sudden temperature rises of 18–27F (10–15C) degrees when the downslope Föhn wind blows. In the Rocky Mountains there is a similar wind called Chinook, an Indian word meaning 'snow eater', because it can melt a foot of snow in a few minutes. A rise in temperature from 11°F to 42°F (− 11·7°C to 5·6°C) was once observed at Harve, Montana in three minutes. Grytviken, South Georgia, Antarctica, experiences rises of 18–22F (10–12C) degrees with SE-WSW winds of 15–20 mph (24–32 km/h).

Air frost is the name given to air with a temperature at or below 32°F (0°C). It is often accompanied by hoar frost (See Chapter 10).

A very rare air frost occurred at Awali, Bahrain on 20 January 1964. Air temperature fell to 32°F (0°C), causing icicles to form over a tree on which a sprinkler had been left all night. The minimum temperature was 38°F (3°C) the day before and the day after. The week before the minimum temperature was 50–52°F (10–11°C).

A frost hollow is low lying ground into which cooling, dense air drains and from which there is no natural outlet, thus making it prone to air frost. Railway embankments frequently act as dams against the free drainage of cold air, and create frost hollows. A typical one exists between embankment and steep sided chalk valley of the river Dour to the north west of Dover, Kent. Here, whole crops of runner beans and potatoes have been ruined by frosts in June.

Valleys in mountainous areas are exaggerated frost hollows and the most notorious in Britain is Braemar, Scotland. It is 60 miles from the nearest coast, situated 1100 ft (335 m) above sea level and is completely surrounded by mountains up to 4000 ft (1220 m) altitude. There is a research station on Morrone 2819 ft (860 m) which towers above Braemar and temperature there is often much higher

Mt Washington Observatory, New Hampshire, USA on a mid-winter day. (Courtesy of the Director)

Napoleon's retreat from Moscow in 1812. **En route from Moscow to Smolensk, 6 December 1812, a temperature of −35°F(−37°C) was registered on a thermometer attached to the buttonhole of a soldier's uniform.** (Mary Evans Picture Library)

than that experienced in the village. The weather station at Braemar was originally set up by Prince Albert in 1855 and has made observations continually for 127 years.

December 1981 was the coldest on record with a mean temperature of 25·9°F (−3·4°C) and 11 days when screen temperatures fell below 14°F (−10°C). During the week 7–13 January 1982, mean temperature was 7·9°F (−13·4°C), minima being below 3·2°F (−16°C) on all 7 nights and below −4°F (−20°C) on 5 nights. On 10 January the maximum did not rise above −2·4°F (−19·1°C) and the minimum fell to −17°F (−27·2°C) to equal the record lowest registered there on 11 February 1895.

A freezing day is one in which the temperature never rises above 32°F (0°C). Places in the centre of continents in high latitudes such as Yukon, Alaska consider a freezing day with this upper limit 'warm' compared with the many much colder days they experience. Freezing days never occur on islands, such as Hawaii, set in the middle of warm seas. The British Isles have mild winters with very few freezing days when the prevailing wind blows from the Atlantic. Cold winters occur when wind blows persistently from the continent of Europe.

The winter season comprises the three months December, January and February in the northern hemisphere, and is dated by the year in which January and February occur. In the southern hemisphere, winter is made up of June, July and August.

Nearly all the inhabited lands with cold winters, having mean temperature of 32°F (0°C) or less, are in the northern hemisphere, though the southern tip of Argentina just enters the appropriate July isotherm in the southern hemisphere.

Winter cold cannot be measured in terms of individual low minimum temperatures, because these often occur under clear skies so that the following day's Sun raises air temperatures to more agreeable levels. Persistent low temperature occurs when cold air streams are accompanied by cloud so that temperatures do not rise appreciably during the day.

Mean minimum temperatures in winter tend to be lower with increasing distance from the sea, as indicated by the following mean January minimum temperatures:

TEMPERATURES NEAR THE GROUND

	°F	°C
LATITUDES 45°–60°N		
London, GB	34	1·7
Paris, France	32	0
Berlin, Germany	26	−3·3
Moscow, USSR	−9	−12·8
Omsk, USSR	−14	−25·5
Winnipeg, Canada	−13	−25·0
Vancouver, Canada	32	0
LATITUDES HIGHER THAN 60°, N OR S		
Fairbanks, Alaska	−21	−29·5
Yakutsk, USSR	−53	−47.0
S. Pole, Antarctica	−81	−62·8
McMurdo Sound, Antarctica	−24	−31·2
Spitzbergen, Arctic Ocean	−4	−20·0

The coldest area of the world is in Antarctica. Vostok, at 78° 26′ S, 106° 52′ E, is 11 500 ft (3505 m) above sea level and is known as 'the pole of cold', having a mean annual temperature of −72°F (−57·8°C).

At the geographical south pole, where an American scientific station has been keeping records for 20 years, the mean July temperature is −75°F (−59°C), and the mean annual temperature is −56°F (−49·2°C). The coldest year was 1976, which had a mean temperature of −58°F (−50°C).

In the northern hemisphere the coldest area is Siberia, where the village of Oymyakon (63° 16′ N, 143° 15′ E) claims to be the coldest permanently inhabited place, recording a minimum of −96°F (−71·1°C) in 1964.

In the United Kingdom winters are generally mild because of proximity to the Atlantic. Cold winters occur when high pressure predominates and wind blows from the continent of Europe.

Mean winter temperatures, December–February, evaluated over the years 1941–70, are:

	°F	°C
N. and W. Scotland	38·5	3·6
E. Scotland	37·6	3·1
N.E. England	38·5	3·6
N. Wales and N.W. England	39·4	4·1
Central England and East Anglia	38·7	3·7
S.E. and central south England	39·9	4·4
S. Wales and S.W. England	41·4	5·2
N. Ireland	39·2	4·0

The lowest minimum temperatures, in each month of the year, have all occurred in Scotland. Braemar holds the record lowest minimum of −17°F (−27·2°C) on both 11 February 1895 and 10 January 1982. It also has the lowest annual minimum temperature, which was less than 0°F (−17·8°C) in eleven years out of 40 between 1930 and 1969. Grantown-on-Spey came near to the record lowest minimum on 8 January 1982, when −16·2°F (−26·8°C) was registered.

In England, two new minimum records were set within four weeks, both in Shropshire. Shawbury recorded −12·8°F (−24·9°C) on 13 December 1981 and Newport −15°F (−26·1°C) on 10 January 1982.

New Year's Day, 1967, was one of the coldest for 16 years in England, and many roads were blocked by drifts of snow. Milk froze in bottles and expanded to push off the foil tops. (Syndication International)

NOTABLE TEMPERATURES IN CENTRAL ENGLAND SINCE 1725

Coldest and warmest months

Month	Year	Mean 24-hour temperature		Year	Mean 24-hour temperature	
		°F	°C		°F	°C
Dec	1890[1]	30·5	−0·8	1934	46·5	8·1
Jan	1795	26·5	−3·1	1916	45·5	7·5
Feb	1947	28·5	−1·9	1779	46·3	7·9
Mar	1785	34·2	1·3	1957	48·5	9·2
Apr	1837	40·4	4·7	1865	51·1	10·6
May	1740	47·5	8·6	1833	59·1	15·0
June	1909	53·3	11·8	1846	64·7	18·2
July	1816	56·1	13·3	1783	65·8	18·7
Aug	1912	55·3	13·0	1975	65·6	18·6
Sept	1807	50·9	10·5	1779	63·7	17·6
Oct	1740	41·5	5·3	1969	55·5	13·1
Nov	1782	36·2	2·4	1818	49·1	9·5

[1] *Provisional figures show December 1981 to have been as cold as 1890.*

Coldest and mildest winters

Year	Mean 24-hour temperature		Year	Mean 24-hour temperature	
	°F	°C		°F	°C
1740, 1963	31·5	−0·3	1869	44·2	6·8
1795, 1814	32·8	0·5	1834	43·7	6·5
1879	33·2	0·7	1796, 1975	43·2	6·2
1830, 1895, 1947	34·0	1·1	1935	42·9	6·1
1891, 1917, 1940, 1979	34·7	1·5	1877, 1943	42·6	5·9

Sequences of cold and mild winters

Mean 24-hour temperature less than 38·3°F (3·5°C)		*Mean 24-hour temperature more than 39·2°F (4°C)*	
Consecutive years	Date	Consecutive years	Date
7	1740–46	8	1732–39
5	1751–55, 1765–69	7	1910–16
4	1783–86, 1808–11	5	1971–75
3	1776–78, 1879–81, 1886–88, 1891–93, 1940–42	4	1747–50, 1866–69, 1882–85, 1920–23, 1925–28

The longest continuous period of freezing days in England this century was 34 days at Moorhouse, Cumbria, from 23 December 1962 to 25 January 1963, and 31 continuous days throughout January of the same year at Great Dun Fell. Both are exposed high level stations, and the cold at Kew, London, during the same period was probably more representative of a wider area. It had nine continuous freezing days, 17–25 January 1963, out of a total 18, a record only broken by a total of 21 freezing days in 1891.

In the United States some coastal areas have mild winters akin to those of the United Kingdom, but extreme continental cold also occurs inland.

Mean January temperature varies from 30–40°F (0–5°C) in northern coastal states to 50–60°F (10–15°C) in southern coastal states. In the central states January temperatures are more like 20–30°F (−8 to 0°C), with frequent minima temperatures very much lower.

The three consecutive winters 1977–79 were particularly severe, and an unparalleled sequence in the history of meteorological records. January 1977 was the coldest since 1895 in 15 states and also nationally (weighted average of the 48 contiguous states). The national mean January temperature was 23·9°F (−4·5°C). The winter of 1978 was the coldest on record in nine states with most, from Montana southward to Texas, having winter temperatures about 10F (5C) degrees lower than normal.

The winter of 1979 broke even the cold records of 1977, it being the coldest both nationally and in six individual states. The national January temperature was 22·8°F (−5·1°C).

Illinois had its three coldest winters on record in 1978, 1979 and 1977, each having mean daily temperatures at least 8F (4·4C) degrees below normal.

The coldest weather station in Canada is Eureka in the Northwest Territory, 380 miles (600 km) south of the North Pole. It is one of five Joint Arctic Weather Stations established by the World Meteorological Organisation in 1947. The mean annual temperature is −2·9°F (−19·4°C) and mean monthly temperature only rises above freezing in June, July and August.

Nevertheless, although winters are very cold, wind is usually light, making it comfortable to work outdoors when suitably clad. The summer is often warmer than other localities in the Arctic and the surrounding country is prolific in plant and animal life, earning Eureka the reputation of the 'Garden Spot of the Arctic'.

February 1979 was the coldest month on record.

		°F	°C
Mean daily temperature		−54·2	−47·9
Lowest minimum, 15 Feb		−67·5	−55·3
Highest maximum, (lowest ever), 21 Feb		−23·8	−31·0
85% hourly readings	⩽	−49	−45
93% hourly readings	⩽	−40	−40
13 consecutive days, minimum	⩽	−58	−50
17 consecutive days, maximum	⩽	−49	−45

Lowest minimum air temperatures

		°F	°C	
World	Vostok, Antarctica	−126·9	−88·3	24 Aug 1960
N HEMISPHERE	Verkhoyansk, USSR	−90·4	−68·0	5 and 7 Feb 1892
CANADA	Snag, Yukon	−81·0	−63·0	3 Feb 1947
SCOTLAND[1]	Braemar	−17·0	−27·2	11 Feb 1895 and 10 Jan 1982
GREECE	Kavalla	−13·0	−25·0	27 Jan 1954
ENGLAND	Newport, Shropshire	−15·0	−26·1	10 Jan 1982
WALES	Rhayader	−10·0	−23·3	21 Jan 1940
AUSTRALIA	Charlotte Pass	−8·0	−22·2	22 Aug 1947
IRELAND	Market Castle	−2·0	−18·9	16 Jan 1881
SOUTH AFRICA[1]	Carolina	5·5	−14·7	23 July 1926

[1] *−23·0°F (−30·5°C) has been claimed for Blackadder, in the Scottish borders, 4 Dec 1879. The temperature was read on an official instrument but the exposure was suspect.*

Notable long sequences of freezing days in the United States

Langdon, N. Dakota	⩽32°F (0°C)	92 days	30 Nov 1935–29 Feb 1936
	⩽0°F (−17·8°C)	40 days	11 Jan–20 Feb 1936
Fort Snelling, Minnesota	⩽32°F (0°C)	60 days	30 Jan–1 Apr 1843

Individual states in the United States having their coldest winters on record between 1977 and 1979[1]

1977	1978	1979
Georgia	Alabama	Colorado
N. Carolina	Arkansas	Kansas
Ohio	Illinois	Missouri
Pennsylvania	Indiana	Nebraska
S. Carolina	Kentucky	Oklahoma
W. Virginia	Louisiana	Wyoming
	Mississippi	
	Pennsylvania	
	Tennessee	

[1] *Many others had their second and third coldest winters in these three years.*

Notable minima in North America

	°F	°C	*Date*
USA			
Maybell, Colorado	−60	−51·1	1 Jan 1979
Parshall, N. Dakota	−60	−51·1	15 Feb 1936
Old Forge, New York	−52	−47	18 Feb 1979
Los Angeles, California	28	−2·2	Feb 1883, 1913, 1949
CANADA			
Watson Lake, NW Territory	−60·9	−51·6	Dec 1978
Dawson, Yukon	−68·4	−55·8	10 Feb 1979
Germansen Landing, Br. Columbia	−55·8	−48·8	Jan 1979

Compiled from monthly weather reviews in *Weatherwise* and from articles by Henry F. Diaz and R.G. Quayle

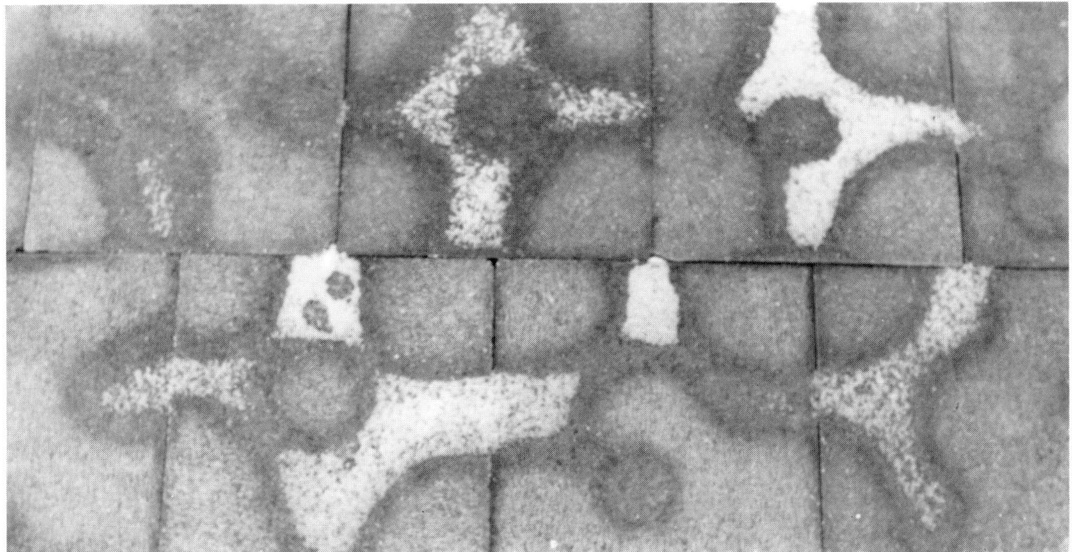

Pattern of melting snow and evaporating water on a terrace whose stones are set on blobs of concrete. The corners and centres of the slabs have benefited from conduction of heat from the soil through the concrete, but the patches of snow are insulated by air from the soil. (Ingrid Holford)

The greatest seasonal fluctuations of temperature occur in the centre of land masses with long cold winters but short hot summers.

Verkhoyansk, north-east Siberia, with a lowest temperature of −90·4°F (−68°C) has also recorded a summer maximum of 98°F (36·7°C), a range of 188·4F (104·7C) degrees.

The smallest fluctuations of temperature occur on small islands where air temperature is determined by surrounding sea temperature. Garapan on Saipan, one of the Mariana Islands in the Pacific Ocean, had an extreme range of only 21·2F (11·8C) degrees during 9 years, 1927–35. The lowest temperature was 67·3°F (19·6°C) and the highest 88·5°F (31·4°C).

Over a longer period of 55 years, 1911–66, the Island of Fernando de Noronha had an extreme temperature range of only 24·1F (13·3C) degrees, the lowest being 65·6°F (18·7°C) and the highest 89·6°F (32°C).

A spectacular weekly fluctuation of temperature in England occurred in the first week of June 1975. On 2 June several screen temperatures fell to below 35·6°F (2°C) and snow fell locally between Scotland and southern England. Ground frost was widespread between 2 and 4 June. On the 6th, temperature climbed to over 70°F (21·1°C), starting a long hot summer.

The greatest daily changes of temperature have occurred in the USA. At Browning, Montana, the temperature fell 100F (55·5C) degrees, from 44°F (6·7°C) to −56°F (−48·8°C) in 24 hours during 23 and 24 January 1916.

Extracts from the Daily Weather Summary, as issued by the London Weather Centre, for 10 January 1982. Record low temperatures occurred that day.

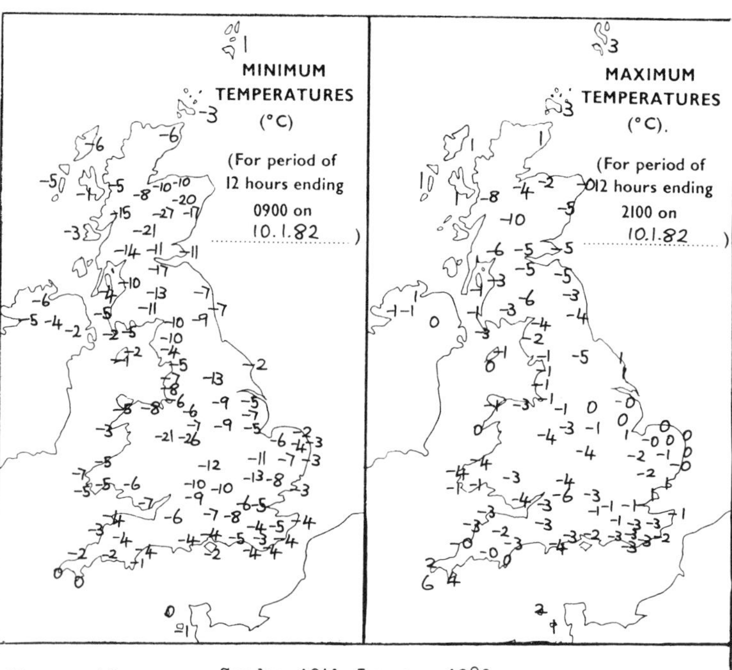

SUMMARY OF BRITISH WEATHER

After a mostly dry night, Northern Ireland and much of Scotland had a dry, bright and frosty day, though there were snow and hail showers in the extreme north of Scotland.

It was very cold, with very severe overnight frost. The temperature at Braemar, in the Grampians, equalled the record,(set at Braemar in February 1895) for the lowest officially recorded temperature in Britain (-27.2°C).

Wales and much of England was dry and bright, though southern counties were cloudy, with rain,sleet or snow in the southwest.

It was bitterly cold with a keen easterly wind adding to the severity of the overnight frost, whilst in Shropshire, sheltered from the wind by hills to the east, the temperature fell to a new English record low of -26.1°C at Newport.

'Extremes' for Sunday 10th January 1982

Highest maximum	:	6°C Scilly
Lowest minimum	:	-27.2°C Braemar
Lowest grass minimum	:	-26.8°C Shawbury (Newport and Braemar not available)
Most rain (24 hours from 0900 h)	:	22.3 mm Jersey
Most sun	:	7.1 hours Ringway, Hemsby

London Weather Centre 284 High Holborn London WCIV 7HX All times are GMT

Average air temperatures at selected places throughout the world

°F to nearest whole degree					°C to nearest half degree			
January		July			January		July	
Max	Min	Max	Min	NORTHERN HEMISPHERE	Max	Min	Max	Min
				Europe				
44	35	73	55	England, London	6·5	1·5	23	13
36	28	72	56	Denmark, Copenhagen	2	−2	22	13·5
43	34	76	58	France, Paris	6	1	24·5	14·5
48	36	88	65	Greece, Athens	9	2	31	18·5
28	19	70	54	Norway, Oslo	−2·5	−7·5	21	12
43	35	65	52	N. Ireland, Belfast	6	1·5	18·5	11
31	22	75	57	Poland, Warsaw	−0·5	−5·5	24	14
43	35	65	52	Scotland, Edinburgh	6	1·5	18·5	11
55	44	82	69	Spain, Barcelona	13	6·5	28	20·5
30	23	72	57	Sweden, Stockholm	−1	−5	22	14
35	26	73	55	Switzerland, Berne	1·5	−3·5	23	13
15	3	73	55	USSR, Moscow	−9·5	−16	23	13
45	36	69	54	Wales, Cardiff	7	2	20·5	12
				North America				
24	2	76	47	Alberta, Calgary	−4·5	−16·5	24·5	8·5
7	−13	79	55	Manitoba, Winnipeg	−14	−25	26	11
17	−2	74	52	Ontario, Fort William	−8·5	−19	24	11
−2	−20	72	48	Alaska, Fairbanks	−19	−29	22	9
55	42	72	54	California, San Francisco	13	5·5	22	12
22	6	83	63	Minnesota, Minneapolis	−5·5	−14·5	28·5	17
32	16	83	63	New York, Albany	0	−9	28·5	17
62	44	92	74	Texas, Houston	17	7	33·5	23·5
				Atlantic Islands				
63	54	76	66	Azores, Santa Cruz	17	12·5	24·5	19
68	59	85	74	Bermuda, Fort George	20	15	29·5	23·5
36	28	57	48	Iceland, Reykjavik	2	−2·5	14	9
				Asia				
33	16	90	73	China, Tiensin	0·5	−9	32	23
83	67	85	77	India, Bombay	28·5	19·5	29·5	25
47	29	83	70	Japan, Tokyo	8·5	−1·5	28·5	21
90	68	90	76	Thailand, Bangkok	32	20	32	24·5
				SOUTHERN HEMISPHERE				
78	65	60	46	Australia, Sydney	25·5	18·5	15·5	8
90	77	87	67	Australia, Darwin	32	25	30·5	19·5
85	63	57	42	Argentina, Buenos Aires	29·5	17	14	5·5
88	75	89	75	Brazil, Manaus	31	24	31·5	24
85	53	59	37	Chile, Santiago	29·5	11·5	15	3
87	73	81	73	Ghana, Accra	30·5	23	27	23
87	75	81	71	Kenya, Mombasa	30·5	24	27	21·5
70	53	50	35	N. Zealand, Christchurch	21	11·5	10	1·5
78	58	63	39	S. Africa, Johannesburg	25·5	14·5	17	4

The most abrupt change in temperature occurred in 2 minutes at Spearfish, South Dakota. Temperature rose 49F (27·2C) degrees between 7.30 am and 7.32 am on 22 January 1943, from −4°F (−20°C) to 45°F (7·2°C).

The greatest daily range in England occurred at Rickmansworth, Hertfordshire, on 29 August 1936, when temperature rose 50·9F (28·3C) degrees in 9 hours, from 34·0°F (1·1°C) to 84·9°F (29·4°C).

In Scotland (24–25 January 1958) the temperature at Kincraig rose 45·6F (25·3C) degrees, from −5·8°F (−21°C) to 39·8°F (4·3°C).

Sea surface temperature determines the temperature of air moving over it for any appreciable distance. Sea temperature varies from 28·5°F (−2°C) in the White Sea and near polar ice, to 96°F (35·6°C) which was once recorded in the Persian Gulf.

Mean February and September sea temperatures in European waters vary between:
54°F and 66°F (12°C and 19°C) in the southern Bay of Biscay
46°F and 61°F (8°C and 16°C) in the Irish Sea
42°F and 50°F (6°C and 10°C) near the Faroe Islands.

During the hot summer of 1976, July and August sea temperature rose to 70·7°F (21·5°C) off the coasts of Dorset and Hampshire. Mean sea temperature in February 1969 fell to 36·5°F (2·5°C) off the coast of south east England.

Land temperature is hottest near the Tropics, in places where the ground material is receptive to the Sun's radiation and dry, so that air pockets deter conduction of the heat into the subsoil. In sand on the coastal plain north of Port Sudan 183°F (84°C) was recorded on 24 September 1960. The temperature of a black cloth laid near the ground at Khartoum on 31 May 1918, was 194°F (90°C), at a time when the shade temperature of air was 109°F (42·8°C). Even in temperate latitudes extremely high surface temperatures can be reached. A black glass exposed fully to the Sun once reached a temperature of 160°F (71·1°C) in Watford, Hertfordshire, when the air temperature was only 70°F (21·1°C).

Permafrost is permanently frozen land, which occurs wherever the mean annual air temperature is about 16°F (−9°C). Any cover, such as moss or tundra, insulates the soil against the benefit of sunshine, so that there may be an appreciable rise in air temperature during the short summer without much effect on the frozen ground.

In Canada, about 50 per cent of the land surface is permanently frozen, to a depth of about 6 ft (2 m) at the southern limit, and to about 900 ft (300 m) at the northern limit.

The greatest measured depth of frozen ground is 4920 ft (1500 m) on April 1968 in the basin of the river Lena, Siberia.

Permafrost 1620 ft (494 m) deep was measured on Melville Island, N.W. Territory, Canada, in July 1963 by the Jacobsen-McGill Arctic Research Expedition.

The only permafrost in England is artificially created, at Canvey Island in the Thames estuary where an underground store contains liquefied gas at subfreezing temperature. The soil around the store has itself frozen, and in places pushed up the ground by 2 ft (0·6 m).

4. Pressure and character of the atmosphere

The pressure of the atmosphere is imperceptible to the human body under normal conditions because it acts both inwards and outwards on everything containing air. It is not surprising, therefore, that atmospheric pressure had to be *discovered*.

Hero of Alexandria, Greek engineer of the 1st century AD, was probably the first to demonstrate that air has weight. He inverted an open-ended vessel full of air downwards on to the surface of water and showed that the water would not fill the vessel unless air escaped as bubbles rising to the surface. He deduced that air was a material substance, probably composed of particles, but the idea was too advanced for his era and he was merely laughed at. The question was not taken up again in a serious manner until the 17th century.

Evangelista Torricelli (1608–47), Italian mathematician and physicist, became a pupil of Galileo in 1641. Galileo set him the problem of why water would not rise in a pump more than about 33 ft (10 m) above its natural level. In seeking the answer, Torricelli experimented in 1643 with a glass tube 4 ft (1·2 m) long. He filled it with mercury, the heaviest known liquid, and inverted the open end under the surface of mercury in another container. The level in the tube fell but not so far as to equalise with the level in the container. Since there was nothing but mercury vapour in the top of the tube he had created the first sustained vacuum, thereafter called the Torricellian vacuum. He concluded that the only thing that could be pushing the mercury in the tube higher than the level in the container must be the pressure of the atmosphere on the surface of mercury in the container.

Blaise Pascal (1623–62), French mathematician and physicist, repeated Torricelli's experiment but used red wine instead of mercury. Since wine is even lighter than water which in turn is 13·6 times lighter than mercury, Pascal's tube had to be 46 ft (14 m) tall to prove that the atmosphere exerted a pressure. In order to confirm the existence of atmospheric pressure, Pascal persuaded his young brother to walk with a Torricelli tube to the 3458 ft (1054 m) summit of Puy de Dôme, in the Auvergne mountains near Clermont Ferrand where he lived. (Pascal himself always suffered from ill health.) The level of mercury in the tube fell 3·33 in (84 mm), showing that 1000 ft (300 m) depth of atmosphere near the surface exerts a pressure of approximately 1 in (25 mm) mercury.

Similar falls in atmospheric pressure are recorded wherever ships rise through the locks of a canal, or an aeroplane climbs into the air.

Evangelista Torricelli, 1608–1647, from an engraving by Tomba. (Mary Evans Picture Library)

THE PRESSURE AND CHARACTER OF THE ATMOSPHERE

Otto von Guerike (1602–86), German physicist and Mayor of Magdeburg for 35 years, demonstrated the logical consequences of atmospheric pressure with a flamboyant experiment in 1651. He made two hollow hemispheres of metal, 20 in (500 mm) in diameter and evacuated the air in between by means of an air pump of his own invention. He then caused two teams of eight horses to pull on each hemisphere, but they could not be separated until some air was admitted between the two parts by a valve. They had been firmly clamped together by atmospheric pressure alone.

Variation in atmospheric pressure, as recorded by the daily fluctuations in the level of mercury in a Torricelli tube, was puzzling for scientists of the 17th century.

Giovanni Borelli (1608–79), Italian mathematician at Pisa and friend of Galileo, was sent a Torricelli tube by the Grand Duke Ferdinand II of Tuscany, and instructed to make constant observations with it. Correspondence between Borelli and the Duke's brother, Prince Leopold, contained the following wild theories.

☐ Pressure might be caused by the weight of clouds or rain. This was contradicted when it was observed that pressure usually *fell* during wet weather.

☐ The clouds might actually support the air above, but that suggestion was dismissed as improbable.

☐ Air might pile up like water waves, but Borelli did not like the analogy with transient water waves because high atmospheric pressure often lasted for several days.

Even Erasmus Darwin, a century later, confessed that he could not imagine how one fifteenth of the atmosphere could apparently 'disappear' and cause a corresponding fall in atmospheric pressure. Nevertheless, Prince Leopold remained convinced, even without explanations, that pressure was an important factor in the weather process and suggested that the Torricelli tube should be given a special name.

Von Guerike's experiment to demonstrate the 'force of vacuum'. (Negretti and Zambra Ltd)

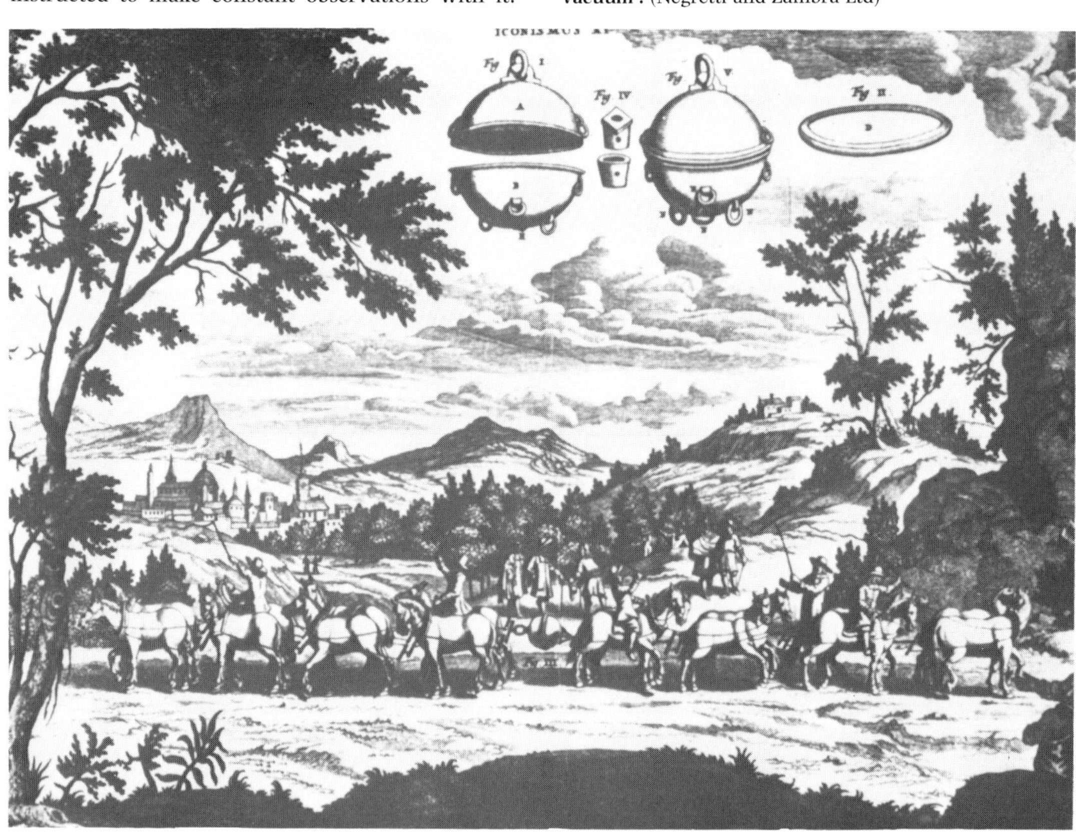

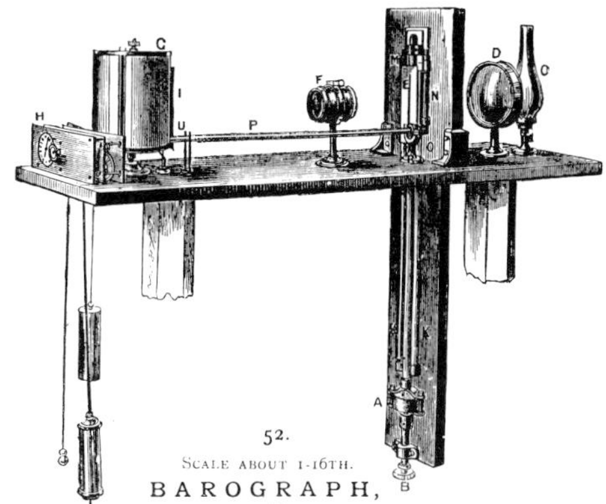

OR

SELF-RECORDING MERCURIAL BAROMETER, £58.

As adopted by the Meteorological Committee of the Royal Society.

122. This instrument is simpler in its arrangement than the Thermograph, but resembles it in recording photographically, not temperature, but the changes in the height of the Barometer. A clock revolves a cylinder, bearing photographic paper, once in 48 hours.

A double combination of achromatic lenses brings to a focus rays passing through a slit placed in front of the mercurial column, behind which is a strong gas-light or paraffin lamp, the rays of which are condensed upon the slit by two plano-convex lenses

Photobarograph from a catalogue, *c* 1874, by O. Comitti and Son, London.

René Descartes (1596–1650), French mathematician and philosopher, was probably the first person to apply a scale to a Torricelli tube and use it for measuring pressure. He wrote a letter to his colleague Mersenne on 13 December 1647:

> 'So that we may also know if changes of weather and of location make any difference to it, I am sending you a paper scale two and a half feet long, in which the third and fourth inches above two feet are divided into lines; and I am keeping an exactly similar one here, so that we may see whether our observations agree.'

Robert Boyle (1627–91), Irish chemist, is accredited with being the first to call an instrument measuring atmospheric pressure a barometer (Greek *báros*: weight, *métron*: measure).

Barometer manufacturers encountered many problems. Mercury is very heavy, and glass is susceptible to breakage. The mercury cistern had to be closed against spillage but remain susceptible to atmospheric pressure, and leather proved the most suitable material. At first it was just tied down over the top of a wooden cistern. Later the whole cistern was made of leather, enclosed in a wooden case and cemented to the neck of the glass tube. A screw device at the bottom could reduce the volume of the wooden box and force mercury to the top of the tube so that it did not sway dangerously during travel. In 1738, Charles Orme (1688–1747) became the first instrument maker to boil mercury in order to expel all air and make a better vacuum within the barometer. Mercury meniscus (curvature) is very pronounced and there were initial difficulties about detecting small changes in mercury level.

The angled barometer was invented in 1670 by Sir Samuel Morland, master mechanic to Charles II, as an attempt to get greater accuracy of measurement. The tube was bent at 28 in (700 mm) above the cistern and a remaining possible 3 in (75 mm) vertical rise in mercury was accommodated in an angled arm 18 in (450 mm) long. These sloping arms were even more liable to break than vertical barometers, a

Wheel

BAROMETER

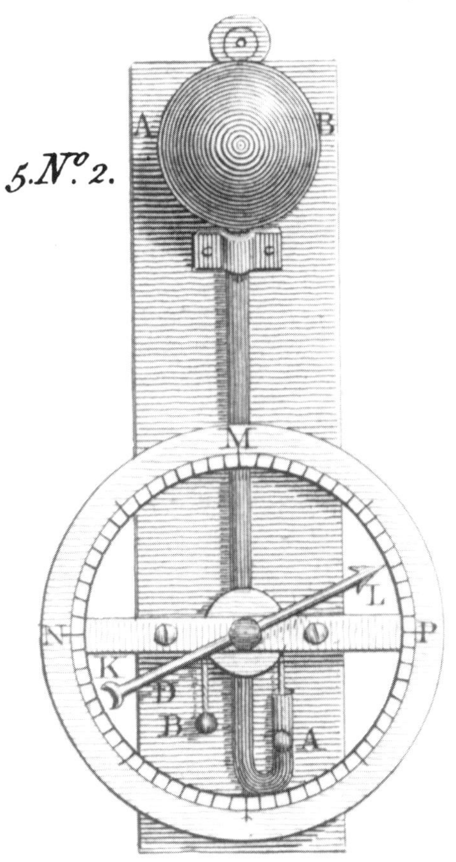

Wheel barometer designed by Robert Hooke and shown in his 'Micrographia' published in 1665. (Ann Ronan Picture Library)

problem which Charles Orme tried to overcome by mounting three angled barometers with *short* sloping arms at staggered heights on a board. Each barometer recorded within certain barometric pressure ranges only.

The wheel barometer was invented in 1665 by Robert Hooke, when curator of experiments to the Royal Society, London. A float attached to a silk cord rested on the mercury in the cistern and the cord passed round a pulley, being kept taut by a counterweight. A needle was attached to the pulley and revolved over a graduated dial as the mercury level changed.

The banjo barometer is shaped like the musical instrument of that name. It was originally designed to accommodate a column of mercury, but the pattern was popular and later used with aneroid mechanisms.

Popular demand for barometers increased enormously during the 18th century and the design of barometer cases became a prestige trade on a par with clockmaking.

Amongst the many weather enthusiasts who owned a barometer was Daniel Defoe (1660–1731), English author, who was living in London at the end of 1703. He experienced the most disastrous storm ever suffered in southern England and wrote a detailed report about it afterwards (See Chapter 7).

Not all barometer owners could afford to treat their instruments with the reverence they deserved as is apparent from a Thomas Hutchin writing from Manitoba in 1771:

> 'The surgeon being in great need of quicksilver, we were obliged to borrow some from the barometer, consequently no observations can be taken from the instrument for some time.'

Mercury was apparently used as a purgative!

The Fortin barometer takes its name from the man who, in 1810, first applied a device to the barometer for setting the zero of the instrument. A screw action

Aneroid barograph showing alterations of pressure recorded during two typical weeks in southern England.

Glaisher and Coxwell get into trouble because of lack of oxygen during their ascent to an estimated 37 000ft (11 300m) on 5 September 1862. (*Travels in the Air* James Glaisher)

alters the level of the mercury in the cistern until an ivory point just rests on its surface.

The aneroid barometer was invented in 1843 by Lucien Vidie (1805–66), French scientist, as a result of pressure gauge research by his countryman Bourdon. It has the advantage of being easily transportable and is sufficiently accurate for most practical purposes. The aneroid consists of corrugated capsules evacuated of air, with the faces kept apart either by the rigidity of the metal or by a separate spring. Changes in atmospheric pressure cause the capsules to expand or contract and the movement is recorded by a needle over a dial. Aneroid movements frequently replaced the mercury columns inside old barometers when repairs were needed. Modern aneroid barometers are often housed in traditional banjo shapes.

A barograph is an instrument which connects a barometer to an inked pen resting on a chart wound round a drum, which rotates by clockwork. This gives a continuous trace of pressure. Self-recording mercury barometers were made but were cumbersome, and modern barographs nearly always use aneroid mechanisms.

An altimeter measures height above ground by the difference in atmospheric pressures there and at ground level. Altimeters are used in aircraft and must be re-set for each flight to accord with surface pressure.

Pressure can be corrected to Mean Sea Level (MSL) by adding an imaginary column of air, equivalent to the height above sea level at which the barometer is read. After thus removing the effect of altitude, pressure differences between one place and another become significant in determining weather.

The millibar (mb) is the modern international unit in which atmospheric pressure is measured, and it can be defined in terms of Pascals (Pa) in honour of Blaise Pascal.

1 mb = 100 Pa = 100 Newtons per square metre
1000 mb = the pressure exerted by 29·53 in (750·06 mm) of mercury under standard conditions at 32°F (0°C).

A standard atmosphere at mean sea level is considered to exert a pressure of 1013·2 mb. This figure

Professor Auguste Piccard in his airtight capsule suspended beneath a balloon. (Dr Jacques Piccard)

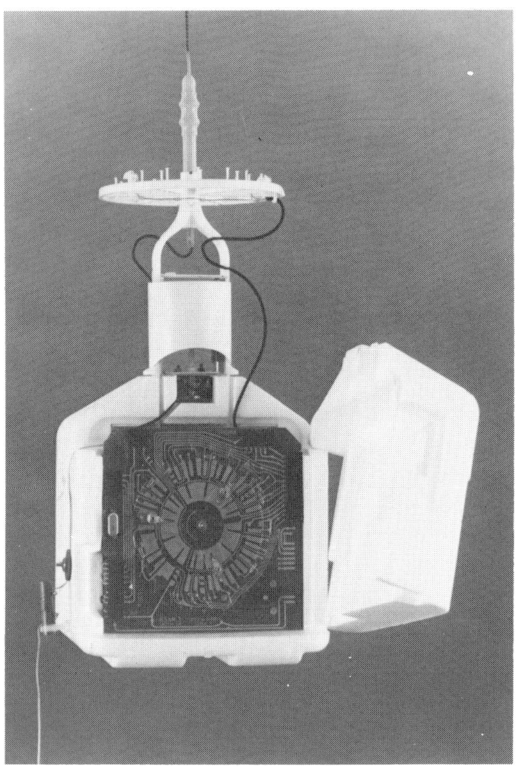

Modern radio sonde for sending aloft by balloon. (Meteorological Office, Crown Copyright)

has little significance in weather matters, but it is the pressure at which all instruments are calibrated.

The character of the upper air, beyond the reach of ground-based instruments, became of crucial interest to scientists discussing the phenomenon of atmospheric pressure. The only way to investigate was to send instruments aloft.

Dr Alexander Wilson of Glasgow made the first serious attempt to measure upper air temperature in 1749 when he flew a thermometer from a kite, but naturally this method was restricted to a fairly shallow layer of atmosphere.

The hot-air balloon was invented by the Montgolfier brothers Joseph Michel (1740–1810) and Jacques Etienne (1745–99). This suggested to scientists that they too might ascend into the atmosphere and make observations. The French physicist Jacques Alexandre Charles went aloft in a hydrogen balloon on 15 October 1783, taking a barometer with him to measure altitude. The first ascent specifically to obtain meteorological data was made in 1784 by Dr John Jeffries and the aeronaut Jean Pierre François Blanchard, when they measured temperature, humidity and pressure up to an altitude of 9000 ft (2740 m).

Joseph Louis Gay Lussac (1778–1850), French chemist, and Jean Biot (1774–1862), French physicist, made an ascent to 23 000 ft (7000 m) in 1804 and found that the atmosphere became drier with altitude, but its chemical composition remained the same as that at the ground level.

James Glaisher (1809–1903), English meteorologist, usually with Coxwell as pilot, made the most important series of ascents between 1862 and 1866 at the request of the British Association. Glaisher made 29 flights, during the most famous of which he and Coxwell recorded 29 000 ft (8840 m) on 5 September 1862 before Glaisher became unconscious and Coxwell so paralysed that he could only open the control valve with his teeth. It seems churlish to quibble at their *estimated* maximum height of 37 000 ft (11 300 m).

Research in subsequent years showed that the stress on their bodies was due to diminished partial pressure of oxygen. The human body can adapt to

Radio sonde receiving equipment at ground station. (Meteorological Office, Crown Copyright)

this only slowly over time and people living at an altitude of 18 000 ft (5486 m) in the Andes, the highest inhabited area of the world, have a deep and rapid breathing system which results in barrel-like chests.

Professor A. Berson and R. Suring made a higher ascent still, on 30 June 1901, in an open gondola suspended beneath the balloon but carrying a supply of oxygen. They reached an altitude of 35 435 ft (10 800 m) and this remained a record for some years during which time Finvielle, Tissandier and Flammarion all continued gleaning material by manned ascents.

Professor Auguste Piccard, Swiss physicist, broke the record in 1931 when he travelled in an air-tight capsule suspended beneath a balloon, with an inside air supply at ordinary pressure of 30·6 in (775 mm) mercury. He reached a height of 53 153 ft (16 201 m) where outside atmospheric pressure was only 3·1 in (78 mm) of mercury.

(The current official record for the highest balloon flight is 113 740 ft (34 668 m) by Cdr Malcolm D. Ross, USNR and the late Lt-Cdr Victor A. Prother, USN in an ascent from the deck of USS *Antietam* on 4 May 1961, over the Gulf of Mexico.)

Meanwhile, these dramatic but cumbersome ascents to obtain information did not blind people to the fact that invaluable data could be acquired on high mountains. These observations referred to more modest levels but could have greater continuity.

The highest weather observatory in Great Britain used to be on top of Ben Nevis at 4406 ft (1343 m) above sea level. It was built by public subscription under the enthusiastic direction of Alexander Buchan (1829–1907) Scotland's foremost meteorologist. He was secretary of the Scottish Meteorological Society, which administered the Observatory, from 1860 until his death. The observatory was manned, and provided regular hourly data, from its opening in 1883 until September 1904 when it was closed.

Two years before the observatory opened, instruments, protected by cages and cairns, were installed at the summit. Between 1 June and 14 October 1881, Clement Wragge, subsequently in charge of the Australian Meteorological Office but then living in Fort William, made a daily ground level weather observation at about 5 am. He then climbed the mountain, making observations en route at 6.30 and 8.15 am; at the summit at 9, 9.30, and 10 am; and on the way down again at 10.50 am and 1 pm. He was given a horse to take him half way up the mountain and a trained assistant to relieve him twice a week.

Meteorograph designed by Teisserenc de Bort, used between 1898 and 1907 and now in the Science Museum, London. (P. Defries)

The highest weather station in the British Isles at present is at the top of the Cairngorms, 4084 ft (1245 m) above sea level.

The highest observatory in the United States is on Mt Washington, 6262 ft (1909 m) high, in New Hampshire. Regular observations started there on 13 November 1870 in an old engine house adapted for the purpose. It blew down in January 1877 in gale winds of 186 mph (299 km/h) and no further observations were made there until better premises were built and more modern equipment installed in October 1932. The observatory boasts the 'worst weather in the world'.

Automatic instruments carried by free-travelling balloons which burst on reaching a certain minimum pressure and descend to the ground by parachute, have generally superseded the need to work at such uncomfortable altitudes in order to observe.

A meteorograph, registering pressure, humidity and temperature on charts attached to revolving drums, was first sent aloft attached to a balloon in France on 21 March 1893. The balloon weighed 40 lb (18 kg) and had a lifting capacity of 77 lb (35 kg). The instrument descended safely the next day after recording a highest flight point of 49 000 ft (15 000 m) where the temperature was −40°F (−40°C). This first balloon was made of gold-beater's skin (cattle gut) so named because of its use when beating gold into leaf thickness, but later balloons were made of varnished paper. A famous balloon, named Cirrus after the highest type of cloud, was made of silk and covered 700 miles (1126 km) from Berlin to Bosnia in July 1894. Mean velocity was 62 mph (100 km/h) and it reached a height of 54 000 ft (16 500 m) where temperature was −63°F (−52·8°C). It bettered its own record in April 1895 by reaching 72 000 ft (22 000 m) where the atmospheric pressure was 1·5 in (38·1 mm) of mercury.

William Henry Dines (1855–1927), English mechanical engineer and meteorologist, invented a lighter and more compact meteorograph which soon superseded the earlier instrument. It consisted of a large disc rotated by clockwork about its centre, on to which three styluses scratched traces recording temperature, pressure and humidity.

A temperature inversion over Christchurch, New Zealand, made evident by trapped smoke. (M. J. Hammersley)

The International Meteorological Congress in Paris in 1896 decided to monitor atmospheric conditions regularly by unmanned balloons. Carrying meteorological instruments, the balloons were released simultaneously from different places and gradually the coverage increased. The Germans started upper air soundings from Samoa Island, Pacific Ocean in 1906. Berson made the first sounding from East Africa in 1908, and the Dutch from Batavia, Java in 1910. Griffith Taylor started upper air soundings from Australia after having accompanied the British Antarctic Expedition from 1910 to 1913, where balloon ascents were made to 22 000 ft (6700 m).

Radio sonde upper air observations were first made in Britain in 1937. A small light-weight radio transmitter is incorporated in the meteorological instruments, sending back to ground-receiving-station readings of pressure, temperature, humidity and wind data in the form of audio frequency notes. This was a great improvement, because information could be received without delay, and was not dependent upon retrieval of the instrument.

Aircraft reports from commercial and meteorological flights supplement radio sonde upper air data in the impossible task of trying to get a complete picture of the atmosphere.

The first satellite to provide useful weather data was the US Explorer VII, launched in October 1959. TIROS I, the first specialised weather satellite, operated from 1 April 1960 and others followed at intervals. ESSA I was the first satellite to transmit cloud pictures, on 3 February 1966.

Sun synchronous weather satellites orbit above each Pole every 2 hours, encircling the Earth a dozen times a day. The Earth also rotates about its polar axis beneath the satellite, which therefore scans only one sixth of the Equator each complete orbit, and the entire Equator twice each day. Places in between Poles and Equator are scanned at intermediate frequencies, depending upon latitude.

The current USA sun synchronous satellites are TIROS-N (Television and Infra Red Observation Satellite), launched in October 1978, and NOAA 6 (National Oceanic and Atmospheric Administration) launched in June 1979. Between the two, most parts of the world are scanned about every 6 hours. Sun synchronous satellites cruise at a height of about 500 miles (800 km).

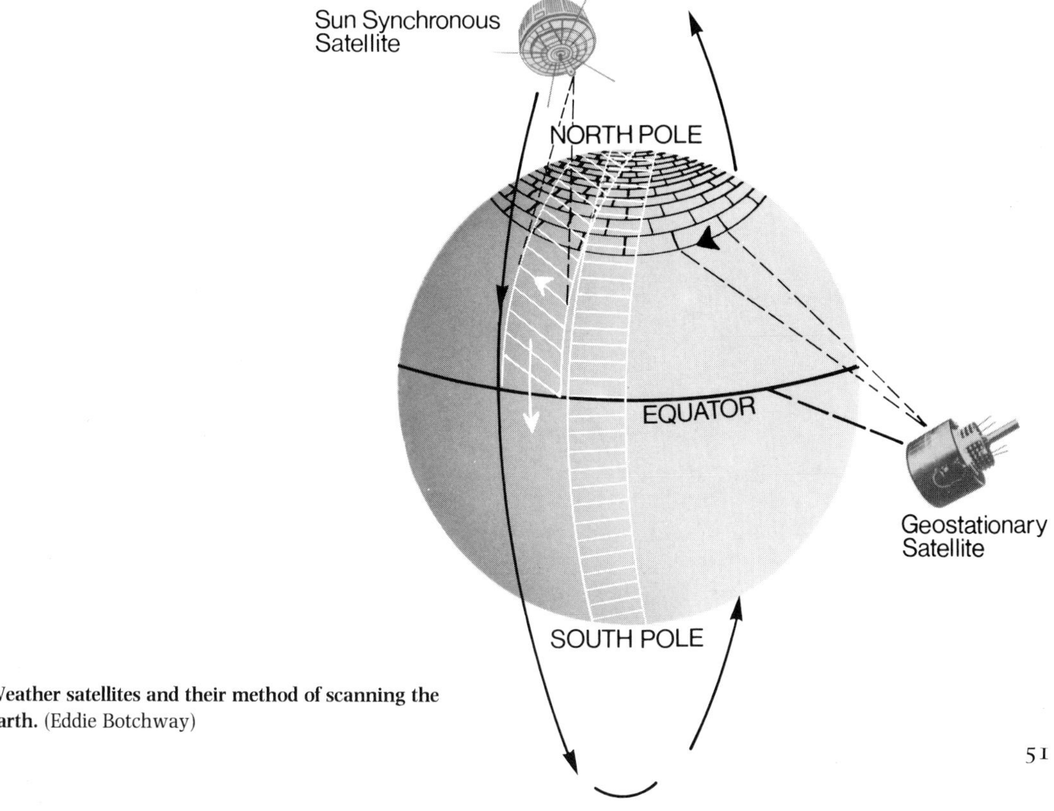

Weather satellites and their method of scanning the Earth. (Eddie Botchway)

Geostationary satellites orbit in the same plane as the Equator and at the same speed as the Earth rotates about its axis. The satellites therefore remain almost stationary relative to the Earth, at the colossal height of 22 300 miles (35 880 km) above the Equator. Sensors and cameras on board move in stepped sequence, scanning the half-globe beneath laterally, strip by strip, so as to build up a complete picture each half hour. Pictures are distorted at the edges, but four or five geostationary satellites, together with a sun synchronous satellite, can cover the whole world satisfactorily.

The United States controls two satellites, GOES-west over longitude 135°W and GOES-east over 75°W. (The acronym stands for Geostationary Operational Environmental Satellite.) *Sunflower*, managed by Japan, is stationed over 140°E. METEOSAT 2, operated by the European Space Agency, is stationary over the Greenwich Meridian and was launched on 19 June 1981.

The temperature profile of the atmosphere is a statement or graph showing temperature at all heights above the ground. Within broad limits, the profile varies from day to day, determining the height to which convection clouds can develop and indicating to forecasters other pertinent changes in atmospheric characteristics. The most accurate temperature profiles are obtained by electronic thermometers sent up in radio sonde apparatus, but satellites also send back valuable information. Sensors operate on wavelengths radiated by carbon dioxide, which is always present in the atmosphere. Fluctuations in radiation, which vary slightly according to the temperature of the gas, are processed by computer into temperature readings.

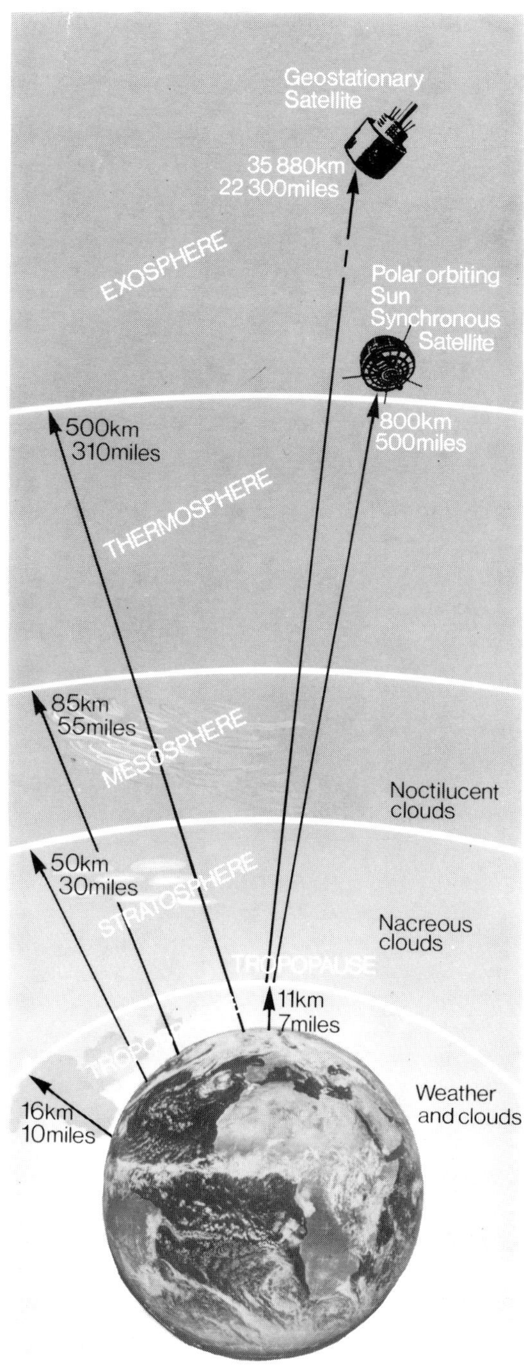

The Earth, its atmospheric layers and beyond. The view of the half world (enlarged on left) was scanned by METEOSAT 1 in half an hour on 7 July 1979. (Eddie Botchway and University of Dundee)

The troposphere is the lowest layer of the Earth's atmosphere, and the region in which weather forms. Temperature within the troposphere generally decreases with height but usually at different rates at each level. Thus the temperature profile of the troposphere varies every day as the result of innumerable modifications, mixtures and confrontations of air masses which originate in one place and move on to another. Glaisher discovered in his balloon flights that there are often quite abrupt discontinuities of temperature in the upper air, and on 12 January 1864 he noted that air was actually warmer between altitudes of 1300 ft and 6000 ft (400 m and 1800 m) than it was at ground level.

A temperature inversion exists in a layer of air when temperature rises with increasing height above ground. This condition is a frequent feature near the ground after a night of radiation cooling under a clear sky. An inversion limits the buoyancy of air, so that smoke, fog or cloud remains trapped beneath a lid of warmer air.

The tropopause is the boundary at the top of the troposphere where temperature ceases to fall with height. The tropopause varies from an average 10 miles (16 km) above ground near the Equator to about 7 miles (11 km) near latitude 50°, reaching only about 6 miles (9 km) over the Poles. The tropopause tends to be higher in summer than in winter.

Temperature at the tropopause is usually much lower over the Equator than over the Poles because air temperature can continue to decrease up to a higher tropopause than it can above the Poles. A temperature at the tropopause of −40°F to −76°F (−40°C to −60°C) is considered comparatively warm; −76°F to −112°F (−60°C to −80°C) is comparatively cold.

During the nuclear tests in 1957 scientists took the opportunity of making meteorological soundings which recorded extremely low temperatures at the tropopause over Christmas Island and the Maldives. Mean monthly temperatures were between −120°F and −126°F (−85°C and −88°C). Five successive readings on 19–22 February showed less than −134°F (−92°C) with one extreme value of −146°F (−99°C).

The stratosphere is the region above the tropopause which has little change of temperature with height, sometimes even a slight increase of temperature with height. This region extends to an altitude of about 30 miles (50 km) above the Earth and its upper boundary is called the stratopause. The stratosphere contains a relatively large amount of ozone, absorbing much of the Sun's ultraviolet radiation which would otherwise be dangerous for plant and human life.

The mesosphere lies above the stratosphere, between altitudes of 30 and 55 miles (50 km–85 km). Here, temperature again decreases with height. The lowest temperature recorded so far was over Sweden between 27 July and 7 August 1963, when −225°F (−143°C) was registered at a height of 50 miles (80 km).

The thermosphere lies above the mesosphere, and there temperature increases with height all the way to our atmosphere's edge, at an altitude of about 310 miles (500 km).

The exosphere lies beyond Earth's atmosphere, where temperature no longer has its customary terrestrial meaning.

Atmospheric pressure is exerted by the sum of all the layers of air which have different temperature and density. Pressure varies comparatively little throughout the world because of the regulating boundary of the tropopause. Surface air, which continually warms and rises over equatorial areas, has to cool over a greater height into the atmosphere than does air which is already cold and dense near the ground at the Poles. The average weights of atmosphere which each area supports are not too dissimilar.

However, hot and cold surfaces are not equally distributed between Equator and Poles but are complicated arrangements of adjacent land and sea. The balance of heat around the world is achieved by means of an alternating sequence of relatively high and low pressure belts, which roughly follow parallels of latitude.

The equatorial low pressure belt lies 15°–20° north and south of the Equator and is partly determined by the high temperatures near the surface.

Semi-permanent high pressure exists around the latitudes 30°N and 30°S.

Seasonal high pressure zones develop over continents in high latitudes during winter because of rapidly cooling air. The most pronounced winter high pressure occurs over central Asia, where average January pressure is between 1026 and 1036 mb.

Seasonal low pressure zones develop over continents in summer because of thermal heating. Since these areas are the same as those having high pressure in winter, they experience the greatest seasonal range in pressure. Average pressure over central Asia in July is about 1005 mb.

Small areas of permanent high pressure exist over both Poles where there is always a layer of very cold dense air.

Fluctuating pressure is characteristic of the oceans and adjacent land in latitudes higher than 40° N or S. Pressure varies from about 970 mb to 1040 mb, sometimes within days. Occasionally, more extreme values are experienced. Low pressure cells, travelling from west to east, create cloud and rain in the conflict between winds from the subtropics and from the polar regions. High pressure systems interrupt low pressure systems, but do not always persist for long.

Diurnal pressure changes happen because of rhythmic temperature fluctuations all around the world. Pressure rises from 4 am to 10 am, falls from 10 am to 4 pm, rises again between 4 pm and 10 pm and falls from 10 pm to 4 am local times. The daily range in the tropics is about 3 mb and is easily detectable on a barogram. In middle latitudes the range is much less, about 0·8 mb, and is usually camouflaged by pressure changes caused by developing weather systems.

Pressure tendency is the rate of change of pressure. In general, a pressure fall indicates the approach or deepening of a low pressure system, while a rapid rise indicates its departure or filling. A slow steady rise for 24 hours or more portends the development of a high pressure system.

A fall or rise in pressure of 10 mb in 3 hours is an almost certain sign of gales. However, a smaller tendency is no guarantee that gales cannot occur.

At the approach of the most disastrous hurricane known in the United States, at Galveston, Texas, on 5 September 1900, pressure fell about 22 mb in 4 hours.

In the worst storm known in southern England, on 27 November 1703, pressure fell about 13 mb in 4 hours.

On 16–17 February 1981, Hellissandur, Iceland, recorded a fall of 19·4 mb in the 3 hours prior to 9 pm and a rise of 20·7 mb in the 3 hours prior to 3 am. There was a deep depression, 940 mb, in the vicinity.

The highest pressure ever recorded was in north central Siberia at Agata, on 31 December 1968,

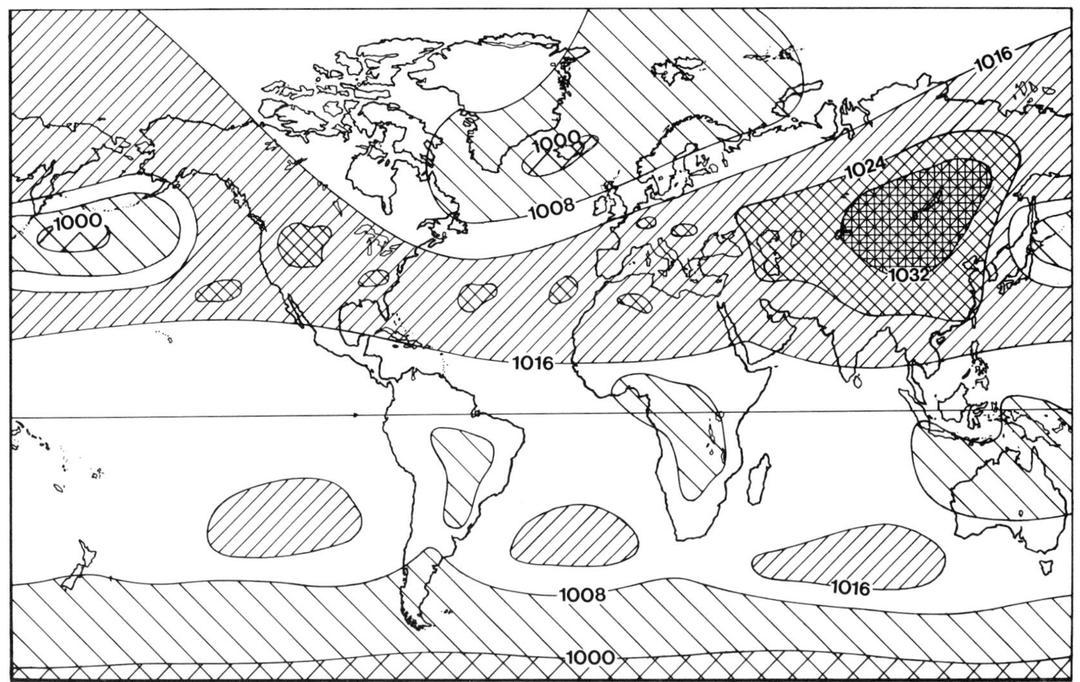

Average January isobars. (P. Milne)

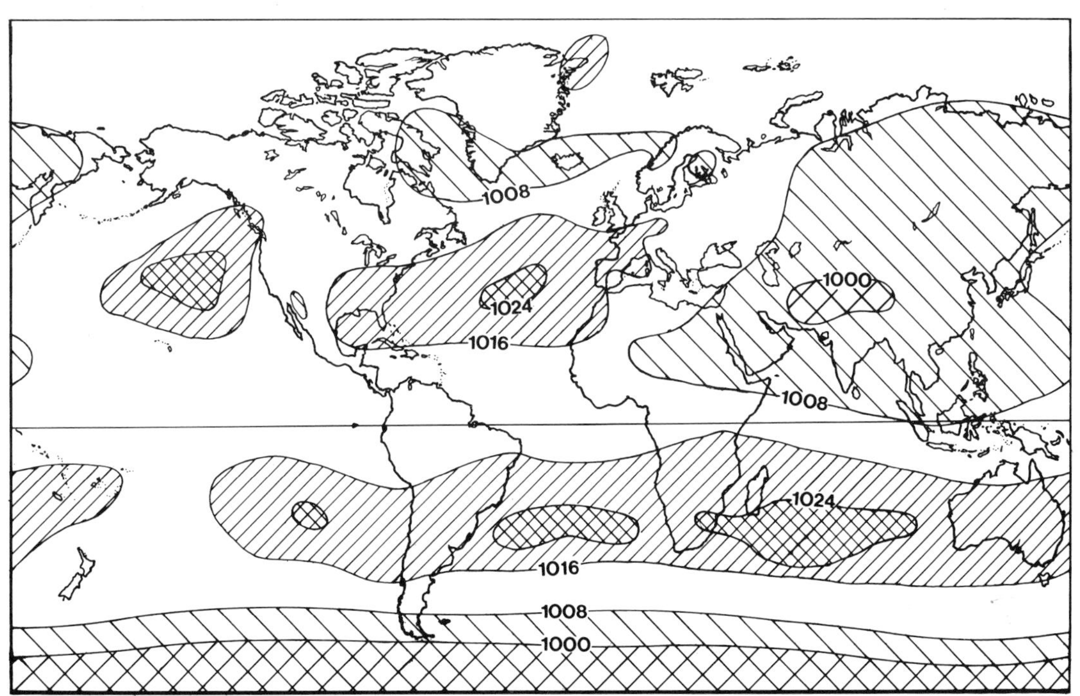

Average July isobars. (P. Milne)

when air temperature was −50°F (−46°C). The pressure was above 1070 mb for 5 days and reached 1083·8 mb. Five other stations in the region had similarly high pressure, discounting any probability of error.

1067·3 mb was registered at Medicine Hat, Alberta in Canada on 24 January 1897.
The highest pressure recorded in the British Isles was 1054·7 mb at Aberdeen, Scotland, on 31 January 1902.

The lowest pressure ever measured was by US Air Force drop sonde in the eye of typhoon *Tip*, some 1000 miles east of the Philippines on 12 October 1979. Sea level pressure was 870 mb.

Lowest recorded in Great Britain was 925·5 mb on 26 January 1884 at Ochtertyre, Perthshire.

The lowest actual atmospheric pressure at mean sea level may never be known, because it occurs in the centre of tornadoes. The chances of a barometer being in the right place at the right time are small, and the chances of the instrument surviving the tornado are less.

Atmospheric pressure conversion table

Millibars	*inches*	*mm*	*millibars*	*inches*	*mm*	*millibars*	*inches*	*mm*
960	28·35	720	990	29·23	742	1020	30·12	765
961	28·38	721	991	29·26	743	1021	30·15	766
962	28·41	722	992	29·29	744	1022	30·18	767
963	28·44	722	993	29·32	745	1023	30·21	767
964	28·47	723	994	29·35	745	1024	30·24	768
965	28·50	724	995	29·38	746	1025	30·27	769
966	28·53	725	996	29·41	747	1026	30·30	770
967	28·56	725	997	29·44	748	1027	30·33	770
968	28·59	726	998	29·47	749	1028	30·36	771
969	28·61	727	999	29·50	749	1029	30·39	772
970	28·64	727	1000	29·53	750	1030	30·42	773
971	28·67	728	1001	29·56	751	1031	30·45	773
972	28·70	729	1002	29·59	752	1032	30·47	774
973	28·73	730	1003	29·62	752	1033	30·50	775
974	28·76	731	1004	29·65	753	1034	30·53	775
975	28·79	731	1005	29·68	754	1035	30·56	776
976	28·82	732	1006	29·71	755	1036	30·59	777
977	28·85	733	1007	29·74	755	1037	30·62	778
978	28·88	734	1008	29·77	756	1038	30·65	779
979	28·91	734	1009	29·80	757	1039	30·68	779
980	28·94	735	1010	29·83	758	1040	30·71	780
981	28·97	736	1011	29·85	758	1041	30·74	781
982	29·00	737	1012	29·88	759	1042	30·77	782
983	29·03	737	1013	29·91	760	1043	30·80	782
984	29·06	738	1014	29·94	760	1044	30·83	783
985	29·09	739	1015	29·97	761	1045	30·86	784
986	29·12	740	1016	30·00	762	1046	30·89	785
987	29·15	740	1017	30·03	763	1047	30·92	785
988	29·18	741	1018	30·06	764	1048	30·95	786
989	29·21	742	1019	30·09	764	1049	30·98	787

5. The nature of wind

Wind is moving air which obeys the normal buoyancy rules of fluids. Dense cold air moves to replace warmer and less dense air which then rises. The weakest winds are draughts in houses but the same basic principle—air temperature difference—determines wind outdoors, from tiny zephyrs along a river bank to the tearing jet streams several miles above ground.

Surface wind blows below a height of 33 ft (10 m) above ground, and is therefore the wind most affecting everyday life. This wind must be the most keenly observed weather element of all time. Hunters have always watched it meticulously in order to avoid betraying themselves by scent when upwind of their quarry.

Personification of wind, ie naming winds after deities, was the natural outcome of lack of understanding about its cause. Aristotle used the allegory of human breath and called wind 'exhalation'. In Athens Andronicus of Cyrrhus (1st cent. BC), Greek astronomer, built an octagonal marble tower, called the Tower of the Winds or Horologium. Each face was decorated with a frieze of figures, carved into the marble, to represent the eight principal winds. Each figure portrayed a deity appropriately dressed and equipped for the weather with which it was associated.

Boreas (from the north) and *Notos* (from the south) were primary and opposite winds which could not blow together. Winds from other directions, *Zephyros* from the west or *Apeliotes* from the east, were able to act in concert with the primary winds. The wind blowing from north east was called *Kaikias*, that from the south east was *Euros*, the south westerly was *Lips* and the north westerly was *Skiros*.

Below these figures, facing the Sun, were sundials indicating the time. Inside the building was a hydraulic clock used when the sky was overcast.

A statue of the sea god Triton, at the top of the Horologium, turned with the wind and thus indicated its direction. This was the first use of weather vanes.

Wind names still persist all over the world, and some are listed on the adjacent page.

Left: The Tower of the Winds at Athens, Greece. (National Tourist Organisation of Greece)

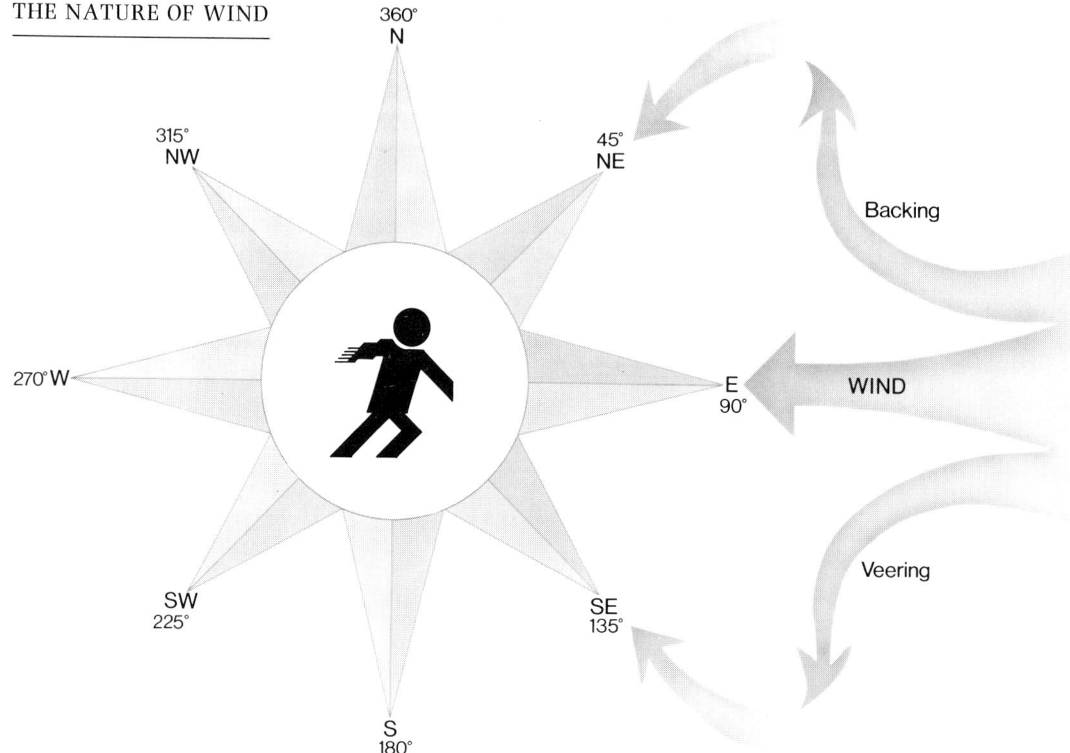

Wind blows from the compass point, given in the description, towards the observer. It veers when changing direction in a clockwise manner and backs when changing counter clockwise. (Eddie Botchway)

Wind description by compass point, or by the number of degrees from north, started after the magnetic compass was introduced into Europe from China in the 12th century. Wind blows *from* the compass point towards the observer; eg a NW wind, or a 315° wind, blows from the north west towards the observer.

Wind *veers* if it changes direction in a clockwise sense and *backs* if it changes in an anticlockwise sense.

A wind vane consists of a fin on the end of a horizontal arm which freely pivots on a vertical spindle. Wind pressure on the fin forces it away from the compass point from which the wind is blowing; the usual arrow on the other end of the horizontal arm therefore points to the direction from which the wind is blowing. Wind vanes have always been popular subjects for artists and craftsmen and evolved as 'house flags' bearing coats of arms or trade symbols.

The weather cock is a wind vane, adopted by the Christian church in the middle of the 9th century. The cock turns its head into the wind, and the choice of symbol was intended as a perpetual reminder of the cock which crowed at Peter's denial of Christ.

A remote-reading wind vane permits wind direction to be read indoors. In the first century BC, Marcus Varro, writer on agricultural matters, had such a wind vane on his roof connected to a dial on the ceiling of the room below. Erasmus Darwin (1731–1802) did the same, thus gaining continual surveillance of the wind. It enabled him to note that wind direction often changes suddenly, quite apart from the small fluctuations of direction which occur all the time. Modern wind vanes have changed little in principle but have improved in precision of construction. Remote vanes record electrically onto dial faces.

Wind speed cannot be evaluated by timing over a measured distance because wind is invisible. A good approximation can be made by timing light articles, such as balloons, blowing in the wind, or by timing the shadows of clouds over water.

NAMED WINDS OF THE WORLD

BERG WIND (Afrikaans, meaning mountain) Hot and dry wind coming from the interior of South Africa and blowing down the mountains and off-shore.

BORA Cold, usually dry NE wind blowing from the mountains in Jugoslavia and north-east Italy.

BRICKFIELDER Very hot NE wind in south-east Australia, blowing during the summer months and carrying dust and sand.

BURAN (Russian *Burán*, Turkish *Borán*) Strong NE wind in Russia and central Asia. Most frequent in winter when it often carries snow and may then also be known as 'purga'.

CHINOOK Warm dry and often turbulent W wind that blows on eastern side of Rocky Mountains.

DOLDRUMS Calm or baffling wind near the Equator where opposing trade winds converge.

FÖHN Warm dry downslope wind experienced in stable atmospheric conditions in the lee of mountain ranges. Named originally for the wind experienced in the European Alps, but now applied generically to all such winds. The warmth of the Föhn is due to adiabatic compression on descent, especially if moisture has been spilled over the mountain, and to the sucking downwards of warmer air from higher altitudes.

GREGALE (Latin *Graerus*: Greek) Strong NE wind blowing in the southern Mediterranean mainly in the cooler months of the year.

HABOOB (Arabic *habub*: blowing furiously) Any wind of a strength to raise sand into a sand storm, particularly in Sudan.

HARMATTAN A dry and relatively cool NE or E wind which blows in north west Africa, average southern limit 5° N latitude in January and 18° N latitude in July. It is often dust laden and so dry as to wither vegetation and cause human skin to peel off. It nevertheless gives welcome relief from the usual humid heat of the tropics.

HELM Strong and often violent cold NE wind blowing down western slopes of Cross Fell range, Cumbria, mainly in late winter and spring. Very gusty.

KARABURAN (Turkish *kara*: black, *curan*: whirlwind) Hot dusty NE wind in central Asia.

KHAMSIN Oppressive, hot, dry S wind over Egypt, most frequent between April and June, often laden with sand from the desert.

LEVANTER (from Levant: land at eastern end of Mediterranean) Moist E wind in region of Straits of Gibraltar, often strong and most frequent June-October.

MISTRAL (Latin *Magistral*: master wind) Dry cold NW or N wind blowing off-shore along the Mediterranean coasts of France and Spain. Particularly violent on the coast of Languedoc and Provence when it funnels down the Rhône Valley.

MONSOON (Arabic *mausim*: time, season) Any markedly seasonal wind, particularly in east and south east Asia.

PAMPERO (Spanish *pampa*: great plain, prairie) Piercing cold SW wind which blows from the Andes across the S. American pampas in Argentina and across Uruguay to the Atlantic.

PURGA Strong NE winter wind in Russia and central Asia, often raising snow from the ground to cause blizzards.

ROARING FORTIES Region between latitudes 40° and 50° S where strong W winds, known as 'Brave West Winds', blow steadily. So named by sailors who first entered these latitudes.

SCIROCCO or *Sirocco* (Arabic *suruk*: rising of the sun) An oppressive hot dry S wind on north coast of Africa blowing from Sahara. By the time this wind crosses the Mediterranean to Europe it has became slightly cooler but very moist. It produces languor and mental debility.

SEISTAN Strong N wind in summer in the Seistan region of eastern Iran and Afghanistan. It can attain velocities of over 100 mph (160 km/h) and carries dust and sand.

SHAMAL Hot dry and dusty NW wind, persistent in summer in Iraq and the Persian Gulf.

SOUTHERLY BUSTER Sudden cold S wind in south eastern Australia, usually strong and succeeding wind from some northerly point. Temperature can fall 36F (20C) degrees or more in a very short time with the arrival of this wind.

TRADES Steady winds blowing between latitudes 10° and 30°, from the NE in the northern hemisphere, from the SE in the southern hemisphere. Of importance to sailing ships, hence called 'winds that blow trade' by navigators in the 18th century. Trade winds change in direction according to the seasonal shift in the high pressure belts.

TRAMONTANA (Latin *trans*: across; *montem*: Mountain; Ital. *tramontano*: between the mountains) — cool dry N wind blowing across the Spanish Mediterranean coast.

WILLIWAW Strong downslope wind in Alaska.

The Beaufort Scale was originated by Admiral Sir Francis Beaufort (1774–1857), a contemporary of Nelson. In 1805 he specified a scale with 13 degrees of wind strength, as well as calm, which related to the amount of canvas which a sailing vessel could carry in those conditions. The next year he modified the scale by labelling both calm and light air Force 1 and combining the two upper wind strengths as Force 12 'a hurricane which no canvas can withstand'.

The idea was good, but the scale was dependent upon the subjective decisions of captains of different ships. Hence the scale was later adapted to relate to the visible effect of wind on sea, which was the same for every vessel afloat. It is still used at sea but gives an approximate value of wind speed only. The state of the sea depends also upon the wind blowing in distant areas and how it has been blowing in the past day or two. The Beaufort Scale has been adapted for land use also.

A knot is a nautical mile per hour, obtaining its name from the old method of measuring a ship's speed through the water. A float, shaped to offer resistance to towage and attached to a long line knotted at equal intervals, was thrown into the water. The number of knots, passing freely through the hand over a period of time as the line spun out, indicated ship speed. Distance and speed at sea are measured differently from the way they are measured on land because the only visible points of reference are the planets and the time recorded by chronometer.

A nautical mile is the length of a minute of latitude and varies from 6046 ft (1843 m) on the Equator to 6092 ft (1857 m) in latitude 60°. The international nautical mile is defined as 1852 metres. (1 knot = 1.15 mph = 1.85 km/h.)

An anemometer (Greek *anemos*: wind) is anything which measures wind speed. Washing blowing on a line acts as a rudimentary anemometer, because the faster the wind, the stronger the force which it exerts and the more nearly is the tethered washing blown to the horizontal.

The Beaufort Scale for use at sea

Beaufort Force	*Description*	*Sea state*	*Knots*
0	Calm	Sea like a mirror	Less than 1
1	Light air	Ripples with appearance of scales, no foam crests	1–3
2	Light breeze	Wavelets, small but pronounced. Crests with glassy appearance, but do not break	4–6
3	Gentle breeze	Large wavelets, crests begin to break. Glassy looking foam, occasional white horses	7–10
4	Moderate breeze	Small waves becoming longer, frequent white horses	11–16
5	Fresh breeze	Moderate waves of pronounced long form. Many white horses, some spray	17–21
6	Strong breeze	Some large waves, extensive white foam crests, some spray	22–27
7	Near gale	Sea heaped up, white foam from breaking waves blowing in streaks with the wind	28–33
8	Gale	Moderately high and long waves. Crests break into spin drift, blowing foam in well marked streaks	34–40
9	Strong gale	High waves, dense foam streaks in wind, wave crests topple, tumble and roll over. Spray reduces visibility	41–47
10	Storm	Very high waves with long overhanging crests. Dense blowing foam, sea surface appears white. Heavy tumbling of sea, shock-like. Poor visibility	48–55
11	Violent storm	Exceptionally high waves, sometimes concealing small and medium sized ships. Sea completely covered with long white patches of foam. Edges of wave crests blown into froth. Poor visibility	56–63
12	Hurricane	Air filled with foam and spray, sea white with driving spray. Visibility bad	⩾ 64

The Beaufort Scale, adapted for use on land

Beaufort Force	*Description*	*Specification on land*	*Speed* mph	km/h
0	Calm	Smoke rises vertically	Less than 1	
1	Light air	Direction of wind shown by smoke drift but not by wind vanes	1–3	1–5
2	Light breeze	Wind felt on face, leaves rustle, ordinary wind vane moved by wind	4–7	6–11
3	Gentle breeze	Leaves and small twigs in constant motion, wind extends light flag	8–12	12–19
4	Moderate breeze	Wind raises dust and loose paper, small branches move	13–18	20–29
5	Fresh breeze	Small trees in leaf start to sway, crested wavelets on inland waters	19–24	30–39
6	Strong breeze	Large branches in motion, whistling in telegraph wires, umbrellas used with difficulty	25–31	40–50
7	Near gale	Whole trees in motion, inconvenient to walk against wind	32–38	51–61
8	Gale	Twigs break from trees, difficult to walk	39–46	62–74
9	Strong gale	Slight structural damage occurs, chimney pots and slates removed	47–54	75–87
10	Storm	Trees uprooted, considerable structural damage occurs	55–63	88–101
11	Violent storm	Widespread damage	64–73	102–117
12	Hurricane	Widespread damage	⩾74	⩾119

Japanese wind sock, being a hollow paper fish which is distended by the wind. (Mary Evans Picture Library)

A wind sock is the simplest practical anemometer, and consists of a tube of cloth fixed to a metal ring which pivots on the top of a pole. It streams out at an angle from the pole according to wind strength, giving practised observers a very good visual indica-

tion of wind *speed*. The wind sock goes one stage further than washing-on-the-line, because it pivots to face into the wind and therefore indicates speed *and* direction, an invaluable aid to aircraft pilots approaching a landing strip.

A pressure plate anemometer was one of the first instruments to measure the force exerted by wind. It was described by Leon Battista Alberti around 1450 and was among many ideas sketched in the notebooks of Leonardo da Vinci (1452–1519). He visualised a metal plate, fixed at the top and free to swing alongside a curved graduated scale. The stronger the wind, the higher it forced the plate towards the horizontal. The idea was sound and was developed by Hooke in the mid-17th century as a standard anemometer.

It is interesting to note that at a wind speed of 100 mph (160 km/h) a person can lean forward on the wind with straight body and legs and almost touch the ground with his hand without falling. This makes him an upside-down pressure plate anemometer, tethered to the ground!

The cup anemometer was invented by John Robinson in 1846, and is still the most widely used instrument for measuring wind speed. Three or four hemispherical cups pivot on a vertical spindle and rotate according to the force of the wind acting upon them. Each rotation makes an electrical contact and the number of turns is recorded by counter.

The anemograph is an instrument which records the movement of an anemometer on a rotating chart. The mechanism is often combined with a wind vane, so as to record changes in wind direction on a different section of the chart. The anemogram is the resulting chart which shows fluctuations in wind speed and direction.

A manometer is an instrument which measures pressure by variation in level of a liquid. A mercury barometer, for instance, is a manometer and so is the pressure tube anemometer invented by W. H. Dines. He was President of the Royal Meteorological Society in 1892.

The Dines Pressure Tube Anemometer has a vane with an open-ended head which constantly faces into

Right: A transmitting cup anemometer on the top of Skylon during the Festival of Britain year, 1951. Current model, with wind vane (left) on the Offices of the General Steam Navigation Co, London. (R. W. Munro Ltd)

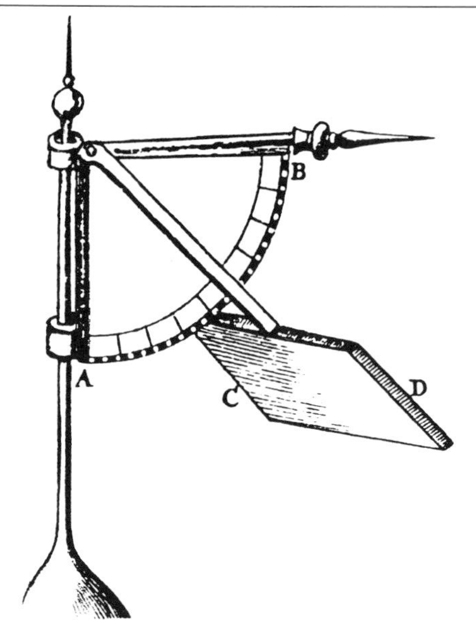

Robert Hooke's swinging plate wind gauge, circa 1664.

wind. The wind blows into the horizontal tube and across a vertical perforated suction tube, connected to the air space at the top of a water tank. As the wind blows across the perforations, air from the chamber is sucked out and the float in the water rises. When wind decreases, the float sinks till the air in the tank is in equilibrium with the wind strength outside. A recording pen is attached to the float and traces wind strength onto a chart on a revolving drum. The instrument was developed in association with the manufacturer, R. W. Munro, who had sole production rights, as a result of the investigation into the Tay Bridge disaster on 28 December 1879.

A Dines Pressure Tube Anemometer, with modifications to prevent choking by snow, was lent to the second British Antarctic Expedition led by Capt. Scott in 1911. It performed admirably, was reconditioned on return and lent to Sir Ernest Shackleton's Antarctic Expedition of 1914. It was lost when the supply vessel *Endurance* was crushed in the ice, causing the expedition to be stranded on a large ice floe.

The Dines Pressure Tube Anemometer is now obsolete, partly because its response to wind changes was rather slow.

The exposure of anemometers was the subject of research by W. H. Dines at the end of the 19th century. He mounted several anemometers on poles at the same level over his house and found they did not read similarly because of turbulence. He then raised them progressively higher till they all recorded the same readings at about 15 ft (4·5 m) above the roof top. Standard exposure for an anemometer is 33 ft (10 m) on the top of a pole, well away from any building, or as high as is practicable above the roof where readings are required.

Wind deviates in a horizontal plane in order to get round solid obstacles such as houses, hills, mountains, and it deviates in a vertical plane to surmount obstacles such as roofs or mountain tops.

Wind eddies backward into the relatively 'empty' space behind solid obstacles, which is called the

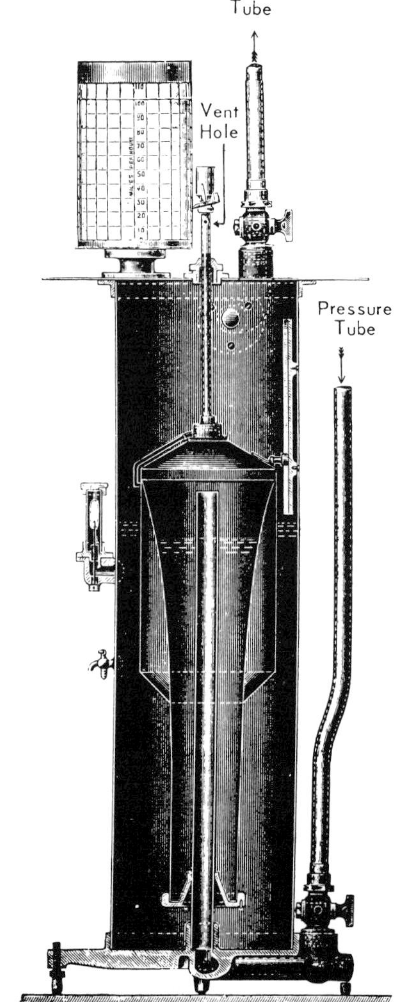

Dines pressure tube anemometer. (R. W. Munro Ltd)

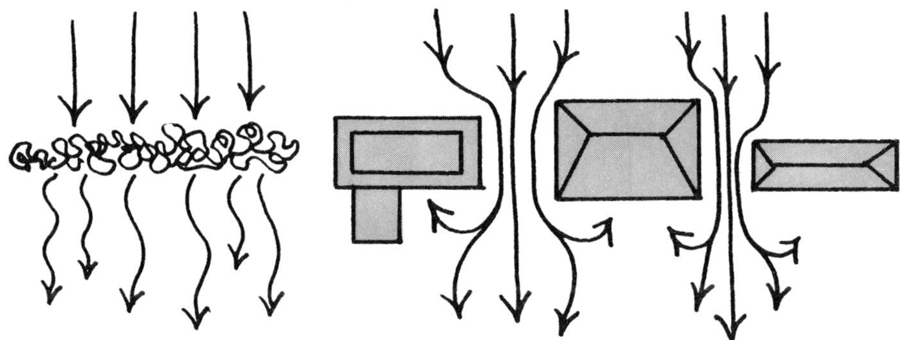

Wind filters through semi-permeable obstructions, such as hedges, so that its impact is lessened. Wind funnels through constrictions between solid obstructions and consequently increases in speed. (Diana Davies)

leeward side. Therefore, the immediate lee of a building or cliff does not always give shelter from the wind.

Wind is said to funnel when it has to squeeze through constrictions (between houses, cliffs or mountains) and increases in speed to do so. It is analogous to the increase in speed of water when forced through the constricting nozzle of a hose pipe.

A wave motion can be induced in an air stream forced over hills and mountains at high speed, and air may undulate in a vertical plane for a considerable distance to leeward, with pronounced crests and troughs similar to water waves. This is thought to contribute to the high speed of winds blowing down the leeward side of mountains in certain instances.

A gust is a momentary increase above the average wind speed, and a **lull** is a momentary decrease below the average speed.

Wind exerts a pressure which is proportional to the square of its speed. A gust to *double* the average wind speed implies a *four-fold* increase in pressure.

The first British wind powered electric generator is to be built on a hill in the Orkneys, and is due to be operational by the winter 1983–4. The machine, 150 ft (50 m) high with a blade 180 ft (60 m) diameter, is designed to produce full power with wind speeds between 37 and 60 mph (60–96 km/h). It will have a capacity of three megawatts.

Turbulence is the irregularity of wind speed and direction caused by obstructions, the drag of surface friction or the superimposition of vertical winds on horizontal winds. There is no precise height at which the roughness of any terrain ceases to be effective on the movement of air, but for meteorological purposes it is considered to be 2000 ft (600 m) above the ground. Turbulence at higher levels often occurs when horizontal winds of different speed or direction blow in adjacent layers of the atmosphere. This is known as clear air turbulence.

Wind eddies in the lee of solid obstructions and may undulate for some distance beyond. (Diana Davies)

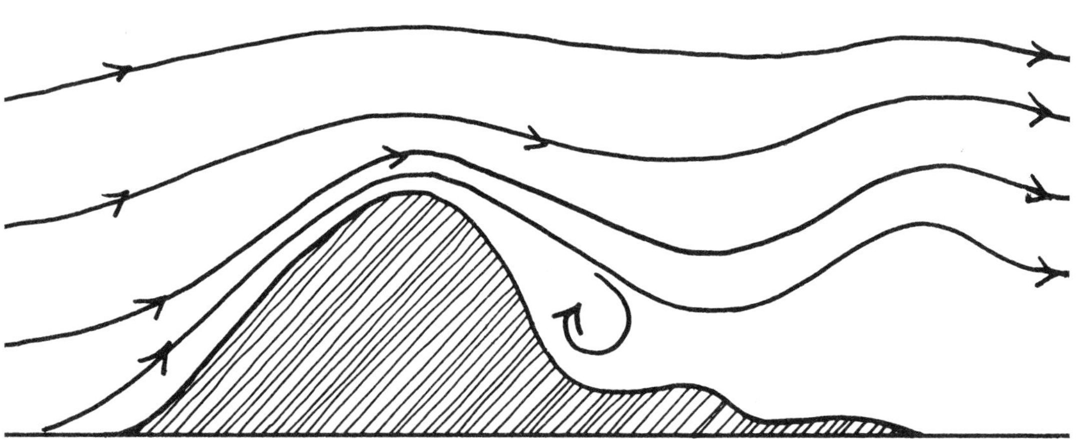

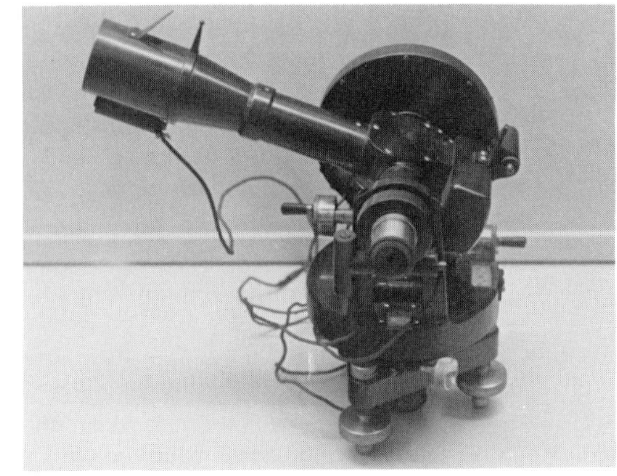

Right: Pilot balloon theodolite, from 1918, in which eyepiece remains horizontal whatever the angle of the telescope. (P. Defries)

Below: Model of a wind turbine, designed by the Wind Energy Systems Group, to be built on Burger Hill, Orkney, for the North of Scotland Hydro Electric Board and the Department of Energy. The rotor will operate at wind speeds between 15 and 60 mph (25 and 100 km/h). (Taylor Woodrow Construction Ltd)

1 60m diam. Rotor

2 Duplicate Wind Speed and Direction Sensor

3 Air Brake

4 Low Speed Gearbox

5 Disc Brake

6 High Speed Gearbox

7 1500r.p.m Generator

8 Service Gantry

9 Detachable Pallet

10 Structural Steel Nacelle Framework

11 Aluminium Alloy Nacelle Cladding

12 Orientation Vertical Support Bogie

13 Orientation Slewing Mechanism

14 Reinforced Concrete Tower

15 Slip Ring System

16 Electrical Power and Auxiliary Cable

17 Control Equipment and Storage Room

18 Switchgear and Transformer Room

19 Underground Power and Auxiliary Cables

20 Construction Apron

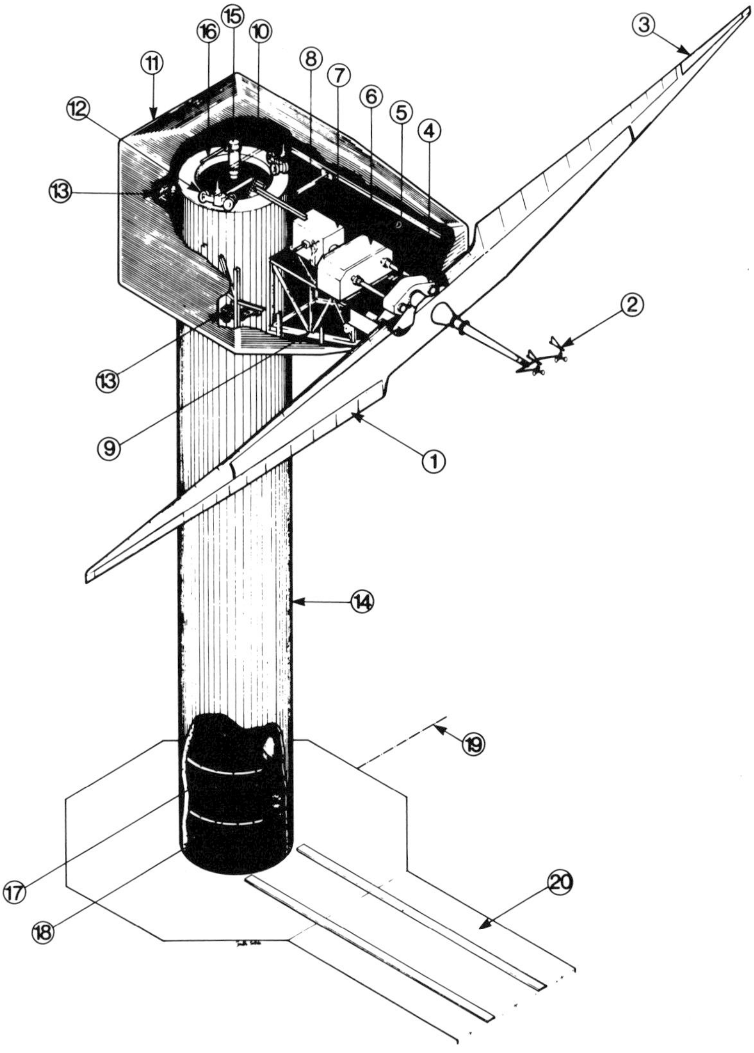

Wind generally becomes stronger with height, increasing rapidly in the first 6 ft (2 m) above ground and then at a steadier and slower rate. An experienced observer can get some idea of wind speed and direction at different altitudes, by watching the movement of clouds. Very low cloud often appears to be moving faster than it is simply because it is relatively near to the eye.

Consecutive satellite pictures of clouds, showing the distance they have moved over a known period of time, give helpful knowledge of upper winds. It has to be remembered, however, that cloud bands are constantly changing and may look very different from one picture to another.

A comb nephoscope (Greek *nephos*: cloud) is a simple device for gauging high level wind. It looks something like a Neptune's trident set into the ground. The upright can be revolved until a selected plume of ice crystal cloud appears to travel along the upper horizontal bar; that determines wind direction. Wind speed is estimated from the time taken by the plume to pass the spaced prongs on the horizontal bar.

A pilot balloon is one which is filled with hydrogen to a predetermined pressure, so that its vertical rate of ascent, when released, is known. The balloon can be tracked by a theodolite, and wind speed and direction calculated from the elevation and azimuth readings obtained. Balloon colour is chosen for optimum contrast to the prevailing sky.

A modern refinement is to attach a radar reflector to the pilot balloon so that echo signals may be received at a station on the ground. This eliminates the need for visual theodolite sightings.

Wind statistics must be assessed in the context of altitude and time. Wind speed is normally greater at high altitudes than at low, and greater in gusts than averaged over longer periods of time. Even moderate wind speeds over a long averaging period may be extraordinary when recorded at low altitude stations. Highest recorded wind speeds make no pretence of being the highest actual wind speeds, which may never be measured. All figures given are for surface wind unless otherwise stated.

The windiest place in the British Isles is Tiree, off the west coast of Scotland which has a mean annual wind speed of 17 mph (27 km/h).

The windiest place in the world is in Antarctica, on the coast of Eastern Adelie Land and West King George Land. A French expedition maintained a station at Port Martin from February 1950 to January 1952, and made valuable discoveries about the inhospitable wind. It nearly always blows from ESE or SSE, which is from the ice cap towards the coast line, and it appears to be an exaggerated katabatic wind. Intensely cold air over the high interior races downwards towards the coast over a 1-in-100 slope, slackening abruptly on reaching the warmer sea. The wind is fairly steady while it blows, but often starts and stops abruptly. It is as if the supply of air suddenly runs out and has to accumulate again for its downhill journey.

In 1951 mean wind speeds at the Port Martin station were:

Annual: 40 mph (64 km/h)
Highest monthly (March): 65 mph (105 km/h)
Highest 24-hour: (21–22 March) 108 mph (174 km/h)

There were 122 days with mean speed above 73 mph (117 km/h) and only 22 days with mean speed below 31 mph (50 km/h).

The highest recorded gust occurred in the USA, at the Mt Washington Observatory, New Hampshire, at an altitude of 6288 ft (1916 m). On 12 April 1934 a speed of 231 mph (371 km/h) was recorded, and gusts to 220 mph (354 km/h) occur there frequently.

The highest recorded gust in the British Isles occurred in Scotland at the Cairngorms Weather Station, altitude 3525 ft (1074 m). Wind gusted to 144 mph (232 km/h) on 6 March 1967. Kirkwall, Orkney, recorded a gust of 136 mph (219 km/h) on 7 February 1969.

The highest mean 24-hour wind speed occurred in the United States, on Mt Washington in New Hampshire. The mean speed for 24 hours between 11 and 12 April 1934 was 129 mph (208 km/h).

The highest mean hourly wind speed in the British Isles has been 99 mph (159 km/h). This was experienced at Great Dun Fell, Cumbria, altitude 2813 ft (857 m) on 15 January 1968 and at Lowther Hill, Scotland, altitude 2415 ft (736 m) on 20 January 1963.

A thermal is a vertical wind, created when air warms on contact with a heating surface, rises, and is replaced by colder air from above, or alongside. Thermals may also develop when air travels over a sea surface which gets progressively warmer with latitude.

Thermal currents are the main power source for gliders and they rise thus:

Weak thermal: $1\frac{1}{2}$–3 ft/s ($\frac{1}{2}$–1 m/s)
Moderate thermal: 3–9 ft/s (1–3 m/s)
Strong thermal: more than 9 ft/s (3 m/s)

Tree shaped by the prevailing wind, a familiar sight on exposed shore lines. (Ingrid Holford)

Gliders require air currents which are rising faster than the craft sink, which means about $2\frac{1}{2}$–3 ft/s (nearly 1 m/s). In Great Britain thermals are usually only strong enough for gliding between approximately 11 am and 7 pm during summer months.

The strongest thermals occur in deep shower clouds. The US army co-operated with the Weather Bureau in daring investigations of these clouds during the 1950s. Pilots deliberately flew into the clouds at various levels and allowed the thermals to take control of the aircraft. Updraughts as strong as 3000 ft/min (1000 m/min) were usual, and 5000 ft/min (1500 m/min) were encountered occasionally in clouds whose tops reached 60 000 ft (18 000 m).

Strong thermal upcurrents delay considerably the fall by parachute from an aircraft. On 26 July 1959 an American pilot ejected from his plane at 47 000 ft (14 400 m) and took 40 minutes to fall through a thunder cloud instead of the expected 11 minutes.

The effect of wind upon sea is particularly important for oil platforms. See chapter 8. (British Petroleum Ltd)

Leeward downdraughts can be hazardous in mountainous areas and may account for hitherto unexplained aircraft accidents. Several instances have been reported by pilots of powered aircraft, of downdraughts greater than 30 ft/s (10 m/s) to the lee of the Little Carpathian Ridge, Czechoslovakia. These caused forced altitude drops between 900 and 1500 ft (300–500 m).

The longest wind-powered flights are achieved on a combination of thermal currents, horizontal pressure wind and uplift in wave motion over mountains. The flight of the mythological Daedalus, some 750 miles (1200 km) from Knossos in Crete to Cumae in southern Italy, is considered to have been possible. There was adequate fabric and woodworking skill available at the time to build a sail-plane and there was suitable topography along the route to give enough lift in some weather. The journey would have needed a high standard of wind detection, which the ill-fated Icarus presumably did not have, so that he fell into the sea and was drowned.

Modern gliders are usually launched by release after tow from a powered aircraft. Record flights have covered distances of more than 1000 miles (1600 km) and soared to altitudes of more than 8 miles (14 km).

Even a heavy aircraft, designed for powered flight,

can find air currents in which to glide. The pilot of a Lockheed F5, with engines dead and propellers feathered, soared for more than an hour between 13 000 ft and 31 000 ft (4000 m and 9000 m) over the Sierra Nevada Mountains, USA, on 5 March 1950.

Hang gliders are launched by running into wind from a hilltop, and an airflow over the wing of 10–13 mph (16–20 km/h) is required. This can be achieved by hard running when there is no wind, or by taking only a few paces forward when wind speed is above 13 mph (20 km/h). Safe hang gliding requires a wind speed of no more than 22 mph (35 km/h). Record flights have covered distances of more than 100 miles (160 km) and achieved altitudes greater than 2 miles.

Free-fall parachuting requires minimal thermal currents and is best accomplished in high pressure weather conditions.

A 60-second free fall in a mean pressure wind of 34 mph (54 km/h) gives the parachutist a drift in the direction of the mean wind of 3000 ft (900 m). Experienced parachutists can control direction and forward speed when the mean wind speed is as high as 11 mph (18 km/h) by day and 9 mph (14 km/h) at night. Safe landings can be made in surface winds up to 22 mph (36 km/h).

An anabatic wind is an up-slope wind, created when air nearest the slope is heated by sunshine more quickly than air at the same horizontal level but further from the ground. The warmed air rises and is replaced by cooler air from alongside. The anabatic wind is most pronounced in early morning, before sunshine has had time to stir up the air more generally.

A katabatic wind is a down-slope wind, created on otherwise calm nights. Air nearest the slope cools, becomes heavier and blows downhill to be replaced by air from the same horizontal level alongside. This, in turn, cools and sinks. Katabatic winds are most pronounced on cloudless nights and when there is no pressure gradient wind to stir up the air close to the ground.

A sea breeze blows on a sunny summer day, from the cool sea surface on to land, where the air is warming and rising. By mid-afternoon a sea breeze can spread as much as 15–30 miles (24–48 km) inland.

A land breeze blows at night when clear skies cause rapid cooling over land, so that the air over the sea is comparatively warmer. Cold air from the land flows out over the sea where the warmer air is displaced.

A monsoon wind changes direction markedly according to season, basically because of temperature differences between adjacent oceans and continents.As early as 1686 Edmond Halley (1656–1742), English astronomer, likened monsoon winds to giant sea and land breezes and the comparison is apt, though not wholly correct. Complicating factors, such as orographic effects of mountain barriers and the interaction between air masses on either side of the Equator, render incomplete our understanding of monsoon regimes.

The Monsoon Experiment, MONEX was a series of regional investigations, begun in 1978 as part of the

Katabatic wind during the night. (Diana Davies)

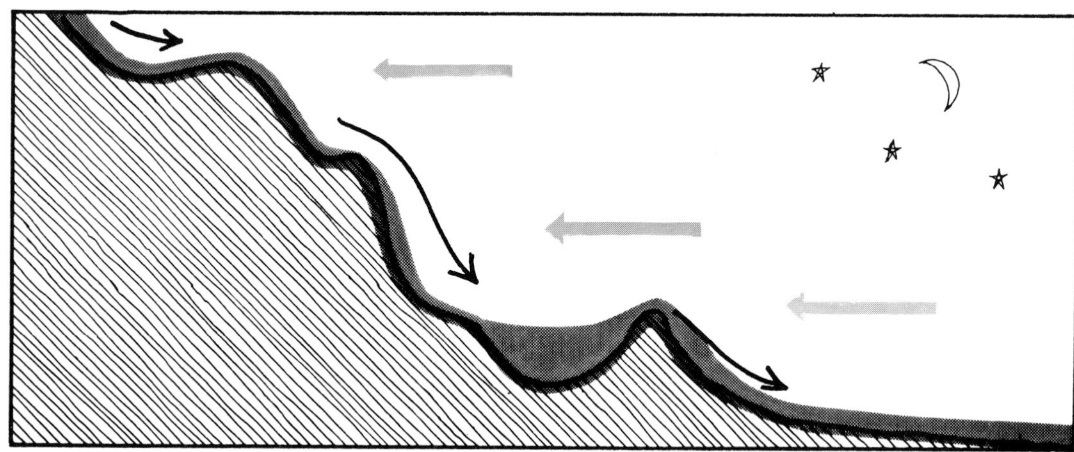

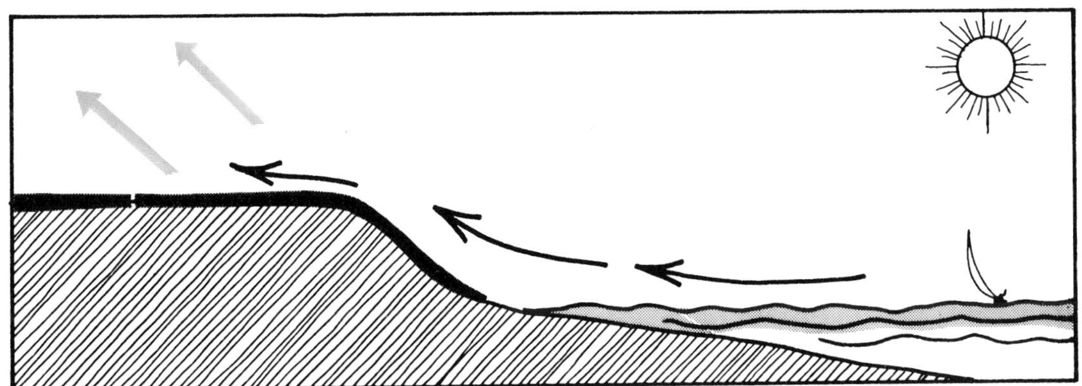

Sea breeze on a sunny summer day. (Diana Davies)

Global Weather Experiment, undertaken by member nations of the World Meteorological Organisation. Intensive observations were made over the Indian Ocean, Arabian Sea, Bay of Bengal, south-east Asia and the South China Sea.

The most dramatic monsoon conditions occur in India which experiences a change to the south-west monsoon at the end of May, and a change again to the north-east monsoon at the end of October.

In the southern hemisphere, the summer monsoon winds come from the north near Mauritius and Madagascar, but on the north coast of Australia they blow from the north-west. The Arabs had an extensive knowledge of monsoon changes at a very early date. A book, written in 1554 by Sidi Ali, about navigation in the Indian Ocean, gave the commencing date of each monsoon at 50 different places.

A jet stream is a narrow belt of high speed wind near the tropopause, whose existence was suspected in the 1920s and confirmed during World War II when pilots started flying at very high altitudes. American bombers, capable of ground speeds of 350 mph (560 km/h) and flying over the Pacific towards Japan, found their speed in the air reduced to about 200 mph (320 km/h). Subsequent research showed that there are usually two westerly jet streams, subtropical and polar in each hemisphere, blowing with speeds of between 100 and 200 mph (160 km/h and 320 km/h). They become stronger in the winter when there is greatest contrast between polar and equatorial temperatures, and 350 mph (560 km/h) has been recorded.

Clear air turbulence occurs when there is rapid change of horizontal wind speed over a relatively small difference in altitude. This causes dry air to turn over vigorously without any 'tell-tale' cloud indicators. This turbulence often happens above or below the jet stream, especially when that is accentuated by passing over mountains. Aircraft can encounter extremely rough conditions without warning. A research flight over the Sierra Nevada, USA, in February 1967 encountered such violent turbulence at a height of 50 000 ft (15 240 m) that it lost control and fell a few thousand feet before being able to recover.

6. Weather charts

Large-scale winds circulating round the world puzzled the early scientists. It was quite obvious that wind did not blow perpetually from the Poles, where the air was cold at the surface, towards the Equator, where it was warm. For want of a *theory*, practical people began assembling observed *facts* in the hope that the correct explanations would then become apparent. It was no accident that many sailors became practised weather observers, because their lives depended upon it. Their keenest concern was often the vicious circular storms which, as new sea routes developed, they encountered in tropical latitudes.

Hurricane was a name probably derived from an Indian word used in the Caribbean meaning 'big wind'. It entered the Spanish vocabulary as 'Hurracan', when 15th-century explorers first encountered these winds which were so much stronger than those they knew in Europe. By meteorological definition the term 'hurricane' is today reserved for winds of Force 12 Beaufort Scale, ie more than 64 knots, 74 mph or 119 km/h.

Typhoon (Chinese *tai fung*: 'wind which strikes'), was the name given to similar violent storms in the China seas. Some people think the word may have derived from the Greek mythological monster Typhon or Typhoeus, the father of storm winds. The name persists today in the Pacific Ocean, so that hurricane and typhoon are merely different names for the same phenomenon.

William Dampier (1652–1715), English buccaneer and scientific explorer, published an informative book about winds in 1697 called *A voyage around the world*. He accurately described a typhoon, and the data from his ocean journeys were an authoritative source of information for many years.

Edmond Halley (1656–1742), English astronomer and mathematician, was the first to sense that the general circulation of air round the world was caused by ascents of warm air in some places and descents of cold air elsewhere. In 1698 he published an account of trade winds and monsoons, with illustrative map, likening the monsoon to a giant sea breeze.

George Hadley (1685–1768), English scientist, was the first to mention, in a paper read to the Royal Society in 1735, that the rotation of the Earth might be a factor determining wind. The idea did not make much impact until John Dalton took it up again 60 years later.

William Redfield (1789–1857), American saddler and transport manager, became interested in hurricanes after the September gale of 1821 in western Massachusetts. He wrote a treatise on West Indian hurricanes, published in 1833, in which he identified hurricane paths as going first towards the west and then recurving towards the north or east.

Matthew Maury (1806–73) was an oceanographer and American naval officer, who was invalided out of the service in 1839. Thereafter, he devoted 9 years to the collection of wind and weather observations at sea, by distributing log books to ships' captains.

Heinrich Dove (1803–79), German scientist, described the essential difference between tropical storms of the two hemispheres. Winds rotate in an anticlockwise manner (when imagined looking down on them) in the northern hemisphere, and in a clockwise direction in the southern hemisphere.

William Reid (1791–1858), Scottish soldier, used the knowledge of circular motion of air to propound sailing rules for avoiding the worst perils of storms at sea. In 1838, he published *An attempt to develop the law of storms by means of facts*, and when he became

Right: The Law of Storms, based on the assumption that a sailing vessel could not travel against hurricane winds, but only with them. (Diana Davies)

governor of Barbados in 1847, he instituted the first system of hurricane warning signals at Carlisle Bay.

The Law of Storms was based on the assumption that a sailing vessel could not travel *against* wind of hurricane strength, but only with it. The dangerous semi-circle of such a storm was that in which the circulating wind carried the ship along in the same general direction as that of the whole storm, thus prolonging the agony of being within it. The most hazardous quadrant of the dangerous semi-circle was the forward quadrant, when a ship running before the wind actually approached the centre of the storm.

The *navigable* semi-circle was that in which the wind was blowing contrary to the movement of the storm centre, and the ship was therefore increasing the distance between itself and trouble.

The clockwise or anticlockwise manner in which wind in the ship's vicinity altered as the storm approached, helped ascertain in which semi-circle the ship lay relative to the storm.

Cyclone (Greek *kuklos*: cycle or circle) was the name first given to intense circular storms by Captain H.

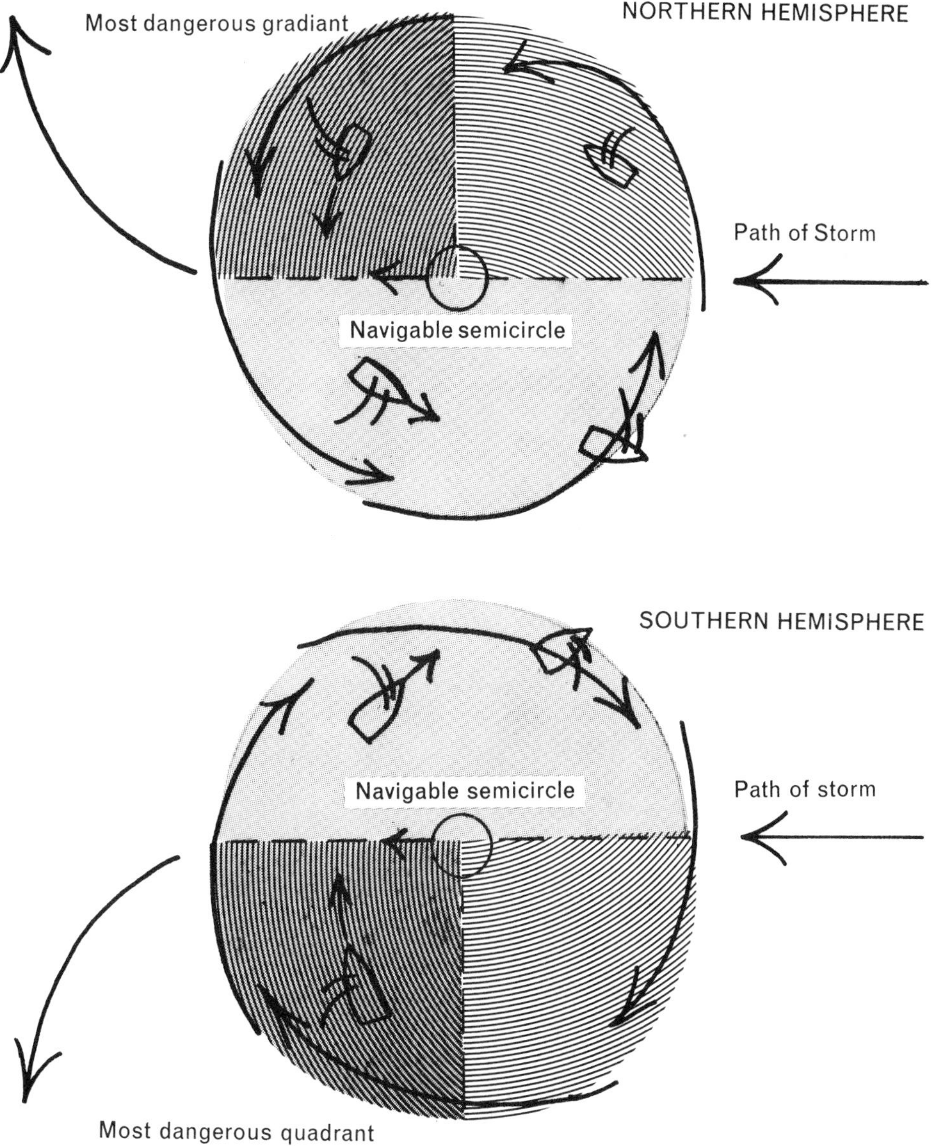

Piddington in 1848, who also recognised that wind converged in towards the centre of storms. The term cyclone is now usually confined to intense circular storms in tropical latitudes which do not attain the status of full hurricane. Circular storms in higher latitudes are called 'depressions'.

Vice-Admiral Robert Fitzroy, from a portrait at the Royal Naval College, Greenwich.

Robert Fitzroy (1805–65), naval officer, was captain of the *Beagle* when it made its famous voyage round the world with Charles Darwin. Of necessity, Fitzroy was a keen observer of the weather and of the barometer. He noted that falling or rising pressure, called tendency, was usually followed by certain types of weather, and he formulated forecasting 'Remarks' which became popular and were often inscribed on barometers.

> 'A fall of half a tenth of an inch or more in half an hour is a sure sign of storm.'
>
> 'A fall when the thermometer is low indicates snow or rain.'
>
> 'A fall with a rising thermometer indicates wind and rain from the southward.'
>
> 'Steady rise shows that fine weather may be expected and in winter, frost.'

These were reasonably sound guidelines, connecting pressure with weather, but they did not recognise the relation between pressure and wind in general, as distinct from hurricane winds.

Fitzroy's barometer was often accompanied by a storm glass, which was a bottle filled with a mixture of camphor, nitre, sal-ammoniac, alcohol and water. Fitzroy believed there was some connection between wind direction and the clarity or crystallisation of this liquid, but this has never been proved.

Reproduction Fitzroy barometer, with the Admiral's Remarks inscribed. (O. Comitti and Son, London)

Right: Section of the weather map published by Robert Fitzroy when investigating the loss of the 'Royal Charter' **on the north coast of Anglesey, Wales, on 25 October 1859. Also a key to symbols used.** (*The Weather Book*, R. Fitzroy)

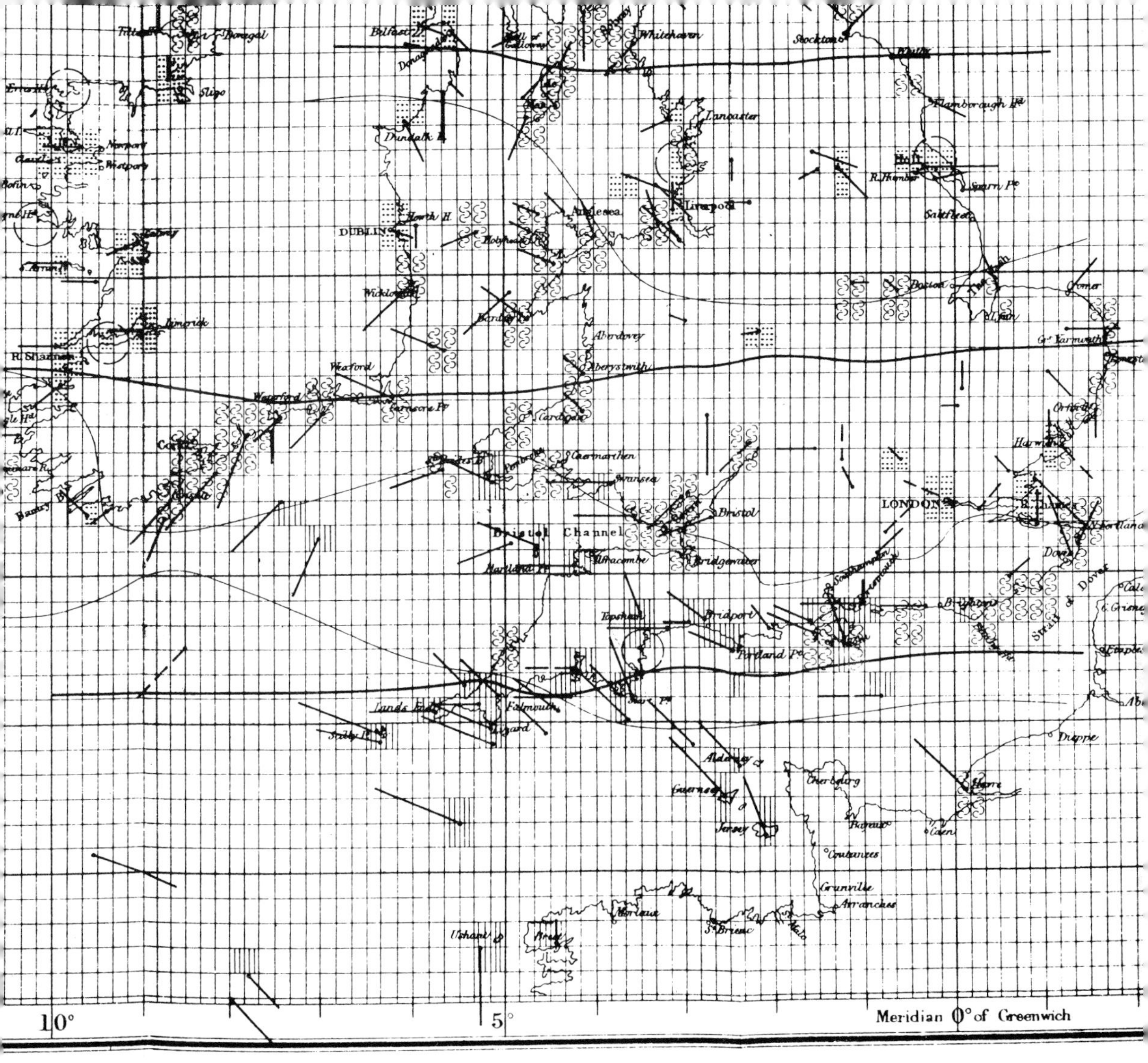

Explanatory.

Wind — *true direction — drawn to leeward of Station — by scale of force; that of a storm being represented by eight spaces of longitude, thus* ———— *West, Storm.*

Pressure — *barometric — single, dark line;* ———— *measured from parallel of latitude below, on inch scale. (marked 28 and 30)*

Temperature — *single, light line,* ———— *measured from the same parallel; one degree being represented by one tenth of an inch. (30°)*

Sky — *blue, clear, (or no recorded observation)* blank paper.

Cloud — *small curves or curls*

Rain — *vertical lines (N & S)*

Snow — *horizontal lines (E & W)*

Hail — *broken alternate lines*

Fog — *dots*

Relative (estimated) prevalence shewn by the number of (oblong) spaces, marked as above, from one, the least, to four, an excess.

Broken wind lines — — — *shew direction alone, not force.*

A broken circle ( ) *denotes calm, or very light variable breeze.*

Weather observers in Europe were meanwhile getting organised. The Lunar Society of Birmingham, The Royal Society of London, The Société Royale de Médecine in France, amongst others, encouraged people to keep weather diaries and to make observations under standard conditions. The Societas Meteorologica Palatine in Mannheim, Germany, was in correspondence with 50 observers in 1778 and with 70 by 1784, including some in Baghdad, New York, Stockholm and St Petersburg. The Société de Médecine had its work suppressed by revolutionary decree in 1793, but the observations collected before then were of a standard high enough to be of use to research workers today.

The first simultaneous weather observations in North America were made daily during 1777 and 1778 by Thomas Jefferson (later the President of the United States) at Monticello, and James Madison at Williamsburg. In 1814 US Army surgeons were ordered to keep weather diaries with a view to investigating the effect of weather on disease, and by 1838 daily weather observations were being made at 13 forts.

The electric telegraph, developed after 1836 by Samuel Morse (1791–1872), American artist and inventor, solved the critical problem of time lag in collecting weather information. The physicist Joseph Henry inaugurated a service by which weather information was collected by the American telegraph companies, and summaries of the weather were fed back to them. By 1857 these reports were being published in the *Washington Evening Star* and some local papers. The *Weather Bureau* was inaugurated on 1 November 1870 as a division of the Army Signal Service and by 1878 was operating 284 observing stations. The Bureau became a part of the Department of Agriculture in 1890 when it became known as the *United States Weather Bureau.*

The daily collection of weather data started in the Netherlands and France in 1855. The British service was inaugurated on 3 September 1860 by Admiral Fitzroy who was then Chief Meteorologist to the Board of Trade, and countries all over the world soon followed suit.

Mathematical codes were devised so that long descriptions of weather could be summarised for quick transmission by telegraph. Today, each weather item is allocated one or more positions within a series of five-figure groups. Measurements, such as temperature and pressure, are transmitted as the numbers themselves: descriptions of weather, cloud etc, are given a numerical code. Experienced meteorologists can read each coded message quite easily, but it is less easy to assimilate a whole sheet of figures referring to widely spaced positions. The numbers are therefore converted to pictorial symbols and plotted on to a map in the position in which the observations were made.

Pictorial weather maps had been talked about since the 18th century. The French naturalist Jean Baptiste Lamarck (1744–1829) and chemist Antoine Lavoisier (1743–94), were both convinced that weather maps might one day form the basis of weather forecasting. The first weather map was made by the German physicist Heinrich W. Brandes (1777–1843) in 1816, using weather data from the year 1783.

Early weather maps differed from those today in the minor matter of symbols used. A greater failing was in the presentation of pressure, which made no visual impact. Brandes used lines of equal deviation from normal whereas Admiral Fitzroy drew undulating lines across his maps, giving barometer readings measured from the parallel of latitude above. Buys Ballot (1818–90), Dutch meteorologist, at first used a system of vertical shading for areas which had pressure higher than normal, and horizontal shading for areas with lower pressure. By concentrating on the undoubted fact that pressure *tendency* seemed a more important indication of weather than the *actual* pressure value, they missed the simple connection between actual pressure and wind.

The first published weather maps were sold to the public for one penny at the Great Exhibition of 1851 at the Crystal Palace, London by the Electric Telegraph Company.

A synoptic chart is a weather map, plotted with synchronous weather observations, that is to say observations made at the same Greenwich Mean Time. Each item has a specified position around a circle and until after World War II plotting was done by hand in red and blue ink. The recognised system was to tie two pens together with a rubber band and rock the hand from one nib to another. An experienced plotter could keep pace with the data being received on the teleprinter. Today, observations received at central forecasting offices are sorted and plotted by computer and then sent to outstations by facsimile machine, as finished charts for forecasters to analyse.

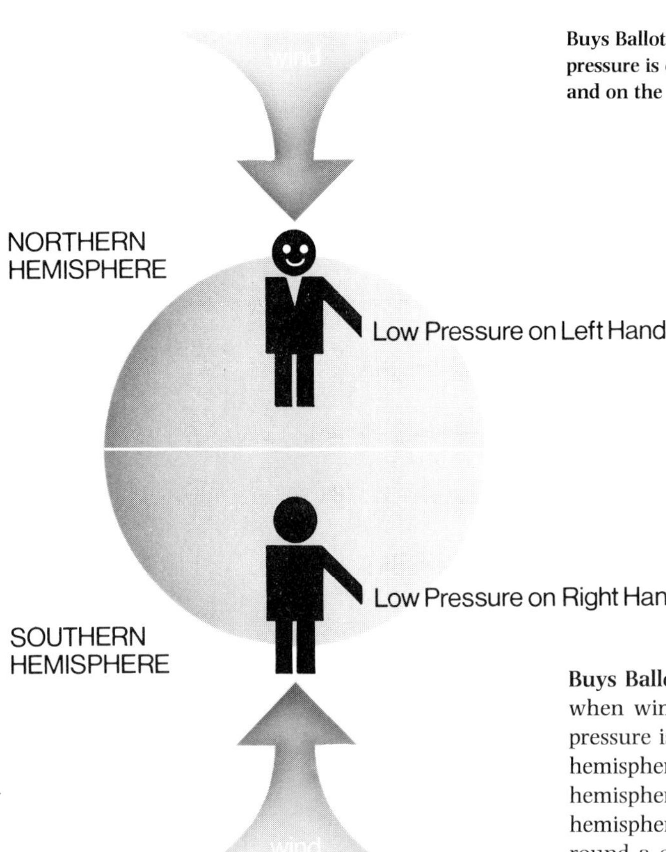

Buys Ballot's Law: when wind blows on the back, low pressure is on the left hand in the northern hemisphere and on the right in the southern. (Eddie Botchway)

A synoptic chart covering the British Isles is relayed within 1 hour of observations being made. A chart covering one half of the hemisphere takes several hours to complete because of the time taken to collect surface and upper air data from distant places.

Buys Ballot made a vital discovery when he realised that wind, like other fluids, tries to move from high pressure to low. But because the Earth rotates, it exerts a force called the Coriolis force, after the French mathematician who first described it. This force deflects wind from its high-to-low path, by 90° to the right in the northern hemisphere and by 90° to the left in the southern hemisphere. Friction keeps a better grip on air near the surface, and the deflection from the high-to-low pressure direction is rather less, about 60°–80°, according to roughness of terrain.

The geostrophic wind is the horizontal wind, caused by pressure differences and the deflecting Coriolis force. It blows according to Buys Ballot's Law.

Buys Ballot's Law, enunciated in 1857, states that when wind is blowing on an observer's back, low pressure is always on the left hand in the northern hemisphere, and on the right hand in the southern hemisphere. Consequently, wind in the northern hemisphere blows in an anticlockwise direction round a centre of low pressure and in a clockwise direction round a centre of high pressure. In the southern hemisphere, wind blows in a clockwise direction round a centre of low pressure and in an anticlockwise direction around high pressure.

Hurricanes are merely special cases of low pressure circulations, all obeying similar wind rules.

An isobar is a line on a map joining places having equal barometric pressure at a specified height above ground. Isobars are drawn for consecutive whole values of pressure, usually at 2, 4 or 8 mb intervals either side of 1000 mb, and are interpolated smoothly between readings received from observers. The resulting chart depicts pressure contours and is analogous to a geographical contour map.

The general public sees isobaric maps of pressures at mean sea level, but the professional forecaster also studies isobaric charts for higher levels of the atmosphere.

The pressure gradient is the difference in pressure between isobars. When the isobars are close together the gradient is steep. When they are far apart the pressure gradient is slack.

Wind direction at 2000 ft (600 m) is considered to be above the influence of surface friction. It blows parallel to the isobars according to Buys Ballot's Law. Winds at higher altitudes also blow according to the same rules, but parallel to the isobars at the specified level.

Surface wind direction differs from that at 2000 ft (600 m) by an angle of 10°–30°. It is backed from the upper wind in the northern hemisphere, and veered from it in the southern hemisphere. In both cases this implies a movement of surface air inwards towards a centre of low pressure, called **convergence**, and a movement of surface air outwards from the centre of high pressure, known as '**divergence**'.

Wind speed is directly proportional to the pressure gradient. The closer together the isobars, the steeper the pressure gradient and the stronger the wind. Wind generally increases with height above 2000 ft (600 m).

Surface wind speed is proportional to the speed of wind at 2000 ft (600 m), about one third over land and about one half over the sea. Speed drops considerably in lulls but in gusts may be nearly as strong as the wind at 2000 ft (600 m).

PLOTTING SYMBOLS

- *Drizzle*
- *Rain*
- *Snow*
- *Hail*
- *Showers*
- *Thunderstorm*
- *Mist*
- *Haze*
- *Smoke haze*
- *Fog*
- *Fog patches*
- *Squall*
- *Thundery showers*

Warm front
Cold front
Occlusion
Direction of movement

Plotting Examples

RAIN
NORTH force 5
24
1024 mbs falling
5
5 mls
200 yds
Visibility MOD / POOR
RAIN at first
SHOWERS later
mp 8
GOOD
SE 6 becoming ENE 4
200
98
998 mbs steady
FOG CALM
mp 9
DRIZZLE
SE 3 becoming CYCLONIC

Plotting symbols and examples for those who wish to make their own weather charts, using Met Maps issued by the Royal Meteorological Society.

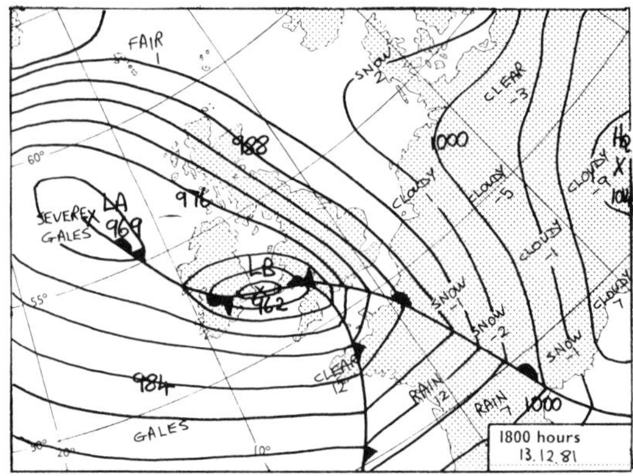

Depressions to north-west and south-east of Ireland; ridge of high pressure over Denmark. From the Daily Weather Summary, as issued by the London Weather Centre.

Coastal wind speed on a sunny day in summer is the resultant of the pressure wind and the sea breeze. Wind near the coast is stronger than elsewhere if the two components act together in the same direction, but is less if the two components oppose each other.

Pressure patterns are those formed by isobars drawn on a weather map. They are fluid patterns around centres of high and low pressure and depict circulations of air around the world. There are four basic patterns:

ANTICYCLONE, a circulation of air round a centre of high pressure. Wind speed is generally light near the centre but can be strong on the outer fringe where it blends in towards a low pressure circulation. Anticyclones are often persistent so that air within them has time to stagnate and modify. The systems drift, rather than travel with measurable speed. Pressure rises steadily when an anticyclone is developing and falls when it is receding.

RIDGE OF HIGH PRESSURE, an extension of an anticyclone, having isobars of exaggerated curvature, concave to the centre of high pressure. Wind is often, but not necessarily, light and there is pronounced divergence of surface air where the isobars curve markedly.

DEPRESSION, a circulation of air round a centre of low pressure, usually between 950 mb and 1020 mb. It is 'deep' if it has a strong pressure gradient and the centre is encircled with many isobars, indicating strong wind. It is 'shallow' if there is little pressure gradient, few isobars and light wind. An embryo depression may deepen to maturity and travel towards the east with a measurable speed, before filling up, slowing down and eventually losing its identity. At other times small circulations may disappear without having made much impact. Pressure falls when a depression approaches, and rises again when it departs. Gales in middle latitudes are nearly always associated with depressions.

TROUGH OF LOW PRESSURE, an extension of a depression, having isobars of pronounced curvature, concave to the centre. Wind is often light but there is a marked convergence of surface air where the isobars have pronounced curvature. Any particularly elongated trough is a likely breeding ground for a new depression, called a secondary depression.

A COL is the calm area between diametrically opposite depressions or anticyclones.

A tropical cyclone is a low-pressure circulation in tropical latitudes, having wind speeds greater than Beaufort Force 8, but less than Force 12.

A hurricane or typhoon is an intense tropical cyclone having average surface wind speeds of 74 mph (119 km/h) or more. Hurricanes form and travel over the oceans, and once they reach land they usually degenerate into depressions.

Upper air pressure patterns are similar to the patterns which feature on surface weather maps, but they are usually less pronounced.

Tornadoes, whirlwinds, dust devils, water spouts and **water devils** are low-pressure circulations of such a small cross section that they are not discernible on normal weather charts. They have winds of great strength (See Chapter 17).

Part of a computer-plotted weather chart, with isobars drawn in by hand. Since pressure readings are rarely an exact whole number of millibars, isobars are interpolated between readings so that higher values fall to one side of the line and lower values to the other.

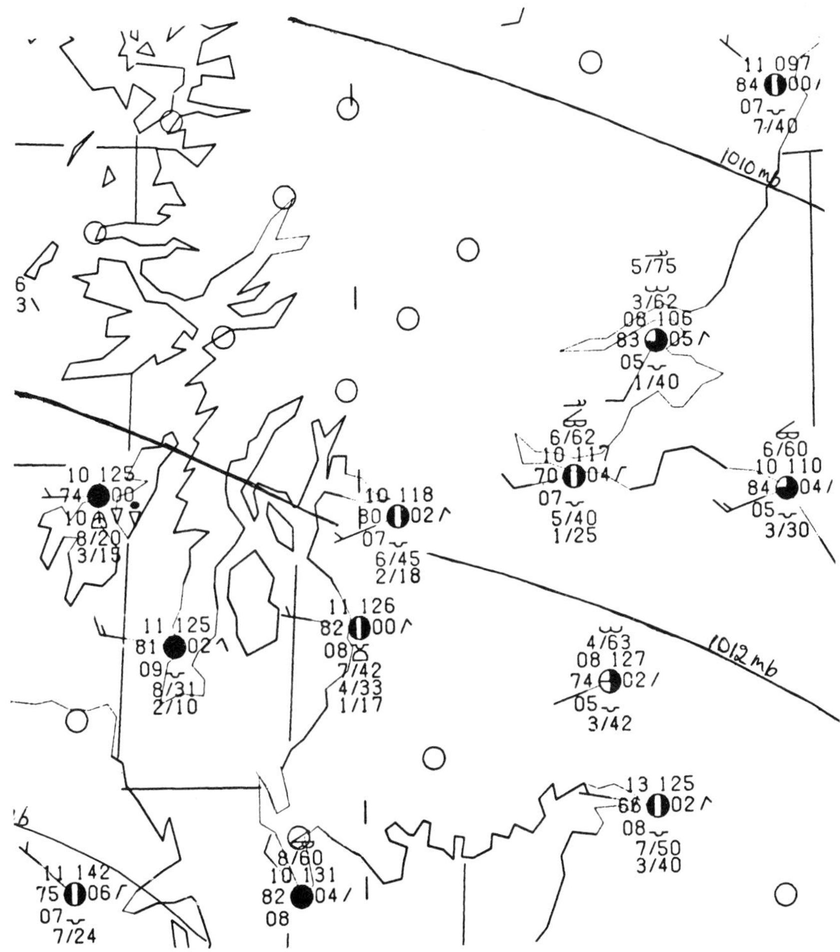

7. Stormy winds

Storm warnings were issued before countries developed proper weather forecasting services. Telegraph operators who were experiencing a storm in their area merely passed the message to other telegraph stations who distributed the warning to whomever they thought fit.

The first national storm warning service was started by France in 1856 as a direct consequence of a weather disaster during the Crimean War. French and English warships were caught close to the coast near Balaclava, in a violent storm on 14 November 1854; they suffered disastrous losses which might have been averted if news of the storm had been transmitted by telegraph, so that the ships could have sought more sea room.

In Great Britain Admiral Fitzroy started a storm warning service in 1860, and telegraph messages were, and still are, conveyed by visual symbols at coastguard stations. A south cone, indicating gale winds from southward, hangs with the apex downwards; a north cone, indicating gale winds from northward, hangs with the apex upwards.

The first radio gale warning to ships in the eastern Atlantic was made in 1911. Shipping bulletins, which began in Great Britain in 1919, always start by enumerating the sea areas where gale warnings are in operation. News bulletins carry gale warnings but, in addition, all radio programmes are liable to interruption at suitable moments for announcements of impending gales. The term 'imminent' means within 6 hours of the issue of the warning. 'Soon' means between 6 and 12 hours from the issue of the warning, and 'later' means more than 12 hours ahead.

In countries affected by hurricanes, constant interruption of radio and television programmes with news of approaching storms has greatly helped minimise damage to property and has reduced casualties.

Areas most susceptible to hurricanes, typhoons and tropical cyclones, are those between latitudes 10° and 30° north and south of the Equator, in the Indian Ocean, in the Caribbean Sea and Gulf of Mexico, in the South China Sea, and off the east and north west coasts of Australia.

Hurricanes have certain general features. They occur most often in summer and autumn when the sea is at its warmest. Their average life span is 9 days, the average forward speed is 12 mph (20 km/h) and the general track is towards the west, recurving again towards the east.

Few hurricane winds can be measured because anemometers normally collapse under the strain, but sustained speeds of 100 mph (160 km/h) gusting to 150 mph (240 km/h) probably occur. Sustained speeds of 150 mph (240 km/h) gusting to 225 mph (360 km/h) may occur occasionally. Wind speed increases steadily to within 20–30 miles (32–48 km) of the centre, which is called the **'eye'**, and then remains at maximum speed within a belt 15–25 miles (24–40 km) wide around the eye. The eye has an average radius of 7 miles (11 km) and within this area wind speed falls to about 15 mph (24 km/h) which seems calm in comparison with that which preceded. The lull is followed by hurricane winds from the opposite direction as the storm moves away.

Rotating winds may extend to a height of 6 miles (10 km), but speed decreases with height. Deep banks of cloud spiral inward around the centre, but the eye itself is cloudless.

Right: Low pitched aluminium roofs were sucked from houses at Hatfield, Herts, during gales on 4 November 1957, mainly because of insufficient fastenings. (Building Research Establishment, Crown Copyright)

RECENT HURRICANES

IN THE ATLANTIC in 1979, there were two devastating hurricanes, *Frederic* and *David*, on the weather map at the same time. *Elena*, a tropical storm in between, died out before attaining hurricane status.

David, 25 August–7 September, attained a maximum sustained wind speed of 130 mph (209 km/h) and a lowest pressure of 924 mb, its path crossing widespread inhabited areas. It was the fiercest hurricane reported in Dominica since 1834 when 56 people died and three quarters of the population of 80 000 were left homeless. In the Dominican Republic there were over 2000 deaths and 200 000 people were made homeless. *David* declined before reaching the mainland, but spawned 34 tornadoes as it moved up the east coast of the United States.

Frederic, 29 August–14 September, attained a maximum sustained wind speed of 132 mph (213 km/h) and a lowest pressure of 943 mb. *Frederic* was less violent than *David* while it was in the eastern Caribbean but it caused torrential rain. *Frederic* regained strength in the Gulf of Mexico and became the most intense hurricane of the century and the first to affect Mobile in Alabama since 1932. Dauphin Island in Mobile Bay was partly destroyed by a peak sea surge 12 ft (4 m) high. This hurricane was probably the costliest in American history but the deathroll was only five persons due to an efficient evacuation scheme.

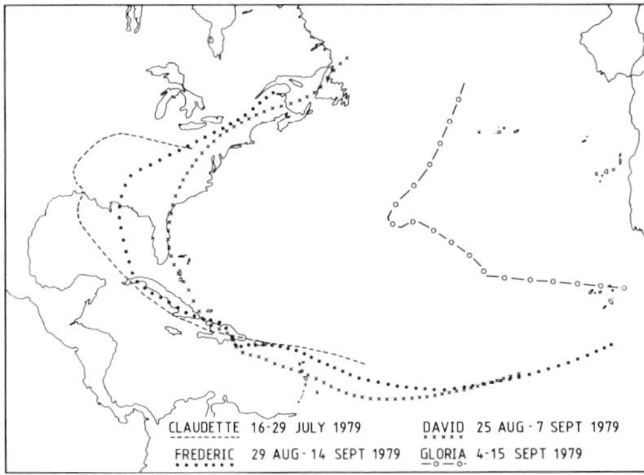

Tracks of 'Claudette', 'David', 'Frederic' and 'Gloria' during 1979. Based on information from the National Hurricane Center, Florida. (K.B. Shone)

In the next year, 1980, hurricane *Allen* was the first, and by far the most severe, of the season. It was unusual in having three separate pressure minima. *Allen* originated near the west African coast and attained hurricane status 500 miles east of Barbados, on 3 August. It passed north of Barbados, causing damage but no deaths, and to the south of St Lucia, killing six people and inflicting disastrous damage. Two hundred miles south of Puerto Rico, pressure fell to 911 mb, its first minimum and the lowest recorded in the eastern Caribbean. Pressure then rose again, as *Allen* weakened for about 36 hours. Nevertheless, it inflicted 220 deaths and made half a million people homeless when it crossed the south east corner of Haiti. Eight people died in Jamaica as *Allen* passed near to the north coast where it disgorged 10–20 in (250–500 mm) of rain; twice as much as in Barbados and St Lucia.

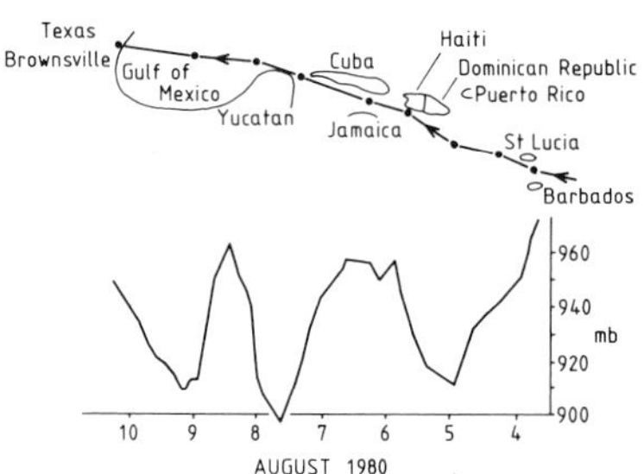

Hurricane 'Allen' developed three distinct minimum pressures during its progress from Barbados to Texas. Based on information from the National Hurricane Center, Florida. (K.B. Shone)

After passing south east of Cuba and over the Cayman Islands, where it caused damage but no loss of life, *Allen* again intensified and pressure fell to a new record low of 899 mb in the Yucatan Channel on 7 August. Pressure rose again once the hurricane entered the south east Gulf of Mexico, but fell again to 909 mb on 9 August, en route for the Texas coast. The storm crossed the coast in a sparsely inhabited area, just north of Brownsville, but nevertheless inflicted considerable damage and produced 10–15 in (250–380 mm) of rain. Two off-shore oil rigs were destroyed and 13 people died in a helicopter crash during the platform evacuation. Half a million people were evacuated from the coastal areas of Texas and Louisiana and no lives were lost there.

The highest wind speed in the Yucatan Channel area was 189 mph (304 km/h).

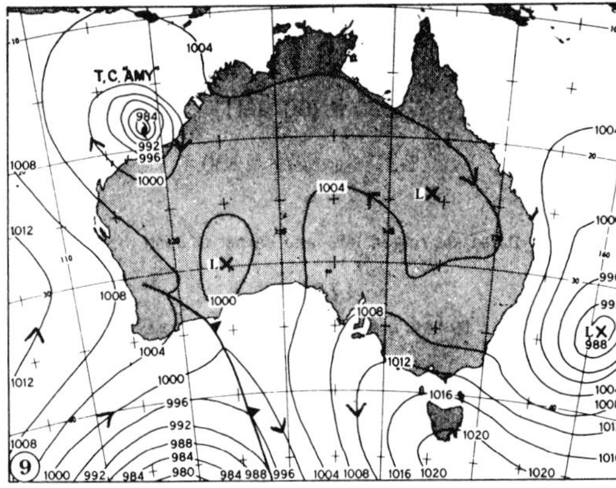

'Amy' at 10 am Australian time on 9 January 1980, one of three storms to cross the coast of north-west Australia in 5 weeks. (Bureau of Meteorology, Australia)

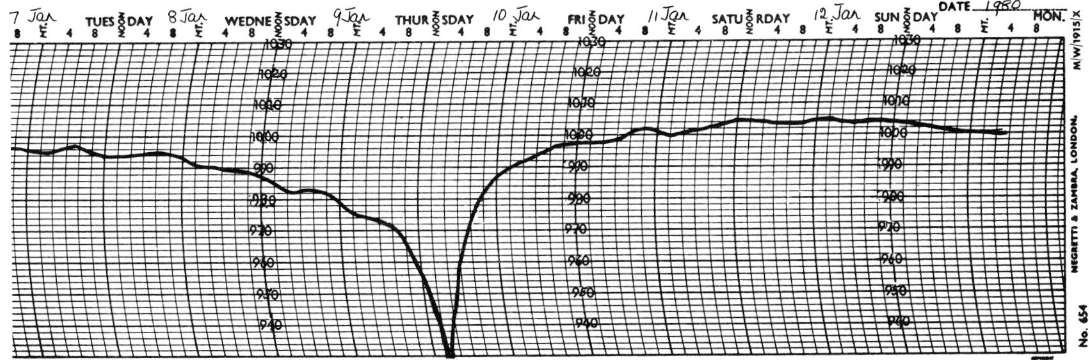

Reproduction of the barograph trace at Goldsworthy, during the passage of 'Amy' on 10 January 1980.
(Bureau of Meteorology, Australia)

IN THE PACIFIC, *Typhoon Alley* is the name given to the waters south west of Japan, which provide a corridor for the passage of typhoons. In 1979, storms plagued Japan and Korea every fortnight of the late summer: *Irving* 14–18 August, *Judy*, 20–26 August, *Owen* 27 September–1 October and *Tip*, 19–20 October. *Tip* was the worst storm in Typhoon Alley for 13 years; its centre pressure of 870 mb on 12 October, when about 1000 miles east of the Philippines, was the lowest ever recorded by drop-sonde from an aircraft.

IN THE EASTERN INDIAN OCEAN in 1980, there was an exceptionally high incidence of three tropical cyclones in 5 weeks, all of which crossed the coast of north west Australia within 90 miles (145 km) of Port Headland in Western Australia.

Amy reached the coast on 10 January, with gusts up to 143 mph (230 km/h) being recorded. There was severe damage to homes, mines, ports and oil platforms, and very heavy rain.

Dean crossed the coast on 1 February, and the eye of the storm passed less than 30 miles (48 km) from Goldsworthy. Many buildings were damaged in Port Hedland. Gusts reached 124 mph (200 km/h).

Enid crossed the coast on 17 February, having developed at sea from a depression which had already affected the coast once. Gusts occurred up to 140 mph (225 km/h), even to 105 mph (170 km/h) as far inland as Nullagine.

The combined rainfall from these three storms caused widespread flooding.

A fourth cyclone *Brian*, also formed off the same coast on 21 January, but remained over the sea, travelling parallel to the coast.

In 1981, cyclone *Max* tore through Darwin in the Northern Territory, Australia, on 12 March, with winds up to 90 mph (144 km/h) and rainfall of 5·5 in (140 mm). Apart from uprooting trees, little damage was done because the light frame houses, which were demolished there by *Tracy* on 25 December 1974, had been replaced by cyclone-proof buildings.

IN THE SOUTH PACIFIC the typhoon *Isaac* devastated the island group of Tonga on 3 March 1982. Windspeeds of more than 95 mph (150 km/h) flattened the majority of houses, uprooted large trees and ruined all the agricultural crops. Four lives were lost.

IN THE WESTERN INDIAN OCEAN tropical cyclones are not unusual, but *Monique*, 25–31 March 1968, was amongst the worst. She was detected by satellite when still in embryo stage at 82° E, 11° S and was traced over a classical track towards west-south-west until she passed close to Rodriguez island, 300 miles (480 km) due east of Mauritius, before curving round again towards the south east. *Monique* reached maturity on 29 March when Rodriguez reported the lowest pressure ever recorded in the Indian Ocean, 934 mb. The maximum known wind gust in the Indian Ocean, 173 mph (278 km/h), was recorded at Rodriguez at 5 pm on the same day. *Monique* destroyed all standing crops and much of the recently planted forest.

IN THE BAY OF BENGAL in November 1977, two cyclones in quick succession caused devastation in the states of Tamil Nadu and Andhra Pradesh.

The first, 7–24 November, crossed the Bay of Bengal and then the coast of Tamil Nadu on the 12th, just north of Sri Lanka. Gales and heavy rain damaged crops, caused many homes to collapse and killed more than 400 people. By 13 November it was travelling west over the Arabian Sea, but after 3 days it deepened again and turned around, to cross the west coast of India yet again, on 22 November bringing with it heavy rain and gales.

This cyclone track was unprecedented for the area, but the damage it caused was overshadowed by another storm crossing the Bay of Bengal at about the same time. By 18 November it was close to the position of the first cyclone, the week before, but then it deepened and turned northwards to inflict a deluge of water upon Andhra Pradesh on 19–20 November.

Satellite view of hurricane 'David' on 31 August 1979, with its centre over the coast of the Dominican Republic. (National Hurricane Center, Florida)

Hurricanes were first given names in Australia. Clement L. Wragge, at the Queensland Weather Bureau from 1887 to 1902, named every identifiable system, high or low, on his weather charts. Some of these names were decidedly exotic — *Ramath, Xerxes, Uphaz* etc—but others were somewhat vindictive.

Wragge was inclined to engage in heated public controversy on all kinds of scientific matters, and politicians who incurred his wrath were liable to find their initials attached to particularly pernicious meteorological disturbances on the weather maps. His adversaries were apt to refer to Clement Wragge as 'inclement Wragge' or 'wet Wragge'. The custom of naming weather systems fell into disuse after Wragge left office.

Hurricane naming was revived in the United States during World War II. One story attributes the initiative to a radio operator who issued a hurricane warning and then started to sing a few bars of 'Every little breeze seems to whisper Louise', and the hurricane was thereafter referred to as *Louise*. Whether or not this was how the christening custom was revived, it was a thoroughly practical idea for accurate transmission of weather information. There are often several low pressure systems over a large area at once, all requiring mention in a forecast.

Atlantic names start afresh at the beginning of the alphabet each year and the names rarely get to M (13 hurricanes) in a year. In the eastern Pacific, however, names frequently reach initial letter P (16 storms). In the western North Pacific names continue to the end of the alphabet regardless of date, and often have more storms during a single year than names available in one list. Until recently, feminine names only were used.

Australia was the first country to use male names for hurricanes, following protests at the hurtful practice of always naming such devious, destructive and demoniacal phenomena after the ladies. From 1975 these aspersions have been cast equally between male and female.

The United States followed suit in 1978, and alternate male and female names are allocated and published in advance.

Designated names for Atlantic hurricanes in 1983 are: *Alicia, Barry, Chantal, Dean, Erin, Felix, Gabrielle, Hugo, Iris, Jerry, Karen, Luis, Marilyn, Noel, Opal, Pablo, Roxanne, Sebastien, Tanya, Van* and *Wendy*.

Hurricanes usually originate between latitudes 7° and 15°, north or south. In the northern hemisphere they generally start moving towards the west before curving north west and later north east at about latitude 30°N. In the southern hemisphere the tracks are generally westward, then south west and eventually towards the south east. Initial speeds of hurricanes are about 10 mph (16 km/h) but this doubles or more, after recurving. There are considerable variations from this basic pattern of behaviour.

In Great Britain, 'hurricanes hardly happen' but remnants of Atlantic hurricanes do sometimes linger on as particularly nasty depressions.

On 17 September 1961, the remnants of hurricane *Debbie* gave severe gales in Scotland and the Shetland Isles. Lerwick Observatory had a mean hourly wind speed of 61 mph (98 km/h) and registered a gust of 88 mph (142 km/h), which was the highest recorded since the Observatory opened in 1921.

On 16 September 1978, the remnants of hurricane *Flossie* merged with another depression in the Atlantic to give an intense low pressure area, centre 959 mb, to the north-west of Scotland. Gusts up to 104 mph (166 km/h) occurred at Fair Isle.

Right: The third cooling tower to collapse at Ferrybridge, Yorkshire, on 1 November 1965. Eight towers had been built in staggered double file, and insufficient allowance had been made for turbulence and funnelling gusts between them. Mean wind speed was 44 mph (71 km/h), with momentary gusts nearer 85 mph (137 km/h). (Central Electricity Generating Board)

STORMY WINDS

In southern England, the worst storm ever documented occurred on the night of 26–27 November 1703 (old calendar). It was described in detail by Daniel Defoe, English author, who was living in London at the time.

A depression approached south-west England and moved north eastward across Wales to south Yorkshire. SSW gales blew across southern England on the afternoon of 26 November, causing great damage and disastrous flooding in the Severn Valley. The Eddystone lighthouse disappeared without trace with all its occupants, including the designer, Winstanley, who was visiting it at the time.

The storm increased in intensity and reached a peak in the eastern English Channel between 2 am and 5 am on 27 November. The average wind speed at the peak of the storm was probably over 100 mph (161 km/h). About 8000 lives were lost, mainly at sea. Many ships were collected in harbours or at anchor in the Channel, awaiting favourable winds after a succession of gales in the previous fortnight. Warships and supply vessels were waiting to sail for Spain or had just returned from the summer campaign in the Mediterranean. Twelve men-o'-war were wrecked on the Goodwin Sands alone and hundreds of ships were tumbled together in harbours, in the Thames and along the south coast. Inland, roofs were damaged, 100 churches were stripped of lead, 400 windmills overturned and about 800 houses were destroyed. Countless trees were uprooted, even really large specimens which are usually able to stand their ground. Defoe counted 17 000 trees uprooted in Kent alone before he tired of the task; he estimated 450 parks lost between 200 and 1000 trees each and the New Forest about 4000. A mean wind of hurricane strength must have persisted for more than 2 hours on this occasion, something which has not happened since.

The calculated wave motion in the air stream crossing the Pennines on 16 February 1962. The compression of air above Sheffield caused wind speeds of much greater strength than were experienced a few miles away. The vertical scale is exaggerated 16 times compared with the horizontal scale. (UK Meteorological Office, Crown Copyright)

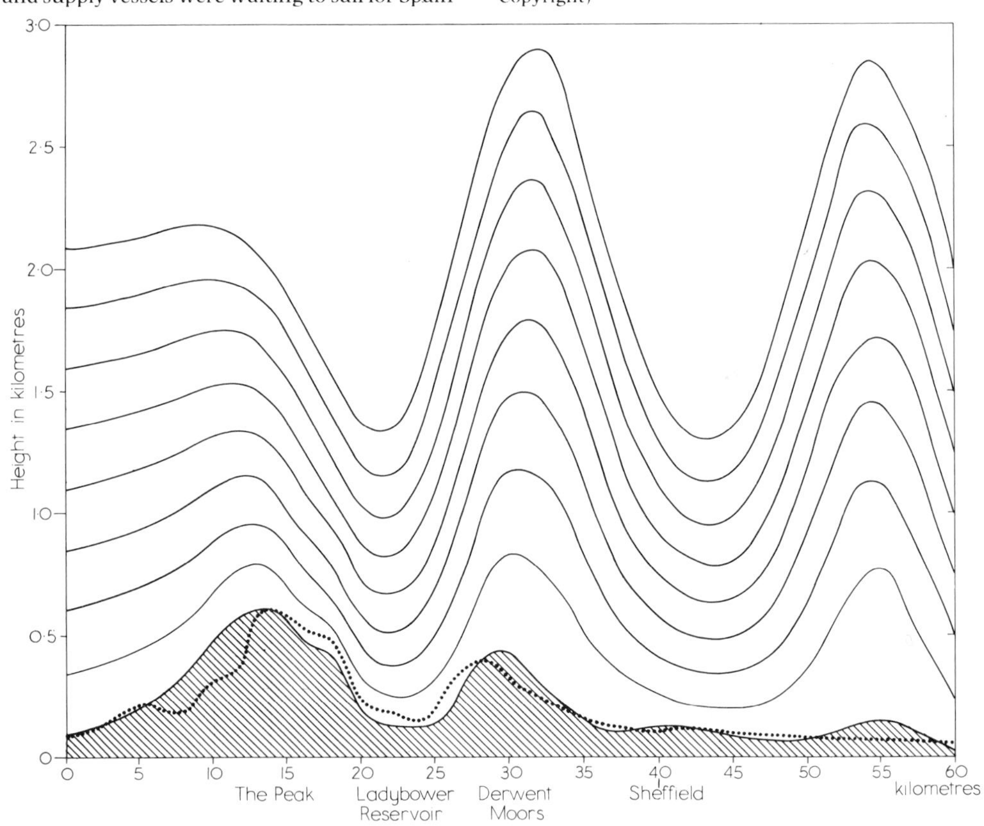

Geographical contours accentuated gales at Sheffield, Yorkshire on 16 February 1962, when enormous damage was done to the city, and prefabricated homes were razed to the ground. A depression was travelling north of Scotland, where some places had a mean hourly wind speed of 65 mph (105 km/h). In the Midlands, average wind speed was 45 mph (72 km/h) and the isobars on the weather map were spaced accordingly. At Sheffield, however, mean wind speed increased to 75 mph (120 km/h) during the early hours of the morning and gusts reached 96 mph (154 km/h). A few miles away from Sheffield, mean wind speed was considerably *less* than 45 mph (72 km/h), sometimes as low as 18 mph (29 km/h).

Subsequent investigation by the Meteorological Office indicated the cause to have been exaggerated wave motion induced by the lift of air over the Pennine Range. Air flow was compressed into the bottom of the wave-trough just over Sheffield, giving exceptionally high wind speed; elsewhere, air flow was stretched out over considerable depth at the wave crest, and surface wind was abnormally reduced.

Wind funnelling up the river Clyde often accentuates gales experienced by Glasgow, situated in low ground surrounded by mountains.

On 28 January 1927, a depression to the west of Scotland caused average wind speeds of 55–60 mph (88–96 km/h) over northern England and Scotland. In Glasgow, wind frequently gusted to 70–80 mph (112–128 km/h) and soon after 4 pm nearby Paisley recorded a gust of 102 mph (164 km/h), the highest since records started there in 1883. Eleven people were killed and over 100 injured. Damage was widespread.

On 15 January 1968, a similar pressure pattern was again giving WSW gales, and Prestwick on the west coast of Scotland recorded a gust of 96 mph (154 km/h). Tiree, in the Western Isles and nearer the centre of the depression, had a gust of 117 mph (188 km/h). Great Dun Fell in Westmorland, at a height of over 2000 ft (610 m), recorded an unprecedented gust of 134 mph (215 km/h). In Glasgow, there was a mean wind speed of 61 mph (98 km/h) between 2 and 3 am, and one gust reached 102 mph (164 km/h). The storm was universally dubbed a hurricane and it probably spawned several tornadoes. The damage done, particularly to the roofs of tenement buildings in the Partick and Maryhill districts of the city, was enormous. Nine people were killed in Glasgow alone, 1700 people were made homeless and 100 000 homes were damaged.

One of many crashing chimney stacks wrecked the interior of this tenement house in Glasgow during gales on 15 January 1968, killing two mothers and two children. (Glasgow Herald)

8. Wind on sea and sand

The effects of wind upon sea are important in meteorology. Weather forecasters and master mariners work together to provide a ship routeing service, advising on wind strength and state of sea and the most advantageous routes to follow.

Sea waves are defined in three dimensions. *Height* is the vertical distance between crest and trough. *Length* is the distance between the crest of one wave and the crest of the next, and wave *period* is the time taken by two consecutive wave crests to pass a fixed point.

Fetch is the uninterrupted distance across the sea over which the wind has been blowing before arriving at the place of observation.

Average wave height is a function of wind strength and duration, as well as the fetch. The stronger the wind and the longer the duration and fetch, the rougher is the state of the sea. However, wind is never constant and each wave varies from the average, both in height and period. The sea is alive with waves travelling at different speeds, and when one catches up another it creates a much larger wave which lasts only momentarily in the combined state.

Statistical calculations on the frequency of these large waves agree remarkably well with the practical experience of seamen.

- ☐ One wave in 23 is twice the average wave height.
- ☐ One wave in 1175 is three times the average wave height.
- ☐ One wave in 300 000 (which is the normal number that a ship encounters during 1 month at sea), is four times the average height.

The *Daunt* light vessel off Cork, Eire, recorded a wave height of 42 ft (13 m) on 12 January 1969. This was 4·1 times the average height.

The maximum likely wave height in a given wave field depends upon how long one watches the sea. The longer the observation time, the higher the biggest wave seen is likely to be.

In an average year, the maximum likely wave height could be 30 ft (10 m) in the southern North

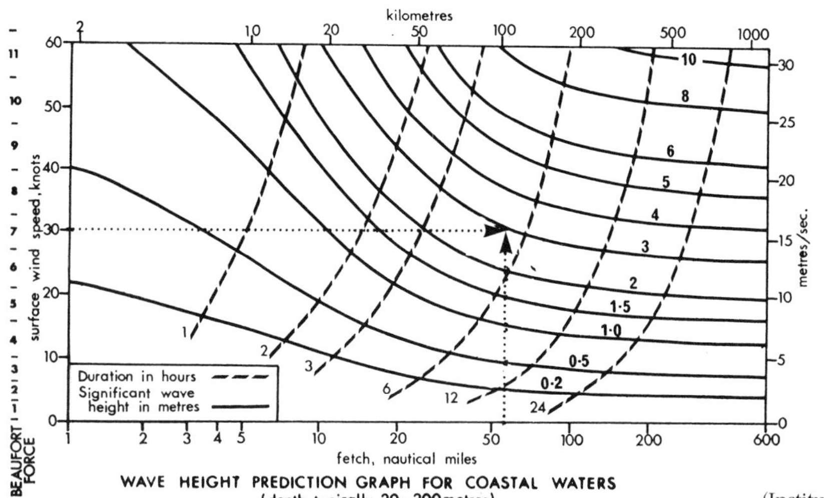

WAVE HEIGHT PREDICTION GRAPH FOR COASTAL WATERS (depth typically 20–200metres)

How to use the Wave Height Prediction Graph.

Example; 30 knot wind blowing for 12 hours over a 60 mile fetch.

Enter from left at 30 kt, moving horizontally to right. The 60 mile fetch limit line is reached before the 12 hours limit line. Read off Significant Height = 3·0 metres.

(Adapted from Darbyshire & Draper, 1963, Engineering, 195, 482-484. q.v.)

(Institute of Oceanographic Studies)

Sea, 50 ft (15 m) in the south-western coastal waters of the British Isles, and 70–80 ft (21–24 m) in the northern North Sea and the open Atlantic.

The significant wave height is what interests seamen. It is the average height of the highest one-third of all the waves being experienced at the time. The average height of all the waves is about 0·63 times the significant wave height.

A working estimate of significant wave heights can be obtained from the accompanying diagram by using values of wind speed, fetch and duration of wind at that speed.

The measurement of waves by eye when at sea is very difficult because the observer's ship pitches with the waves. It requires a steady nerve to study a huge wave dispassionately and record a reliable result. This quality certainly applied to Admiral Fitzroy: during a gale in the Bay of Biscay he 'measured' the crests of waves against the centre of his main mast when the ship was upright in a trough. He deemed several waves to be higher than 60 ft (20 m), and some were probably even bigger.

A Waverider Buoy floats on the surface of the sea and measures wave height by means of an accelerometer. It gives reliable measurement, providing it is moored at least half a mile (800 m) from an obstruction such as an oil platform. It can, however, sometimes tear loose in rough weather.

A Shipborne Wave Recorder measures the height of waves by a combination of accelerometer and water pressure sensor which is welded to the bottom of the ship below the water line. It gives best results on deep seas when waves are high and long.

Extreme wave heights have been measured in only a few of the huge seas. Nevertheless, traditional tales of monstrous waves may have some basis in fact.

The highest reliably-observed wave was 112 ft (34 m), experienced by the USS *Ramapo* in the North Pacific on the night of 6–7 February 1933. Average wind speed was 78 mph (126 km/h).

The Weather Ship *Famita* recorded a 61 ft (20 m) wave, and estimated the maximum to be 76 ft (23 m), when she was 160 miles (260 km) east of Peterhead, Aberdeenshire, during the winter 1969–70. In the same area, a Dutch vessel recorded a wave of 72 ft (22 m) on 21 October 1970.

The highest wave ever measured was 86 ft (26 m), on the ship *Weather Reporter* in the Atlantic at 59° N 19° W on 30 December 1972.

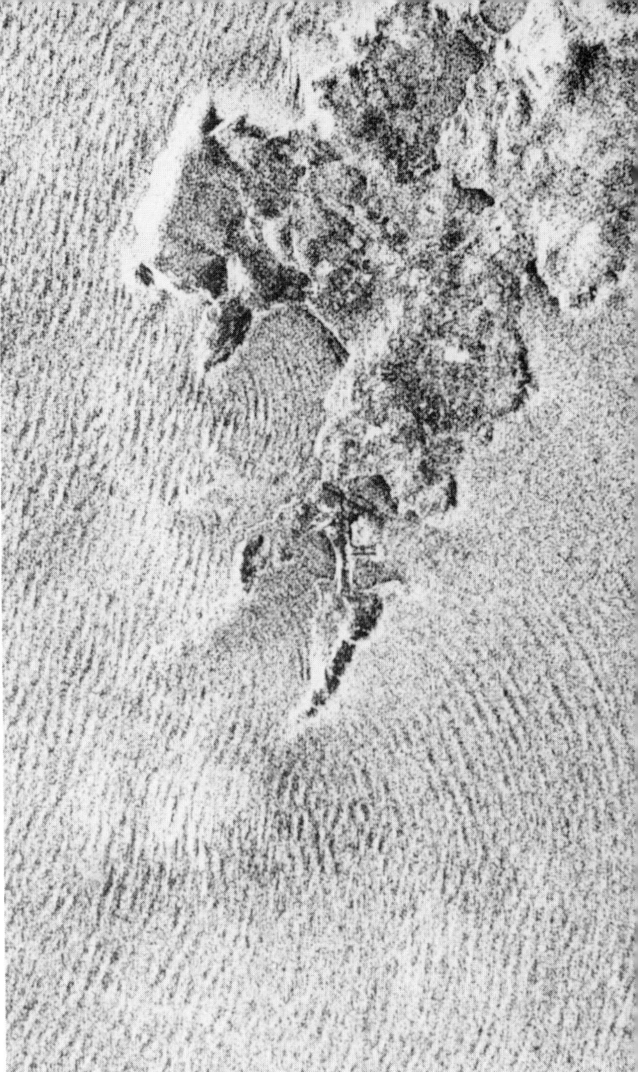

Atlantic swell, 15 September 1978, approaching the southern tip of the Shetland Isles, showing wave pattern radiating from the headland. Image taken from SEASAT, the first satellite dedicated to the study of the ocean's surfaces, using Synthetic Aperture Radar. This operates like an array of radar transmitters, coherently summing up echoes received from the sea surface while it scans a known distance. (Institute of Oceanographic Studies)

A 'sea' is the state of waves set up by wind blowing at that place and time of observation.

On 15 February 1982 the 84-man crew of the oil exploration rig *Ocean Ranger* were lost when the rig capsized 170 miles (273 km) off the coast of Newfoundland. Wind speeds of 80 mph (129 km/h) created 50 ft (15 m) waves which battered the rig. Fifty three of those drowned came from Newfoundland.

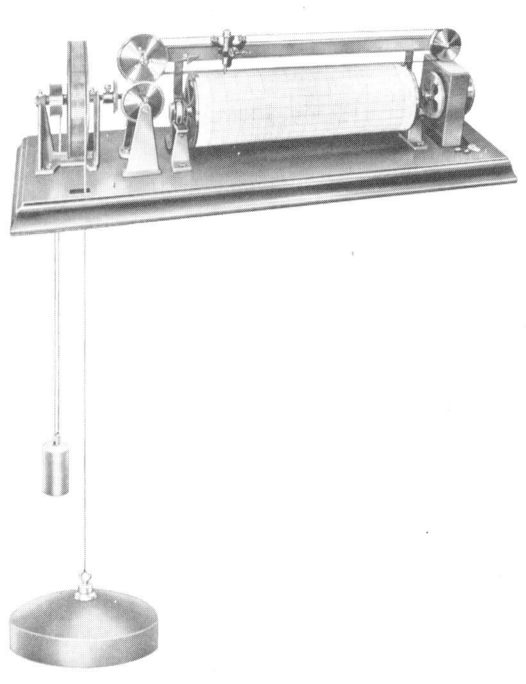

Swell is wave motion in the sea caused by wind which is blowing elsewhere. Swell may persist long after the original disturbance has died away, particularly in the southern Atlantic Ocean and the southern Indian Ocean where there are few interrupting land masses. Huge swell waves in these areas are called South Atlantic Rollers.

Swell has been detected off Cornwall, England, as a result of storms off the Falkland Islands, latitude 52° S in the South Atlantic Ocean.

A tsunami is a wave generated by an earthquake and not by the wind or tide. It is incorrect, therefore, to call a tsunami a 'tidal wave'.

The highest recorded tsunami was one of 220 ft (67 m) which appeared off Valdez, south west Alaska, after the great Prince William Sound earthquake of 28 March 1964. Tsunami (a Japanese word which is singular and plural) have been observed to travel at 490 mph (790 km/h). Since about 500 BC 286 instances of devastating tsunami have been reported.

In France, a freak wave swamped a stretch of the Côte d'Azur on 16 October 1979, sending yachts and parked cars spinning across the sea front. Eleven

Left: Recording tide gauge, providing for changes in level up to 12 metres. The float rides on the surface of the water in a submerged cylinder, open to the sea.
(R.W. Munro)

A Cockerell Raft, one tenth scale model, undergoing tests in the Solent during wind conditions of Force 6–7. This is an idea of Sir Christopher Cockerell, inventor of the hovercraft, which is being investigated by Wavepower Ltd of Southampton as a possible source of energy. Diagram right shows how the wave contouring raft floats on the surface of the water and follows the wave profile as each successive crest passes beneath. Individual sections are joined together by hinges and power is extracted at the hinge points from the relative motion of adjacent sections.
(Wavepower Ltd.)

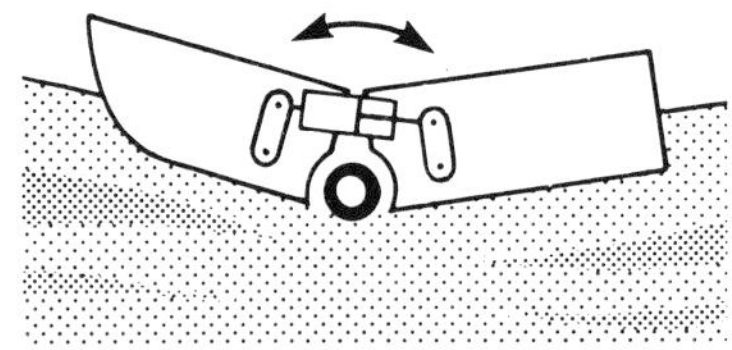

Tide gauge stations, with approximate time of travel of high tide between stations. (Storm Tide Warning Service)

people were drowned, of whom ten were men working on a breakwater under construction at Nice. The cause of the wave was sea bed subsidence.

A storm surge of water is caused by a deep and fast-moving low pressure system travelling across the sea. It is additional to the turmoil stirred up on the sea surface by the changing wind directions within the circulation. Pressure falls ahead of the system and rises behind it, thereby allowing the sea level to rise or fall. When this occurs slowly it is hardly noticeable—a matter of half an inch change in sea level for 1 mb change in pressure. But when it occurs rapidly it has a plunger effect upon the sea and creates a large-scale undulation. This may be noticeable as swell in the open sea many miles away from the place it originated. If such a storm surge is driven into the closed confines of land, it forms inflated waves and floods over the land. This is often called a tidal wave, erroneously because it has nothing to do with the tides caused by the pull of the moon. However, the most damaging storm surges are those which occur at the same time as a predicted high tide.

A negative surge occurs when the wind is driving water away from a shore, so that actual tides are lower than those predicted for astronomical reasons. Negative surges can be dangerous for shipping using shallow waters.

A Storm Tide Warning Service was inaugurated in Great Britain after the 1953 east coast floods. It is operated by members of the Hydrographic Department of the Navy, housed in the Meteorological Office at Bracknell. Tides progress up the west coast of the British Isles and down the east coast, with known time delays between various reference ports. Any major difference between actual high water, measured by tide gauge at these ports, and the predicted tide can be tracked down the coast. The development of the surge at the northern ports is calculated to take note of all the geographical and meteorological factors involved.

Close co-operation is maintained with Belgium, Holland and Germany, which suffer from storm surges in a similar way.

In the United States the most disastrous storm surge occurred at Galveston, Texas, on 8–9 September 1900. The city is sited on a low-lying island strip across Galveston Bay, some 2 miles off the mainland. An approaching hurricane caused a surge which had already inundated the island before the centre of the storm arrived. Wind increased to about 100–120

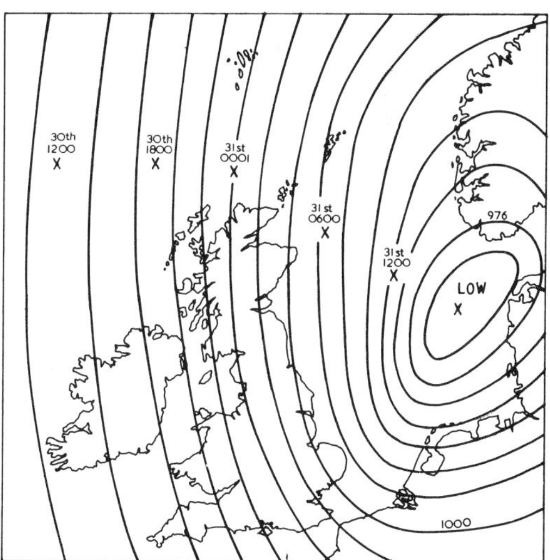

Synoptic situation at 1800 GMT, 31 January 1953, with previous positions of the depression centre. A surge of water, driven by northerly gales into the southern North Sea, caused extensive floods in eastern England and in Holland.

mph (160–190 km/h) and the city of 38 000 people was doomed. Six thousand people were drowned or killed by flying debris and collapsing homes, and thousands more were injured. Over 3600 houses were destroyed, and the whole city had to be rebuilt behind massive sea walls.

India has suffered many storm surges moving into its low-lying deltas. Near the mouths of the river Ganges 300 000 lives were lost at Calcutta in 1737; 100 000 people died at Backergunge in 1876; and more than 200 000 died in the same area in 1970.

On 18 November 1977, a storm in the Bay of Bengal intensified to give hurricane winds within a radius of 60 miles (100 km) of the centre which had a pressure of 940 mb. It was heading for the delta of the rivers Kistna and Godavani in Andhra Pradesh, and as the storm surge was driven across the rapidly shelving sea floor it developed into a wall of water 12–18 ft (4–6 m) high. This travelled inland for about 10 miles (16 km) washing away completely more than 30 villages, damaging 50 others very badly, and causing more than 15 000 deaths. Crops were destroyed and the soil was left contaminated by salt.

In Great Britain the worst storm surges occur when northerly gales blow behind a depression moving down the North Sea, piling up water into the constriction at the southern end. The most notorious disaster occurred on 1 February 1953. Sea walls were breached all along the east and south-east coasts of England, but fortunately for London the surge into the Thames estuary preceded high tide there by about 3 hours. A total of 307 lives were lost, of which 58 were drowned on Canvey Island and 35 at Jaywick, both in Essex; 30 000 were made homeless, and a quarter of a million acres of land were contaminated by sea water.

The Netherlands received direct impact from water piling down the North Sea, so that innumerable dykes, protecting reclaimed land, collapsed: 1800 people drowned, over 50 000 people were evacuated from low-lying areas, and it took over 9 months before sea walls were finally repaired.

On 11–12 January 1978, similar weather conditions resulted in extensive flooding and damage along the east coast of England from Humberside southwards. Towns worst hit were Cleethorpes, Kings Lynn, Wisbech and Deal. Piers were destroyed at Margate, Skegness and Hunstanton, and others on the East Anglian coast were damaged. Flood warnings were issued by the Flood Centre for London, but the capital escaped inundation by 19 in (0·5 m). Steel and rubber flood gates, designed to seal off the five major London docks, were closed for the first time since their completion in 1972.

London is increasingly at risk from storm surges because Great Britain is slowly tilting downwards from north west Scotland to south east England, at about 1 ft (0·3 m) every 100 years. Consequently, the effective tide height in London has been steadily rising, and over past centuries river walls have often been raised after floods. It is no longer feasible to build up the walls further, hence the Thames Barrier is under construction across the river at Woolwich. Hopefully it will be finished before the next dangerous weather situation.

On 6 January 1928, a storm surge travelled up the Thames to London. The river topped the embankments, which collapsed in several places, roads were torn up and the Tate Gallery was flooded almost to the tops of the ground floor doors. Fourteen people drowned in basements because of the rapidity of the inundation, and 4000 people were left homeless.

Storm surges in the English Channel may travel from east to west as a result of a North Sea surge penetrating the Straits of Dover. On other occasions a surge may originate from the west as happened during the *Morning Cloud* storm of 2 September 1974, when the yacht of that name foundered off Brighton, East Sussex, with the loss of two lives. A deep depression travelled from the south west into the Celtic Sea, giving prolonged southwesterly gales most of the day. The differences between predicted and actual tide heights on the English and French coasts, corrected for a variety of local factors, were plotted onto maps by the School of Maritime Studies at Plymouth. The sequence showed the progress of the surge up-Channel, the maximum height of that alone being about 27 in (700 mm).

It has been estimated that *Morning Cloud* could

Right: The Thames Barrier, nearing completion, across the river at Woolwich, built to protect London against the likelihood of flooding by a storm surge. In dangerous conditions the massive main gates will be lifted from their normal horizontal position, which does not interfere with shipping, into their vertical position against the sea. (Greater London Council)

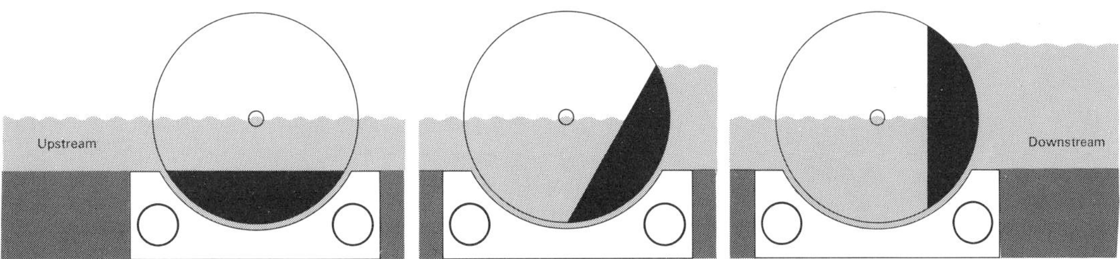

Gate in normal lowered position

Gate rising

Gate in flood defence position

have encountered a wave of 26 ft (8 m) during the 3 hours of the gale, and that there was a 1 per cent chance of a wave of 30 ft (10 m) or more.

The Fastnet storm, 13–14 August 1979, approached south west Ireland just as many of the 303 yachts, racing from Cowes, Isle of Wight, were half-way to the Fastnet Rock which they had to round. The depression deepened, one yacht recording 979 mb, and wind gusted at times to hurricane strength. Most of the yachts could have coped with that alone, but the turmoil of the sea was overwhelming. Abrupt changes in wind direction, as the depression travelled, were part of the cause; but there were probably secondary cell disturbances of a tornadic nature as well. Waves were estimated to have reached 44 ft (13 m) in height. Fifteen yachtsmen were drowned. Five yachts sank, 19 were abandoned but later retrieved, and only 85 yachts of the 303 finished the race.

The sea invaded the South Devon coast on 4 January 1979, when gales from ESE piled water into Start Bay at high tide, invading Torcross and Beesands. Huge boulders were tossed into the streets by 30 ft (10 m) waves, water several feet deep rushed through houses and 200 people were evacuated to safer areas.

The nearby village of Hallsands was completely engulfed by the sea in 1917, when driving gales coincided with high tide.

Haboobs are violent sand storms, caused by strong wind disturbing loose sand in deserts. They occur in advance of large convection clouds or cold fronts, when strong horizontal wind combines with vertical wind to make particularly turbulent conditions. Cold down-draughts of air from within the cloud spread out over hot dusty ground, and then convect upwards into a dense turbulent roll of air carrying sand which often reduces visibility to nil.

In the United States frequent dust storms occurred in the 1930s during the prolonged years of drought which created the Dust Bowl of the central plains. Dirt not only obscured visibility locally, but was often carried aloft and transported at high altitudes. It was carried to the ground by rain or snow in distant areas, creating curious colouring effects. The Great Dust Storm of 12–13 November 1933, carried dust from as far as Montana State all the way to the Atlantic seaboard. 'Black rain' fell in New York State, and 'brown snow' in Vermont. In 1934 there were four major dust storms, the most widespread on 9–12 May and christened 'Black Blizzards'.

In Europe, sand falls occasionally, usually after being carried from the Sahara on high altitude winds. Fine red sand from that desert fell with rain over the Home Counties, Hampshire and Isle of Wight on 11 February 1982.

A cloud of yellow dust, known locally as a 'Calina', obscured the Sun over Madrid and the central plain of Spain on 21–23 August 1980 causing widespread eye irritation.

Yellow dust from the Sahara was reported from Ireland, the Midlands and Scotland on 28–29 November 1979. A scientist estimated that about 60 000 tons must have fallen in the Cork region.

In Denmark, gales whipped up agricultural soil during a storm on 20 April 1980. Thousands of tons of newly sown soil were carried aloft to form a dust cloud rising to 7000 ft (2 km) and turning the sky brown or yellow.

A disastrous sand storm occurred in Scotland, at the end of the 17th century.

Culbin used to be a rich estate on the shores of the Moray Firth, Scotland, but sand banks and dunes had started to shift by the 1690s, because the coarse binding grass was depleted for use in thatching. In the autumn of 1694, a deep depression caused a yellow blizzard of sand which lasted all night and drifted high against the houses. The inhabitants had to dig themselves out and fled inland with as many cattle as they could gather together. After a short lull there was a renewal of the storm which finally submerged the whole village in sand. An arid desert 8 miles^2 (21 km^2) was left, with rolling billows and some sand mountains 100 ft (30 m) high. Storms in subsequent centuries remoulded the sand into different shapes, and in the 19th century the tips of some of the houses were temporarily uncovered.

The last sand storm in the area occurred in May 1920, when huge billows of sand rolled inland to submerge a wood. Since then the Forestry Commission has planted grass, brush wood and young trees as a successful three-line defence against wind and sand.

Right: The Fastnet storm approaching Ireland at 1537 GMT on 13 August 1979. The alignment of clouds, ahead and behind the cold front, indicates the wind changes which contributed to the enormous seas; TIROS-N, Vis. (University of Dundee)

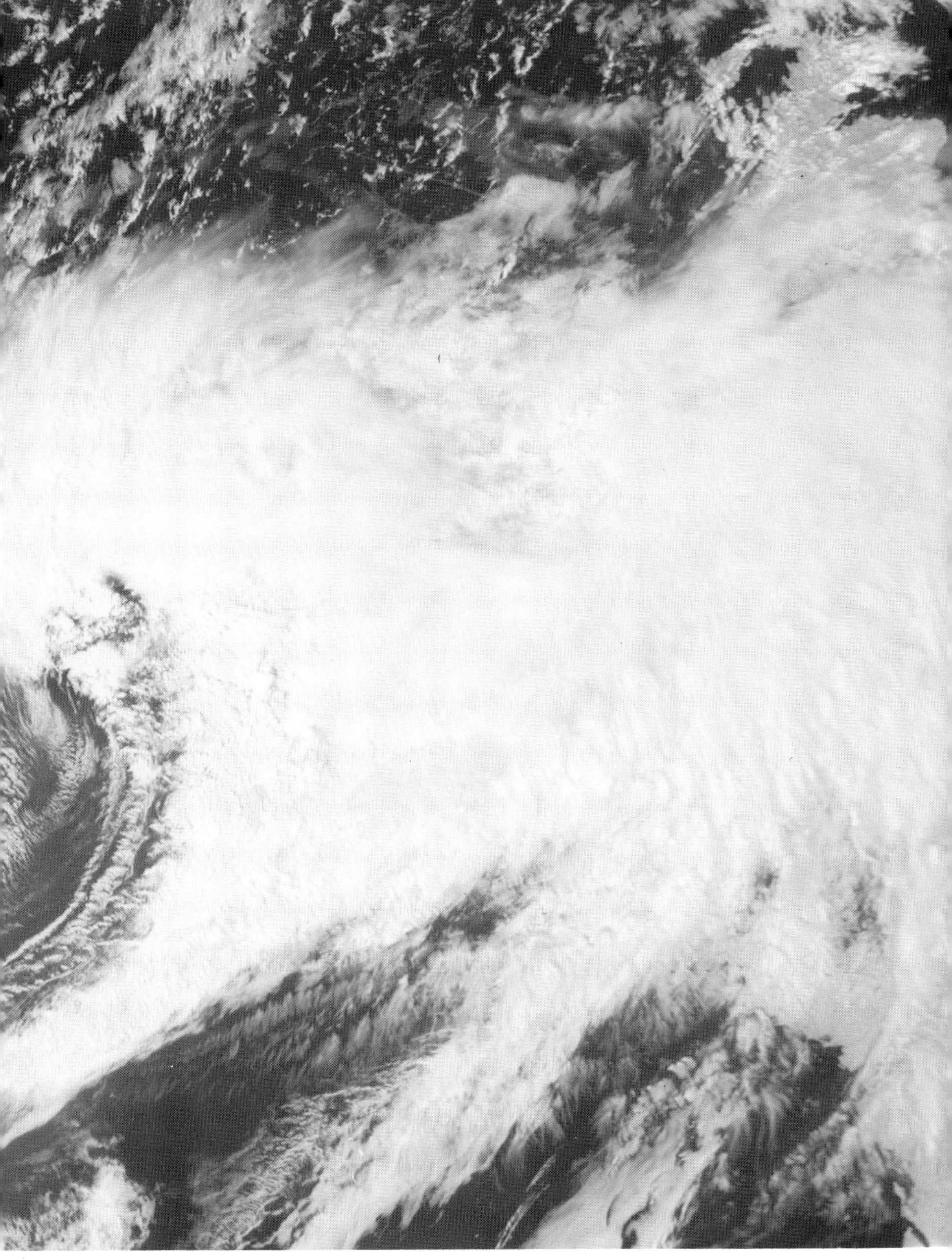

9. Water in its three disguises

Water is the raw material from which all visible weather is created. Both liquid and solid states are so familiar that they need no introduction, but the advent of thermometers permitted the discovery of many new facts about the properties of water.

Water is a compound of one volume of oxygen and two volumes of hydrogen, chemical formula H_2O. Although water is colourless when clean, it is a versatile solvent and therefore easily gets dirty. Rainwater accumulates organic matter, salts, minerals and other soluble ingredients during its run across land to the sea but is still considered comparatively fresh when it reaches its destination.

The density of water is greatest at a temperature of 4°C when it equals 0·99997 grams per cubic centimetre. It is sufficient to remember the density as 1 gram per cubic centimetre, which it was originally thought to be.

The density of fresh water increases with fall in temperature till the maximum is reached at 39·2°F (4°C). Thereafter the density decreases until water solidifies, forming ice.

Fresh water in bulk starts to freeze at a temperature of 32°F (0°C). Because of upside-down convection (See Chapter 1) it may take quite a time for a river to cool to 39·2°F (4°C) throughout its depth. Once that stage has been reached, however, water becomes less dense if it gets colder, so that surface ice soon forms.

River ice forms most readily on inner curves where the flow is slowest, and least readily wherever the stream increases along an outer bend or around an island.

Lake Titicaca, Peru, which has a maximum depth of 1214 ft (370 m) maintains a steady temperature of 50°F (10°C) by upside-down convection despite the bitter cold of the air at the altitude of 12 506 ft (3811 m).

Individual water drops can remain liquid when 'supercooled', that is, when they have temperatures

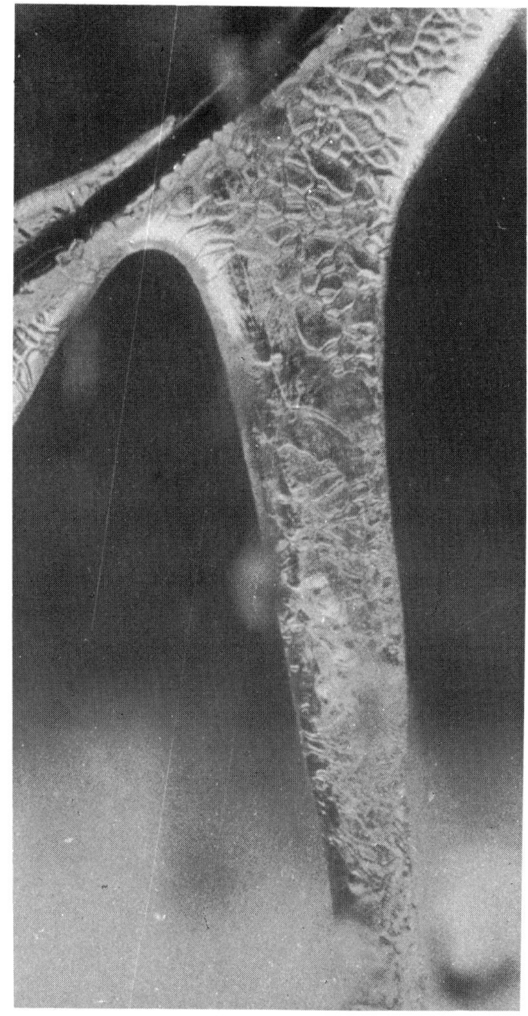

Icicle hanging from a line, showing cellular pattern of air bubbles and channels. (K.B. Shone)

Right: Icicles formed where dripping stream water has emerged from cover into sub-freezing air. (M.J. Hammersley)

below the normal freezing level of 32°F (0°C). Supercooled drops can exist in clouds at temperatures as low as −40°F (−40°C), but the condition is precarious. Droplets freeze instantly on contact with ice crystals or other particles having sub-zero temperature.

Sea water contains approximately 3 per cent salt as well as other minerals, but the proportion varies considerably, according to the ground over or through which the water has been fed. The most saline sea, and therefore the most dense, is the Dead Sea, which is a large inland lake 1296 ft (395 m) below the level of the Mediterranean. It is the lowest stretch of water on the Earth's surface and contains about 25 per cent salts, of which 7 per cent is common salt (about 12 650 million tons). No life is possible and normal salt water fish die at once when put into this lake.

The density of sea water increases continuously with falling temperature until freezing occurs.

Sea water freezes at a lower temperature than fresh water, between 29°F and 28°F (−1·5°C and −2°C) according to salinity. It precipitates its salts on freezing and becomes a mixture of fresh water ice, brine and air. The brine gradually gravitates out, so that water just below sea ice may be more salty than the rest.

Deep oceans do not freeze, because surface sea water becomes more dense as it gets colder; therefore it continually sinks to be replaced by warmer, less dense water from below (upside-down convection). Sea ice does form in shallow water which has a chance to cool to freezing level throughout its depth. Sea ice breaks loose from shallow water because of mechanical pressures or driving wind and then travels into deep water as ice floes.

Estuary water is a mixture of sea water and fresh river water and is therefore less saline than the sea. Consequently, estuaries freeze more readily than the sea but stay open to shipping for longer than rivers during cold winters.

Slippery water is a shallow surface layer of warm water which slides with very little friction over denser cold water below. Under such circumstances the wind easily drives the top layer over the bottom one, a feature first used to good advantage by the British Yachting team at the Olympic Games at Acapulco, Mexico, in 1968.

The 'Notts County' aground near the shore in Isajordur, Iceland. All the ice had accumulated from spray falling over the vessel in sub-freezing air temperature. (Topix)

The oceans and seas cover 139 670 000 miles² (361 740 000 km²), which is seven-tenths of the Earth's surface. The Pacific Ocean alone covers almost half the world's surface, and nearly all the land is in the other half. Early cartographers did not believe such inequality of distribution possible, and because they lacked factual evidence often added imaginary land in the southern hemisphere to 'balance' the world.

Ocean currents are permanent movements of water driven by wind and deflected by land masses, until they arrive in regions where their temperature is different from that normal for the latitude. Currents were first discovered by Matthew Maury who aptly described them as 'rivers in the ocean'.

Ice is the solid state of water. It appears white when broken or frozen unevenly, because of the refraction and scattering of light by the many faces of the ice pieces.

Satellite view of the glaciers and sea ice on the coast of Greenland. Note the sea eddies, traced out by slush and water mixture, at the outer edge of the ice belt; TIROS-N, Vis, 1245 GMT, 3 June 1979. (University of Dundee)

Black ice is not really black, but a transparent frozen film of water which takes the colour of the surface on which it forms. The name probably originated from the dark colour of roads which appear normal even though slippery with ice.

The density of ice is 0·92 grams per cubic centimetre, and is achieved abruptly when water solidifies. Freezing is accompanied by an equally abrupt increase in volume of about one-tenth. This gives ice its terrific power when formed in confined surroundings: bottles, metal pipes, and cleft rocks can all burst with the expansion of freezing water. Ice is as hard as metal at about −40°F (−40°C).

Frazil ice (French-Canadian *fraisil*: cinder) consists of small pieces of ice in seas or rivers which are flowing too fast to permit formation of a solid ice sheet.

Ice floes are slabs of ice which have broken free from the places where they formed and then travel along rivers or with ocean currents. In the Soviet Union on 6–7 January 1979, a huge ice floe broke loose in Vladivostok Bay, following a sudden rise in temperature and a strong off-shore wind. Some 2840 Russians, who had ignored warnings and gone on to the ice to bore holes for fishing, had to be rescued by 20 ships and three helicopters.

The largest extent of sea ice in the northern hemisphere occurs north of latitude 60° N during winter. It persists all the year in the Arctic Ocean, which is centred around the North Pole and consists of a restless circulating mass of ice floes of an average thickness of 10 ft (3 m). For this reason, discovery of the North Pole was not just a question of planting a flag into the ice as proof of arrival. The ice travels the whole time, taking any discovery flag with it. The Arctic Ocean is a perpetual challenge to explorers because of the dream of using it as a commercial route.

The first to claim arrival at the North Pole were the Americans Dr Frederick Albert Cook (1865–1940), on 21 April 1908, and Commander Robert Edwin Peary (1856–1920), on 6 April 1909.

The first indisputable claim, independently checked by a weather aircraft, was that of Ralph Plaisted, also American, and his three companions. They reached the North Pole on 19 April 1968 after a 42-day trek in snow-mobiles.

The first surface ship to reach the North Pole was the Russian nuclear-powered ice breaker *Arktika*, 18 172 tons, in August 1977. The voyage from Murmansk took 9 days and despite the summer season the *Arktika* had to break through ice 12 ft (4 m) thick in places.

The first vessels to cross the Arctic ocean beneath the ice were the American nuclear submarines *Nautilus*, in August 1958, and *Skate* which broke through ice to surface at the North Pole in 1959.

The first trans-Arctic crossing by sledge and dogs over the ice was made by a team led by Wally Herbert between 21 February 1968 and 29 May 1969. The distance covered, as the crow flies, was 1662 miles (2674 km). However, drifting ice increased that distance by a further 700 miles (1126 km), quite apart from diversions on the ice due to open leads of water. Temperature fell to −47°F (−44°C) during the trek.

Members of the Transglobe Expedition, Sir Ranulph Fiennes and Charles Burton, arrived at the North Pole on Easter Sunday, 11 April 1982, after a welcome spell of cold weather. Unseasonally high temperature, about 28°F (−2°C) during early March had broken up much of the ice and impeded the team's progress. Later in March, air temperatures fell to about −33°F (−36°C) and the water lanes re-froze.

The most southerly limit of North Atlantic sea ice in recent years was reached during spring 1968, when a bridge of ice between Iceland and Greenland provided uncomfortably easy access for polar bears to renew acquaintance with Iceland after 50 years' absence. Consequent gloomy predictions about the likelihood of an immediate new Ice Age were confounded by the spring of 1976 when the Arctic ice edge had retreated almost to the coast of Greenland and up to the west coast of Spitzbergen.

Summer sea ice in the northern hemisphere generally retreats towards the 78th parallel of latitude, but Canada and the USSR have difficulty in keeping any sea routes open along their northern boundaries—even in summer.

Skating in Hyde Park in the winter of 1857. Skating is easiest when the temperature is not too far below freezing level, because melt water created by the pressure of the blades acts as a lubricant. (Illustrated London News)

Sea ice in the southern hemisphere surrounds the continent of Antarctica, and in winter may extend

well north of the 60° S latitude. Some of the ice is formed in shallow coastal waters, but much is compacted snow which has gradually crept off the continent and broken into icebergs which travel the sea.

Shallow seas, which are confined by land and do not benefit from stirring by strong tides and currents, freeze more readily than open sea. The Hudson Bay, the Bering Sea and the northern Baltic Sea between Sweden and Finland are all ice-covered during winter. Much of the Atlantic in the same latitude remains free of ice because of the North Atlantic Drift current. In the southern Baltic Sea, the severity of winter in Sweden and Demark is judged by whether or not they become ice bound.

The most dangerous form of sea ice occurs in regions where warm sea currents enable ships to remain afloat during winter, but where air temperature falls below freezing level when wind blows off frost-bound continents. A ship afloat in such conditions risks the danger of capsizing as the sea spray sets solid on to the sub-freezing superstructure, altering the vessel's centre of gravity.

On 4 February 1968, trawlers from Hull, Humberside, were fishing west of Iceland when a deep depression caused wind in the fishing grounds to become easterly and of hurricane strength. Spray from mountainous seas filled the air whose temperature was 12°F (−11°C), and ice accumulated on the trawlers, making them increasingly difficult to handle. The *Ross Cleveland* eventually capsized and sank within a few seconds, only one of the crew surviving.

Rivers in the centre of large land masses north of latitude 50° N are always liable to freeze in winter. Exceptionally hard winters result in polar scenes considerably further south. North America was exceptionally cold in January and February 1977, and by the beginning of February the normally busy Hudson River was thick with ice floes near New York (41° N).

Rivers in the British Isles freeze only in exceptionally cold winters when the wind predominates from the continent of Europe.

The most recent occasion on which the Thames was frozen, so that people could cross above Kingston-upon-Thames, was in February 1963. Below Kingston, the river remained at a temperature of about 45°F (7°C) all winter, because of waste heat from power stations.

Most winters yield ice on puddles and in many winters ponds freeze over. Occasionally, sea ice forms along the east coast, most recently in December 1976.

In order to melt ice, heat is required—an obvious fact that could only be quantified after thermometers were invented. Scientists then discovered some rather extraordinary features of the melting and freezing processes.

Ice always starts to melt at 32°F (0°C). It takes as much heat to melt 1 gram of pure ice at a temperature of 0°C as it takes to raise the temperature of 1 gram of liquid water by 80C degrees. Yet all that heat is used entirely for melting the ice, and not for raising the temperature of the mixture of ice and melt water. That remains at a constant 0°C until all the ice has melted. Such a mixture is therefore useful for calibrating thermometers.

The reverse process, freezing, causes a similar amount of heat to be released, 80 calories per gram of water. This is why bulk water solidifies slowly. Every time a little freezes, it releases heat to delay the solidification of the rest. Even at air temperatures as

The quantities of heat involved for water to change its state. (Diana Davies)

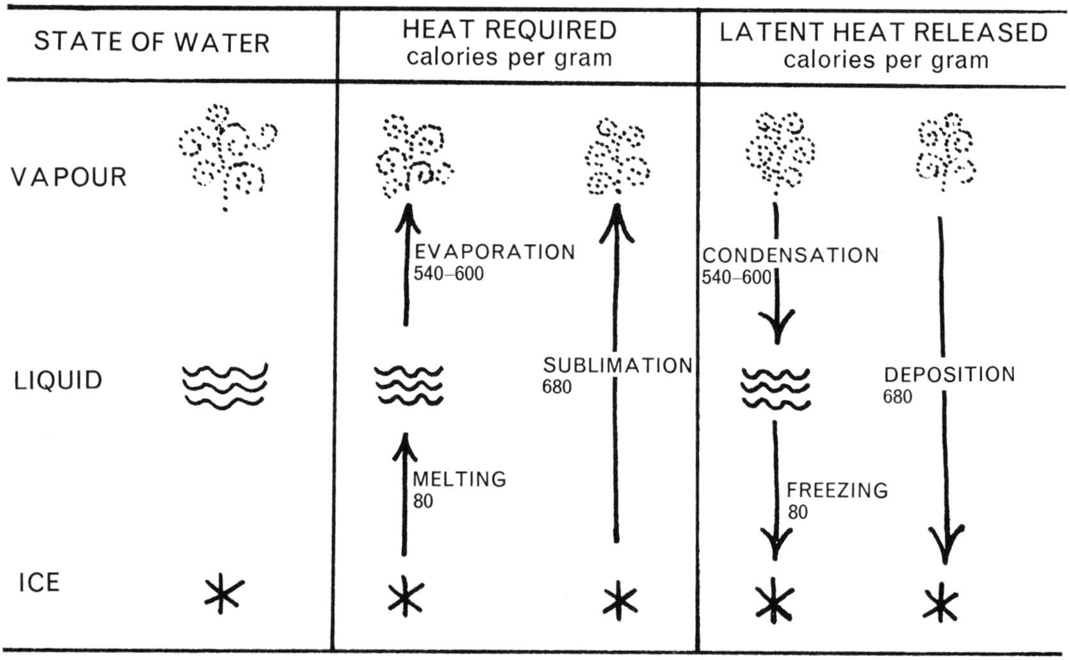

Ice floes blocking London Bridge in February 1870. (Illustrated London News)

The Thames above Kingston Bridge, frozen over during the 1963 winter. Open water persists near the edge of Raven's Ait, around which the river divides and therefore runs faster. (Ingrid Holford)

low as −40°F (−40°C), which is frequently experienced in polar regions, a cup of water poured on to the ground will take some moments to freeze. If the water is first thrown into the air to split it into smaller amounts, however, it explodes into a dazzling shower of ice crystals, which also emit an audible hiss at temperatures as low as −60°F (−51°C).

Latent heat is that heat which is released during a change of state of a substance without causing any change in temperature.

Latent heat of fusion of water into ice can be put to practical use for frost protection. If blossom is sprayed with a fine jet of water when air temperature reaches 32°F (0°C) it becomes encapsulated in ice. Providing the spray continues to maintain a mixture of ice and water over the blossom, its temperature will fall no lower than 32°F (0°C). This means it can often survive even when air temperature falls much lower. Apart from practical and financial problems of this method, an obvious hazard is that the blossom may break off under the weight of accumulated ice, even if it does not die of cold.

The melting point of ice is lowered by the application of pressure. This means that if ice is already near the normal melting temperature of 32°F (0°C), any pressure applied to it may tip the balance and cause it to melt. Therefore, skating is easier on comparatively warm ice than on ice at very low temperatures, because the melt water created by the pressure of the skate blades acts as a lubricant.

Regelation is the refreezing of melt water once temporary pressure is withdrawn. A weighted wire will go through a block of ice without apparently cutting it, due to regelation. Separate pieces of ice, which become coated with melt water when under pressure, bond together as one piece when pressure is released. Ice floes, which rise out of river or sea under the initial impact with others, re-freeze again as pack ice with a humpy appearance.

Cutting ice on the Hudson River, New York, at the end of the 19th century, for storage in ice houses. (Illustrated London News)

The last Frost Fair on the Thames in 1814 was made possible because of regelation. During the very cold month of January, ice floes drifted down to London from the upper reaches of the river. Old London Bridge was still standing and its archways were too small to allow the ice to pass through. The pressure of one floe behind the other caused them all to bond together as humpy ice. On 31 January, the first people ventured on to the ice and for 5 days a Frost Fair, with entertainments and stalls, was the focus of everyone's attention. On 5 February the wind shifted to the south; it then rained in the evening and the thinner bonding ice was the first to melt. The river became a mass of crashing ice floes, separate entities once again; several lives were lost, and an enormous amount of damage was done to moored vessels.

Domestic ice in warm weather is a precious commodity. Before the invention of refrigerators ice was cut from ponds in winter and stored in ice houses until the summer (See Chapter 19). In climates without persistent cold weather, ice was made artificially whenever still clear nights augured air temperature near freezing level. Radiation cooling together with evaporation cooling of water stored in porous jars, permitted ice to be made at Cawnpore in India, in 1846 when the air temperature was 43°F (6°C).

The ice pits at Allahabad, India, described by Mrs Fanny Parkes, the wife of the Manager, in her book 'Wanderings of a pilgrim in search of the picturesque' (1850):

'The shallow square beds were covered with a black-looking straw, which had to be kept perfectly dry. At each corner stood earthen jars filled with water which kept cool by evaporation. The old foreman who was in charge of ice-making watched the weather to assess the possibility of a cold night. If the breeze was fresh there was no point in going to the expense of filling the shallow pans. But if there was a crisp frosty feel in the still air, he beat his tom-tom about 6 pm to summon the coolies in the bazaar. They filled the pans, by means of cups on long sticks, with cool water from the jars on the pathways, and they were then dismissed. About 3 am next morning the foreman would test the pans for a sufficient thickness of ice, and then again beat the tom-tom to rouse the coolies from sleep to return to the pits. The ice was knocked out of the pans into baskets which were emptied into the deep pits under thatched roofs. The ice was beaten down, covered with straw and the door locked. Pits were opened for sale of ice on the first of April or May, and ice often lasted till the middle of August.' (India Office Library)

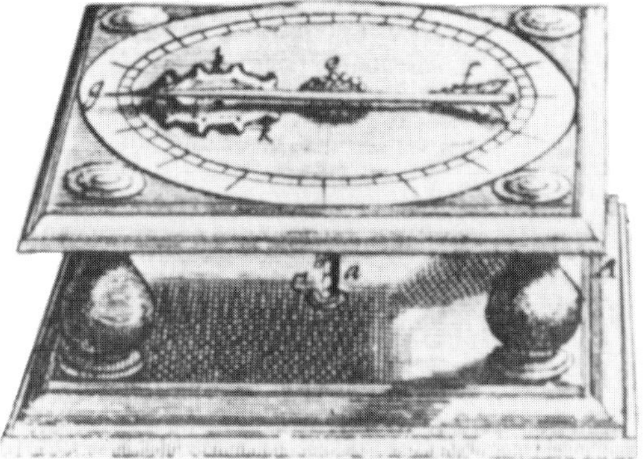

Right: Oat-beard hygrometer, shown in R. Hooke's 'Micrographia'. The oat-beard twists and untwists as humidity changes. Each twist advances one tooth of the starwheel by means of a tiny pin fixed beneath the pointer. (Ann Ronan Picture Library)

Mason's hygrometer, with the muslin covering the wet bulb dipping into a reservoir of distilled water. (Casella)

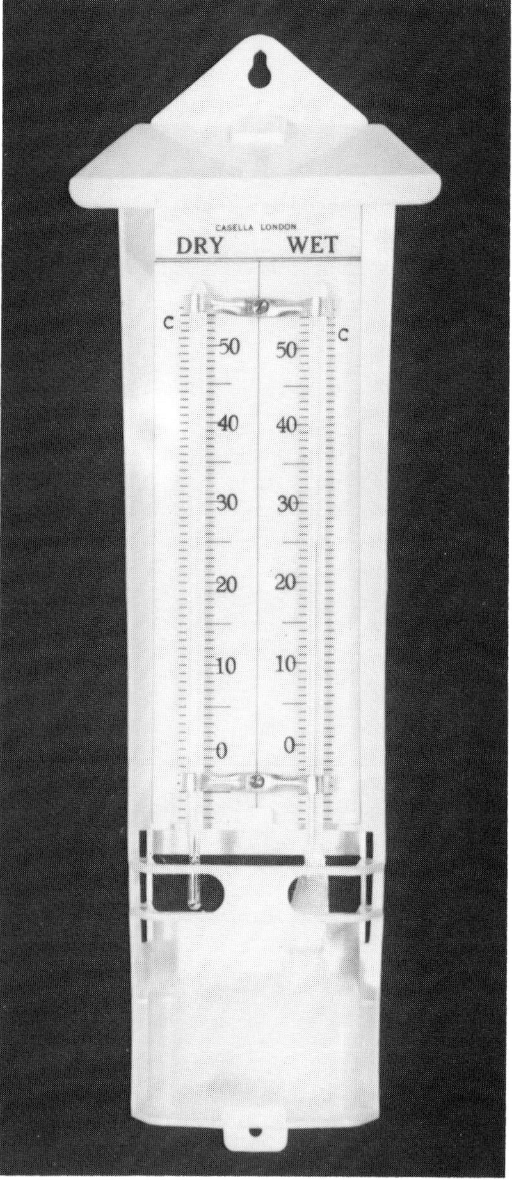

Water vapour, the invisible state of water, was not understood until the 18th century. The word 'vapour' had been used since classical times but it described mist and moisture which was *visible*, actually tiny drops of liquid water. People also talked about 'exhalation' implying that the Earth breathes moisture like themselves. Everyone knew that water sometimes disappeared, either by prolonged boiling or by uncovered exposure to the air, but they didn't know why.

Robert Boyle (1627–91), Irish-born chemist and physicist, pioneered the study of gases. He went to Italy to study the works of Galileo, and on return to the family estates in Dorset, devoted himself to science. In 1662 he formulated Boyle's Law which states that when temperature remains constant, the volume of a given mass of gas is inversely proportional to the pressure acting upon it.

Jacques Alexandre César Charles (1746–1823), French physicist, discovered Charles' Law, which states that when pressure is constant, the volume of a gas is proportional to the temperature. Gases at constant pressure lose 1/273 part of their volume at 0°C for each 1C degree that their temperature falls. Hence, at −273°C the volume of a gas should in theory be reduced to zero which is called absolute zero.

New gases were meanwhile discovered

Oxygen was independently discovered between the years 1771 and 1774 by Carl Wilhelm Scheele, the Swedish chemist and Joseph Priestley, English chemist. Priestley was the first to isolate oxygen from atmospheric air and, because it was the inflammatory constituent, he called it 'dephlogisticated air'. This was named oxygen a few years later by the French chemist Antoine Lavoisier (1743–94).

Hydrogen was discovered by Henry Cavendish (1731–1810), English chemist and physicist, who described it to the Royal Society in 1776. It was named hydrogen 20 years later by Lavoisier. Hydrogen is the lightest gas, and its discovery opened the ballooning era. However, hydrogen is highly explosive and helium was used instead after its discovery in 1895 by Sir William Ramsey.

Nitrogen was discovered in 1772 by Daniel Rutherford (1749–1819), Scottish chemist.

Dry air proved to be a composition of 78 per cent nitrogen and 21 per cent oxygen, together with small proportions of other gases.

John Dalton (1776–1844), English chemist, was keenly interested in the weather. He kept careful

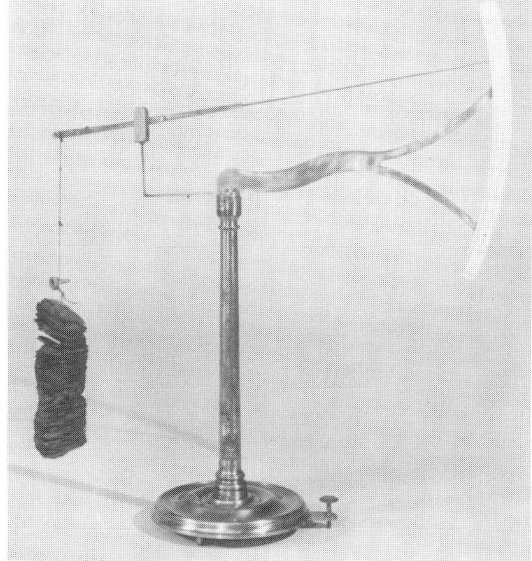

Absorption hygrometer. Discs of paper, probably impregnated with salt, absorb moisture from the atmosphere and register the amount by a pointer passing across a graduated scale. (Crown Copyright. Science Museum, London)

records for 46 years, often using self-made instruments, and accumulated some 200 000 weather observations. He applied his own theories of the atomic properties of matter to the new laws of gases and thereby laid down the fundamental meteorological principles governing water vapour in the atmosphere.

Atmospheric air is dry air together with water vapour, which exists as an independent gas in variable quantities. Each of the constituent gases contributes its own independent pressure to the total exerted by the atmosphere. Nitrogen exerts a pressure of about 750 mb and oxygen about 230 mb. The maximum pressure exerted by water vapour varies from as little as 0·2 mb, when air temperature is as low as −40°F (−40°C), to as much as 42·4 mb when air temperature is 86°F (30°C) and saturated.

Evaporation is the escape of water molecules from the surface of water into gaseous disguise. Evaporation can only take place until a certain maximum vapour pressure, called *saturated vapour pressure*, has built up over the surface of the water, and this amount is different for every air temperature. Warm air is more hospitable to vapour than cold air.

Condensation is the return of vapour to the liquid state. It happens when air, which is already saturated with vapour, cools still further, so that its moisture content is more than the maximum possible at that lower temperature.

Air at a temperature of 86°F (30°C) can hold 27·69 grams of vapour per kilogram of air, approximately 2·8 per cent of its mass. This amount is nearly 240 times as much vapour as air can contain at a temperature of −40°F (−40°C). All water vapour is a potential source of wet weather.

Dewpoint is the temperature of air at which condensation takes place when that air has a given vapour content.

Sublimation is the escape of water molecules direct from a surface of ice into gaseous form. The molecules are more rigidly structured in ice than in liquid water, and the saturated vapour pressure possible over ice is slightly less than over water. If air contains both ice crystals and supercooled water drops, there

Cotton, in one pan of the scales, absorbs moisture from the air and weighs it against wax in the other pan, which does not absorb moisture. (Crown Copyright. Science Museum, London)

can be saturation vapour pressure with respect to ice, but not with respect to water drops.

Deposition is the return of vapour direct to ice form. It takes place when air has already saturated vapour pressure and a temperature below 32°F (0°C), and then cools further.

Latent heat is released during condensation and amounts to 540–600 calories per gram, which is the same as the amount of heat required to change one gram of water to vapour.

Latent heat is released during deposition and amounts to 680 calories per gram — the same amount of heat as is required to change ice direct to vapour.

Air is said to be moist or dry, according to whether its vapour pressure is near saturated level or well below. The more moist the air, the more readily a given amount of cooling produces condensation.

The relative humidity of air (RH) is the actual vapour pressure expressed as a percentage of the maximum possible at that temperature.

When RH is high, then comparatively little cooling will bring air temperature down to dewpoint and produce condensation. When the RH is low, temperature can fall a long way before dewpoint is reached.

Relative humidity usually increases during the night, because temperature falls even though the amount of water vapour may remain constant.

A hygrometer measures the humidity of air, but the earliest instruments merely weighed the amount of water which dry fibrous material absorbed.

An absorption hygrometer was sketched by Leonardo da Vinci in one of his notebooks. It consisted of a pair of sensitive scales, holding a piece of cotton fibre in one pan and an equal weight of wax in the other. In moist air, the cotton became heavier while the wax did not, so that the depression of the balance arm from the horizontal indicated the moisture content of the air.

A paper hygrometer in the Science Museum, London, dating from about 1790, consists of a series of paper discs, probably impregnated with salt to attract moisture, suspended at one end of a pivoting arm. The other end of the arm moves against a graduated scale to indicate the weight of water absorbed by the papers.

Expansion hygrometers utilise the known property of fibrous materials to swell when wet. A very simple one in the Science Museum, dating from about 1700, consists of two strips of wood secured together in a common base. Each strip is two-ply, having the longitudinal grain on the inside and the cross grain on the outside, the strips having been assembled when thoroughly moist. Wood shrinks more across the grain than along it, so that the drying out process causes the strips to splay apart, according to the dryness of the air.

Seed 'beards', which twist and untwist as they become dry or moist, were also used in expansion hygrometers.

The first hair hygrometer was devised in 1783 by Horace-Bénédict de Saussure (1740–99), Swiss physicist and geologist. A hair, fixed at one end to a brass frame, passed over a wheel carrying a long arm which moved over a graduated scale. Humidity was indicated by the position of the pointer between two fixed points. One was determined when the hair was saturated with water and therefore fully expanded, and the other when it was absolutely dry and at its shortest.

The first wet bulb experiments were made by the Scottish geologist James Hutton (1726–97) in 1792, when he was researching the subject of rain. He mounted two thermometers side by side and moistened the bulb of one with water. As the water evaporated, the level of mercury in the wet bulb thermometer fell below that in the dry bulb thermometer, and remained lower as long as its bulb was kept moist. Hutton concluded that heat had been stolen from the bulb itself, thereby providing an explanation to a phenomenon which had been known for years. A porous container holding water permits evaporation from the outer surface during hot, dry weather thus keeping the inner contents cool. The human body is like a wet bulb instrument, because it can lower its temperature by the evaporation of sweat.

Mason's hygrometer was developed, by Sir John Leslie of Edinburgh and Mason of London, from Hutton's original wet-and-dry-bulb idea, and it remains popular. The wet bulb is covered with muslin, tied on with a wick which dips into a container of distilled water.

A whirling psychrometer consists of a wet-and-dry bulb thermometer, packed into a wooden frame which pivots on a handle and resembles a football match rattle. It is used with the same degree of vigour, by whirling, in order to ensure a steady maximum flow of air across the two thermometer bulbs.

A hygrograph is a self-recording hygrometer which provides a continuous trace of humidity, usually by pen on a clockwork rotating drum.

James Glaisher, who was chief meteorologist at Greenwich and became the first secretary of the Royal Meteorological Society in 1850, made thousands of temperature observations over a period of years. He compared dewpoints with wet and dry bulb values, eventually compiling tables which specified the relationships between them and with relative humidity.

The wet bulb temperature is always lower than the dry bulb temperature, except when the environment air is saturated so that no evaporation can take place from the wet bulb. The two thermometers then register the same. The highest wet bulb temperature recorded was 93·2°F (34·0°C) at Bahrain International Airport on 16 August 1972.

The dewpoint of unsaturated air is always lower than the wet bulb temperature, because the microclimate around the wet bulb itself is always saturated. When the general atmosphere, too, is saturated, then dewpoint, wet and dry bulb temperatures are identical.

Relative humidity in the British Isles usually varies between 60 per cent and 95 per cent, and is often higher; 40 per cent is rare even in summer, and the lowest recorded was 9·5 per cent on 24 May 1901 at Parkstone, Dorset.

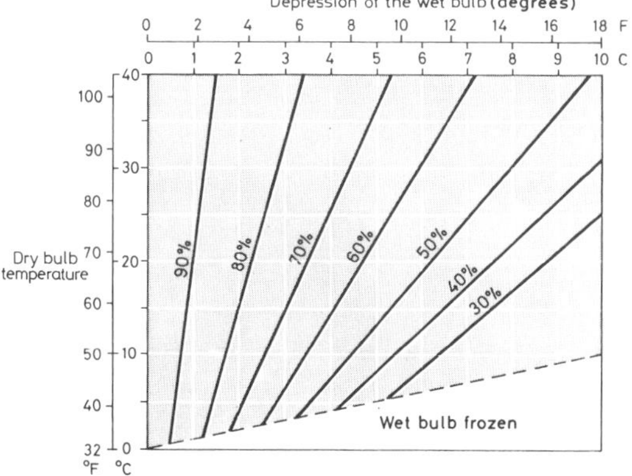

Table showing relative humidity of air according to the depression of the wet bulb thermometer below the dry bulb reading. (G. Arnold)

Relative humidity in high latitudes in winter is nearly always above 80 per cent. The water vapour content at very low temperatures can only be small, and the additional vapour exhaled by people is sufficient to cause condensation near the face. Dog teams in polar regions are often signalled by long trails of mist which can persist for a long time, especially when there is no wind.

Relative humidity in low latitudes falls well below 40 per cent during the day in regions removed from the sea and hardly ever rises to 100 per cent. In coastal areas it can become very humid. Bahrain has one of the most uncomfortable climates in the world. It is hot and surrounded by shallow sea which can warm to 95°F (35°C). In July 1978, the mean daily temperature was frequently above 95°F (35°C), with a mean relative humidity above 60 per cent. On 20 July, the maximum temperature soared to 113°F (45°C) and the mean relative humidity was 59 per cent.

Relative humidity, in Föhn conditions, falls as the air temperature rises. When this wind blows in Switzerland, relative humidity may fall to 30 per cent or less for perhaps 3 or 4 days. This sudden dryness has an aggravating effect upon the human constitution, affecting both the blood circulation and the nervous system. Mental stability suffers, and there is an increased tendency to suicide. Fire risk also increases as the exceptionally dry air greedily sucks moisture from wooden buildings and vegetation. The history of the country is full of tales of fire disasters which have reduced villages to ashes, and householders now have a statutory obligation to fire-watch during Föhn conditions.

Indoor relative humidity is materially affected by artificial heating systems. Unless steps are taken to increase the water vapour in the air discomfort to persons and damage to fibrous materials may result (See Chapter 19). Extreme examples occur in places like Whitehorse in Alaska, where outdoor temperature sometimes falls to −50°F (−45°C), with relative humidity near 100 per cent. When such air is warmed indoors to 75°F (24°C), it suffers a fall in relative humidity to 5 per cent. The air is then so dry that it evaporates too much moisture from the skin so that people feel colder than the temperature alone warrants. Even humidifiers have difficulty in raising the vapour content of air to a comfortable 50 per cent RH under such conditions.

10. Dew, frost and fog

Dew, frost and fog are formed when air in contact with a colder surface cools to below dewpoint. Hoar frost, like dew, is direct condensation from air, but it occurs in ice crystal form when dewpoint is less than 32°F (0°C).

Radiation cooling at night, when there is no cloud cover and only light wind, often provides suitable surfaces on which vapour in air can condense. Metal radiates heat very quickly, so that parked cars, for instance, easily induce condensation. Dry soil cools less quickly than metal but more quickly than wet soil, which can conduct heat from the subsoil to counteract surface cooling. Grass collects condensation rapidly, partly because it transpires vapour itself and thus makes its particular micro-environment especially moist. Moreover, the air spaces between the blades insulate grass from the benefit of heat in the soil below.

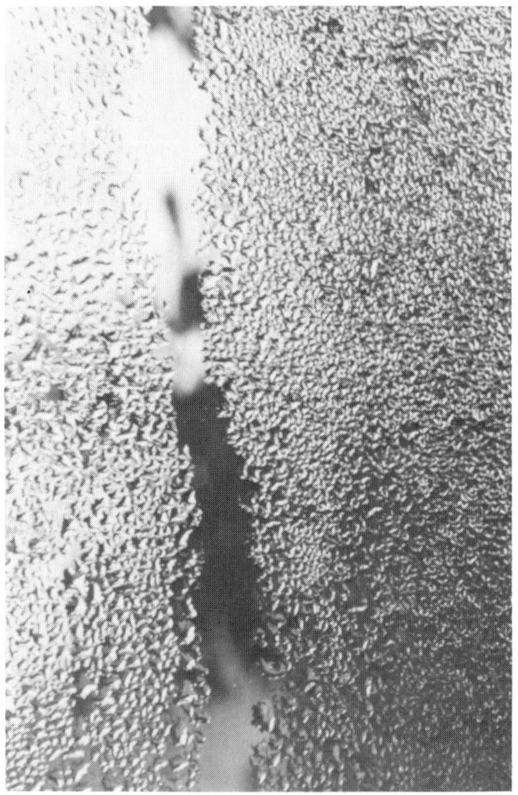

Guttation is transpired water, which is unable to evaporate because saturation vapour pressure has already been reached. It hangs as single large drops at the tips of grass blades. Dew, however, is condensed from the air and consists of much smaller drops all along the flat surface of the blades.

Measurement of dew can be made by weighing the amount deposited on a given surface or by photographing drops and comparing size and quantity with known deposits. However, the measurement does not have great significance, because quantities vary considerably according to the material on which dew forms. The amount produced at any one place in the British Isles is thought to be less than 0·4 in (10 mm) per annum.

A dew pond is one which retains water throughout all but the most severe droughts. The name is misleading because dew is quite inadequate to keep the ponds filled. They rely upon rain together with fog and cloud drip, and are not fed by spring or stream. Dew ponds are situated on high ground, which is probably the reason why 'Jack and Jill went *up* the hill to fetch a pail of water'; a few are natural hollows but the majority are man-made as watering holes for livestock. Excavated soil from the centre is used to make a raised edge round the circumference. The inside is lined with watertight materials such as clay, puddled chalk or concrete, and often overlaid with rubble or broken chalk.

Left: Dew on a cold window, condensed from the warmer air indoors. (M.J. Hammersley)

Above: Hoar frost on a car key hole, when air was comparatively moist. (M.J. Hammersley)

Dew traps in Lanzarotte, a small volcanic island in the Canary Isles, are extremely efficient. The craters are approximately 10 ft (3 m) in diameter, and 6 ft (2 m) deep in the centre, and are clustered together to give the impression of a lunar landscape. They contain a top layer, 2–4 in (50–100 mm) thick, of glass-like volcanic ash, called picon or lapilli. This insulates the soil in the craters from the heat of the Sun during the day, and also presents an admirable cooling surface for condensation at night. Frequent warm and moist winds from the south-west provide ample vapour for condensation as dew, invaluable for an island whose annual rainfall is normally less than 8 in (200 mm). Each crater has a vine growing in the centre, and semi-circular low walls protect these from the east winds, which are the driest and therefore most greedy to evaporate water. In 1975 and 1976 practically no rain fell, but the vines generally struggled through on dew alone. There is no artificial irrigation on the island at present.

Below: Fern frost on a car, formed in relatively dry air. (M.J. Hammersley)

Advection dew forms when moist warm air moves over surfaces which are already very cold. After a cold spell, when the wind suddenly changes to a warmer direction, walls and furniture in unheated rooms 'bloom' with minute drops of dew. The windows of cars taken from cold garages cannot be cleared of condensation until they warm to the new higher temperature.

Supercooled dew sometimes forms in very cold weather, but this liquid state is very unstable. Any attempt to rub a window clean merely provokes rapid freezing of the droplets and more opaque glass.

Dewdrops freeze when air temperatures fall below 32°F (0°C), after condensation has already occurred at a higher temperature. Frozen dewdrops are usually mixed with hoar frost which forms *after* air temperature has fallen below freezing level.

Air frost exists when temperature is 32°F (0°C) or less, measured at 4 ft (1·2 m) above ground. If the air is also saturated then hoar frost, fern frost or rime will form as well.

Hoar frost is deposition of vapour directly from air whose dewpoint is lower than 32°F (0°C). It consists of ice crystals, usually needle-shaped, which appear white because of multiple reflection and refraction of light. Hoar frost occurs under the same conditions as dew: most frequently through radiation heat loss on calm cloudless nights, and, in the first instance, on surfaces near the ground where cold air has settled. It can whiten the ground beneath trees whose tops remain considerably warmer, a fact which has often saved fruit blossom in the spring.

Hoar frost is a visible symptom that temperature in the immediate environment has fallen to 32°F (0°C), but it is not a necessary symptom. There can be an air frost when air is not saturated, and then there will be no hoar frost.

Air frost is the enemy of plant tissue, rather than hoar frost crystals themselves, which may even act as a protection in cold weather. If thickly encrusted over a cold frame they may allow the temperature beneath to remain 4F (2C) degrees warmer than it would be if the glass remained clear.

Fern frost often occurs inside windows during severe weather. First, dew forms and remains supercooled for some time after its temperature falls below 32°F (0°C). The first ice crystals which form trigger off a chain reaction throughout all the supercooled drops, which freeze one by one to form beautiful patterns like ferns, Christmas trees or curled feathers. If water drops are large they freeze more slowly because of the release of latent heat from the initial crystallisation. Patches of sheet ice then appear on the glass instead of a spontaneous crystalline pattern.

Radiation mist or fog forms when the air is moist, when the ground cools by radiation under clear skies and when a wind speed of about 5 mph (8 km/h) ensures the stirring of cooled air above the ground.

It occurs most often inland during long winter nights and forms most quickly over open country where vegetation or rivers provide extra moisture. Fog is experienced most frequently in hollows or valleys into which cooling air drains, but is thickest in industrial areas where dirt particles facilitate condensation. Winter fog may persist during the day, because the Sun is too low to counteract the cooling effect of long nights, but in summer radiation fog usually clears soon after dawn.

A micron or micrometre is a conveniently small unit for measuring the size of fog droplets.

1 micron = 0·001 mm = 0·000039 inches

Fog consists of droplets with radius between 1 and 10 microns. Mist consists of droplets measuring less than 1 micron.

Visibility in fog is less than 1 km (1100 yd), according to international definition. However, for practical purposes a lower classification is needed which more closely relates to traffic disruption. The word 'fog' is often reserved for a visibility of 600 ft (180 m) or less, and 'mist' covers any greater visibility up to 1 km.

Radiation fog forms patchily, because relative humidity and ground surfaces vary over quite short distances. Air cools quicker to fog level at one place than at another, so that good visibility alternates with blinding fog patches, which only slowly merge into one dense cover. Fog is also liable to disperse in a patchy manner the next day.

One of the worst fog accidents in Britain occurred on 29 November 1971, when fog patches stirred belatedly from moist fields alongside the M1 motorway, long after the rest of the fog had cleared. Vehicles were travelling at speed in bright sunshine when the first plunged into a fog patch, braked, and

Above right: Rime edging leaves. (M.J. Hammersley)

Below right: Dew formed on the flat surface of grass blades, with guttation (transpired water) hanging as single large drops from the tips of the blades. (Ingrid Holford)

caused the rest to pile up behind. Fifty vehicles were involved; seven people died and 45 were injured in those few moments.

Similar accidents have happened elsewhere and it is difficult to devise an effective warning system. Lighted signals can only advise that fog already exists or is about to form, but cannot indicate the exact position where clear air may abruptly change to fog.

The most significant increases in radiation fog took place during the years of the industrial revolution, when pollution from chimneys provided many more dirt particles on which condensation could take place. 'Pea-soupers' of the Victorian era were so named because the fogs were coloured by chemical pollutants.

The foggiest year in London in the last century was 1873, which had 74 days with thick fog. The worst month was December 1879 having 17 days with periods of fog.

In the 20th century London has twice suffered 114 hours continuous fog, from 26 November to 1 December 1948 and from 5 to 9 December 1952.

Smog combines the two words 'smoke' and 'fog', and is the modern equivalent of the 'pea-souper'. The most lethal smog occurred in the London area between 5 and 9 December 1952. It formed in an easterly drift of air, and brought a maximum concentration of dirt from industrial areas; some estimates put the amount as high as 1000 tons of dirt particles. The colour of the smog became steadily more evil, and sulphur dioxide combined with water drops and oxygen to form sulphuric acid. Deaths during this period were seven times greater than usual for that time of year. Probably 4000 people, mainly the aged and ill, died in the London area because of the smog, though the certified causes of death were usually bronchitis or pneumonia. The Clean Air Act of 1956 was introduced to combat smog. Britain is gradually converting to smokeless fuels, and fogs have become less frequent, and noticeably cleaner.

Fog stirring out of valleys in the mountains of New Zealand shortly after sunrise. (M.J. Hammersley)

Thick rime on the windward side of a gate on a hill on Banks Peninsula, New Zealand. The accumulation formed when supercooled cloud covered the hill top.
(M.J. Hammersley)

Supercooled fog exists when air temperature is below 32°F (0°C). Droplets remain liquid while suspended in air, but freeze at once on contact with cold objects. Supercooled fogs with temperature below 14°F (−10°C) have been known in the British Isles, but usually air is moist enough to condense to fog long before temperature has fallen that far.

Rime is the crust of ice which builds up on twigs, branches, fences etc., when in a supercooled fog. The first frozen droplets freeze the next supercooled drop which touches them, and if there is no wind, rime builds up evenly all round exposed objects. When wind speed is appreciable, then rime accumulates on windward surfaces. Rime is white like hoar frost and has the same loosely packed appearance, but it is granular rather than crystalline. It tends to whiten the whole landscape and not only ground surfaces. In countries like Britain, where supercooled radiation fog occurs infrequently, the greatest incidence of rime is on high ground which is enveloped in supercooled cloud.

Ice fog consists of minute ice crystals deposited directly from the air at temperatures lower than −22°F (−30°C). Such fog scintillates in filtered sunlight and has therefore earned the name of 'diamond dust'. It does not occur in Britain, but occasionally ice crystals form on suitable nuclei in supercooled fog. At Burton on Trent, on two occasions in November and December 1978, enough ice crystals fell from supercooled fog for children to make 'rime balls'.

Frequent ice fogs in Alaska afflict the town of Fairbanks. Air temperature is often −40°F (−40°C) or less in winter, and little vapour can be contained in air. Power plants, factories, and automobiles all discharge water vapour into the atmosphere, and the inhabitants, too, exhale moisture, so that between them they create their own ice fog. The situation is made worse by the fact that the town lies in a shallow basin, and cold air stagnates very close to the ground. Even katabatic winds blowing down the Tanana valley slither *above* the cold pool of air instead of sweeping it away. One of the more dangerous aspects of being out of doors in an ice fog is that ice crystals may accumulate around one's nose when inhaling and cause suffocation.

Advection fog occurs when the wind brings warm air across a cool surface. In Britain this usually happens after a cold winter has left the ground snow covered or frozen hard, and the wind then changes suddenly to the south west. Fog forms temporarily until the encroaching warm air has had time to raise the temperature of the ground.

Sea fog is an advection fog, formed when warm air cools to dewpoint over a cold sea. It usually persists until there is a change in wind direction, because sea surface temperature does not alter much in the short term. Sea fog may be patchy, however, because there are always slight local variations in sea temperature due to upside-down convection. Any fog which drifts across warming land during summer usually disperses a short distance inland. Sea fog can exist in wind speeds up to 15 mph (24 km/h), because turbulence merely brings more warm air into contact with the cooling surface. Any stronger wind usually lifts fog off the surface to give very low cloud.

Sea fog around the British Isles occurs most frequently, on the west and south coasts, during spring when the sea is coldest but south westerly winds may bring warm air across it. On the east coast, sea fog forms in summer when warm continental wind cools over the North Sea. (In winter the North Sea usually warms cold continental air.)

Cold ocean currents cause sea fogs, even in regions bordering hot deserts.

On a sunny morning in Los Angeles, when the Mojave Desert further inland heats up and causes a sea breeze to blow, sea fog from above the cold California current rolls onshore like a tide. It disperses as it spreads over the warming land.

The same happens regularly along the edge of the Namib Desert in South West Africa. Sea fog, formed over the cold Benguela current, rolls onshore with the sea breeze, clearing as the sand heats up during the day. The fog provides enough water to sustain animal life there. Lizards, snakes and the sand-burrowing blind mole come out from hiding in the sand and lick the fog which falls upon themselves. One species of beetle has adapted to foggy conditions with particular efficiency. It stands on its front legs so that its shiny back, turned into the wind, collects fog drip which runs down into its mouth.

When warm winds blow from the Sahara over the cold Canaries current, the Canary Islands become enveloped in sea fog.

Mixture fog occurs when ocean currents of widely different temperature meet, and the air streams above the current mix. The Grand Banks, off Newfoundland, suffer more than 120 days of fog each year. There, the cold Labrador current from the north meets with the warm Gulf Stream from the south-west, and the air above them may be as much as 30F (17C) degrees different. The temperature of the mixed airs often cannot contain their combined moisture, so that fog forms and may persist for weeks at a time.

Steam fog forms when very cold air passes over water which is at least 18F (10C) degrees warmer than the air. Evaporation from the warmer water condenses again in the colder air above, and forms a shallow layer of swirling fog.

In Britain, steam fog occasionally forms over rivers and lakes on very cold nights and in cold winters. However, it is a more frequent manifestation of microclimate, in unheated bathrooms when hot baths are drawn.

Arctic sea smoke is steam fog in polar regions, and happens when intensely cold air, from above pack ice or snow, blows over open stretches of comparatively warm water.

A photochemical fog is caused by the reaction of sunlight on hydrocarbons in the atmosphere. Visibility may be reduced to fog level, even though no water droplets are present.

Photochemical fogs are a special problem for cities which experience frequent temperature inversions that keep pollution near the ground. In the case of Los Angeles, photochemical fog is worst when cold air from above the California current remains trapped beneath warm air from the Mojave desert. Power stations sometimes have to run at reduced capacity in order to decrease the danger from stagnant poisonous fumes. The authorities are also investigating methods to control car exhaust emission.

Fog dispersal had been a major challenge since the development of aviation. In Britain FIDO was the Fog Investigation and Dispersal Operation during World War II. Fuel burners along runways raised air temperature enough to improve visibility in the immediate vicinity, despite adding pollutants from the burning fuel. The method was expensive and it was nerve-racking for pilots to land between flames. Nevertheless, some 2500 successful landings were made in fog during the last 2 years of the war. The system was then dropped because of expense and the stringency of safety regulations for commercial flying. Helicopters can clear small areas of fog by creating downdraughts of drier air to mix with fog below, but they cannot clear fog on a large scale.

In France a fog dispersal system called Turboclair

Only the tops of the bridge across the Firth of Forth were visible above the fog on 3 October 1973. (Aerofilms)

has recently been used at Orly and Charles de Gaulle airports with considerable success. Jet engines project heat and turbulence over the runway and approach zone, warming and blowing away the fog. In the USA the Cornell Aeronautical Laboratory has seeded fog with salt in order to provide extra nuclei on which vapour can condense. They have managed to improve visibility eight-fold by changing a fog of small droplets into a thinner fog of larger droplets; but the resultant salt fog is too corrosive for practical use.

One of the worst fog disasters at sea in recent years occurred on 25 July 1956. The Italian luxury liner *Andrea Dorea* (29 000 tons) was approaching the American coast in the vicinity of the Nantucket Lightship off Massachusetts, in thick fog. The Swedish liner *Stockholm* (12 644 tons) was moving east at 18 knots in clear moonlight, when suddenly the *Andrea Dorea* came out of fog and across her bows. After collision, the *Andrea Dorea* slowly sank and disappeared beneath the sea 12 hours later. Fifty-two people were either killed by the impact or were drowned.

11. Clouds

Clouds were described and classified long before the reasons for their formation were properly understood. The only clouds which can be explained by radiation cooling are very low sheets of cloud, called stratus, which is really lifted fog.

Erasmus Darwin, 1731–1802. (Mary Evans Picture Library)

Jean Baptiste Lamarck (1744–1829), French naturalist and pioneer of the theory of evolution, was one of the first to propose a classification of clouds into three levels and five types which was published in the *Annuaire Météorologique* in 1802. He emphasised that clouds do not form by chance but because of some combination of circumstances which it would be useful to recognise. He did not press his ideas and in the same year Luke Howard made a similar suggestion with greater impact.

Luke Howard (1772–1864) was an English manufacturing chemist, who attained enough success in business to be able to concentrate on his other interests, of which meteorology was the foremost. He was a member of the Askesian Society of London intellectuals, who took it in turn to read papers to each other on scientific matters. In 1802, Howard read his *Essay on the Modification of Clouds*, which was published with sketches in a limited edition in 1804. It remains the basic classification of clouds today, even though Howard admitted at the time that he did not understand why such clouds formed.

Three main types of cloud were named by Howard in Latin for international use.

CIRRUS (curl of hair) Parallel, flexous or diverging fibres, extending in any or all directions.

CUMULUS (heap) Convex or conical heaps increasing upwards from a horizontal base.

STRATUS (prostrate) Widely extended continuous horizontal sheet increasing from below upwards.

These terms are still used, with further subdivisions.

Cloud amount is measured in oktas, which are the number of eighth parts of the sky covered by a particular cloud type. For instance, 7/8 of the sky within the range of vision may be covered with cirrus, with an additional 3/8 cover of cumulus below.

Cloud base height can often be adequately estimated by practised observers. More accurate measurement is made by releasing a small balloon, filled with a known amount of hydrogen, and timing its rise from

Right: Cumulus clouds over distant mountains in New Zealand. Over the plain in the foreground, stratocumulus breaking up into small cells. (M.J. Hammersley)

ground level into the cloud base. At night, a searchlight directed vertically upwards makes a bright spot on low cloud, whose angle of elevation from the horizontal can be measured by an alidade. The height of the spot, and therefore the cloud base, can be calculated by trigonometry, using the angle of elevation and the known distance of the instrument from the light beam.

Erasmus Darwin (1731–1802), English physician, was the first to suggest that lift of air into heights above the ground was an important natural cooling mechanism. His essay, called *Frigorific Experiments on the Mechanical Expansion of Air* was published in the *Philosophical Transactions* of the Royal Society in 1788. His experimental equipment was simple but effective, and his conclusions were vital.

Darwin charged an air gun (without using any pellets) and then allowed it to rest for a while until it acquired the temperature of the room. He then discharged the gun on to the bulb of a thermometer, and the reading fell. He reasoned that the sole cooling agent must have been the sudden expansion of the air as it was released from compression in the gun, and that a similar reduction in pressure imposed on air, which is forced to lift over mountains, could account for cloud frequently seen over heights.

John Dalton was aware of Darwin's experiments, which may have nudged him towards his own famous work on the behaviour of gases.

Christian Leopold von Buch (1774–1853), German geologist, expressed the opinion in 1816 that rising currents of one sort or another could probably explain all weather phenomena.

Heinrich Brandes (1777–1834), German mathematician and meteorologist, concentrated his attention on thermal upcurrents as a lift mechanism. He propounded the theory of convection and also realised that convergent air masses with different temperatures and humidity characteristics must

CLOUD CLASSIFICATION

Genus (with abbreviation)	*Height of base* ft	m	*Description*
Cirrus (Ci)	16 500 to 45 000	5 000 to 13 700	Detached clouds in the form of white, delicate filaments, patches or narrow bands. They have a fibrous, hair-like, appearance and often silky sheen.
Cirrocumulus (Cc)	16 500 to 45 000	5 000 to 13 700	Thin, white patch, sheet or layer of cloud without shading, composed of very small elements like grains, ripples, etc., merged or separate, and more or less regularly arranged.
Cirrostratus (Cs)	16 500 to 45 000	5 000 to 13 700	Transparent, whitish cloud veil of fibrous or smooth appearance, totally or partly covering the sky, and generally producing halo phenomena.
Altocumulus (Ac)	6 500 to 23 000	2 000 to 7 000	White or grey patch, sheet or layer of cloud, generally with shading, composed of laminae, rounded masses, rolls, etc., which are sometimes partly fibrous or diffuse, and which may merge together.
Altostratus (As)	6 500 to 23 000	2 000 to 7 000	Blue-grey cloud sheet or layer, with striated, fibrous or uniform appearance, totally or partly covering the sky, and having parts thin enough to reveal the Sun at least vaguely.

Genus (with abbreviation)	Height of base ft	m	Description
Nimbostratus (Ns)	3 000 to 10 000	900 to 3 000	Grey cloud layer, often dark, appearing diffuse because of falling rain or snow. It is thick enough to blot out the Sun. Low, ragged patches frequently occur below the layer.
Stratocumulus (Sc)	1 500 to 6 500	460 to 2 000	Grey or whitish patch, sheet or layer of cloud which has dark parts, usually composed of non-fibrous tessellations, rounded masses, rolls, etc., and which may merge together.
Stratus (St)	surface to 1 500	surface to 460	Whitish-grey cloud layer with a fairly uniform base, which may give drizzle, ice prisms or snow grains. When the Sun is visible through the cloud its outline is clearly discernible. Stratus does not produce halo phenomena (except possibly at very low temperatures). Sometimes stratus appears in the form of ragged patches.
Cumulus (Cu)	1 500 to 6 500	460 to 2 000	Detached clouds, generally dense and with sharp outlines, developing vertically in the form of rising mounds, domes or towers, of which the bulging upper part often resembles a cauliflower. The sunlit parts of these clouds are brilliant white; their bases are relatively dark and nearly horizontal.
Cumulonimbus (Cb)	15 to 6 500	460 to 2 000	Heavy and dense cloud, with a considerable vertical extent, in the form of huge towers. Part of the upper portion is usually smooth, fibrous or striated, and nearly always flattened; this top often spreading out in the shape of an anvil or plume. Beneath the base, which often appears very dark, there are frequently low ragged clouds and precipitation, sometimes in the form of virga.

maintain identifiable boundaries until they have had time to mix together.

James Espy (1785–1860), American meteorologist, focused attention in 1830 on the importance of latent heat of condensation as a factor prolonging the upward rise of thermal currents.

Adiabatic is a word derived from Greek. *A*: not, *diabano*: pass. Adiabatic therefore means impassable to heat, occurring without heat entering or leaving the system.

Adiabatic changes of temperature occur without any external sources of heat or cooling, when a gas is either compressed or expanded. The temperature of air in a bicycle pump rises because of its compression when the pump is being used. The temperature of gas in a cartridge falls when it is released from compression into a soda syphon.

In the atmosphere, when air is lifted into regions of lower pressure it expands and thereby cools, irrespective of the surrounding atmosphere and its temperature. Air which sinks into regions of higher pressure warms because of compression alone.

The dry adiabatic lapse rate is the rate at which dry air cools when forced to rise into regions of lower pressure. The rate is always the same, 5·4F degrees per 1000 ft (1C degree per 100 m). Dry and sinking air warms at the same rate.

The saturated adiabatic lapse rate is the rate at which air cools when forced to rise *after* it has cooled to dew-point. Condensation releases latent heat to counteract cooling by the adiabatic process. The saturated lapse rate is therefore less than the dry lapse rate, according to the amount of vapour available for condensation. The saturated lapse rate is very small when air temperature is high, but it increases to approximately the same as the dry lapse rate when air temperature is as low as −40°F (−40°C).

The temperature profile of the atmosphere states the temperature at all altitudes above a particular place at the time of observation. These temperatures vary each day, according to the origin of the air mass and how it has been modified by pressure changes or mixing during the previous days. On average, air cools at a rate of 3·5F degrees per 1000 ft (0·6C degrees per 100 m), but it does not do so smoothly. It cools more quickly at some levels than at others, and there may even be an inversion zone where air gets warmer with height. If the values are plotted against the height at which read, the resulting graph gives a profile of the atmosphere for that day which is as individual as the profile of a human face.

However, air which is forced to rise *within* such an environment does cool at a known steady rate, as if it were behaving under laboratory conditions. At any given altitude, such a rising parcel of air may be warmer or as cold as its surroundings.

Buoyant air is air which, when forced to rise from the surface, continues rising within the environment because it is warmer (even after cooling at the adiabatic lapse rates) than its surroundings.

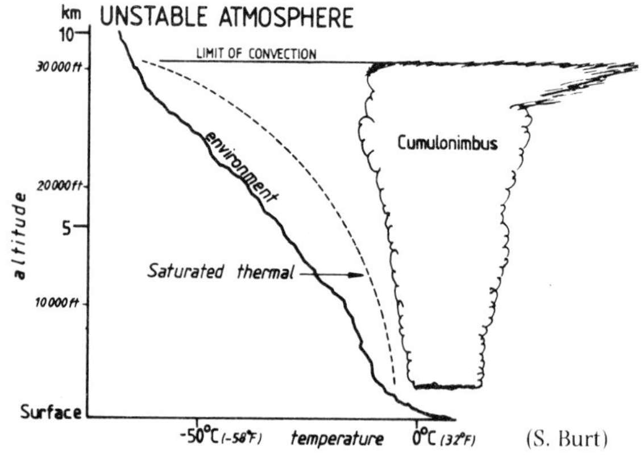

(S. Burt)

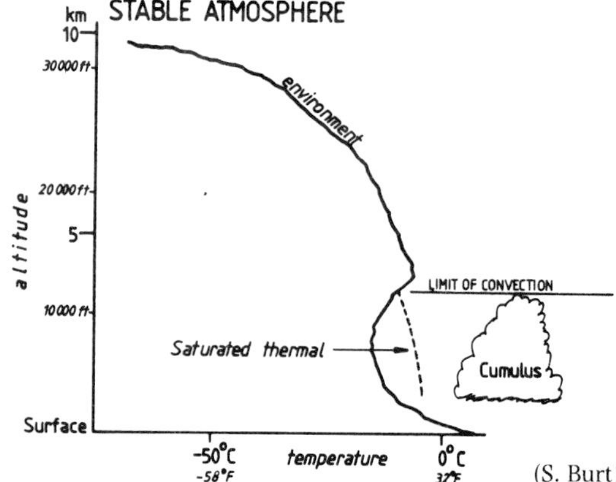

(S. Burt)

Non-buoyant air is air which, after being forced to rise from the surface, stops rising because it becomes colder (after cooling at adiabatic lapse rates) than its surroundings.

An environment is said to be unstable if rising air can remain buoyant to great heights. Air masses which originate in polar regions and are particularly cold aloft, but which have warmed in the lower levels by travelling into lower latitudes, are usually unstable environments.

An environment is said to be stable if rising air quickly becomes non-buoyant. Air masses which originate from tropical regions and are warm aloft but have cooled in the lower levels by travelling into higher latitudes, are usually stable environments.

The most stable air is that beneath an inversion of temperature, such as occurs near the ground after a night of intense radiation cooling.

Water drop cloud consists of both warm and supercooled drops whose size varies between 1 and 50 microns. Supercooled water drops can exist at temperatures as low as −40°F (−40°C), but an increasing number of ice crystals occur in cloud at temperatures below −4°F (−20°C). There is no visible difference between a warm cloud and a supercooled water drop cloud.

Glaciation is the sudden change from supercooled water drop cloud to ice crystal cloud, making its appearance more intensely white. Glaciation occurs when cloud temperature falls to about −22°F (−30°C) or below and the process can be facilitated by seeding, that is introducing cold nuclei into the cloud. Glaciation is an important factor in the production of rain.

Entrainment is the mixing of cloudy air with the clear

environment at the edges of a cloud. Some evaporation of water drops occurs, using heat from the boundary air in the process. Consequently, boundary air becomes colder and starts to sink, causing some blurring of the outline of cloud.

There are four major lift mechanisms which cause air to cool to dewpoint and cloud to form turbulence, orographic lift, convection and convergence. These mechanisms may work separately or in combination one with another.

TURBULENCE alone may cause cloud when the air is moist. The low level variety, called *stratus*, is shapeless and forms either as a continuous sheet (lifted fog), or as patches (scud) beneath thicker cloud from which rain is falling. Turbulence at higher levels, where there may be abrupt changes in wind direction or speed within a shallow zone, may also create cloud.

OROGRAPHIC LIFT over hills or mountains results in several kinds of cloud:

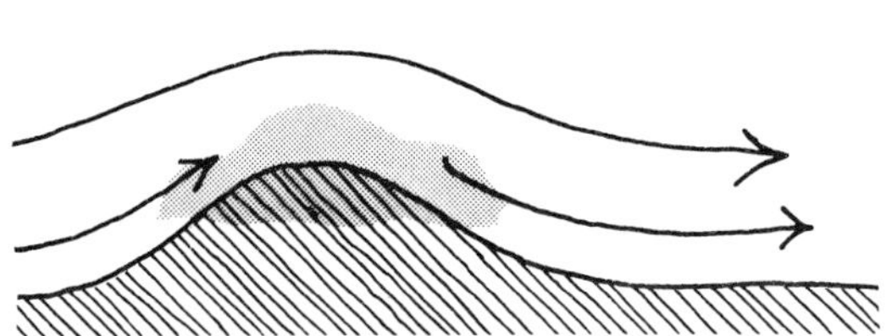

Hill fog is very moist air which cools to dewpoint before reaching the top of the hill. Cloud clings to the windward slopes and to the summit, and is fog to anyone caught within it. Hill fog has various local names. For example, Scotch Mist, Mizzle (in Devon and Cornwall), and the Table Cloth (over Table Mountain, Cape Town).

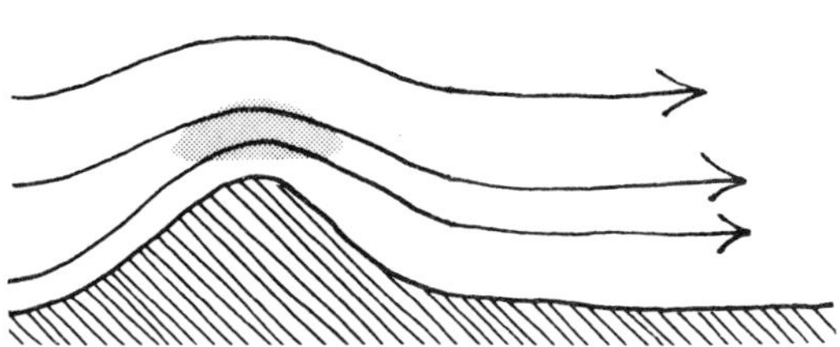

Cap cloud forms when air is comparatively dry and cools to dewpoint only after being lifted clear of the hill top. The cloud remains above the summit, apparently stationary despite the wind. In reality it is not the same cloud all the time, but one which continually forms on the windward side and disperses again to leeward.

A typical cap cloud is the Helm which sits above Crossfell, Cumbria, in NE winds.

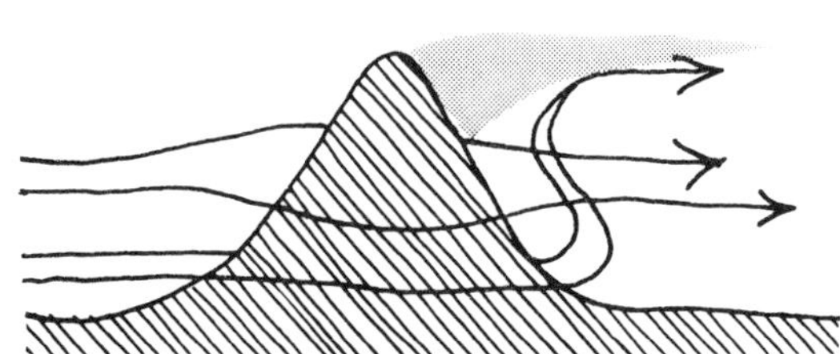

Banner cloud can be seen on the leeward side of mountain peaks which force the wind to divide either side. This causes eddying on the leeward side and sufficient turbulent lift to produce cloud in moist air streams. After forming behind the peak it blows with the wind and gradually evaporates, so that it appears like a tapering flag hoisted at the peak.

Well known banner clouds include those streaming from the Matterhorn (Switzerland), Mount Everest (Nepal), Mount Teide (Tenerife, Canary Islands), and Mount Fujiyama (Japan).

Lenticular wave clouds appear in the crests of an air stream which undulates after being forced over a mountain when the environment air is stable. The cloud tops have a smooth lens shape indicating lack of buoyancy, and the clouds get smaller in each progressive crest as the wave motion dampens down.

Rotor cloud is produced in the turbulent eddy to leeward of mountain ranges. The cloud may be shaped like a long cylinder, having its horizontal axis parallel to the range.

One such cloud is the Helm Bar which forms to leeward of Crossfell, Cumbria, sometimes as much as 4 miles (6 km) away.

(Diana Davies)

CONVERGENCE of different air streams often creates cloud. The airs cannot mix together immediately, so the colder undercuts the warmer which rises, cools and condenses. On a small scale, a sea breeze may bring cold air inland to confront warmer air over the land moving in the opposite direction. A roll of shallow cloud often forms at the junction known as a sea breeze front. Similar rolls of cloud may form at the end of valleys whose mountainous sides separate airs of different natures.

However, the most vigorous convergence occurs when winds from different quarters bring extensive air masses together in confrontation. Persistent, slow lift of warm air ahead of the cold causes flat sheet cloud extending from horizon to horizon, for several hundred miles. First, wispy *cirrus* which gradually consolidates to a continuous film, dimming Sun or Moon and often encircling it with a halo. This sheet thickens and lowers to become *altostratus*, giving rain or snow. The precipitation usually lasts for several hours but is only occasionally as heavy as that which falls from cumulonimbus. This cloud sequence can occur at any time of day or night.

Above: Altostratus almost obscuring the Sun. Rain imminent. (Ingrid Holford)

Left: Cirrus increasing and thickening near the horizon to altostratus. Almost certain sign of rain to come. (M.J. Hammersley)

Below: Altostratus, giving rain, with stratocumulus below covering mountain tops. (Ingrid Holford)

CONVECTION in thermal upcurrents causes *cumulus* clouds to develop. They have billowing upper contours, like cauliflowers, while they are growing vertically. Each has a relatively small base area, and each cloud is separated from the next by clear air. That is where down-currents, balancing the up-currents, cause compression and warming of air, and dispersal of cloud.

Over land, cumulus are diurnal, forming and dispersing as the land warms and then cools again with the rising and setting of the Sun.

Over the sea, cumulus are non-diurnal because it is not the Sun, but the sea temperature, which triggers off thermals in the air blowing across it. Sea temperature does not change over short periods, so if it is warm enough to cause convection in the daytime it is also warm enough to do the same at night.

Cumulonimbus are the huge towers which give rain, hail and thunder. They often have anvil shaped tops, flattened out at the limit of convection.

Cumulonimbus, are tallest in tropical latitudes where the Sun is most powerful and the tropopause is highest. There is an abundance of vapour in the rising air to provide latent heat of condensation and prolong buoyancy. Cloud tops often reach heights of 9 miles (15 km), and up to 11 miles (18 km) has been recorded.

The tallest cumulonimbus in temperate latitudes form over land in spring, when the Sun is high enough to heat the ground rapidly but air streams of polar origin are still very cold aloft. Cloud tops may then reach a height of about 8 miles (13 km).

Large cumulus are rare in Antarctica and form mainly over the sea or the dry valleys of ice-free rock inland from McMurdo Sound. The cold air contains so little vapour that cumulus rarely give showers and tops hardly ever extend higher than $1\frac{1}{2}$ miles (2·5 km).

Above right: Large cumulus, typical of unstable low pressure weather. (Ingrid Holford)

Below right: Cumulonimbus with anvil tops, giving showers over the distant shore. (Ingrid Holford)

Below: Small cumulus, typical of stable conditions in high pressure weather. (Ingrid Holford)

Vilhelm Bjerknes (1862–1951), Norwegian physicist and his son **Jakob** organised a network of weather observing stations in Norway during the 1914–18 World War. From the extensive observations which accrued, they developed the frontal theory which is still used in forecasting. When large masses of air, having different characteristics, confront each other after travelling from different parts of the world they cannot mix together at once. In the convergence zone, the cold heavier air undercuts the warmer, which rises and forms extensive cloud sheets. They called the boundaries between such air masses 'fronts'.

Polar Fronts form where warm winds from the subtropical high pressure belts meet with much colder winds from polar regions. Wave motion along the Polar Fronts results in depressions which carry along with them sectors of warm air, trapped between cold air behind and cool air ahead. Warm air makes the only escape possible, by slithering forwards over the cool air ahead, and by lifting vigorously when undercut by following cold air.

A warm front is the surface boundary between warm air and cool air ahead. It is drawn on weather charts either as a red line or as a black line with semicircles on the side towards which the front is advancing.

A cold front is the surface boundary between warm air and pursuing cold air. On charts it is indicated in blue, or by a black line with teeth on the side towards which the front is advancing.

The warm sector is the fold of warm air between the cold and warm fronts.

Plan view of typical fronts lying across the British Isles. (Eddie Botchway)

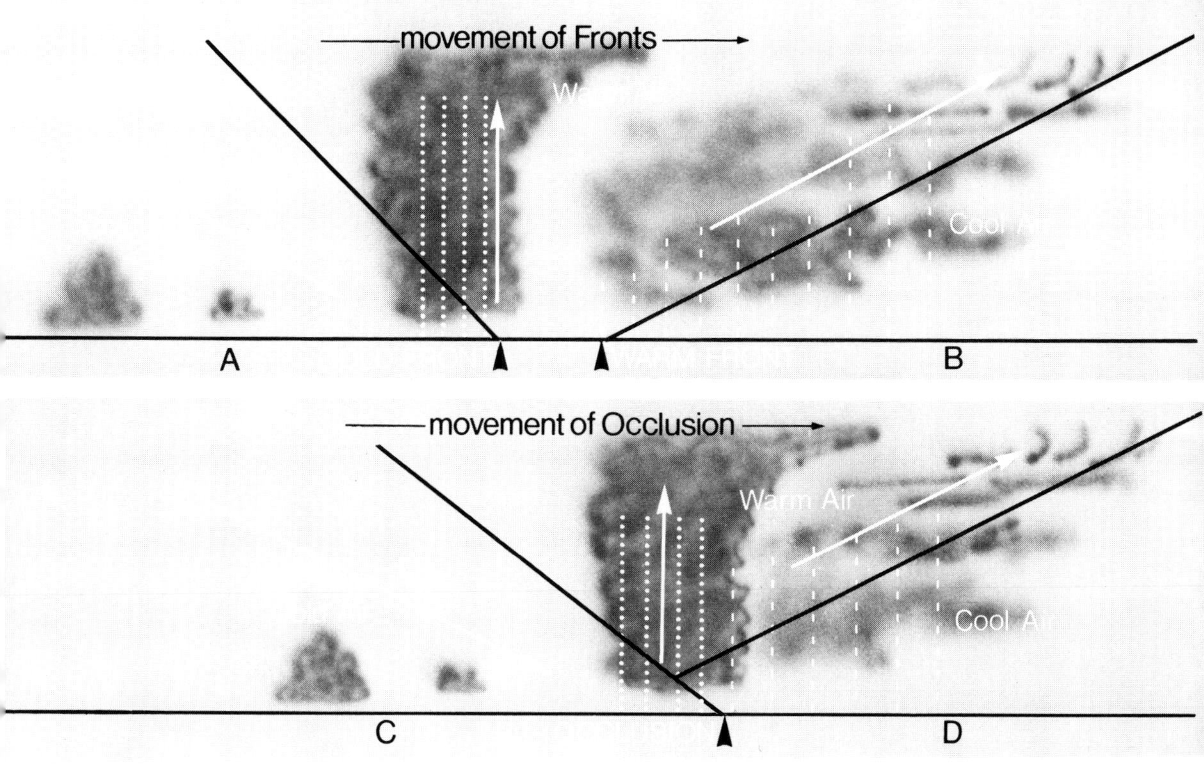

Vertical cross sections through warm and cold fronts, and through an occlusion. (Eddie Botchway)

A cold front travels faster than a warm front, eventually overtaking it. The warm sector is then lifted off the surface and the fronts are said to be occluded. An active cold front may travel at about 30 mph (50 km/h), but a trailing occlusion in a trough may remain stationary.

An occlusion is the surface boundary between new cold air and modified cool air ahead. Weather charts show an occlusion in purple colour or as a black line with alternating semicircles and teeth on the side towards which the occlusion is advancing.

Contrails (condensation trails) are high clouds which form in straight lines behind aircraft because of water vapour ejected from the engines. When the environment is very dry, contrails disperse quickly, but when air already has a high humidity the cloud can persist. A succession of persistent contrails may merge together to form a large sheet of cloud obscuring the Sun.

Distrails (dissipation trails) are paths of clear air evaporated from cloud by the passage of aircraft when heat from the engines is a more important factor than the emission of water vapour.

Fallstreak holes form in cloud when the passage of an aircraft induces freezing of some of the supercooled drops which then fall from the cloud. The circular shape of such a distrail is caused by the chain-reaction of freezing amongst other supercooled drops radially outwards from the initial crystallisation.

Castellanus (Latin *castellum*: castle) are cumulus clouds which develop rapidly in an unstable layer of air above a lower stable level. It requires an excessive build up of heat in the lower layer or the additional forced lift over mountains to break down the barrier between the two layers. Their high bases are often obscured by the haze of a heat wave.

Stratocumulus forms when cumulus clouds reach a stable layer and then spread sideways into a continuous sheet.

Mammatus, udder like protuberances from the base of cloud, formed by upside down convection. Some droplets evaporate into the clear air, causing rapid cooling and the descent of blobs of cloud. These features are temporary only because their descent itself causes warming, mixing with clear air and evaporation.

Pileus cloud is a smooth cap cloud which forms in a stable layer above a cumulus when air is temporarily forced upwards by the vigorous thermal below.

Virga are streaks of ice crystal cloud or water drops which trail below the main base of a cloud, but evaporate before reaching the surface.

Nacreous clouds, often called mother of pearl clouds because of their iridescence, form in the stratosphere and are visible at night when illuminated against a dark sky by the Sun shining from below the horizon. They have a lenticular shape, and result from wave motion over mountains which is transmitted throughout the troposphere and into the stratosphere. This occurs when the wind is consistent with height throughout the troposphere.

Nacreous clouds are frequently sighted in Antarctica and were first described in 1911 by Sir George Simpson, when he was a meteorologist with Scott's last expedition. He drew attention to the fact that they did not produce halo phenomena. They were therefore unlikely to consist of ice crystals. Subsequent observations have confirmed that

Right: Cumulus clouds over the British Isles at 1515 GMT on 23 August 1980. Some clouds are arranged in 'streets', downwind of pronounced thermal sources. Others are arranged symmetrically by wave movement over mountains, into 'billows' and regular patterns resembling 'mackerel' skin. Some of the west coast is free of cumulus because wind is blowing off the sea and clouds only start to build up some way inland. (University of Dundee)

Lenticular wave clouds in a stable airstream over Christchurch, New Zealand; and below: virga falling from the base of a cumulonimbus. (M.J. Hammersley)

nacreous clouds probably consist of supercooled water droplets, despite the fact that air temperatures at altitudes of 11–18 miles (18–30 km) are usually as low as −112°F (−80°C). It is not known why the drops can remain liquid at such low temperatures; possibly it is because of lack of nuclei to induce freezing, or because the droplets only exist for a very brief period in the crest of the wave motion.

Nacreous clouds have been seen on several occasions over Scotland, usually in deep cold air streams at the rear of a depression.

Noctilucent clouds are seen, usually around midnight in latitudes higher than 50°. They resemble cirrostratus clouds, with a blue or yellow tinge, and appear to form at altitudes of about 50 miles (80 km). They are thought to consist of ice crystals or meteoric dust. A network of 15 observing stations in Britain, Sweden and Iceland reported 43 sightings of noctilucent clouds in 1979 and 32 in 1980.

Mammatus cloud, below the base of a cumulonimbus. (S. Burt)

A Morning Glory roll cloud, photographed from the air on 4 October 1979. This is a spectacular cloud which accompanies early morning squalls around the south coast of the Gulf of Carpentaria, northern Australia. (D. Reid)

12. Rain

Rain is merely one phase in the perpetual recycling of the world's constant supply of water. Vapour in the air condenses as cloud, from which falls rain, snow or hail. The water goes into temporary storage in the ground, from whence it evaporates again or feeds streams and rivers which carry it to the sea. There, vast quantities of pure water vapour escape again into the atmosphere, leaving behind the salts and impurities which they acquired on land. The question of how cloud droplets, suspended in air, manage to acquire a large enough size to fall to ground, is complicated.

James Hutton (1726–97), Scottish geologist, thought that rain resulted from the mixture of air streams with different temperatures and humidity. Mixture, however, only produces water drops in suspension. Even the lift mechanisms producing deep clouds are not sufficient to explain the occurrence of rain, and the theories which have evolved in the 20th century are still not entirely adequate.

One important clue resulted from some careful study of cloud behaviour. Individual cumulus clouds, which are well separated from their neighbours, can often be observed to their full vertical extent. Their tops gleam white in the sunshine when they become glaciated, and in the 1920s it was noted that glaciation was frequently followed by rain.

Tor Harold Percival Bergeron (b 1891), Swedish meteorologist, suggested in 1933 that the presence of ice crystals in cloud was a necessary precondition for rain; and this idea was further developed by the German physicist, Walter Findeisen (1909–45).

The Bergeron-Findeisen theory of rain concentrated on the fact that the saturated vapour pressure over ice is less than that over water:

A large cloud contains supercooled water drops, therefore saturation vapour pressure exists with regard to water.

Ice crystals introduced into such a cloud experience *super*saturated vapour pressure with regard to ice, and therefore grow because of deposition from the immediate environment.

The deposition of crystals releases latent heat which lowers the relative humidity and permits evaporation from adjacent supercooled drops.

Ice crystals grow at the expense of supercooled drops till the cloud becomes glaciated. Crystals coalesce because of collisions within the cloud and when large enough fall as snow against the rising air currents within the cloud.

Snow melts to rain soon after the descending flakes reach surroundings which have a higher temperature than 32°F (0°C). Hence the only condition that precipitation should reach ground as rain, is that the air temperature near ground level should be above freezing.

The Bergeron theory was not entirely confirmed by observation because rain sometimes falls from warm clouds containing no ice crystals.

Irving Langmuir (1881–1957), American physicist and Nobel Prize winner for chemistry, drew attention to the range of drop size which can exist in a water cloud because of different nuclei present. Water drops accelerate under the force of gravity until a **terminal velocity** is achieved, when the weight of the drop is counterbalanced by the upthrust of rising air and frictional drag. Terminal velocity is greater for large drops than for small ones, which may hardly achieve any speed at all.

The Langmuir chain-reaction theory suggests that large water drops overtake slower small drops and coalesce on collision. The resulting bigger drops acquire higher terminal velocity and gather up more drops in the process until they fall as rain.

Drizzle drops have a radius of 0·002–0·02 in (0·05–0·5 mm), reach a terminal velocity of 2·3–6·6 ft/s (0·7–2·0 m/s) and are just heavy enough to fall out of cloud.

Rain drops have radius of 0·02–0·1 in (0·5–2·5mm) and reach a terminal velocity of 12·8–30 ft/s

(3·9–9·1 m/s). Drops with a radius larger than 0·1 in (2·5 mm) usually break up under aerodynamic forces.

The smell of rain is a widely experienced sensation for which there is no certain explanation. It may be caused by substances or gases given off by vegetation or soil in wet conditions or when atmospheric pressure is low. On the other hand it could be an increased awareness of our own sense of smell when the atmosphere is moist.

Rain is measured in linear units, which indicate the depth of rain which would cover absolutely flat impermeable ground in a specified period. Such natural surfaces do not exist, so sample rainfalls are collected in graduated vessels. One inch of rain over one square mile weighs about 64 700 tons (25 mm of rain over one square kilometre weighs about 25 000 tonnes).

A very early rain gauge was described in an Indian manuscript from 400 BC. It was a simple bowl about 18 in (450 mm) in diameter, and the writer suggested that the sowing of seeds should be regulated according to the amount of rain registered in the bowl.

The first tipping bucket rain gauge which emptied itself when full, was made in 1662 by Sir Christopher Wren (1632–1723), the English architect. The design was later perfected by William Henry Dines (1855–1927), the English meteorologist.

Richard Townley, of Townley near Burnley, Lancashire, was the first person in Britain to keep a continuous record of rainfall, between 1677 and 1703.

George James Symons (1838–1900) was the first to appreciate the value of a rainfall review over the whole country. His interest was stimulated by the drought years of 1854–8, and he started collecting rainfall statistics from observers in England and Wales. He had already published figures from 168 such observers, when he joined the Meteorological department of the Board of Trade in 1860. He extended his chain of observers to embrace the whole of the British Isles, and in 1863 resigned his job with the Board of Trade in order to devote himself entirely to rainfall work. He was secretary, and twice President, of the Royal Meteorological Society, whose highest award, the Symons Memorial Gold Medal, bears his name.

The British Rainfall Organisation was the title given to the body of 1500 rainfall observers who were contributing to Symons' annual publication *British Rainfall* at the time of his death in 1900. The organisation was taken over by the Meteorological Office in 1919 and the number of observers is now more than 6000. Of these, one third are private individuals, reporting either to the Meteorological Office or to various water authorities. One family alone provided a continuous daily record of rainfall for 98 years, at Belleek, County Fermanagh, Ireland. John Beacom began readings in April 1879, and when he died his nephew and wife, and their daughter, in turn, continued to report rainfall until she died in 1977. The final volume of *British Rainfall* published statistics for 1968. Rainfall data are now compiled by computer and published as *Monthly and Annual Totals of Rainfall for the United Kingdom*.

Accurate rainfall measurement is not as easy as it might seem, a suspicion confirmed in research by Dr Heberden in London and published by the Royal Society in 1769. He mounted a rain gauge on a roof 30 ft (9 m) high, and discovered that it caught only 80 per cent as much rain as a gauge set at ground level. A gauge on top of a 150 ft (45 m) tower caught only half the amount of rain collected at ground level. The discrepancy was caused by wind eddies.

A natural syphon rain gauge was first patented by F. L. Halliwell in 1920. Rain falls through a funnel into a vessel. A float, bearing a rod and pen, rises on the surface of the rainwater and records on a rotating drum. Water is discharged by a syphoning tube when the container is full.

The standard specification for a modern rain gauge is a funnel 5 in or 8 in (125 mm or 200 mm) in diameter with a sharp-edged rim, bevelled outside to prevent runback into the funnel, and with vertical walls inside. The rain-collecting tube is narrow in order to minimise evaporation of rain already collected. The height of the rim above ground is 11·8 in (300 mm), enough to prevent splashback from the ground, but not enough to cause undue wind eddying. The rain gauge must be sited well clear of obstructions.

Rain falls unevenly, particularly from cumulonimbus clouds. These have erratic but strong vertical currents which may reach 40 mph (65 km/h) in Britain. Therefore it is not possible to interpolate with accuracy between two rain gauges very distant from each other to obtain a reliable estimate of rain at some intermediary place. A close network of cheap

Right: Rain drops on river, one phase in the continual recycling of the world's water supply. (M.J. Hammersley)

rain gauges, even at the expense of some inaccuracies, gives a better picture of total rainfall than a sparse network of more expensive instruments.

Exceedingly cheap rain gauges were used in an experiment to obtain an instantaneous picture of rainfall over Britain at 6.30 pm on 30 May 1979. Dr Magnus Pyke, in his Yorkshire television programme 'Don't just sit there', asked viewers to expose a piece of soft toilet paper to the rain for 5 seconds as soon as the transmission ended. Nearly 1200 letters were later received, reporting on the number of wet patches produced by the rain drops and their maximum, minimum and average sizes. Fortunately for the experiment, there was a rain belt lying across the country, sufficient to drench some papers. Despite inaccuracies the resulting rainfall map proved of value to those studying the erratic nature of rain.

Falling rain can be detected by radar and measured by the echoes which vary according to the diameter of the rain drops. These signals from a network of radar stations can be processed by computer and transmitted as an immediate picture of rainfall over a wide area. The impact of the picture can be enhanced by the use of colour coding for different intensities of rainfall. The result is very suitable for view data systems, offering an immediate warning of abnormal rain.

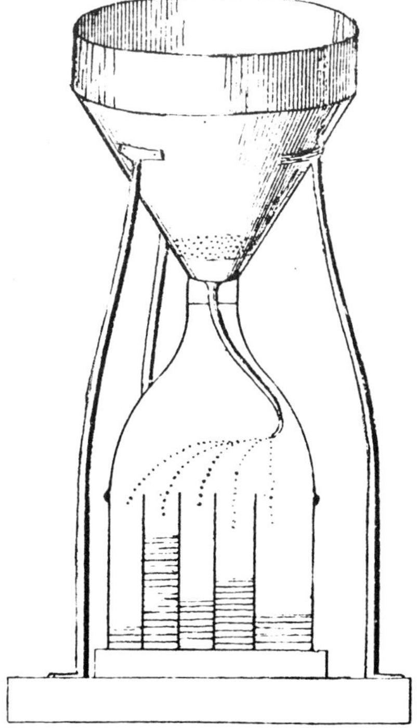

Rain intensity gauge, designed by P.H. Maille, French amateur meteorologist, in 1853. The funnel leads into a tube which bends towards the horizontal. The heavier the rain the further it is projected into the separate collecting compartments.

Modern tilting rain gauge. Rain enters the funnel passage through a protective mesh into the bucket below. When one bucket is full it tilts and discharges, and the other bucket starts to fill. The bucket mechanism operates a switch below, which registers electronically and can be transmitted to a remote recording chart. Some models incorporate a heater for melting snow. (R.W. Munro Ltd)

A rain day is a period of 24 hours, usually starting 9 am GMT, during which 0·01 in (0·2 mm) of rain falls.

Point rainfall is the quantity of rain measured at one particular place. Rainfall quoted for a large area is the average of the various point rainfalls measured within the area.

Intensity of rain is classified as:

Light if falling at less than 0·02 in/h (0·5 mm/h)

Moderate if falling at 0·02–0·16 in/h (0·5–4 mm/h)

Heavy if falling at more than 0·16 in/h (4 mm/h)

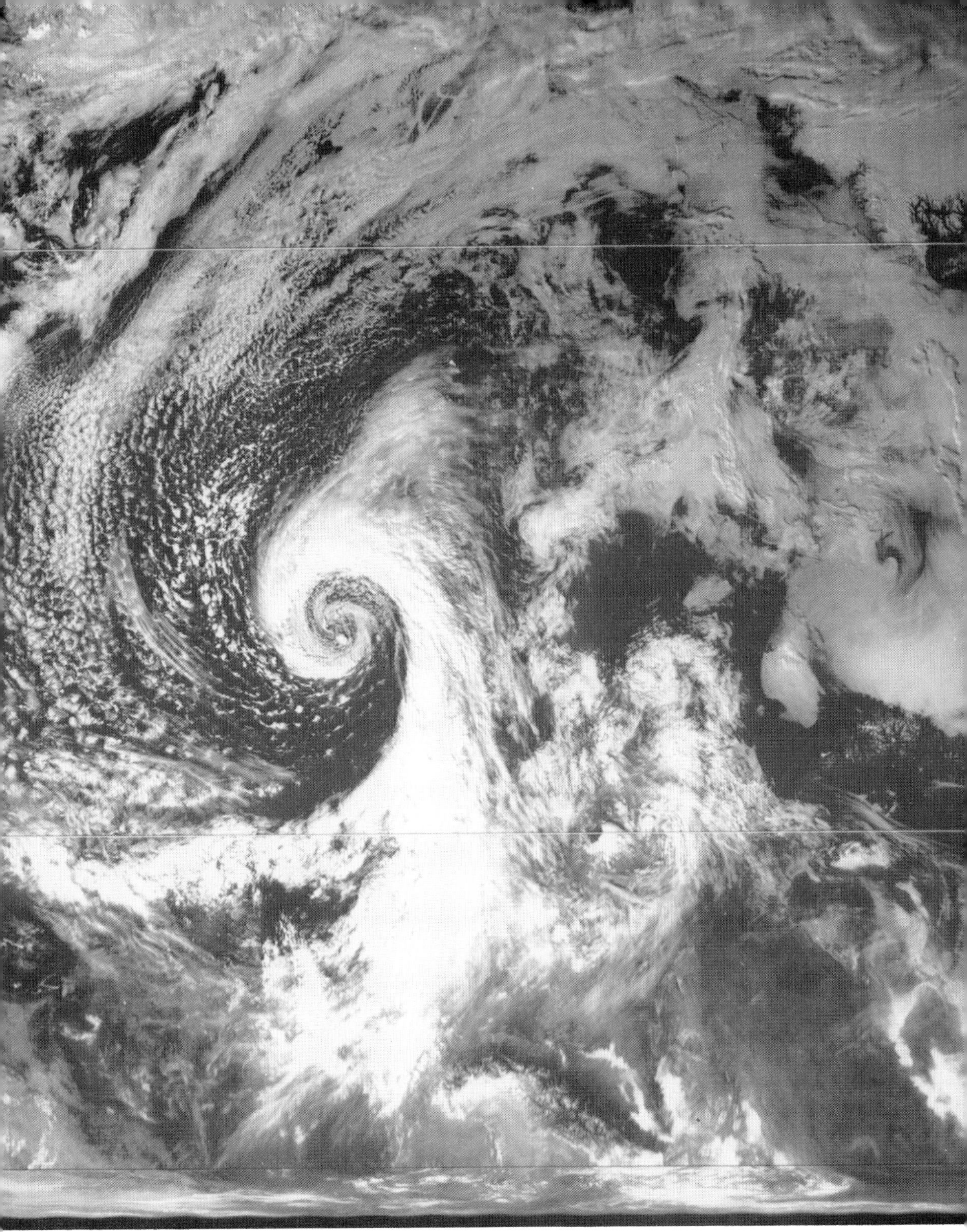

Satellite view of the two major types of rain-bearing cloud. Individual cumulonimbus pour southwards from the Arctic, growing over the sea. The thick white swirl of cloud is associated with a depression and fronts. (University of Dundee)

A rain shadow is an area of below average rainfall on the leeward side of mountains which obstruct rain-bearing winds. The forced ascent of air over the mountains intensifies rain on the windward slopes and over the summit. Air is consequently drier when it starts its descent again down the leeward slopes. The drying-out process is accentuated down steep mountains by adiabatic warming, so that rain may be almost unknown in some regions. The Atacama desert in Chile is a rain shadow desert because prevailing winds blow from the interior, beyond the Bolivian Andes.

Death Valley in California has a meagre 1·7 in (43·2 mm) mean annual rainfall, whereas San Francisco, only 250 miles (400 km) away, but on the prevailing windward side of the mountains, manages an average rainfall of 22 in (559 mm). The Pacific coast, about 800 miles (1290 km) to the north west, receives approximately 140–150 in (3560–3800 mm) of rain per annum.

Rain-bearing clouds are deep cumulonimbus and thick altostratus, which occur separately or together in low pressure systems. Rainfall statistics therefore mirror the transient, seasonal or permanent location of low pressure, as well as the latitude and topography of an area. The lower the latitude, the greater the amount of vapour available for precipitation in warm air which has travelled far across the sea. The higher a mountain barrier, the greater the exaggeration of the meteorological factors which are squeezing vapour out of air.

The most consistently wet place in the world is Mount Wai-'ale-'ale on Kauai in the Hawaiian Islands. The mountain is 5148 ft (1569 m) high and the island is situated at latitude 20° N. This is on the fringe of the equatorial low pressure convergence zone, at longitude 156° W, in the middle of the Pacific Ocean, and therefore constantly enveloped in warm moist air. Rain falls an average 335 days per annum, sometimes as often as 350 days, and the mean annual rainfall is 451 in (11 455 mm). These figures are not representative of the populated areas of the region. At sea-level in Kauai, only a few miles away from Mount Wai-'ale-'ale, as little as 20 in (500 mm) per annum is recorded.

Right: Cumulonimbus over the Tasman Sea, near Karamea, New Zealand. (M.J. Hammersley)

Regular daily showers occur over land in equatorial regions, where there are consistent air masses, abundant vapour content in warm air and maximum solar radiation. In the basin of the Amazon River, Brazil, for instance, convection clouds build up regularly each morning, release heavy showers for a couple of hours in late afternoon and then disperse. The region never has less than 60 in (1520 mm) of rain per annum and usually has 180 in (4570 mm).

Showers are consistently light within the Arctic and Antarctic circles where there is little vapour content in the cold air, and cumulonimbus tops do not reach great heights.

In temperate latitudes, showers are most frequent in unstable air streams, moving from polar regions into warmer latitudes. They are heaviest over land during spring, when polar air streams are still at their coldest but land masses warm up rapidly in the Sun. They are heaviest over the sea during autumn, when the sea is at its warmest and provides the best heating source.

Cherrapungi holds all records for more than 15-day point rainfalls. Situated on the crest of the southern range of the Khasi Hills, India, it receives rain in late spring or summer during the S.W. monsoon. Lift over mountains is accentuated by additional squeeze through deep constricting valleys.

Period	*Point rainfall* in	mm
2 consecutive calendar years 1860, 1861	1605	40 767
12 months (some overlapping of monsoon seasons)		
1 Aug 1860–31 July 1861	1042	26 467
1 calendar year 1861	905	22 987
6 months April–Sept 1861	884	22 454
31 days July 1861	366	9 296
15 days 24 June–8 July 1931	189	4 801

Mean annual rainfall over a period of 5 years was 426 in (10 820 mm) at one site at an altitude of 4307 ft (1313 m), and 498 in (12 649 mm) at another site, altitude 3000 ft (915 m).

Réunion holds records for 9-hour to 8-day point rainfalls. The island lies in the Indian Ocean, 400 miles (650 km) east of Madagascar and is very mountainous. Slopes rising to 10 000 ft (3050 m) border deep valleys, through which wind can funnel, giving extra lift to moist air. The minimum sea temperature, in March, is about 81°F (27°C), so there is always an abundance of moist warm air. The heaviest rainfalls occur with tropical cyclones between November and May. Two such cyclones produced record point rainfalls:

	Period	*Dates*	*Point rainfall* in	mm
CILAOS	8 days	11–19 Mar 1952	163	4140
	4 days	14–18 Mar 1952	138	3505
	2 days	15–17 Mar 1952	98	2489
	24 hr	15–16 Mar 1952	74	1880
BELOUVE	18 hr	28 Feb 1964	66	1676
	12 hr	28 Feb 1964	53	1346
	9 hr	28 Feb 1964	43	1092

Exceptional point rainfalls of very short duration usually result from individual cumulonimbus.

	Duration of rainfall minutes	date	*Point rainfall* in	mm
USA Holt, Montana	42	22 June 1947	12·0	305
Roumania, Curtea-de-Arges	20	7 July 1889	8·10	206
Jamaica, Plumb Point	15	12 May 1916	7·80	198
Bavaria, Fussen	8	15 May 1920	4.96	126
USA, Unionville, Maryland	1	4 July 1956	1·23	31

Every possible check was made before accepting the phenomenal Unionville 1-minute fall recorded on a Freiz Universal rain gauge. Nevertheless, the whole storm produced only 2·84 in (72·1 mm) in 50 minutes, considerably less than many recorded 50-minute falls. It is reasonable to suppose that other places may have had similar exceptional 1-minute falls without having a rain gauge positioned to record them.

Seasonal rainfall with monsoon winds.
India receives rain during the summer S.W. monsoon which blows across the Indian Ocean from the far side of the Equator and into the low-pressure area over the warm con-

Extreme monthly rainfalls in England and Wales since 1873

	Mean 1941–70		Wettest		Driest	
	in	*mm*	*year*	*% of mean*	*year*	*% of mean*
Dec	3·4	86	1914	236	1873	30
Jan	3·3	83	1948	214	1880	21
Feb	2·4	62	1923	246	1891	4
March	2·2	57	1947	303	1929	13
April	2·2	56	1920	209	1912	14
May	2·5	63	1967	218	1896	16
June	2·3	58	1879	228	1925	4
July	2·7	69	1888	221	1911	22
Aug	3·3	84	1912	221	1947	15
Sept	3·1	79	1918	231	1959	10
Oct	3·2	80	1903	264	1947	22
Nov	3·7	93	1929	210	1945	22
Winter	9·1	231	1915	189	1964	36
Spring	6·9	176	1979	180	1893	40
Summer	8·3	211	1912	191	1976	37
Autumn	9·9	252	1960	174	1978	50

Remarkable point rainfalls

Place	*Date*	*Period*	*Amount*	
		hr	in	mm
Martinstown, Dorset	18 July 1955	15	11	279
Long Barrow, Exmoor, Devon	15 Aug 1952	12	8·9	228
Horncastle, Lincolnshire	7 Oct 1960	5	7·2	182
Cannington, Somerset	16 Aug 1924	4½	8·5	216
Hampstead, London	14 Aug 1975	2½	6·7	170
Hewenden Reservoir, Yorkshire	11 June 1956	2	6·1	155
Wisley, Surrey	16 July 1947	1¼	4·0	102
Ilkley, Yorkshire	12 July 1900	1¼	3·75	94
Littleover, Derbyshire	9 July 1981	1⅙	3·1	80
Hemyock, Devon[1]	5 July 1963	1¼	3·1	79
		1	2·5	64
		¾	2	51
		¼	1	25

[1] *Recorded on a Dines tilting rain recorder and probably representative of the worst British downpours.*

tinent. Rain starts at the end of May and continues for 2–3 months with only brief respites, often augmented by tropical cylones.

Mean annual rainfall:

Delhi: 25·2 in (640 mm), of which 85 per cent falls between June and September.

Bombay: 71·2 in (1800 mm), of which 98 per cent falls between June and September.

Calcutta: 63·0 in (1600 mm), of which 84 per cent falls between May and October.

Northern Australia gets rain with the summer N.W. monsoon.

Darwin's mean annual rainfall is 58·7 in (1491 mm), of which 80 per cent falls between December and March.

Chile, S. America, has some winter rain.

Valparaiso has a mean annual rainfall of 19·9 in (505 mm), of which 91 per cent falls between May and September.

Grass weighed down by glazed frost, formed by freezing rain. (M.J. Hammersley)

A combination of moist monsoon wind, convergence and hurricane can produce rainfall which is exceptional even for wet regions. The Island of Luzon in the Philippines, Pacific Ocean, experienced such a deluge in July 1972, when the vigorous typhoon *Rita* was 1500 miles (2400 km) away, just south west of Japan. Manila Port, with an average July rainfall of 13·9 in (354·3 mm), recorded nearly three times that amount in the 4 days, 17–21 July, with a total for the month of 68·9 in (1751 mm).

Tropical cyclones and hurricanes often produce exceptionally heavy rain, particularly when they reach a coast and are influenced by heating of the land or by uplift over mountains. The ferocity of the wind may then start to wane, while rain often intensifies.

Connie and *Diane*, 12–19 August 1955, poured 19 in (480 mm) rain into rivers from Virginia to Massachusetts, causing widespread floods. These were worst in the Delaware Valley and Connecticut, where 187 lives were lost. Westfield, Massachusetts, received 19·4 in (493 mm) rain on 18–19 August.

Flora, 4–7 October 1963, jettisoned more than 60 in (1524 mm) rain on some places in Jamaica, West Indies. Six stations recorded more than 20 in (508 mm) in one day.

Camille, 20 August 1969, emptied 25–28 in (635–710 mm) of rain in 8 hours over places in Virginia, a couple of days after the hurricane had arrived at the Mississippi coast. Devastating damage was caused above ground and there was much erosion by flood water in underground caves.

Claudette, 16–29 July 1979, gave torrential rain while looping in south east Texas. A 24-hour rainfall of 42 in (1067 mm) was reported near Alvin, topping the previous local record of 38·7 in (983 mm) in 1950.

Tip, dumped 24 in (610 m) over some parts of Japan in the two days, 17–19 October 1979.

Mac brought 32 in (813 mm) to southern China in two days, 23–25 September 1979.

Allen produced 10–15 in (250–380 mm) over southern Texas, when it reached land on 10 August 1980.

Danielle, 4–7 September 1980, which only attained the status of a tropical storm, nevertheless produced very heavy rainfall: 25 in (635 mm) in 24 hours was recorded at Junction, Texas.

Normally arid countries can experience heavy rainfall from chance hurricanes. Two, on average, develop each year over the Arabian Sea, and 27 October 1972 was the first time for 75 years that such a storm travelled along the Gulf of Aden. There, it gave 9 in (229 mm) of rain in Djibouti, (mean annual rainfall 5 in (127 mm)) and 6 in (152 mm) in Aden, (mean annual rainfall 1 in (25 mm)).

Average monthly rainfall

Inches					Millimetres			
Jan	Apr	July	Oct		Jan	Apr	July	Oct
				NORTHERN HEMISPHERE				
				Europe				
2·0	1·8	2·0	2·3	England, London	51	46	51	58
1·9	1·5	2·8	2·3	Denmark, Copenhagen	49	38	71	59
2·2	1·7	2·3	2·0	France, Paris	56	43	59	50
3·2	1·2	0·7	1·9	Greece, Athens	81	30	18	47
1·9	1·7	3·2	2·9	Norway, Oslo	48	43	82	74
3·1	1·9	3·7	3·3	N. Ireland, Belfast	80	48	94	83
1·1	1·5	3·8	1·5	Poland, Warsaw	27	37	96	38
2·5	1·6	3·1	2·9	Scotland, Edinburgh	63	14	79	74
1·2	1·7	1·1	3·4	Spain, Barcelona	31	43	27	86
1·7	1·2	2·4	1·9	Sweden, Stockholm	43	31	61	48
2·4	2·7	4·9	2·8	Switzerland, Berne	61	68	119	70
1·5	1·5	3·5	1·8	USSR, Moscow	39	39	88	45
4·6	2·5	3·4	4·5	Wales, Cardiff	117	63	86	114
				Canada and USA				
0·7	1·4	2·3	0·9	Alberta, Calgary	17	35	58	23
1·0	1·2	2·9	1·5	Manitoba, Winnipeg	26	30	73	38
2·2	2·0	2·9	2·4	Ontario, Fort William	55	50	76	62
0·9	0·3	1·9	0·8	Alaska, Fairbanks	23	8	48	20
4·0	1·3	<0·1	0.7	California, San Francisco	102	33	<1	18
0·8	1·9	3·3	1·6	Minnesota, Minneapolis	18	48	84	41
2·5	2·8	3·5	2·8	New York, Albany	63	71	89	71
3·7	3·4	5·2	3·6	Texas, Houston	94	87	131	91
				Atlantic Islands				
7·1	4·3	2·3	4·7	Azores, Santa Cruz	181	108	58	119
4·2	4·2	4·4	6·4	Bermuda, Fort George	107	107	112	162
3·5	2·2	2·0	3·7	Iceland, Reykjavik	89	56	50	94
				Asia				
0·2	0·5	7·4	0·6	China, Tiensin	5	13	188	15
0·1	<0·1	24·3	2·5	India, Bombay	3	<3	617	64
1·9	5·3	5·6	8·2	Japan, Tokyo	48	135	142	208
0·3	2·3	6·3	8·1	Thailand, Bangkok	8	58	160	206
				SOUTHERN HEMISPHERE				
15·2	3·8	<0·1	2·0	Australia, Darwin	386	97	<3	51
3·5	5·3	4·6	2·8	Australia, Sydney	89	135	117	71
3·1	3·5	2·2	3·4	Argentina, Buenos Aires	78	89	56	86
9·8	8·7	2·3	4·2	Brazil, Manaus	249	221	58	107
0·1	0·5	3·0	0·6	Chile, Santiago	3	13	76	15
0·6	3·2	1·8	2·5	Ghana, Accra	15	81	46	64
1·0	7·7	3·5	3·4	Kenya, Mombasa	25	196	89	86
2·2	1·9	2·7	1·7	N. Zealand, Christchurch	56	48	69	43
4·5	1·5	0·3	2·2	S. Africa, Johannesburg	114	38	8	56

British rainfall, compared with world extremes, is not as heavy or prolonged as it is reputed to be.

A wet day is defined as one which has 0·04 in (1 mm) rain.

The wettest days of the year yield, on average, 1 in (25 mm) in south-east England but 2 and 3 in (50 mm and 75 mm) respectively over hills and mountains in western and northern areas.

Showers from cumulonimbus in deep unstable air are most frequent in the spring; heavy downpours from cumulonimbus clouds in upper layers of unstable air occur mainly in summer; and rain from depressions is generally more frequent in winter than in summer.

The average frequency of rain days per annum is 250 in the west of Ireland, west and central Scotland and the Shetland Islands; 200 in south-west England, Wales, northern England and central and eastern Ireland; 175 in the Midlands, south and east England and eastern Scotland.

The highest number of rain days experienced in the British Isles occurred at Ballynahinch, Galway in the Republic of Ireland in 1923 when there were 309 rain days.

Annual rainfall, averaged over the years 1941–70, was 34·2 in (870 mm) in England and Wales, 45·5 in (1157 mm) in Scotland and 40·8 in (1037 mm) in N. Ireland.

The highest annual totals were:

England and Wales	50·7 in (1288 mm) in 1872
Scotland	67·5 in (1715 mm) in 1872
N. Ireland	51·1 in (1300 mm) in 1928

Location of the 50 heaviest 2-hour rainfalls in the 20th century:

Southern England	34
Midlands and N. England	9
Wales	4
Scotland	2
N. Ireland	1

Only two of these exceptional rainfalls occurred outside the warmer months of May–September, both being in October. The figures indicate that although northern mountainous areas of the British Isles have the highest annual rainfall, it is because they are most frequently near the centres of fast moving depressions.

Short period rainfalls happen mainly in southern areas where there is greatest thermal activity in summer, often accentuated by convergence in troughs of low pressure.

Freezing rain turns into glazed frost and usually occurs during the transition from a very cold winter spell to a mild one, bringing frontal cloud. Rain from the advancing upper cloud falls to ground where temperatures are still below freezing. The rain freezes on contact with all surfaces, coating everything in ice. The condition usually lasts only a short time, until the warm front arrives to engulf everything in milder air.

In Britain freezing rain is not often experienced, but a particularly long spell hit southern England and Wales from 27 January to 3 February 1940. Glazed frost accumulated until branches of old trees snapped while more supple trees bent to the ground, where they became welded by ice. Telegraph poles collapsed under the weight of tons of ice. Ponies on Plynlimon, Dyfed, were frozen to death in coffins of ice, and millions of birds died.

In the United States freezing rain occurs frequently. During the very severe winter of 1978, three snowstorms in Illinois between 2 and 9 December 1977, were preceded by freezing rain. More fell on 24 January and 12 February 1978 and again, during 24 and 25 March, ice up to 2 in (50 mm) thick accumulated over trees and telegraph lines, bringing many down.

Portland, Oregon, was transformed into an ice encrusted city on the night of 9 and 10 January 1979, with much damage done.

Freezing rain in Leningrad, Russia, on 12 March 1981, coated cars, buildings and streets in ice a quarter of an inch thick. No one could keep his balance in the streets.

Rain sometimes carries extraneous matter with bizarre and often unpleasant results. In Europe, coloured rain is usually caused by sand and dust from the Sahara, carried on high level southerly winds.

In Switzerland, on 14 October 1755, 9 in (225 mm) of blood-red rain fell at Locarno, of which 1 in (25 mm) was estimated to be dust. Rain fell over an area of approximately 360 miles² (936 km²), and over the Alps the precipitation lay as red snow.

At Aberdare, Glamorgan, Wales, rain brought minnow and smooth-tailed sticklebacks to ground on 9 February 1859. There were two showers at 10-minute intervals, after which an area of 240 × 36 ft (80 × 12 m) was covered with fish.

At Acapulco, Mexico, a fall of maggots accompanied a heavy storm on 5 October 1968. Awnings, cockpits and dinghies, assembled for the Yachting Olympics, were littered with maggots about 1 in (25 mm) long.

All these creatures must have been sucked up by vertical winds into shower clouds.

Acid rain brings to ground industrial or natural pollution which has been carried by the wind. The rise in acidity in some Norwegian lakes, with consequent damage to fish stocks, has been attributed to pollution carried in South-Westerly winds from Britain. Atmospheric tests, using instruments in aircraft, are currently investigating the claim.

Volcanoes eject considerable sulphur into the atmosphere, often increasing the acidity of rain for a while.

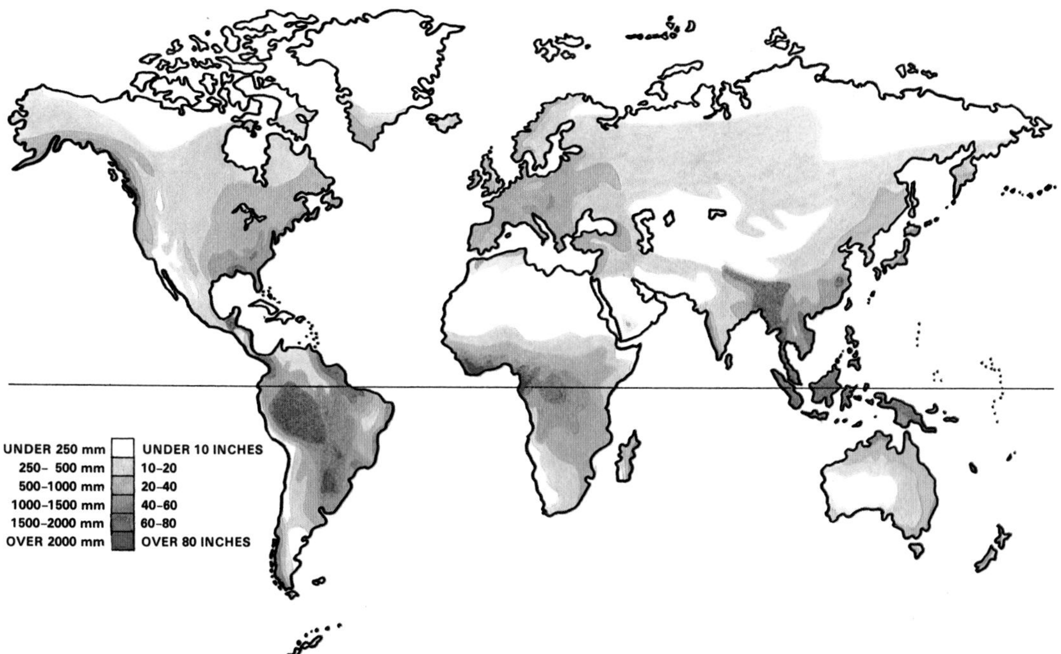

1 **Average annual rainfall.** (D. Davies)

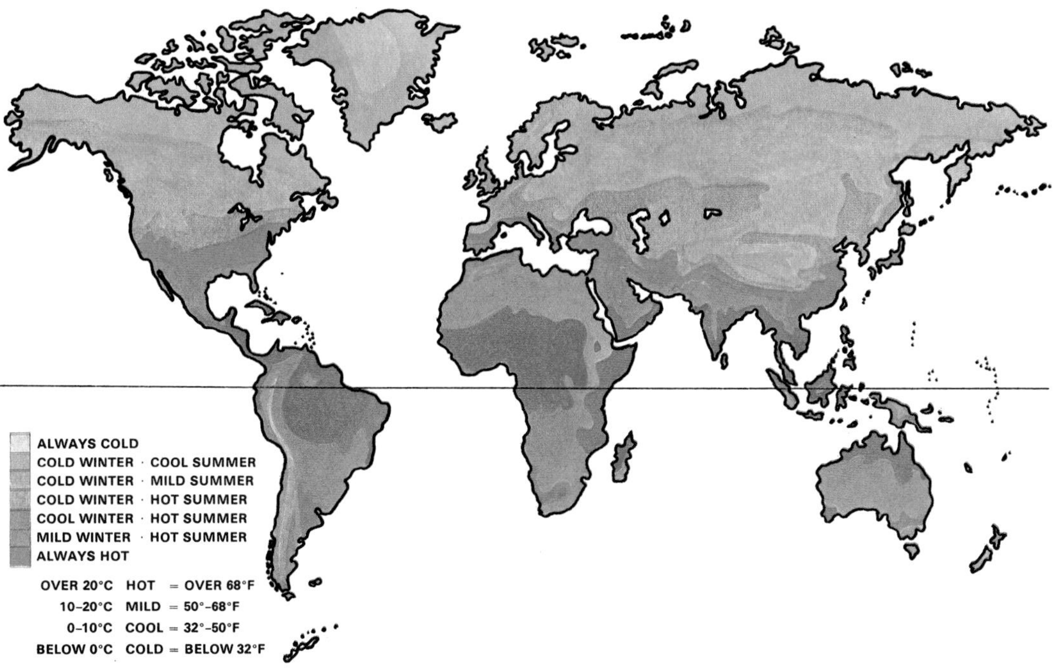

2 **Seasonal regimes of the world.** (D. Davies)

3 The Cairngorms automatic weather station, at a height of 4084 ft (1245 m). Beneath the mound of snow is a hut, protected by walls of granite slabs, which is primarily a radio relay station for mountain rescue work. It also houses the weather station electronics and radio equipment. The weather instruments are in a heated cylindrical housing and are normally completely enclosed. Every half hour the instrument platform rises automatically for a 3-minute exposure to ambient weather, then descends again till the next reading is due. The station logs $2\frac{1}{2}$-minute mean wind, 3-second maximum gust, wind direction and temperature, together with time of observation, on to cassette tape. The information is broadcast by VHF radio (T shaped ariel) to Heriot-Watt University at Edinburgh, where the signal is displayed by micro-computer. Further sensors will be added when instruments can be designed to give reliable readings within the 3-minute exposure and yet be robust enough to withstand heavy riming and very strong wind. (J. S. Barton, Heriot-Watt University)

4 *(above right)* The Christchurch Bay Tower (mark 1) weathering a severe storm. This is a bottom standing tower, unmanned, used for carrying out instrument tests under sea conditions. (National Maritime Institute)

5 *(below right)* Two marine thermometer screens, fixed to the 49–27A Amoco Gas Platform in the North Sea, off Great Yarmouth. The meteorologist is checking instruments, which record temperatures on a digital display panel inside the platform. These and other meteorological measurements can also be transmitted automatically to weather centres inland. (P. Budgen)

6 **Eureka Weather Station, latitude 80°N, in the North West Territory of Canada. It is 600 miles (960 km) from the North Pole and further north than any Eskimo settlement. The station has all 'mod cons', including a greenhouse where the staff grow plants during the 5 months continuous daylight. The first sunrise of the year is on 24 February. This photograph was taken during February 1979 with a 5-minute exposure by moonlight on Kodachrome 25 film. The viewpoint was 300 ft above sea level, looking across frozen Slidre Fjord.** (A. Hurlbert)

7 **Icebergs drifting in the Vaigat past Disko Island, Greenland.** (E. Kay)

8 **Franz Josef Glacier, New Zealand.** (M. J. Hammersley)

9 **Sea fog viewed from a sunny cliff top.** (I. Holford)

10 **Stratus, or lifted fog, breaking up in the sunshine.** (I. Holford)

11 **Dew pond just south of Liddington Hill Fort, with Swindon, Wiltshire seen in the distance.** (B. C. Frost)

12 **Dew traps, each containing a vine, in Lanzarotte, Canary Isles.** (J. T. Holford)

13 *(above left)* **Sea smoke off the coast of Quebec.** (K. C. Scott)

14 *(below left)* **Hill fog spilling over the crest of Mt Rolleston, New Zealand.** (M. J. Hammersley)

15 *(left)* **Cumulus 'coiffure' is the apt description to this towering cloud top seen from an aircraft.** (G. Uveges)

16 *(below)* **Sun and sun dog, with their reflections on the sea, seen through altocumulus cloud.** (J. Thompson)

17 *(above left)* **Pileus cloud formed in the stable air immediately above the top of a cumulus cloud.** (I. Holford)

18 *(below left)* **Lenticular clouds — or flying saucers? — over Scottish hills.** (I. Holford)

19 *(above)* **Passage of a cold front, revealing the top of a cumulonimbus in the colder air mass approaching.** (I. Holford)

20 *(left)* **Cumulus created by Wemyss Bay power station, Firth of Clyde.** (E. Kay)

21 *(left)* **Primary (inner) and secondary (outer) rainbows at Inverurie, Scotland.** (S. Andrews)

22 *(top)* **The Levanter banner cloud over Gibraltar, 5 July 1978.** (J. Hulbert)

23 *(above)* **Brockenspectre and glory, seen from the summit of Tryfan, N. Wales.** (A. J. Samson)

24 *(left)* **Cornice of overhanging snow.** (F. Ross)

25 *(top)* **Altostratus, ahead of approaching warm front, almost obscuring the Sun.** (Ingrid Holford)

26 *(above)* **A wintry scene in a Kent summer. Sevenoaks School on 25 June 1980 after a severe hailstorm.** (A. Theaker)

The Earth moves around the Sun, and also about its own axis.

Heat is distributed around the Earth by vertical and horizontal winds.

Rain is part of the re-cycling process of the Earth's water supply.

Hourly temperature readings contribute to synchronous weather knowledge everywhere at ground level.

Regular balloon ascents carry radar reflectors and radio sonde, reporting on upper air conditions.

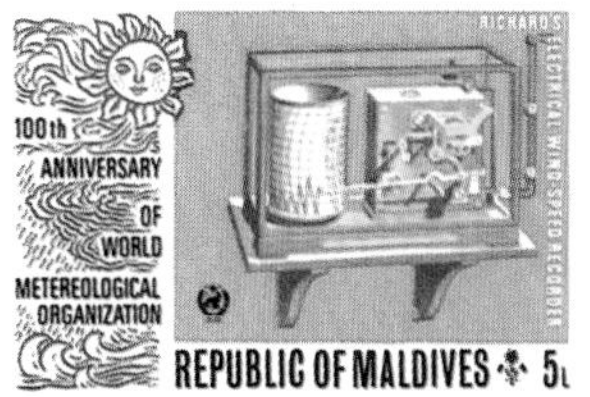

Wind speed and direction can be recorded, as a continuous trace, fro remote anemometer.

Weather ships at fixed positions, and commercial shipping, report on conditions over the sea.

Aircraft are equipped with instruments and report on conditions at flying height.

Weather satellites monitor cloud systems from enormous heights a the Earth.

Radar can be used to detect falling rain and vortices in storm clouds.

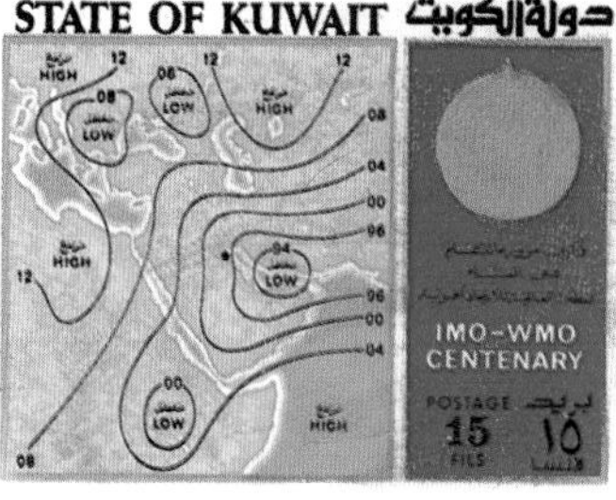

Information is plotted on to isobaric charts, for use in forecasting.

Computers process data and calcula weather maps up to 7 days ahead.

27 Stamps issued for the centenary of the World Meteorological Organisation in 1973.

13. Rain flood and drought

A rain flood is an accumulation of rain-water which is too great to be disposed of by the normal means. The absolute quantity of rain is therefore less important than the duration or rate of fall compared with that normally experienced.

Soil is an important regulator for rain disposal. Water clings by surface tension to the top layer of soil particles and then is gradually forced downwards by the weight of further rain. Percolation is slow, so that soil acts most efficiently as a receptacle when the rain falls lightly but persistently, and least efficiently during heavy falls.

Soil becomes a blocked channel, and therefore a potential cause of flooding, when it is either baked hard by the Sun, frozen solid by frost or when it is already saturated with water. Any rain falling under such conditions runs off the surface as it would do from impermeable concrete. Soil is most receptive when it is moist.

Below: Drying a home after the Molesey floods in September 1968 with an RAF heater. (Surrey Comet)

Rivers and streams have been gouged by centuries of rainfall to cope with normal quantities of water only. The rivers with the biggest catchment areas in the wettest countries are as liable to flood as smaller rivers in dry countries, because any area is liable to experience abnormal rainfalls occasionally. Many disasters occur because debris forms a dam across a river or stream, and then later bursts under the weight of accumulated water.

In urban areas drains carry rain-water away from impermeable surfaces and they are designed to cope with *probable* heavy falls over various periods of time. It is economically impractical to budget for every *possible* rainfall, and therefore the gamble must fail sometimes. Blockage of drains by leaves and debris often causes floods which could not have been expected because of the quantity of rain alone.

A flash flood is one which occurs very suddenly.

In Yorkshire, England, on 24 June 1967, a heavy thunderstorm ended dry weather. Without the benefit of porous soil, rain-water rapidly ran off into underground streams and caverns at Mossdale. The sudden rise in water level below ground drowned five potholers before they could scramble to the surface.

Calama, Chile, situated in the rain shadow desert of Atacama, enjoyed the reputation of being the driest place in the world, having had virtually no rain for 400 years. On 10 February 1972, the town lost its record when torrential rain fell during mid-afternoon, causing catastrophic floods and landslides. The town was cut off by water, mud swept down from the hills and electricity supplies were short-circuited in the town and local mines.

In Big Thompson Canyon, Colorado, on 31 July 1976, a flash flood followed heavy rain which fell into two tributaries of the Thompson River. Some 10 in (250 mm) of rain fell in 4 hours at the high end of the Canyon, where peaks reach 9000 ft (2740 m). The rainfall was considered a once-in-

100-years chance. Officials warned holiday-makers of the danger of a flash flood but these warnings were not heeded. When the flood water arrived, it cut a 15-mile (24 km) swath through the countryside, making it look like a refuse dump. Acres of trees were smashed; the road, where the canyon narrows to a gorge, collapsed to make a precipice 50 ft (15 m) deep, and 80 people lost their lives; 1000 people had to be lifted to safety by helicopter.

At Hampstead, London, a local but exceptionally heavy storm caused 6·7 in (170 mm) of rain to fall in approximately $2\frac{1}{2}$ hours. It happened on 14 August 1975, after a 3-week heat wave, and was probably the biggest point rainfall in the last 100 years. Drains were unable to cope with the water, and cars floated along the streets. Basements and subways filled, and dozens of families had to be evacuated from badly damaged homes. One man was drowned and two struck by lightning.

Right: Small blockages in waterways can lead to extensive floods. (I. Holford)

Opposite page: Scenes from the Devon floods, 12 July 1968. Many roads were torn up and every bridge over the river Otter was damaged or destroyed. (K. Sansom)

Below: Flood water often flows too swiftly to be navigable by small boats. This picture was taken during the west country floods, 12 July 1968. (Syndication International)

River banks and dams sometimes burst, or are flooded over during periods of abnormal rainfall.

In South Africa, on 25–27 January 1981, gales and torrential rain afflicted the Cape Province and Karoo regions, some places having 10 in (25 mm) rain in less than 24 hours. Bridges were washed away, roads were blocked and crops damaged. In Lainsburg, the dried-up bed of the river Buffels became a raging torrent and burst its banks, causing a 6 ft (2 m) high wall of water and mud to engulf the town. About three-quarters of the town was destroyed and more than 150 people were drowned.

In northern India exceptionally heavy monsoon rain during July and August 1980 culminated in serious floods. By the end of the first week of August, the Ganges and several smaller rivers had burst their banks and submerged 12 000 villages. By the end of the month, in Uttar Pradesh alone, floods had affected 20 million people and had wrecked or damaged 580 000 homes. A total of 940 lives were lost.

In Gujarat State, the Machchu Dam burst on 11 August 1979, after a fortnight of incessant rain. A wall of water 12 ft (4 m) high swept over the town of Morvi, washing away two-thirds of all the houses and drowning more than 1000 people.

Northern Italy had already experienced a very wet October in 1966. In Florence, on 3 November, the river Arno was within a few feet of the embankment which protected the 14th-century part of the city and its many treasures. Continuous rain fell during the day, and in the early hours of 4 November the river overtopped its banks. Drains choked with debris, power supplies failed and art treasures were covered by mud. The water coursed through the town for 18 hours before subsiding, to leave many irreplaceable works of art ruined and enough restoration work to occupy specialists for years. Floods also affected many other towns, including Venice and Pisa, and 170 lives were lost altogether.

In the north of England and in Wales on 26–28 October 1980, torrential rain caused three rivers in Wales and the Ribble in Lancashire to burst their banks. Preston was virtually cut off by water, motorists were stranded over a large area and many homes were flooded. In Blackpool 3 in (76 mm) of rain fell in 3 hours.

In the United States, Arizona was declared a major disaster area after heavy rain between 17 and 20 December 1978. Up to 8 in (200 mm) fell in places and almost every river overflowed its banks. The dykes of the Gila broke and sent 12 ft (4 m) of water through the town of Duncan. Ten people were drowned and some 8000 people in the state were left homeless.

In 1972, hurricane *Agnes* reached Panama City, Florida, on 19 June and for the next 6 days travelled up the eastern seaboard. Nearly every river basin north of Georgia and east of the Appalachians, up to New York State, flooded to record or near record levels. Enormous damage was done to property and 118 lives were lost.

Debris in flooded rivers sometimes causes greater damage than the water carrying it.

Lynmouth in Devon lies at sea level, immediately below precipitous heights rising 1000 ft (300 m) up to Exmoor. On 15 August 1952, the ground was already sodden after a wet

Right: Water tumbling down the two steep Lyn rivers, carried huge boulders which carved a passage through houses in Lynmouth on 15 August 1952.

Below: Snow thaw flood augmented by rain and driven by a SW gale caused this breach in the dyke at Over Cambridgeshire on 20 March 1947 (see p. 187). (Both Syndication International)

summer. Then, 12 hours' continuous rain from a slow-moving depression caused 9 in (228 mm) of rain to accumulate in the rivers and streams lacing the moor. Torrents of water and debris in the East and West Lyn rivers shattered narrow bridges which then acted as battering rams against houses downstream. Approximately 200 000 tons of giant boulders were carried down into Lynmouth by the swollen river, 34 lives were lost and up to 400 people were rendered homeless; 28 bridges were destroyed, 93 houses ruined or later demolished as unsafe, 28 cars were wrecked and 38 more disappeared out to sea.

Incoming high tide plus down-river floods is a lethal combination for coastal towns at the mouths of rivers.

South Wales had its worst flooding for 100 years after 2 days incessant rain in December 1979. The ground was already wet and additional rainfall of $2\frac{1}{2}$–4 in (60–100 mm) on both 26 and 27 December resulted in extensive flooding by the 28th. River banks broke, hundreds of people were evacuated from their homes and a bridge collapsed at Port Talbot. Some of the worst-hit areas were those where steep rivers from the mountains passed through towns. At Cardiff, a residential area was flooded when the down-flowing torrent in the river Taff met high tide from the Bristol Channel. Four people died in the floods and 2000 homes were damaged in mid-Glamorgan.

Flood water often flows fast enough to carry away vehicles, and too fast to be navigable by boat. Cars stationary in dips in a road can be death traps. By the time water reaches window level, the outside pressure is too great to allow an occupant to open the door. The window must be opened and the car allowed to fill in order to equalise water pressure both inside and out.

Kansas City had two record-breaking storms on 12 September 1977: 5·5 in (140 mm) fell in 6 hours early in the morning and, after an 8 hour break, a further 6–7 in (150–180 mm) fell over nearly the same area. Disastrous flooding resulted and of 25 deaths, 17 occurred in motor vehicles.

The Solway Moss Flood was one of the most unusual to have occurred in Britain. On 14 November 1771, incessant rain started in the north of England, so that by the 19th the Tees had risen 20 ft (6 m). Floods swept away half of the north Yorkshire market town of Yarm, and only one bridge out of 14 was left standing across the Tyne; the village of Bywell, 6 miles (10 km) from Hexham was almost destroyed and three collieries in Sunderland were filled with water; 34 ships were wrecked on Sunderland Bar.

Ten miles north of Carlisle lay Solway Moss, an area of moss covering a hill about 2–3 miles (3–5 km) in length and 1 mile (1·6 km) wide. The hill contained many springs which maintained the surface as a quagmire even in the driest summers. In the time of Henry VIII, tradition recounts that it sucked down a considerable part of a Scottish army. In the November rains of 1771 the moss swelled and breached the shell of solid earth which retained it at the eastern end of the hill. Moss and mud poured down into the valley, choked a stream at the bottom and formed a lake which extended a mile to the banks of the Esk. Cattle and sheep were suffocated, salmon were killed in the Esk and Solway Firth and about 14 farms, consisting of four or five houses each, were ruined. Although no human lives were lost, since the flood occurred at midnight when everyone was indoors, some 900 acres of good farming land were left covered in moss to depths of up to 20 ft (6 m), submerging all the hedges.

Drought, in the meteorological sense, is lack of rain (or snow) and it is the predominant characteristic of high-pressure systems, known as 'anticyclones'. Upper air subsides and warms over the centre of the anticyclones, thereby restricting the vertical development of cloud. When air is moist and suffers radiation cooling, shallow low cloud or fog may form, but there is no rain. There are certain definitions used for statistical purposes and geared for climates which can expect some rain at all times of the year.

Absolute drought A period of 15 consecutive days without rainfall of more than 0·01 in (0·2 mm).

Partial drought 29 consecutive days with *mean* rainfall of 0·01 in (0·2 mm) or less. Such a period may include a short duration of appreciable rainfall which disappears into insignificance when averaged over 29 days.

A dry spell 15 consecutive days, none of which has more than 0·04 in (1·0 mm) rainfall.

Deserts are regions where virtually no rain falls, either because of permanent high pressure or because of protection from prevailing moist winds by high mountain barriers.

The principal deserts of the world are:

The Sahara and Libyan Deserts, stretching across north Africa, and the adjacent Arabian Desert

The Gobi Desert of central Asia

The Great Western Desert of North America

The Great Victoria Desert of central Australia

The Kalahari Desert of southern Africa

The Atacama and the Patagonia Desert in South America

A hydrological drought is an insufficiency of water supply to meet demand. This can occur anywhere in the world, because lifestyles have evolved on the basis of average rainfall and not absolute quantities of rain. For instance, an Indian monsoon is said to *fail* if it brings too little rain, or rain at too late a date, for the proper growth of the rice crop. This requires ankle deep water in the paddy fields at planting times, and it is needed by mid-June. There has never been an occasion when the monsoon has failed to bring *any* rain, but many instances (the latest in 1972) when the rainfall has been markedly below average, and insufficient for a good harvest. A hydrological drought in India may, therefore, appear strange when considered purely in terms of rainfall; 50 per cent of normal rainfall in Bombay, for instance, is approximately 35 in (890 mm) in 4 months, which is still much more than London gets on average in a whole year, 23 in (584 mm).

Left: Water disrupting traffic in August 1977.
(London Express News Service)

Natural water reservoirs

Impervious basins of rock below ground, retaining water from which air is excluded and called 'groundwater'. The top level of groundwater is the 'water table', and its depth below surface varies according to local geological features and the wetness of the season. Groundwater is pumped to the surface at bore holes, and one of the problems during drought is that one cannot *see* how much water is left.

Springs, which are underground supplies rising naturally to the surface.

Lakes, streams and rivers which eventually discharge into the sea, and from which artificial reservoirs are stocked.

Snow, which is a frozen stock of water, released during spring.

The soil, which is said to be at field capacity when it holds as much water as possible, by surface tension and capillary action, as far down as the water table. Soil moisture deficiency occurs when water extraction is not compensated by rain or artificial watering. Waterlogged soil contains so much water that air is expelled from the soil and the level of the water table rises.

The most important water consumers

The atmosphere, which absorbs enormous quantities of water each year, estimated at 100 000 billion gallons. Probably two-thirds to three-quarters of Britain's annual rainfall is lost by evaporation, mainly during the summer. Even a wet summer provides only for current needs and not for replenishing reservoirs.

Vegetation, which consumes directly from the soil, principally during spring and summer when evaporation is also at a maximum.

Mankind, which has countless domestic, agricultural and industrial requirements for water at all times of the year, and particularly heavy demands in summer to make up artificially for what the clouds fail to provide.

Artificial reservoirs and irrigation channels are the means by which water authorities attempt to balance an irregular supply of water with a continuing voracious demand. It is economically impossible to cater for every *possible* drought and every *possible* increase in demand. Therefore hydrologists have the unenviable task of planning reservoir capacity on the basis of *probable* rainfall, and inevitably realistic compromises sometimes go awry.

The critical period of a reservoir is the time in which it will reach its lowest level, if not replenished by rain or from rivers. Most surface reservoirs in Britain have critical periods of 9 months, but the largest have 18 months. In general, any number of dry summers can be accommodated without hardship providing the intervening winters are wet enough to replenish reservoirs.

From November 1980 to February 1981 only about half the normal amount of rain fell in south east England and anxiety was being felt about the level of reservoirs. The matter was corrected in March, which gave more than twice the normal rainfall in the country generally, with areas of Wales and north west England having three to four times the normal amounts.

The major high-pressure systems of the world shift seasonally in fairly regular manner, but their boundaries are by no means precisely defined. Sometimes they encroach further north, sometimes to the south, and being sluggish systems they often persist longer than desired. Moreover, anticyclones seem to form cyclical habits of straying from their usual position, with consequent long-period abnormalities of rainfall. However, meteorologists are no nearer to defining the periodicity accurately than were astute weather observers in Biblical times.

One of the earliest predictions of drought, based on awareness of cyclical tendency, was that made by Joseph to Pharaoh, and recounted in Genesis. He said that seven lean years would follow seven fat years, and he advised that corn be stored when it was plentiful, in order to cope with the food crisis which would follow in the drought years. There is no absolute validity to the period of 7 years, but it does appear to be the right order of magnitude for that part of the world.

A recent cycle of 'lean years' affected the Sahel, a marginal area situated between the rainless Sahara and the lush equatorial forests of west Africa. Average rainfall is 10–20 in (250–500 mm), enough to encourage quick-growing sparse grass. This supports sheep and goats belonging to tribes who make a regular circuit from one grazing-ground to another. The Sahel had virtually no rain from 1973 until the autumn of 1976, because the subtropical high pressure belt stretched further south than usual. Many herds died of starvation, and whole communities of nomadic people suffered famine. It was a measure of their plight that many accepted help in settling into communities in more hospitable areas, and some will never return to the Sahel. A further drought, 1977–78, again spread famine through the region, emphasising its marginal capacity for supporting life.

One of the most notorious droughts caused by monsoon failure resulted in the plagues visited upon the Egyptians prior to the exodus of the Israelites under the leadership of Moses, some time between 1290 and 1224 BC.

Egyptian agriculture depended upon heavy seasonal rain over the mountains of Ethiopia and in the region of Lake Victoria to flood the Nile all the way down to the sea. At that time there were no controlling dams along the river. In the year of the plagues the shift of the high pressure belt must have so reduced rainfall in the source region that, by the time the northward flowing Nile had been further depleted by evaporation, the Egyptians were left with nothing more than a trickle. Insects abounded in stagnant pools and carried disease among the population; algae made the water unfit to drink and coloured it red; and frogs, which usually bred only when the Nile floods receded, multiplied at a faster rate than the predatory ibis could cope with. It must have been an exceptional drought, even worse than the lean years predicted by Joseph.

In the United States the most infamous sequence of droughts took place during the 1930s when the great Dust Bowl was created in the central plains. The first serious drought occurred in the middle of 1930 and extended into 1931, by which time most of the northern and central plains experienced a shortage of water. Every year thereafter till the end of the decade some region or other was affected by drought, and in 1934 and 1936 the area extended from Texas to the borders of Canada. Normal rainfall returned in November 1940.

California had its worst drought of the century following a very dry year, 1976, and the driest year on record in 1977. There was little winter snow in the Sierra Nevada mountains because of dominant

Right: Soil polygons in the dried out bed of the Pitsford reservoir Northampton, in July 1976. (London Express News Service)

high pressure and rivers and reservoirs were reduced to unprecedented levels. Houseboats on the shores of Lake Shasta were marooned like stranded fish 200 ft (70 m) from the lowered water line, the shrunken Sacramento river became too warm for the healthy spawning of salmon, and thousands of newly drilled wells were further depleting underground stocks of water. Serious loss of crops was compounded by frequent fires which destroyed brush and standing timber. The drought ended with prolonged heavy rain in mid-December, when the crisis of drought turned to one of flood.

Australia faced its worst drought in living memory by early 1980, the third drought year running in Western Australia. By January the water in some dams was as low as 9 per cent and by April there was scarcely any grass to be seen from the Indian Ocean to the Pacific, except where the land was irrigated. Thousands of kangaroos died, and sheep and cattle suffered badly.

China suffered drought in 1980–81 in the Hebei province where half the cultivated land depends upon artificial irrigation. By April 1981, 15 out of 16 main reservoirs were closed after 18 months of record drought. For the first time the government called upon international help to provide food. Spring wheat withered, the soil having only 1 per cent moisture instead of the required 17 per cent. Heavy rain in July and August relieved the drought but caused extensive flooding, particularly of the Yangtze. An estimated 3000 deaths resulted and some 400 000 people lost their homes.

In Britain, absolute droughts are relatively infrequent, as illustrated by figures from Rugby, Warwick, which is representative of central England. Rugby rainfall records have been kept since April 1871, and since that date there have been 128 absolute droughts of 15 consecutive days or more. Of these, 47 lasted 20 days or more but only five reached 30 days. The longest period was 34 days, 4 August –6 September 1947.

The longest absolute drought in Britain was 73 successive rainless days from 4 March to 15 May 1893 at Mile End, in the east end of London.

Historic British droughts, which happened before the compilation of rainfall statistics, can be glimpsed from written descriptions.

In 55 BC Julius Caesar was waging his second campaign in south east England and recounts in Book V of *de Bello Gallico* that his supply problems were much aggravated by the smallness of the autumn crops 'propter siccitates', on account of the dryness. He mentions persistent northerly winds, indicating a blocking anticyclone extending to Britain from the Azores.

Churches were repositories for fire buckets and hooks to pull thatch down from burning roofs, and frequent entries in church accounts for renewal or repair of fire-fighting equipment always accompanied periods of drought.

The year of the Great Plague 1665, began with a cold, dry winter and spring; and as early as 11 April, King Charles reminded the Lord Mayor of London of the danger of fire because of wooden houses closely overhanging narrow streets. In south east England, every month from November 1665 to September 1666 was dry, and by August the Thames at Oxford was a trickle. London buildings were as dry as tinder when the Great Fire started on 2 September 1666, destroying 13 000 houses, churches and public buildings. A rainy spell started on 9 September and there was almost incessant heavy rain for 10 days early in October.

The worst drought in England and Wales since rainfall records began occurred during 1975 and 1976. Weather was dominated by high-pressure systems, which only withdrew occasionally to permit the approach of depressions bringing rain. These years saw the driest 12, 16, and 18-month periods in England and Wales since 1820. Moreover, they followed the driest 5-year period since the 1850s, 1971–5 having a mean rainfall of only 32 in (826 mm) per annum. Absolute drought lasted for extremely long periods, none of which constituted a record, but which were phenomenal because experienced over a widespread area.

A Drought Bill was passed by Parliament on 15 July 1976, giving far-reaching powers to local authorities to control the use of water. Dennis Howell MP was appointed Minister of Drought, the first such ministerial post, and on 25 August the Department of the Environment opened an emergency centre to advise on water problems. The National Water Council maintained that it would take a wet winter, a normal summer and a further wet winter to restore reservoirs to proper levels. In fact, that had already happened by February 1977.

THE BRITISH DROUGHT 1975–76

1975

The year 1975 was the fifth driest of the century. Most of England, from South Devon to Yorkshire, and also eastern Scotland had less than 70 per cent average rainfall.

MAY Rainless spells started and continued through to December, excepting only September.

JUNE Herefordshire, Gwent, Dorset, Devon and Cornwall were all experiencing water cuts or restrictions, and in South Yorkshire the drought was considered to be the worst for 100 years.

SEPTEMBER Rain fell on ground baked hard in the hot summer and came generally too late to be of use to farmers, and was of no consequence for the reservoirs. It did, however, prevent a threatened water rationing in Sheffield.

DECEMBER Stand pipes were set up in the streets of Barnsley, South Yorkshire.

1976

The early months of 1976 were dry in many areas of England and Wales, although some northern districts had 150 per cent average rainfall. In particular, Sheffield's problems were alleviated by the wettest January since 1960. The crucial winter months in the Midlands and southern England passed without replenishment of reservoirs or ground water.

APRIL which often produces heavy showers without suffering undue evaporative loss, failed to live up to its reputation.

MAY was changeable with heavy rain at times in the north. Southern areas had 15 or more days with some rain, but the total was still below average.

JUNE and JULY produced remarkably little rain over the whole of the British Isles which had an even hotter summer than the year before. Rain which did fall consisted mainly of spasmodic deluges from thunderstorms. These swelled rainfall statistics but did not materially affect the drought situation.

AUGUST Reservoirs in Devon and Cornwall were as low as 23 per cent capacity, the Mendip reservoirs between Avon and Somerset were losing water by evaporation at the rate of 5·5 million gallons (25 million litres) per day, and rivers were at record low levels. Stand pipes were operating in South Wales and North Devon, and general rationing was expected by 15 September. The source of the Thames dried up for 9 miles (14 km) and water at Molesey Lock, the last but one before the tidal reaches, was being pumped *up-river* over the lock. Even the Scottish River Spey was 14 in (356 mm) below normal summer level; between the towns of Grantown and Cromdale, Grampian, a series of stones dated 1851, 1868, 1911, 1921 and 1955 record exceptional low levels of the Spey in past years, and every stone was clearly visible above the level of water in August 1976.

On 29 August, heavy rain fell over the south of England.

Duration of absolute drought at representative places in England and Wales, in days

Teignmouth, Devon	44
Thorney Isle, Hampshire	41
Aberporth, Dyfed	39
Guildford, Surrey	38
Edgbaston, Warwickshire	37
Sidcup, Kent	36
Scilly Isles	33
Valley, Gwynedd	29
Borrowash, Derbyshire	28
Liverpool, Merseyside	27
Pickering, North Yorkshire	25
Hull, Humberside	24

Random cirrus, which if it starts to spread over the whole sky, may herald the end of a drought. (M.J. Hammersley)

The driest spells in England and Wales for specified periods since 1820[1]

Period	Year	Start Month	Rainfall in	Rainfall mm
6 month	1921	Feb	7·0	179
	1976	Mar	8·1	208
	1887	Feb	8·7	221
12 month	**1975/6**	Sept	22·4	571
	1854/5	Feb	24·3	618
	1920/1	Nov	24·3	618
16 month	**1975/6**	May	29·8	757
	1854/5	Feb	31·9	811
	1933/4	Apr	33·6	855
18 month	**1975/6**	Mar	35·7	909
	1853/5	Dec	36·7	933
	1887/8	June	39·2	997
24 month	1932/4	Nov	56·6	1439
	1853/5	Oct	56·6	1439
	1862/4	Nov	57·5	1461
	1887/9	Feb	58·7	1493
	1972/4	July	58·9	1497
	1974/6	Sept	58·9	1497

[1] *Highlighting the years which affected the 1976 drought*

The break in the 1976 drought came on 29 August, when high pressure retreated to start a wonderful autumn in the Mediterranean while heavy rain fell over the south of England.

In England and Wales, September was the second wettest since 1873. Mean rainfall was 6·3 in (160 mm) compared with the record September figure, 7·2 in (183 mm), in 1918. The total from mid-September to mid-October was the highest ever, 6·8 in (172 mm).

This whole pattern was unusual because, since 1840, 14 out of 17 hot summers, with mean temperature more than 60°F (15·8°C) and rainfall less than 7·8 in (200 mm), were also followed by dry Septembers. Between 1727 and 1840 the trend was different; none of the summers comparable to 1976 was followed by a dry September.

Much flooding resulted throughout September and October, and the succeeding months continued wet. By January it seemed certain that, if another hot dry summer should materialise in 1977, it could be faced with equanimity. By February, Chew Valley Lake and the Blagdon reservoir on the Avon-Somerset border were full to overflowing, and millions of gallons of water were running over spillways into the rivers Chew and Yeo.

A blocking anticyclone is one which persists in latitudes normally travelled by depressions, which are therefore diverted in other directions. Hence drought in one area is usually adjacent to abnormally high rainfall in another.

There was a notable drought throughout north west Europe during 1976, exceptional dryness in Britain being mirrored by similar conditions in France, where many rivers, including some as fast flowing as the Loire, dried up. The blocking anticyclone diverted depressions southwards during July, causing normally fine Mediterranean weather to be replaced by a wet summer more typical of Britain. Mediterranean rainfall in July 1976, expressed as a percentage of normal, was:

	%
Parts of southern Italy	150
Malta, record 18·9 in (480 mm) Jan–July	200
Parts of eastern Greece	800
Parts of southern Turkey	800
Algiers	2000
Parts of north western Algeria	3200

Cloud seeding is an experimental method of attempting to wring rain from clouds. Therefore it arouses tantalising, but as yet unproven, hopes amongst people in drought-stricken areas. Silver iodide crystals, solid carbon dioxide (dry ice) or salt are injected into clouds, in order to speed the freezing or coalescence of supercooled water drops, an apparently necessary preliminary to precipitation.

In Australia in August 1979, the Commonwealth Scientific and Industrial Research Organisation (CSIRO) began a 5-year experiment to discover how successful seeding really is. Aeroplanes fly into suitable clouds over the Wimmera district of Victoria, burning silver iodide from special burners underneath the fuselage. The planes carry sophisticated instruments, by which it is hoped to document the change in cloud characteristics after seeding.

A rather different experiment took place in Australia at the beginning of the century. Clement Wragge, Queensland Government Meteorologist, thought an explosion in a vapour laden cloud might release rain, and in September 1901 trials started with a Stiger Gun in the Botanic Gardens, Brisbane. This resulted in one fractured gun, no rain, a wet season at the end of 1902, and consequent wane of interest.

14. Snow and thaw flood

Snow is beautiful to look at but an unmitigated nuisance to traffic. Moreover, the manner in which it often arrives in a blizzard and departs by avalanche or thaw flood means that snow must be considered a treacherous enemy.

Snow falls over every continent in the world, but in low latitudes only on the tops of high mountains. In such countries snow may be familiar only by hearsay, and millions of people have yet to 'discover' snow personally. In high latitudes snow is a familiar and regular visitor, but the individual crystal is a comparatively recent discovery.

Olaus Magnus (1490–1558), Swedish historian and Archbishop of Uppsala, was the first person known to have studied individual snow crystals. His drawings were reproduced by woodcut in a book published in Rome in 1555.

René Descartes (1596–1650), French philosopher and mathematician, sketched some dozen different crystals.

Johannes Kepler (1571–1630), German astronomer, was the first to describe in a pamphlet in 1611 the characteristic six-sided symmetry of every snow crystal.

William Scoresby (1789–1857), English Arctic explorer, worked in the right environment to pursue the study of snow further, and he published a book with precise drawings of still more patterns of crystals.

James Glaisher, English meteorologist, published a paper in 1858 about the severe winter of 1855, which was illustrated with drawings, by his wife, of 151 types of snow crystal.

William A. Bentley (1865–1931), was the first person to photograph ice crystals using a camera fitted with a microscope. He was an American farmer who was only 20 years old when his fascination with snow began, and he devoted the next 40 years of his life to building up a collection of 6000 photomicrographs of snow crystals, all being different. However, even this great number omitted many which he ignored, because they did not conform to his idea of beauty. Bentley died in 1931, just before his book *Snow Crystals*, containing 2000 of his best photographs, was published.

Vincent Schaefer (b 1906) was the first to make perfect replicas of snowflakes in plastic in 1940, when he was research assistant to Irving Langmuir at the General Electric Company in Schenectady, New York. The coating material is a synthetic resin, dissolved in a liquid which not only evaporates readily at low temperatures but creeps up over all the surfaces of the snow crystal, giving a three-dimensional replica. The technique is simple and widely used for studying and recording different types of crystal. Replication is also possible by using an aerosol plastic spray, but the spray must be used sparingly for success.

Signposts are little use in this depth of snow.
(M.J. Hammersley)

The formation of snowflakes in clouds was studied in the 1930s by both Langmuir and Schaefer. During winter visits to the summit of Mt Washington, where temperature was often down to −4°F (−20°C), they discovered that the clouds covering the mountain top always consisted of supercooled water drops, rather than snowflakes. In experiments with a freezer chest, it was a simple matter to create a miniature supercooled cloud by breathing into the chest, but impossible to convert these drops into individual ice crystals. The drops tended to freeze to a film of ice on the side of the chest.

The first artificial snow was produced by Schaefer in July 1946, by accident. He put a piece of dry ice into the freezer chest in order to lower the temperature. Immediately the supercooled cloud converted to a shower of ice crystals which fell on to the black velvet at the bottom of the chest. He had proved that intensity of cold, alone, changes supercooled drops to ice crystals, these spontaneous conversions taking place at about −38°F (−39°C).

Four crystal types, all formed at −4°F(−20°C) in a supercooled water drop cloud, and reproduced in Formvar plastic for study under the microscope. (V.J. Schaefer and R.J. Cheng, Atmospheric Sciences Research Center, State University of New York at Albany)

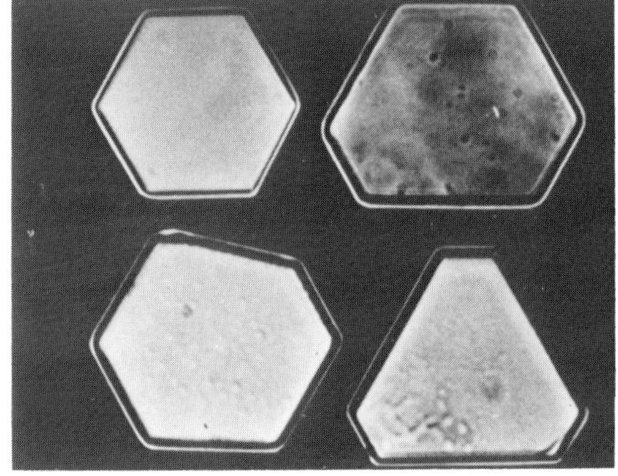

(*a*) Plain and thin hexagonal plates formed spontaneously by cooling with dry ice or by popping plastic bubbles containing pressurised air. When light passes through these plates beautiful interference colours result, as with soap bubbles.

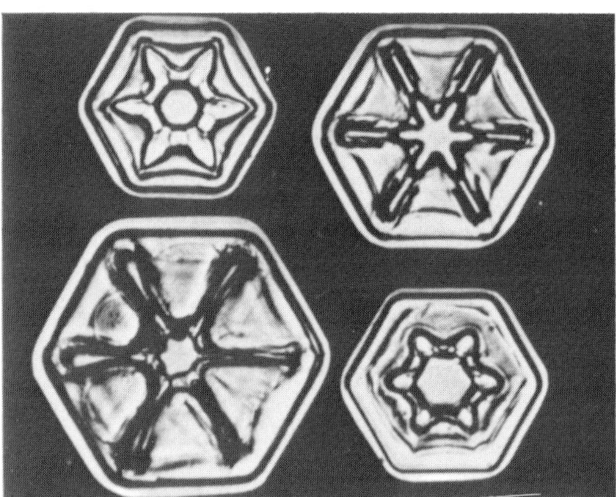

(*b*) Very symmetrical crystals but with infinite variety of detail, formed around embryo seeds of silver iodide crystals or lead iodide crystals.

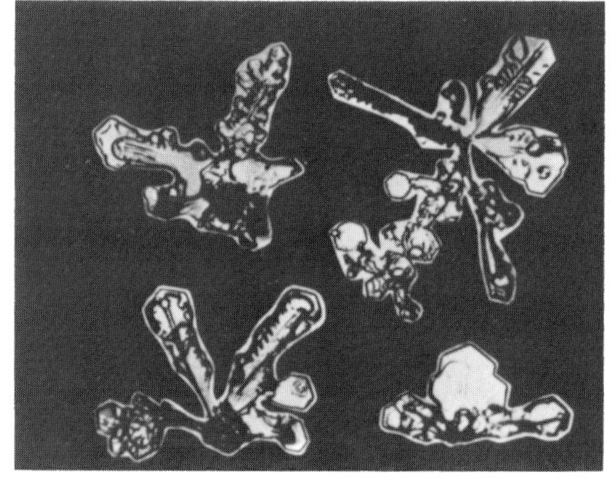

(*c*) Irregular crystals formed around irregularly shaped particles of volcanic dust or clay.

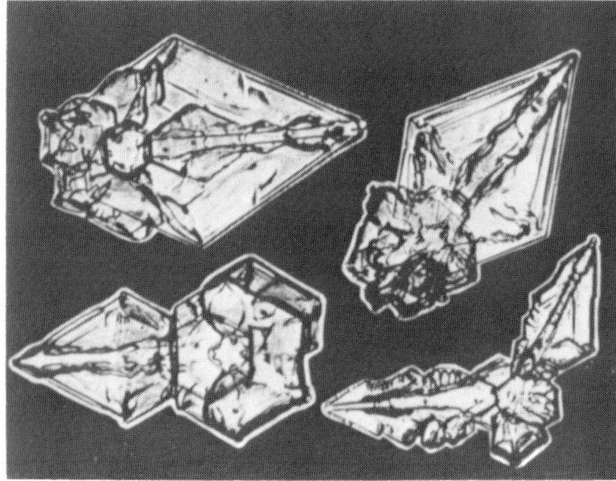

(*d*) Exotic jewel shapes, called 'flare crystals', because they often occur whenever pyrotechnic devices are used to seed cloud with silver iodide smoke.

lines at the side indicate 100 μ
1 μ = 1 micron

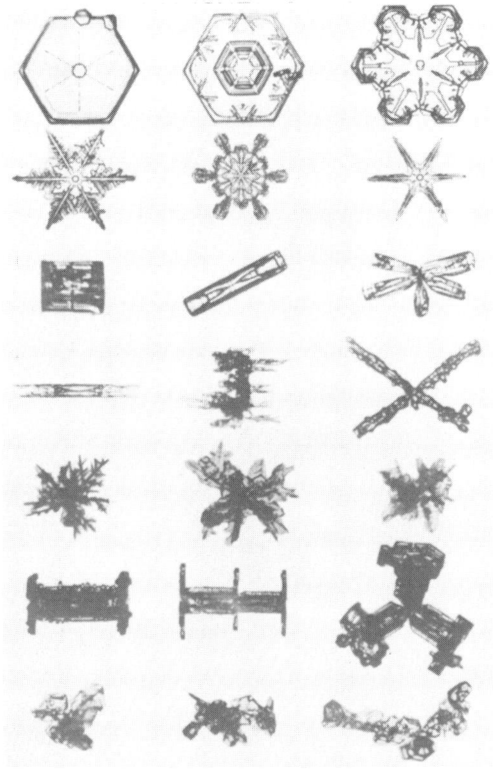

PLATES Thin, solid or semi solid, often including air pockets. Smallest form, known as 'diamond dust', less than $\frac{3}{16}$ in (5 mm), rarely clumped.

STELLARS Single crystals or clumps in wide variety of form and size. Cottony flakes sometimes 2 in (5 cm) in diameter.

COLUMNS Generally flat ended, transparent or translucent, usually with air inclusions. Group of columns sometimes radiate from common source.

NEEDLES Long slender shafts with hexagonal cross section, often with sharp irregular points along edges. Often clumped.

SPATIAL DENDRITES Complex ice crystal with fern like arms extending in many directions from central nucleus.

CAPPED COLUMNS Hexagonal columns with both ends terminated by hexagonal plates; plates sometimes positioned midway. Sometimes clumped.

IRREGULAR CRYSTALS Small balls or pieces of ice, falling separately or as an agglomeration into irregular lumps.

Basic hexagonal shapes in snowflakes (V.J. Schaefer)

The first natural cloud was seeded on 13 November 1946, when Schaefer dispensed 3 lb of dry ice from an aircraft flying into cloud at 14 000 ft (4267 m) and having a temperature of −4°F (−20°C). Long streamers of snow fell from the base of the cloud and after a second run with a further 3 lb of dry ice, snow crystals glittered throughout the cloud. Dry ice can cool a thin layer of cloud to about −94°F (−70°C).

The discovery of silver iodide as an effective seeding agent was made 1 day later, on 14 November 1946, by Bernard Vonnegut, of the same research team and using the same freezer chest. Since then both dry ice and silver iodide have been the most important seeding agents, effective in clouds with temperature 19°F (−7°C) or less.

Ukichiro Nakaya (1900–62), of Hokkaido University, Japan, was the first to study snow with modern X-ray equipment and to demonstrate, in 1954, that the hexagonal symmetry of individual crystals is due to molecular structure.

An infinite variety of crystal shapes exists, around the basic hexagonal symmetry. Thin plates, hollow prismatic columns, needles, dendrites and stellars result from complicated sequences of evaporation, condensation, sublimation and deposition. Temperature and humidity are influencing factors, but in addition the nature of the nuclei on which the crystals form may habitually lead to shapes of a particular type.

Dry snow consists of very cold crystals, which do not bond together by regelation and which therefore remain small. The crystals may latch together if suitably shaped, though inevitably many break under impact with each other.

Dry snow is typical of continental land masses well removed from the sea and, when freshly fallen, it has a density of less than 0·1 g/cm³. If driven by strong winds, dry snow penetrates the smallest cracks in window and door frames, bringing a snow storm literally indoors. Moreover, particularly fine and powdery snow can cause suffocation. The same consistent powdery quality makes dry snow amenable to clearance by 'suck-and-blow' machines, because it does not solidify by regelation under pressure inside the machines. Likewise, dry snow is an ideal surface on which to ski because it does not clog on the under-surface.

Wet snow occurs at temperatures high enough to bond crystals into large snow flakes by regelation. It is typical of maritime borders of continental land masses between latitudes 40° and 60°, where intensely cold air streams from inland can clash with mild air carrying abundant vapour from the sea. Fresh wet snow has a density of approximately 0·3 g/cm³. One m³ of newly fallen snow may therefore weigh 300 kg, and 1 yd³ about 500 lb.

Wet snow is ideal for making snowballs because the flakes bond together easily under hand pressure. For the same reason it cannot be cleared away by a blower machine, but only by snowplough or shovel.

Dirty snow may fall at a considerable distance from the source of its pollution. During the winter of 1962–3, bulldozers slicing through snow drifts in a 3-mile (5 km) wide belt inland from Torquay, Devon, revealed a layer of soot a few feet above the soil. Analysis showed that the dirt had been carried all the way from Stuttgart, Germany.

Graupel (German word for soft hail) is snow which has partly melted and refrozen, usually by being tossed in layers of different temperature, and falls to the ground as compressible pellets of thin ice with a soft core, rarely larger than 0·2 in (5 mm) in diameter.

The terminal speed of snow flakes is considerably less than the terminal speed of rain drops because snow presents a greater area of resistance to the wind. Large flakes having a diameter 0·4–1·6 in (10–40 mm) only reach a terminal velocity of 3–5 ft/s (1–2 m/s) which is not as fast as the speed of the smallest rain drops. Snow cover on the ground is therefore considerably affected by wind speed.

Snow flakes may attain a size of several inches in diameter, and were reported 8 in × 12 in (200 mm × 300 mm) at Bratsk, Siberia, during the winter of 1971. Any snow flakes as large as that are probably caused by being swirled up and down within the cloud in air currents, accumulating more and more ice crystals, till they are in effect snowballs.

A snow cover contains air, and only has even depth over the ground after snow has fallen in calm or very light wind. The depth is then measured, as soon as possible after the fall, by graduated rule over a level surface well away from obstructions.

For purposes of climatological records, depth of snow is translated into rainfall at the average rate of 1 in of rain for every 1 ft of snow (25 mm rain for every 300 mm snow). Actual rates, however, vary considerably with type of snow. Very cold and feathery snow, whose crystals interlock so lightly that air constitutes 95 per cent of the snow cover, may only yield 1 in of water for every 3 ft of snow (25 mm rain

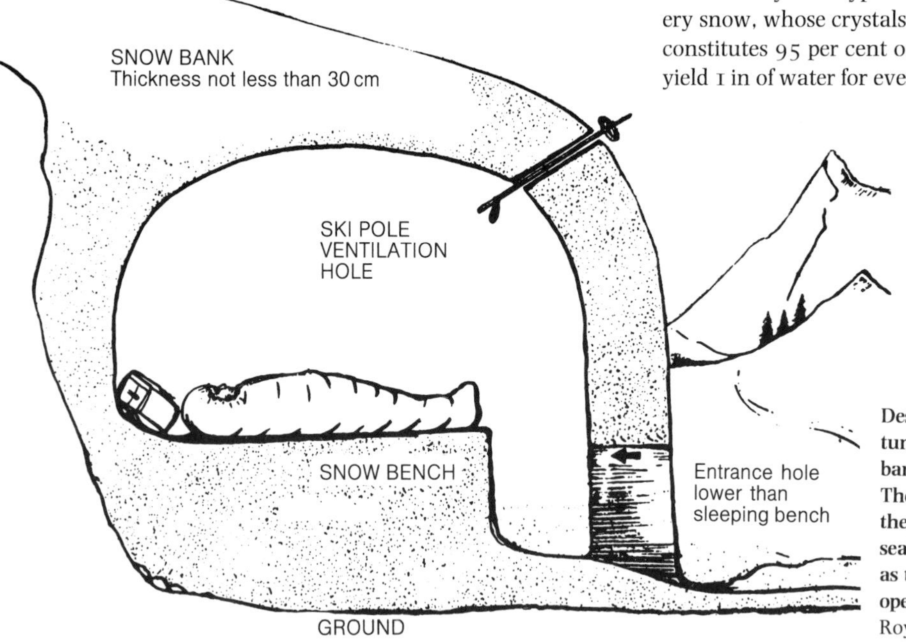

Design for a snow hole, by tunnelling directly into a snow bank and excavating the snow. The entrance must be lower than the sleeping bench and can be sealed with a snow block, so long as the ventilation shaft is kept open. (Crown copyright, courtesy Royal Marines)

for every 900 mm snow); whereas wet snow may give five times as much water for the same depth. A fresh, wet snow cover contains about 75 per cent air, but soon compacts further.

The insulation value of a snow cover varies with its air content, and therefore is most efficient when new. It insulates the ground against excessive cold above the snow and prevents conduction of heat from the soil to the top of the snow cover.

Corn germinated and grew to 3 in (75 mm) beneath a sudden snow cover in the Devon blizzard of 1891, because the ground was warmer than normal when the snow fell.

Sheep can survive for several weeks in snow because their own coats insulate them against loss of body heat until they become completely covered by snow. Snow then melts near their bodies to form small caves in which lambs are sometimes born and survive until rescued.

On 19 January 1982, three sheep were rescued alive near Evesham in the Cotswolds after having been buried for 12 days in a 15-ft snow drift. Very many, however, were not lucky enough to survive and there were particularly heavy casualties in Wales. Some sheep were drowned in melt water near the ground while still covered by snow.

A man and his son survived a blizzard in the Cairngorms, Scotland, on the night of 11–12 December 1977. They had no sleeping bag, but dug themselves into a snow hole to retain their body heat.

The nuisance value of level snow is considerable. Road traffic is usually disrupted by about 4 in (100 mm) and the railways by about 6 in (150 mm). Cattle will nuzzle through 6 in (150 mm) of snow but not through 12 in (300 mm). Sheep can walk through 12 in (300 mm) of snow but are defeated by 24 in (600 mm).

A blizzard is a snow storm in which strong wind causes drifting of snow on the ground and extremely poor visibility. Snow blowing across open ground may remain suspended in air, so that very little settles. Snow, however, accumulates in huge drifts near obstructions, making frozen sculptures which illustrate the normally invisible behaviour of wind. It piles up against windward surfaces; it is carried backwards in lee eddies and it traces aerodynamic flow patterns over slopes.

In the second week of March 1891, after a sudden blizzard over Dartmoor in Devon, narrow roads between hedges were filled to the top with snow but a few exposed fields had hardly any snow cover at all.

Lincolnshire, in the severe winter 1963. (Automobile Association)

The countryside lost all its usual contours and those trudging the snow were as likely to find themselves walking over hedge tops as over roads.

Depth of snow drift gives an unrealistic value of total snow fall, but a very cogent impression of disruption of traffic.

After the blizzards experienced in Buffalo, New York State during the end of January and the beginning of February 1977, the town was left with snow drifts 20 ft (6 m) high, which were compacted so hard by the wind that the blades of snow ploughs broke on them.

During 1947, which was the snowiest winter in Britain this century, drifts accumulated to 15 ft (5 m) depth in many places, and farms and isolated villages were cut off for days.

Traditional reports in Devon, that the ravine Tavy Cleave on the west side of Dartmoor was filled with a giant drift 200–300 ft deep (60–100 m) during the March blizzard of 1891, are no longer considered to be a wild exaggeration, but a realistic possibility.

Wind flow patterns over roofs often cause irregular loading of snow, particularly on the lee side. British building specifications require that a roof pitch of less than 30° must be able to carry a load of 2 ft (0·6 m) of snow, but other countries which have regular falls of heavier snow make more stringent regulations. Northern Japan had an exceptionally cold January in 1977 and the heaviest snow for 14 years: over 200 roofs collapsed under the weight of snow.

In Cardiff, Wales, the roof of the city's largest centre of entertainment collapsed under the weight of snow in the first week of January 1982.

A cornice is a wave shaped sculpture of snow projecting, without material support, over a vertical drop, such as cliff or house wall. It is formed by violent lee eddies, carrying snow backwards into the side of the obstruction after blowing over the top surface.

A snow cushion is a mound of snow which forms in back eddying wind over lee slopes. Windward slopes are frequently less snowy, so that sheep are better able to graze. For this reason, Devon farmers do not burn gorse from the moors which face the east, the direction from which the heaviest English snowfalls come.

Snow rollers are aggregates of snow flakes which are driven along the ground by the wind to form snowballs or cylinders.

A white-out blurs normal perception in a snow storm, or over a snow cover, when cloud merges into snow without a visible horizon. Normally distinguishable contours of the landscape disappear, multiple reflection from ice crystals and cloud prevents shadows, and all sense of direction and balance may be lost.

Snow rollers at Coningsby, Lincolnshire on 2 January 1979, formed after a minor front passed through the area with a freshening wind. Although the air temperature had been 12.2°F(−10.9°C) a few hours previously, when snow was dry, it rose to 32°F(0°C) as the front passed. Snow then became wet and malleable. The rollers persisted for several days, the largest having a diameter of about 7 in (180 mm). (P.R. Goldthorpe)

Snow lies on the ground whenever the air temperature is below 37°F (3°C). It may reach the ground still frozen in air temperatures up to 44°F (7°C) but then melts at once.

When air temperature is near 32°F (0°C) small variations in altitude can make surprising differences to the weather. On 3 November 1958, rain fell on 34th Street, New York, while guards at the top of the Empire State Building at 1150 ft (350 m) were making snowballs!

Snow lies for most of the winter wherever the temperature of the coldest month is less than 27°F (−3°C). It lies intermittently every winter wherever air tem-

peratures are 27° to 39°F (−3° to 4°C). Snow covers approximately 23 per cent of the Earth's surface either permanently or temporarily.

Between the poles and latitudes 66½° precipitation is nearly always in the form of snow, but with little vapour content in the cold air, the quantity of snow is not great. Over Antarctica snowfalls are exceedingly difficult to measure because strong winds continually blow old snow and make it indistinguishable from new falls. The annual amount is thought to be less than 5 in (125 mm) equivalent rainfall.

In latitudes lower than 40° snow falls wherever there are high enough mountains projecting above the freezing level of the atmosphere.

Snow moulded by the wind in the New Zealand mountains. (M.J. Hammersley)

Among such mountains are Mt Fujiyama, Japan, 33°N; Mt Teide, Tenerife, 28°N; and on the Equator, Mt Kenya, 17 058 ft (5199 m).

At low altitudes, the occasional snowfalls cause considerable excitement. Snow fell at Mackay, Queensland, 21°S, on 20 July 1965. It snowed in and around Riyadh, Saudi Arabia, 25°N, on 1 January 1973, clinging to the trees but not settling.

Snow fell in the Kalahari desert on 1 September 1981, the first time in living memory. Temperatures of about 23°F (−5°C) were recorded in the territory's capital, Windhoek.

Tampa, Florida, 28°N, had enough snow for child-

(cont. on p. 182)

SNOW IN GREAT BRITAIN

Side road in Nottingham on 15 March 1964.
(M.J. Hammersley)

The average number of days per annum with snow lying on the ground is 50–100 in the Scottish highlands, 10–20 days in northern England, the Scottish lowlands and central England. Coastal areas and southern England have only 1–10 days per annum of lying snow.

Snow on low ground occurs most often during January, February and March. White Christmases, such as 1981, are uncommon. The heaviest falls of snow yield about 2 ft (60 cm) in 24 hours, apart from drifts.

Snow sometimes falls in April and May; on 17 May 1935 snow lay in many areas of England and South Wales. In June and July snow has only rarely been observed in the south. It was seen in London on 12 June 1791 and on 2 June 1975 but melted at once on reaching ground. Any white cover seen in summer is usually hail.

The earliest snow to fall in London was on 25 September 1885. Generally, the first falls there during the years 1811–1930 were between 18 and 25 November, but from 1931 to 1960 they were a little later, about 8 December.

On 7 November 1980, overnight snow in the Dover area lay 2 in (50 mm) thick by morning. Further snow between 28 and 30 November made the month the snowiest for 25 years in that area.

The most snowy winter of the 20th century was 1947. Between 22 January and 17 March snow fell every day somewhere in the country. There were several daily falls of over 2 ft (600 mm), drifts 15 ft (5 m) high were frequent, and the temperature remained at or near freezing level most of the time so that snow accumulated over the whole period. Many areas were cut off for days on end, and the armed services were called in to drop supplies by helicopter to isolated farmsteads and villages, and to open up roads. An accumulated level fall of 60 in (1524 mm) was recorded in Upper Teesdale and in the Denbighshire Hills, Clwyd.

The winter of 1963 was even colder, and the snow cover also lasted for many weeks but the quantity of snow was slightly less.

Severe blizzards do occur even in winters which are not generally very snowy.

In 1978 a blizzard in Scotland lasted for 50 hours between 27 and 29 January. Even towns on low ground had falls of 14–28 in (350–700 mm). Snow was dry at first but became wet on the 28th, when gales compressed it into drifts more than 30 ft (10 m) deep. This occurred so rapidly that many people were trapped in cars and three trains were buried. Many areas were isolated for days and 300 people were lifted to safety by helicopter. A travelling salesman, buried in his car, survived by doing all the right things: he stayed in his car, maintained a fresh supply of air by poking a stick up through the snow, kept starvation at bay with a meagre supply of biscuits, and kept warm by wrapping himself in the product he was selling — ladies tights!

On Saturday night, 19 February 1978, a blizzard struck southern England and Wales and caused many people to be marooned in places of entertainment. Snow drifted to the first floors of houses and the road to Barnstaple, between high hedges, was filled to the brim. It took 6 days to clear a road through to Lynton, Devon, and seven lives were lost.

In the spring of 1981, a blizzard swept the Midlands, Wales and south-west England during the weekend 25–26 April. The snow was wet and weighed down many power cables, so that thousands of homes were without electricity for more than 24 hours. Trees, in leaf, were badly damaged. Traffic was dislocated, with more than 50 vehicles halted by drifts on Salisbury Plain and 300 people stranded. The thaw came quickly, causing flooding in many areas.

On 11 and 13 December 1981 heavy snow fell over many parts of Britain and drifted several feet thick. It severely hampered rescue work after a train crash near Beaconsfield, Bucks, and made hundreds of miles of roads impassable.

In the first week of January 1982 blizzards turned south Wales and the west of England into a white hell. Roads became impassable, sheep were buried under snow for many days and villages were isolated. Temperatures plummeted and Aberystwyth harbour in Cardigan Bay froze over for the first time in living memory.

Railway cutting through a snow drift in Wales, February 1947. (British Railways)

ren to make snowballs in January 1886 and again in February 1899, when snowflakes were also seen in the air at Fort Myers, Florida, 26°N.

Within latitudes 40° and 66½° snow regularly falls during the winter, but in comparatively small quantities in the heart of large land masses. It also falls copiously if less regularly in maritime regions where moist air from the sea confronts cold air streams over the land.

Mountain barriers such as those of Scandinavia, central Europe, the eastern ranges of North and South America and the Southern Alps in New Zealand, all experience particularly heavy snowfalls because they are accessible to moist airstreams.

The world's greatest recorded snowfalls have all happened in the United States, which has more high altitude reporting stations than other countries.

The Rocky Mountains in general have an annual average snowfall of 300–400 in (7·6–10 m). Paradise Ranger Station, in particular, has an average annual snowfall of 575 in (14·6 m). Even this was more than doubled between 19 February 1971 and 18 February 1972, when there was a total snowfall of 1224·5 in (31·1 m).

The greatest 1-day snowfall occurred at Silver Lake, Colorado, 14–15 April 1921, with 74 in (1870 mm). The greatest 5-day snowfall occurred at Thomson Pass, Alaska, 26–31 December 1955, producing 175·4 in (4455 mm).

The character of a snow cover continually changes, by the same processes which determine the snowflakes which fall from the sky. Some crystals break while others bond together by regelation. Some melt,

Accumulation of snow on trees or bushes often causes them to break under the unnatural weight.
(M.J. Hammersley)

either because they are close to warm ground or because they lie on a rock which warms in sunshine. Convection, too, takes place within a layer of snow, because air may be considerably warmer near the ground than nearer the icy winds. Warm air convects upwards; evaporation, condensation, sublimation or deposition take place until the ice crystals become rounded so that they pack more closely. Air is driven out of the layer until eventually it forms solid ice with only occasional bubbles of air.

Firn is old and compacted snow, containing less than 20 per cent of air. It is less white than fresh snow, because the closely packed crystals reflect less light, making it look more like plaster.

A **glacier** is an extensive sheet of ice formed when permanent deposits of firn snow compress over hundreds of years. The process is accentuated by compression down constricting valleys, so that glaciers become rivers of ice which travel slowly downhill. Glaciers cover 6 million miles^2 (15 million km^2) of the Earth's surface. In warm latitudes they melt when they reach the appropriate altitude and feed rivers which might otherwise be dry.

The longest glacier is in Australian Antarctic Territory. The Lambert Glacier was discovered by an Australian aircrew during the summer of 1956–7 and is up to 40 miles (64 km) wide and at least 250 miles (402 km) long. Together with the Fisher Limb, the Lambert Glacier forms a continuous ice passage of 320 miles (514 km).

In India the longest glacier is the Siachen, which covers a distance of 47 miles (76 km) in the Karakoram range. Two others, the Hispar and the Biafo, combine to form an ice river measuring 76 miles (122 km).

New Zealand has several glaciers creeping down the Southern Alps and finishing as sluggish streams near luxuriant warm forests. This unusual combination is

SNOW IN THE UNITED STATES

The greatest falls of snow occur in sparsely populated mountainous regions of the west. The average number of days with snow lying on the ground is 90–140 per annum in the north eastern states but only 1–10 days in the southern states.

The snowiest populated region is east and north-east of Lakes Ontario and Erie, where proximity to both sea and lakes feeds moisture into the atmosphere.

The 1970s were particularly snowy, and the snowiest of the larger metropolitan areas were Buffalo, with a 10-year snowfall of 1110 in (28·2 m), Rochester 1074 in (27·3 m) and Salt Lake City 818 in (20·8 m).

The snowiest winter in the eastern and mid-western states, in some cases for 100 years, was 1977–8, when significant snow began to fall in October. The main characteristics of that winter were:

1 The number of individual storms. For instance, Illinois had 18 compared with the previous record of 12 and a normal number of 4.
2 Mean air temperatures, about 8F (4C) degrees below normal, from December to March, though there were a few exceptionally low individual minimum temperatures.
3 Very prolonged snow cover. For instance, Antioch in Illinois, had one for 118 days, on 95 of which the depth was more than 1 in (25 mm).
4 Very severe individual snowstorms. Boston, Massachusetts, had two record breaking storms in 3 weeks; 21·4 in (543 mm) snow fell at the end of January and 27·1 in (688 mm) at the end of the first week in February. Chicago, Illinois had three particularly bad storms in January and a total snowfall for the month of 32·3 in (807 mm).

By the end of January an emergency had been declared in New York State, New Jersey and Ohio. More than 60 people died in blizzards, transport was paralysed by snow drifts and the excessive cold caused an acute shortage of fuel. Not until the middle of February did the 'Great American Winter' ease sufficiently to permit a general return to work and school. By the end of February, Buffalo had recorded 183·1 in (4651 mm) snow, compared to its former record of 126 in (3200 mm) in 1909–10.

Snow drifts in many places were reported to be 20–30 ft (6–9 m) high, and were hard enough to damage snow ploughs. Even when the snow could be moved, the problem was how to dispose of it before a thaw made it a flood hazard. Thousands of tons of ice hard snow was loaded aboard goods trains in Buffalo, to be taken out of the paralysed city for dumping wherever it would cause no trouble.

Exceptionally little snow fell in the western states in the 1977–8 winter, while the east was suffering from too much snow. The Rocky Mountains had hardly enough snow to provide a living for the regular skiing resorts, and Alaska was not thickly enough covered for the troops of the Army's Arctic Test Center to stage manoeuvres.

Exceptionally early snow fell in western states in 1846. During October 8-day snow storms caused drifts of 40 ft (12 m) to accumulate in the Sierra Nevada Mountains, North California, trapping a party of emigrants till the following February, by which time 40 of the original 87 had died.

caused by high snowfall at the head of the glaciers and an extremely steep descent, so that the ice is fast moving. In 1943 an aircraft crashed on Franz Joseph Glacier and the wreckage moved at an average rate of 5 ft (1·5 m) per day for the next 6 years.

In Canada, the Glacier National Park, British Columbia, contains 60 separate glaciers which are fed by winter storms and maintained by sub-freezing temperatures at the high altitude. The largest, Sperry Glacier, covers about 300 acres (121 hectares).

In Central Europe, there are many glaciers whose average speed is about 6–15 in (150–380 mm) per day, and which melt at an average altitude of 6000 ft (1830 m) above sea level into turbid rivers.

In Great Britain permanent snow is confined to a small number of gullies on Ben Nevis 4406 ft (1343 m) in Scotland. Rock formations worn smooth by travelling ice indicate that glaciers did exist in Britain centuries ago. In order that semi-permanent snow beds in Scotland should become glaciers, about 25 summers with temperatures 4F (2C) degrees lower than the present average would be needed, and there is no evidence that this is about to occur.

An avalanche is a mechanical break in a snow or ice cover caused by a weakness in a particular area or layer. Snow may slide over a film of melt water or roll over granular crystals, even accelerate as if on lubricated ball bearings if both conditions apply. A cornice overhanging a precipice is particularly liable to crash to the ground as a result of even the slightest fissure.

A slab avalanche is a whole layer of snow which breaks loose along a weak boundary, leaving a break-off wall.

A loose snow avalanche is a mass of snow which breaks from a particular weak point and fans outwards into a pear-shaped track downhill.

Avalanches can become *airborne* and jump dense timber barriers, particularly when the snow is dry and powdery, and when a strong wind is blowing. Steep slopes frequently avalanche in heavy snow storms because of the additional weight of snow falling upon them. Gentle slopes manage to carry a greater quantity of snow before avalanching, but worse damage is caused when the final break occurs. Attempts are sometimes made to cause frequent, but less damaging, avalanches by means of explosives.

The speed of avalanches may reach 50 mph (80 km/h) along the ground, and thereafter the snow tends to become airborne. Speed increases whenever falling snow is channelled down narrow gulleys.

Amongst measured avalanches, one of the fastest occurred at Glärnisch, Switzerland, on 6 March 1898. Snow travelled down a 44° slope at a mean speed of 217 mph (349 km/h), achieving a distance of 4·3 miles (6·9 km) in 1 minute 12 seconds. After crossing a valley more than a mile wide the avalanche ran some distance up the opposite slope before returning into the valley. Snow dust took 7 minutes to settle.

Avalanches are most frequent in spring, or during winter when there is a sudden change to milder air. They occur wherever there are snow covers on slopes, and most happen unnoticed in uninhabited areas.

The most dangerous aspects of an avalanche

- ☐ Weight of snow, particularly in a wet snow avalanche.
- ☐ Risk of suffocation, within a dry powder airborne avalanche or when buried within snow. The risk is greatest in wet snow, and least after a slow-moving avalanche of dry snow which retains air pockets. Twenty minutes is the average time in which rescuers must trace the tell-tale coloured threads carried by skiers in order to find victims alive. An Austrian postman once survived an exceptional 3 days buried in snow.
- ☐ The pressure wave which builds up ahead of a fast moving avalanche, enough to demolish houses before they are engulfed in snow.
- ☐ The explosion of air within the avalanche when it is suddenly brought to a halt.
- ☐ The partial vacuum behind a fast-moving avalanche which attracts a violent inrush of air, enough to carry a man along with it, even though he escapes the forward blast of the avalanche.
- ☐ Temporary adiabatic heating on the descent, so that snow melts but refreezes at once when brought to a halt.

A man was once carried along by an avalanche and covered in melt water which froze immediately when the avalanche came to rest. His life was saved by the lucky presence of people who were able to assist him out of his prison of ice.

The Cascade and Rocky Mountains have plenty of avalanches but relatively few disasters because they have not been much inhabited except for the gold rush of the 1860s. In 1874 a mining camp near Alta, Utah, was almost entirely destroyed by an avalanche but in the next 35 years only 67 people met their deaths.

The European Alps, however, have deep valleys containing many farms and villages, so that avalanches often result in disaster.

On 13 December 1916 more than 100 avalanches crashed down in the Dolomite valley of Northern Italy. Some 10 000 Austrian and Italian troops were killed and bodies were still being found in 1952.

January and February 1951 saw many avalanches after massive quantities of snow fell between 19 and 21 January, when warm air from the Atlantic converged with cold polar air from over the Alps. Houses were crushed at Andermatt, Zermatt, and Vals in Switzerland, and at Innsbruck and Heiligenblut in Austria. A train in the eastern canton of Grisons, Switzerland, was blocked up in a tunnel by simultaneous avalanches at either end. Over 100 people were killed by snow that season, and many forests were destroyed.

In France, on 10 February 1970, a chalet was buried at Val d'Isère, killing 39 people; eight persons lost their lives near Mont Cenis a fortnight later; and on 15 April a sanatorium was engulfed in snow at Plateau d'Assy resulting in 72 deaths.

Nordenskjold Glacier, South Georgia. The ice edge is about 60 ft (20 m) high and constantly calving into the sea. (Crown copyright, courtesy HMS Endurance)

On 31 January 1982 an avalanche engulfed a party of 18 teenagers in Austria. The instructor and all but six of his pupils were killed. The weather had been treacherous for days and avalanche warnings well publicised.

In England the only disastrous avalanche occurred on 27 December 1836, in the unlikely place of Lewes, Sussex. Heavy snow started to fall on Christmas Eve, and easterly gales were blowing over the top of Cliffe Hill and slamming backwards in vicious eddies over the 200 ft (60 m) chalk precipice at the far end. A cornice of snow gradually built outwards so that it overhung a row of houses which stood below. Next day, when the inhabitants saw what had happened they merely regarded the cornice as a snow sculpture to be admired and not as a serious threat to their safety. Two days later bright sunshine caused a fissure in the cornice, which was noticed by one man who gave the alarm. The householders ignored the warning, and the snow broke away in two separate avalanches, one in the morning and the other in the afternoon. The houses were demolished and eight people were killed.

The chalk cliff was excavated to a safer distance from the road, and a public house was built on the site of the accident and named 'Snow Drop Inn' in commemoration.

Notorious ice avalanches: on 14 August 1919 an estimated one million tons of ice broke off from a glacier near Chamonix, France, and plunged over precipitous rocks. A flood of ice and stone resulted, 2500 ft long, 70 ft wide and 60 ft deep (760 × 21 × 18 m), in which nine visitors from Paris were engulfed without any hope of rescue.

On 10 January 1962 an estimated four million tons of ice avalanched from the 22 205 ft (6768 m) peak of Nevado de Huascaran in Peru. The ice ricocheted from side to side of the valley below and buried four mountain villages and the town of Ranrahirca. As the avalanche continued downhill it gathered up rocks and mud as well, travelling a distance of 11 miles (18 km) at an estimated speed of 60 mph (100 km/h) in about 15 minutes. About 3500 persons were killed in this short space of time, as well as an estimated 10 000 livestock.

Ablation is a general term for the conversion of snow and ice back to vapour and water, and thus returned into the world's water cycle.

Sunshine is not very efficient at thawing a thick snow cover because of the reflective qualities of snow. Some melting may take place on the surface in warm sunshine, but the water often refreezes again at night. Curious shapes may result from uneven melting in sunshine.

Snow penitents are pillars of firn or ice, which sometimes form when there is high insolation over a snow cover, and when air is below 32°F (0°C) and dry. Small amounts of surface snow melt wherever the snow density is least and form tiny hollows in the snow. These hollows concentrate the Sun's rays like a concave mirror and increase the absorption of heat at the bottom of the hollows. The air temperature in these depressions rises, allowing more snow to melt until the centres are laid bare. Eventually only columns of ice project into the cold air. The penitents gradually become undercut, and finally collapse.

Warm air is more effective than sunshine at thawing large quantities of snow. In Britain a sudden change from cold easterly winds to mild Atlantic air streams bringing temperatures of 40°–45°F (4°–7°C) may melt snow at a rate of 2·5 in (65 mm) per day. If warm air is accompanied by sunshine the rate of ablation may be about 7 in (175 mm) per day, but it will be considerably more in rain.

Wet snow is best for building snowmen, and this giant lasted many days after the ground snow had disappeared. (I. Holford)

The 'snow eater' is the name often given to very dry föhn winds which descend on the lee side of mountains and evaporate a snow cover as rapidly as 2 ft (600 mm) per day.

Countries with the least to fear from thawing snow are those like Switzerland, which have regular snow every year, so that centuries of excessive water during spring have carved streams and rivers of adequate width. Mountain streams become torrents of rushing water in spring, but often dry out by the end of summer awaiting the next spring floods.

Countries with the most to fear from thawing snow are those, like Britain, where heavy snow is infrequent and rivers have been gouged by steady rain all through the year. Drainage generally keeps pace with the rate at which rain falls, and rivers and streams are narrower than they would be if they had to cope with a huge stockpile of snow released suddenly in spring. Consequently, an abnormally snowy winter may result in a greater press of water during the thaw than rivers can accommodate.

Severe thaw floods in England and Wales followed the snowy winter of 1947. Warm air and rain nudged its way into south-west England on 10 March and flood water covered vast areas by the 13th. A severe SW gale on the night of 16 March drove water ahead and breached dykes in the Fens of eastern England. Many areas from Yorkshire to Essex were submerged, and one of the worst hit towns was Selby in Yorkshire. Three-quarters of all its houses were under water and the population was fed by field kitchens in one of the few dry places, the market square.

Again in January 1982, the same town suffered from snow thaw. The river Ouse overflowed its banks at Cawood, up river from Selby, creating a lake over thousands of acres of farmland. At least 160 homes and farms in or near Selby were inundated. One man in Cawood has been flooded out 20 times in the 47 years he has lived there.

Widespread flooding in the eastern United States started on 17 January 1937, after a sudden thaw was accompanied by unseasonal and very heavy rain. The Ohio flooded along its entire length, the Mississippi basin was awash, complete towns were engulfed, and ten states became emergency areas. Louisville was entirely marooned and Cincinnati had water 80 ft (24 m) deep in places. Over 100 people lost their lives, and more than $1\frac{1}{2}$ million people were driven from their homes.

Snow cannot thaw in very high latitudes, where air temperature does not rise above freezing level. Small annual quantities of snow accumulate for centuries into dense sheets of firn snow and ice, and then gradually inch their way downhill towards the sea.

The largest expanse of permanent sheet ice, 85 per cent of the world's total, covers the mountainous continent of Antarctica over the South Pole, an area equivalent to the size of Europe and the United States together, or twice the size of Australia. In the northern hemisphere, Greenland has the greatest expanse of permanent ice, about 10 per cent of the world's total. It is estimated that in the unlikely event of these ice sheets melting, they would together raise the level of the oceans approximately 225 ft (70 m). Fortunately there is little likelihood of this happening.

Ice sheets creep downhill at speeds which vary from 50 to 1500 ft (15–450 m) per annum. They crack open into crevasses when moving over rock obstructions and portions may be lifted above the general level of the ice sheet to become domes on top of underlying rocks.

The first expedition to reach the South Pole led by the Norwegian, Captain Amundsen, arrived on 16 December 1911, after a trek of 53 days with dog sledges.

The first trans-Antarctic crossing, of 2158 miles (3473 km), was completed on 2 March 1958 by a British party led by Sir Vivian Fuchs, using sledges and dogs.

The British Transglobe Expedition arrived at Scott Base, Antarctica on 11 January 1981 after a record crossing via the South Pole of 66 days, 40 ahead of schedule. The team used snow mobiles. The expedition is crossing the Arctic Ocean at the time of going to press. (See also Chapter 9)

Ice shelves are ice sheets which have reached the coast line and then continue floating out to sea. Once the ice shelf gets into deep enough water the movement of the sea causes it to fracture and break away at an ice front. Ice shelves vary in thickness from 450 ft (140 m) at the seaward edge, where they suffer

Rock balanced on a pillar of snow at Morsarjokull, SE Iceland. Sun and warm air has gradually melted the snow beneath the rock and the precarious edifice will soon topple. (L. Draper)

considerable melting, to 4000 ft (1200 m) at the shore boundary. Average thickness of the ice sheet over Antarctica is estimated to be 6500 ft (1980 m) and the greatest measured thickness over Antarctica is 14 000 ft (4267 m).

Fast ice is that which has broken from the ice shelves and grounded in shallow water. It offers anchorage to sea ice and extends in a belt around the continent as far as the 900 ft (300 m) depth of sea contour, beyond which the ice floats free to roam the ocean. In some areas, notably between longitude 136°w and 158°w around Antarctica, fast ice may be persistent and extend over a width of about 60 miles (95 km).

Tabular icebergs are broken sections of shelf ice. They are flat topped, the striations of individual annual snowfalls are clearly visible throughout the depth of the break line and they have a white lustre colour like plaster of Paris. They float with four-fifths of their volume below water, present a sheer cliff of ice about 90 ft (27 m) above the sea, and often measure 20–30 miles (30–50 km) in length.

Captain Robert Scott, British explorer, sighted a tabular berg 138 ft (42 m) high on his last expedition in 1911.

Irregularly shaped icebergs are usually calved from glaciers when these reach the sea. They often contain crevasses which the sea and wind open up into caves. Icebergs themselves often calve again and may capsize because of a new centre of gravity.

Glacier icebergs are generally dull white, but occasionally dazzling when the right conditions of light reflect from air bubbles near the surface. They are more dense than tabular bergs, and are better able to resist weathering. Black bergs are darker because of mud and stone embedded within, or because of final expulsion of air in the melting process.

Bergy bits are remnants of large icebergs which are still visible above the sea. One was sighted as far north as 26° 30′S, 25° 40′W by the Russian ship *Dochra* on 30 April 1894.

Growlers are small remnants of icebergs, which are almost entirely submerged beneath the water, but which cause considerable damage to ships when dashed by heavy waves.

Icebergs are a hazard to shipping and satellite photography is used to monitor their progress. Two adjacent giants were photographed off Antarctica in the Weddell Sea during January 1969. They measured 25 × 55 miles (40 × 90 km) and 38 × 100 miles (60 × 160 km) and were separated by only a few miles of open water. They travelled 300 miles (480 km) in 4 months.

An iceberg, 45 miles long and 25 miles wide (72 km × 40 km), drifted 300 miles out into the Weddell Sea from April to July 1977, threatening the shipping route round Cape Horn. However, it became frozen again into the pack ice during the Antarctic winter. It was estimated to contain enough fresh water to supply drought-ridden California for 1000 years!

A ship approaching Antarctica during summer may expect to see approximately 300 bergs before reaching the coast, the first visible evidence of their proximity being a dampening down of the sea to give an oily appearance.

Greenland's icebergs drift into the North Atlantic via Baffin Bay. One of these sank the *Titanic* at 41° 16′N, 50° 4′W on her maiden voyage. It was the night of 14/15 April 1912 and the iceberg was one of the dark variety and not seen until the ship was within about 500 yd (450 m). The *Titanic* was holed in collision and 1503 people out of the 2201 aboard were drowned.

Icebergs could be a source of fresh water for the arid regions of the world, a recurring dream which is unlikely to be realised for some time. It is difficult to secure towing lines to a berg, which changes shape as it melts and becomes liable to capsize. More than 50 per cent might melt en route to low latitudes and there is no obvious way of converting the residue back into water before further melting. Moreover, a berg cannot be docked alongside land because nine-tenths of its volume is below the water line.

15. Hail

Hailstones are ice crystals, which have been tossed up and down by strong vertical currents in a cumulonimbus cloud, acquiring one coating of ice after another until they are heavy enough to fall to ground. Crystals attain coatings of clear ice when in contact with large supercooled water drops which freeze only slowly, and get covered in rime when amongst small supercooled drops. Hailstones are usually spherical but are sometimes distorted by the manner in which they spin in the air currents.

Soft hail or graupel is small and opaque, having frozen speedily enough to trap air within the ice. It has a soft nucleus, surrounded by a coating of clear ice where the freezing process has been slowed down by the release of latent heat.

Large hailstones have alternate rings of clear and opaque ice. Cross sections reveal details of the hailstone's journey up and down in the cloud as clearly as concentric rings in the trunk of a tree reveal weather conditions during growth. Twenty-five separate layers have been counted in one hailstone.

Ice meteors are large pieces of ice, fallen from the sky, whose origin is uncertain. Often they have not been made available to persons competent to dissect them or determine their chemical composition. Ice meteors could be super hailstones, carried in exceptionally powerful small-scale vortices like tornadoes, or they could be congealed masses of small stones. Alternatively, some may have broken from aircraft, after forming on the outside by passage through supercooled cloud or by leakage from some inside domestic installation. The inexplicable ice meteors are those which fall from clear skies. An American study carried out in 1960 showed that in one third of the cases investigated no clouds were within 600 miles from where the ice fell.

Ice meteors, unlike hailstones, usually fall singly, but three fell within a mile of each other from a clear sky at Timberville in Virginia on 7 March 1976.

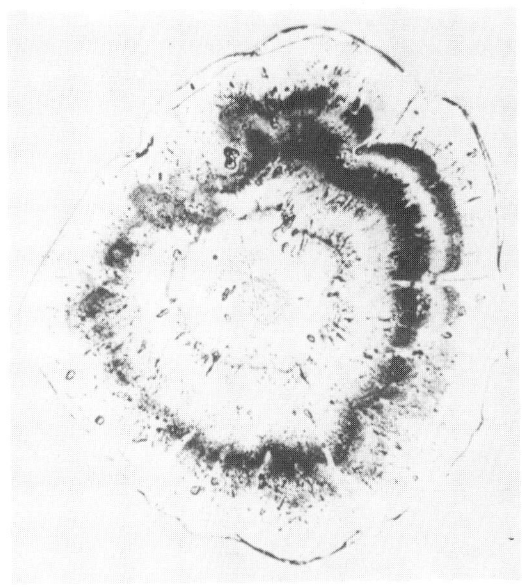

Cross section through a typical hailstone. (Crown Copyright, Meteorological Office)

Research continues and the golden rule for anyone finding an ice meteor is to consign it to a deep freezer. Then report the find to a local meteorological office.

The largest authenticated single hailstone fell in the United States at Coffeyville, Kansas, on 3 September 1970, weighing 1·67 lb (758 g). It measured $7\frac{1}{2}$ in (190 mm) in diameter and $17\frac{1}{2}$ in (444 mm) in circumference when photographed and could have been as big as 8 in (200 mm) in diameter when first picked up.

The heaviest recorded hailstone in Britain, weighing 5 oz (141 g), fell at Horsham, Sussex, on 5 September 1958.

The most closely scrutinised ice meteor was one which providentially dropped at the feet of R. F. Griffiths, a lightning observer for the Electrical Research

Association, who was immediately aware of the importance of the sudden evidence from the sky. On the evening of Monday, 2 April 1973, strong northerly winds were blowing in the Manchester area, and the sky was half covered with clouds with a base of 2000 ft (600 m). At 7.54 pm there was a very bright flash of lightning — and one only — which was seen over a wide area of Manchester. About 10 minutes later a huge lump of ice fell to the ground in Burton Road, Manchester, mostly shattering into small pieces. One large lump remained, which Griffiths hurriedly took home and deposited in the freezer. Later, in laboratory tests, thin sections of the block were cut and photographed by both reflected and transmitted light. They were found to have 51 layers of clear ice separated by thinner layers of trapped air bubbles. The fragment was 5·5 in (140 mm) in length, weighed 20 oz (567 g) and appeared to have broken off at the nucleus of growth, which was less than 0·4 in

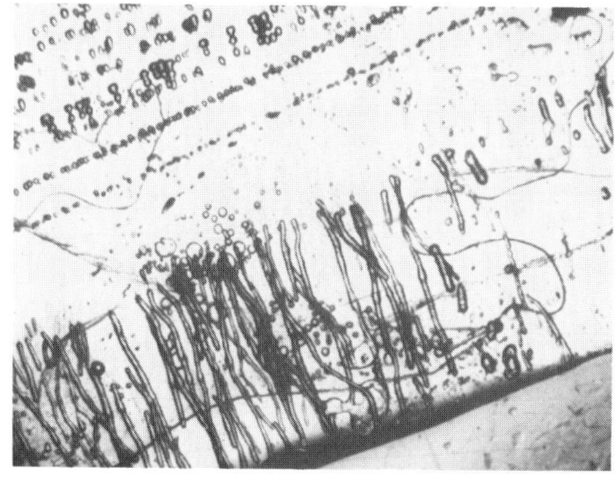

(10 mm) in diameter. It was estimated that the complete ice meteor might have weighed 2–4 lb (1–2 kg), thus comparing favourably with the Coffeyville record hailstone. Analysis of a sample of melt-water from the ice meteor indicated that it was composed of cloud water. Close questioning of personnel at the nearby airport revealed that none of the aircraft in the vicinity had experienced any icing and no other hail was reported nearer than Wilmslow, several miles away. The origin of the meteor remains a mystery.

In equatorial regions hail is mainly experienced over mountainous country, where altitude ensures a temperature low enough for hail to remain frozen until reaching the ground.

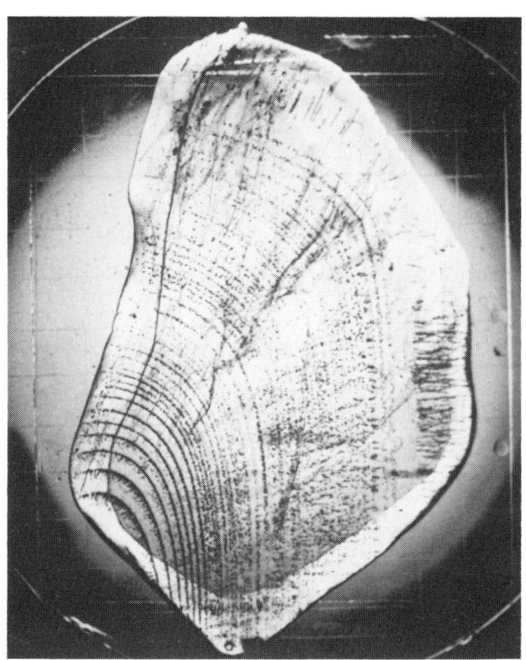

Cross section of the ice meteor which fell at Manchester on 2 April 1973, viewed by transmitted light. Left: an enlargement from the outer rim. (R.F. Griffiths)

In polar regions hail does not occur because cumulonimbus do not develop to great heights, and temperatures within the clouds are too low to contain large supercooled water drops.

In middle latitudes, during the warmer months of the year, hail forms mainly over large land masses. Thermal up-currents in cumulonimbus are then at their strongest, and contain an abundance of supercooled water drops on which small ice crystals can feed.

Hailstone diameter is usually between 0·2 and 2·0 in (5–50 mm), anything over 0·4 in (10 mm) being termed 'large'. Any stones greater than 2·0 in (50 mm) are usually conglomerates of smaller ones, bonded together by regelation in the same way as ice floes bond together into pack ice. Hailstones are more often described by their similarity to known objects, like peas, golfballs or grapefruit.

The frequency of hail is difficult to assess, because stones often melt before being noticed or before they can be measured. Many hailstones bounce out of the apertures of rain gauges, and those which fall inside melt to become indistinguishable from rainfall.

A simple hail indicator can be made by stretching uncreased aluminium foil tightly across a frame or an

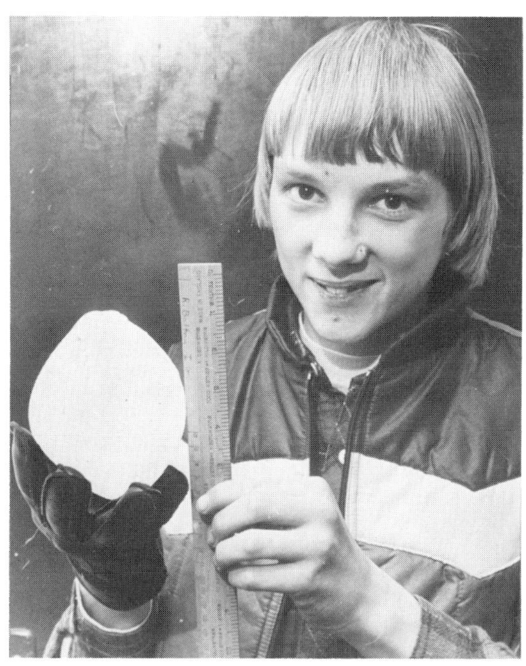

Ice lump weighing $1\frac{1}{2}$ lb (608 g) which fell in Hawkshaw, Lancashire in 1980, in the hand of R. Bolton who found it. (E. Webster)

Below: Unusual hailstone which fell at Sydney, Australia, on 3 January 1971. The scale is in centimetres. (S.C. Mossop)

Foot of page: Hail stopped play at Wimbledon on 26 June 1980. (Keystone Press)

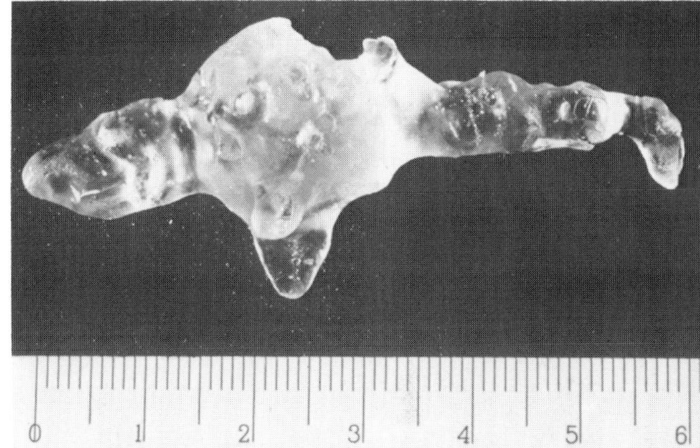

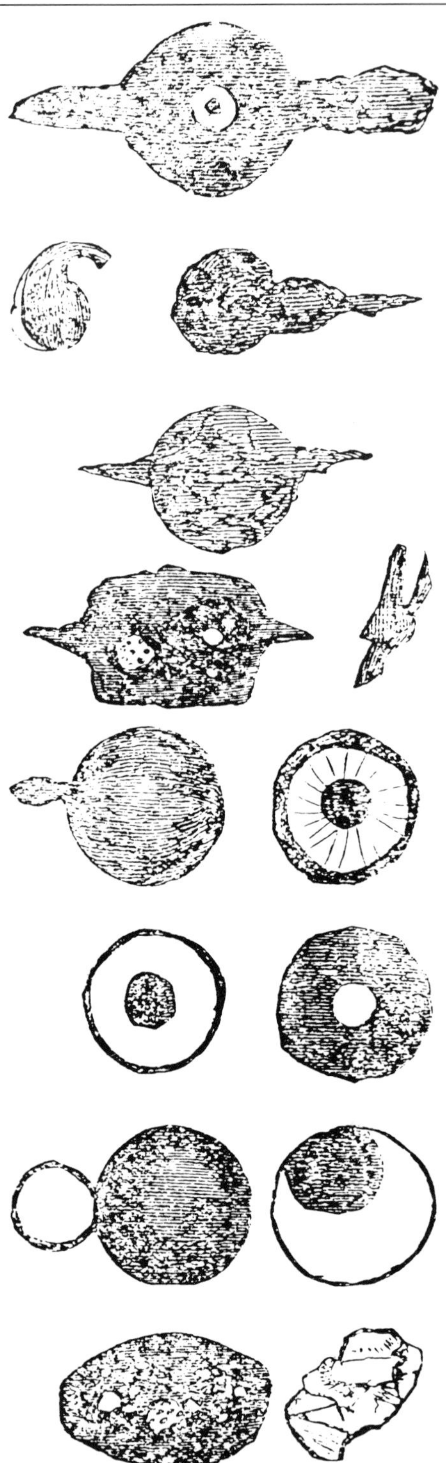

open tin, and leaving it in an unsheltered exposure. Hailstones striking the foil leave readily visible imprints.

In South Africa this idea has been developed further. Imprints made by hail have been compared with dents made by pellets of known size and fired at a known velocity onto the measuring substance. Hail size is then deduced.

In Italy, a hail storm in August 1977, made shallow dents of $\frac{1}{2}$–$\frac{3}{4}$in (10–15 mm) diameter, on 1 mm thick metal bodies of several new cars in transit to Britain.

The oldest known hailstone imprints are fossilised, and date from about 160 million years ago. They were discovered in the cliffs of north east Yorkshire, south of the Peak Fault at Ravenscar. Hail fell originally into mud of plastic consistency, soft enough to give way under the falling hailstones, but stiff enough to retain the impressions of the stones after they had melted.

In Britain hail does not usually remain on the ground for long because air temperatures tend to be above melting level. Nevertheless, on 6 August 1956, hail which fell in Arundel, Sussex, to a depth of 2 ft (60 mm), was swept aside by road sweepers on to a grass verge beneath a dense cover of trees. The hail survived in this shade for more than 3 days, despite maximum screen temperatures locally of 65–74°F (18–23°C). It became steadily more disguised as dirt was thrown over it by passing traffic.

On the afternoon of 25 June 1980 there was a severe, but local storm in Kent which lasted 1$\frac{1}{2}$ hours. There was almost continuous thunder and 4·5 in (116·1 mm) of rain mixed with pea-sized hail. The hail lay on level ground, looking like snow, but in

On 29 May, 1859 there was a violent hailstorm over the Beeston Observatory, Nottingham just before 6 pm. Hailstones fell very thickly, some transparent, some opaque or semi-opaque, some veined and some with minute air bubbles within. Mr Lowe, from the Observatory, collected and sketched the sample on the left, the largest of which measured 1$\frac{1}{4}$in (32 mm). Larger stones must have fallen because one was reported, 23 minutes after the storm had ceased, which measured 1$\frac{3}{8}$ by $\frac{5}{8}$in (35 by 16 mm).

The stones fell very gently, considering their extraordinary size, so that many of the grotesque shapes were unbroken by their fall. Only half a mile away, at the Highfield House Observatory no hail fell at all.

The wind that day was easterly and several thunderstorms had occurred during the afternoon.
(Illustrated London News)

Death and damage caused by hail

ARGENTINA 16 September 1832
Charles Darwin reported a severe hailstorm near the foot of the Sierra Tapalguen. He was told that most of the local wild animals had been killed as a result, something he doubted until he was shown carcases of deer, ostriches and small birds, which he knew could not have been hunted in such a short time.

CANADA 14 July 1953
Hailstones as large as golfballs fell in Alberta and covered an area 140 × 5 miles (225 × 8 km). Thousands of birds were killed, many having their skulls crushed.

CHINA
On 19 June 1932 a hailstorm killed 200 people in Western Hunan Province, and thousands were injured. Hongkong, which has had only six hailstorms since 1940, had two on consecutive days, 5–6 March 1980. Hailstones as big as golfballs caused considerable agricultural damage.

BRITAIN
On 8 June 1957 an estimated equivalent of 1 in (25 mm) of rain fell as hailstones at Camelford, Cornwall. They were bouncing 3 ft (1 m) high and 12 ft (4 m) horizontally. It had been wet all day, with a total rainfall of 7·1 in (180 mm), and the hailstones were washed along in flood water, coalescing into masses of ice. The inn yard at Camelford was piled knee deep with solid blocks of hailstones.

A comparatively rare winter hailstorm occurred at Kingsbridge, Devon, on 13 December 1978. Hail like 'mothballs' fell for 15 seconds during which time greenhouses and skylights were broken and cars damaged. One hailstone went right through a roof, and insurance brokers were inundated with claims.

Recent ice meteors
On 23 January 1972, a block of ice more than 3 ft (1 m) square smashed into the ground in Shirley, Surrey.

On 9 January 1973, an ice meteor weighing 10 lb (4·5 kg) fell out of the sky shattering a porch at West Wickham, Kent.

On 2 January 1977, ice weighing about 110 lb (50 kg) smashed through the roof and into a bedroom in a house in Ponders End, Middlesex.

On 2 October 1980, a huge chunk of ice crashed through the roof of a house in Plymouth, Devon, leaving a 2-ft hole in a bedroom ceiling. At the same time another block fell through a roof in nearby Roborough.

On 10 December 1980, an ice lump fell into a garden in Birmingham during the night. It measured 12 in (30 cm) in circumference and weighed 22 oz (626 g).

INDIA
On 30 April 1888 hailstones as large as cricket balls fell in Moradabad and Beheri. About 250 people were killed and more than 1600 sheep and goats.

On 27 May 1959, hailstones battered holes 10–15 in (250–375 mm) in an aircraft at Delhi.

SOUTH AFRICA 15 January 1980
A hailstorm over Jan Smuts airport, Johannesburg, damaged more than a dozen aircraft and disrupted international flights. Cars were also damaged, windows were smashed and traffic was brought to a standstill.

SYRIA 2 June 1978
A severe hailstorm hit the Jablah coastal area. Stones weighed up to $\frac{1}{2}$ lb (220 g) and 40 of the 53 villages affected lost all their crops. It was the worst hailstorm for 100 years and caused 60 000 people to face starvation.

UNITED STATES
On 30 June 1979 Fort Collins, Colorado, was pounded by hailstones the size of grapefruit. Students who were playing football at the time were lucky to be wearing helmets, but one 3-month-old baby died from a fractured skull, hit by the hail.

In April 1977 a DC-9 aeroplane crashed in New Hope, Georgia during a violent hailstorm while making a descent for landing. Sixty-eight people were killed.

On 8 May 1926 at Dallas, Texas, hailstones the size of cricket balls caused damage amounting to 2 million dollars in just 15 minutes.

A conglomerate of hailstones, and one cross section, drawn after a storm over Messina, Italy, on 17 August 1857. Many ice stones weighed over 3 lb (1.4 kg) and in the mountains weights up to 8 lb (3.6 kg) were reported. Much damage was done to roofs and vegetation, many people were hurt and one child was killed. Some fishermen in an open boat survived by jumping into the sea and sheltering under their boat. (Illustrated London News)

places it was swept by water into huge drifts about 2 ft (60 cm) deep. Some of these did not melt away till the evening of the 26th. During the storm air temperature fell from 60°F (15·6°C) to 44°F (6·7°C). Soft fruit crops were badly damaged.

Unusual hailstones are sometimes reported from different parts of the world.

In Australia knobbly stones with icicle extensions fell in the northern suburbs of Sydney on 3 January 1971. They consisted almost entirely of clear ice but had small opaque centres.

In Germany tragic human 'hail' occurred on two occasions over the Rhön mountains. In 1930, glider pilots, caught in a thundercloud, baled out of their gliders and were carried up and down within the supercooled cloud till they fell to earth, frozen within ice prisons. Only one man out of five survived the ordeal. Another pilot died in a similar manner in 1938.

In the United States at Dubuque, Iowa, on 16 June 1882, hailstones up to 5 in (125 mm) in diameter fell during a 13-minute storm, and in two stones small living frogs were found. They had been carried up in the vertical currents of the storm, and acquired coatings of ice before becoming heavy enough to fall back to earth.

Guinand's anti-hail device, similar to the Stiger Gun, illustrated in 'Petit Journal', 1901. (Mary Evans Picture Library)

Protective measures against hail have been sought throughout history. Farmers in particular despair at the way hail can strip leaves from vineyards and tea plantations, batter crops of cereals to a useless pulp, and cause irremediable damage to young citrus fruits.

Primitive tribes used to shoot arrows into clouds, in order to frighten away the evil spirits, which they thought inhabited the clouds and were making hail.

Christian communities started ringing church bells in the 8th century in order to exorcise the evil spirits in the clouds. It was a dangerous procedure because hail often falls in thunderstorms and church towers were vulnerable to lightning. However, despite an unfortunately high number of deaths, bell-ringing remained popular as a hail prevention method.

Cannons were first fired into clouds over central Europe during the 16th century, but there were no conclusive results from the experiments. There was considerable wrangling about whether storms were merely diverted from satisfied vineyard owners to aggrieved ones.

The Stiger Gun was introduced in 1896 by Albert Stiger, burgomaster in the Steirmark district of Austria, after a series of disastrous hailstorm years. In order to protect the valley, 36 stations were established and equipped with cast-iron muzzle loading mortars. These had 3 cm bore, were 20 cm long, charged with 180 g powder and mounted on stout wooden platforms to fire vertically. Metal smoke stacks were mounted above the muzzles to act as sounding boxes and to make more noise. The following year, there was no damaging hail at all in the valley, and the gun defence attained immediate fame. By the turn of the century, 7000 stations protected north Italy alone, and Stiger guns had been sent to Russia, Spain and the United States. This method was not without its dangers, and it was the direct cause of eleven deaths and 60 serious injuries in 1900 alone.

Meteorologists were divided in opinion about whether the whole idea was nonsense or not, and a conference on the matter was held in Graz, Austria, in July 1902. The Austrian and Italian governments set up two test areas, equipped for even bigger barrages, but within 2 years both areas had disastrous storms. The idea was discredited once more, but all

Reed matting protects this orange grove at Sorrento, Italy, from damage by hail. The semi-permeable palisade acts as a wind break. (V.D. Shaw)

that had really been proved was that the method was not infallible. Rockets continued to be fired experimentally elsewhere.

Modern rocket trials started in July 1963, in the Kericho area of Kenya, where the tea plantations on high ground suffer badly from hail. Results showed that despite a higher than usual incidence of storms, hail caused less damage since it was often 'mushy'.

In 1969, Soviet scientists claimed to have reduced hail damage by up to 80 per cent in selected agricultural test areas of the Caucasus by firing artillery shells, carrying seeding chemicals, into storms. The size of hailstones was reduced from an average 2 in (50 mm) diameter to an average 0·4 in (10 mm).

Possible explanations for the success of some rocketry experiments to prevent hail:

Nuclei introduced into clouds, either by the rocket's own explosives or special chemical seeds, encourage more supercooled drops to freeze, and thus they remain small.

Pressure waves from the rocket explosion may cause cracking of large hailstones which contain air pockets. Such stones have been known to explode with loud reports when falling to the ground.

Shock waves may speed the freezing of water drops and increase the proportion of soft hail in a cloud.

Overhead cover provides more practical protection for the orange groves in Sorrento, Italy. Permanent vertical pallisades shelter the groves against the wind and these are surmounted by a horizontal framework of cross bars. Tidy piles of rush mats sit astride the framework at intervals, capped with two mats at an angle, like the roof of a dovecot. At the first indication of hail, the mats are spread out to make a roof for the orange trees below. The hail melts and seeps through as water instead of being destructive ammunition.

16. Electricity in the atmosphere and thunderstorms

Electricity is the hallmark of modern living, yet the word itself derives from a substance whose electrostatic properties were known even in classical times.

'Elektron' is the Greek word for amber — a fossilised resin — which used to be much prized as a material for ornaments. From the writings of Thales, a philosopher of the 6th century BC, we know that the Greeks were aware of the fact that amber, when rubbed, acquired the property of attracting small particles of light weight. This fact did not at the time appear to have any connection with thunder and lightning, which were considered to be the visible and audible expressions of displeasure by the gods. Aristotle (384–322 BC) attempted a more materialistic explanation, suggesting that thunder was the noise made by air which was ejected from one cloud and then hit another, and that lightning was the ejected wind burning.

Dr William Gilbert (1540–1603), English physician, discovered that many other materials besides amber acquired the ability to attract small particles when rubbed. In 1600 he published a treatise *De Magnete* (things which attract) in which he introduced the terms 'electrics' and 'electricity'. He distinguished two kinds of 'electrics': vitreous electrics produced when glass was rubbed with silk; and resinous electrics produced when amber or sealing wax was rubbed with fur. Gilbert noted that the presence of moisture lessened the attracting abilities of the substances which were rubbed. 'Non-electrics' were defined as materials which remained unaffected by rubbing.

Other scientists continued the experiments, and by the end of the 18th century it was known that similar electrics repelled each other and dissimilar electrics were attracted. Moreover, electrics tended to collect more easily around points or curved contours of the substances rubbed.

Benjamin Franklin (1706–90), American scientist and statesman, was convinced that lightning was a form of electricity, and in 1746 he began his researches.

In July 1752, on a suitably cloudy day, which experience told him might result in a thunderstorm, he flew a kite made of a silk handkerchief stretched taut over two crossed sticks. Near the end of the anchoring hemp twine he attached a metal key, and, between the key and his hand, he used a silk ribbon which he kept dry by standing inside a shed doorway.

Many clouds passed overhead without providing Franklin with the evidence he wanted but eventually rain fell. The kite twine became wet and a few loose threads moved apart, as if containing similar 'electrics'. Franklin stretched his hand towards the key and sparks jumped the gap between. He had proved that 'electrics' had been collected from the cloud, but without the rubbing of vitreous or resinous substances.

The old descriptions of the two kinds of 'electrics' became inappropriate and Franklin renamed them positive electric charge (+ve) instead of 'vitreous electric', and negative electric charge (−ve) instead of 'resinous electric'. The two together are known collectively as static electricity or electrostatic charges. Non-electrics were later renamed conductors when it was discovered that electric current would flow through them.

Michael Faraday (1791–1867), English chemist and electrical engineer, discovered that electrostatic charges always collect on the outside of a hollow object. His own experiments were carried out with a cage, but any hollow object may be described as a 'Faraday cage' when its reaction to electrostatic charge is discussed.

Right: Lightning over Nottingham. (M.J. Hammersley)

Sir Joseph John Thomson (1856–1940), British physicist, discovered the electrical nature of the atom. Every atom consists of a nucleus of particles called 'neutrons' (without electric charge) and particles called 'protons' which have positive electric charge. Electrons are negative charges, which revolve around the nucleus and which are equal in number to the protons in the nucleus. The electrons of some materials can transfer their allegiance when stimulated by heat or friction. Atoms which gain electrons then have more negative charges than positive, and are said to be 'negatively' charged. Atoms which have lost electrons then have more protons than electrons and are said to be 'positively' charged. Insulating materials have electrons, which are firmly bound to their own atom and cannot move independently.

Separation of electric charge by friction occurs all the time, by people walking over the ground, by particles rubbing together in the air, and by road vehicles travelling rapidly over the ground. Normally, charge separation is small and one charge leaks to earth unnoticed, while the other is neutralised gradually by ions in the air.

Ions are particles in the atmosphere which have acquired separated charge by various natural processes. There is a concentration of these particles in the ionosphere, the region 40 miles (60 km) above ground; they also occur in the troposphere. Any small electric charge which collects on objects attracts ions of opposite charge, and they neutralise each other. When the charge is greater than normal, for instance at the sharp point of a conductor, a more violent discharge is made, with a visible spark. This is often accompanied by a crackle or hissing noise, and the whole phenomenon is called a brush discharge.

Brush discharge, as defined above, has become a particular feature of daily living ever since synthetic materials, which are nearly always insulators, started to predominate over natural fibres and leather which are usually conductors. Clothes fizz and spark when pulled off quickly, gyrate around the hand, and become so attracted to each other that they are hard to separate.

In July 1980, prior to a violent thunderstorm, nine people were fishing 6 miles (10 km) off the coast of North Yorkshire. The sea was very smooth and the air warm and oppressive. Suddenly the men's hair, even their moustaches, stood on end until the storm began 20 minutes later when it fell flat again. The boat was the only protuberance on an otherwise flat sea.

A frequent situation for electrostatic shock is when sliding across car seats to enter or leave the vehicle. Charge clings to the body, unable to earth through synthetic fabric, but then discharges painfully when the hand stretches to shut the door.

Busy secretaries, too, scuffing their feet across synthetic carpets, accumulate an electrostatic charge which may jump, as a shock, to a metal filing cabinet.

People who are prone to such shock can ameliorate the problem by wearing clothes made of natural fibre and by presenting broad areas of the body, rather than pointed fingers, towards known conductors. However, there are some unfortunate people who find this no solution and who dread the moment when they must unlock their car door.

Relative humidity is the chief factor in determining indoor brush discharge. The lower the relative humidity the smaller the chance of electrostatic charges leaking away to the air. The worst problems arise in very cold climates. For example, in Whitehorse Yukon, Canada, air temperature outdoors is often below −30°F (−34°C) and relative humidity usually above 80 per cent. When such air is heated indoors to a comfortable 70°F (21°C), relative humidity falls to around 5 per cent. Even humidifiers cannot raise relative humidity enough to prevent shocks.

St Elmo's Fire is a brush discharge which takes place in the atmosphere when there exists a strong electrical field. The discharge occurs from protuberances, such as ships' masts, wind vanes or aircraft wing tips, and is usually blue-green in colour, or sometimes whitish. The Fire is often accompanied by a crackling noise.

This brush discharge has traditionally been regarded as an omen of good fortune, and was at one time called 'the fire of Castor and Pollux', sons of Zeus. Later the fire was named after St Elmo, who was Bishop of Gaeta, Italy, in the 4th century, and became the patron saint of fire whose protection was much invoked by mariners.

In the late 12th century, St Elmo's Fire appeared at the masthead of a ship in the fleet of Richard I and was thought to be an apparition of the Virgin Mary.

Andes Glow or Andes Lights is a brush discharge, sometimes seen in the vicinity of mountain peaks.

Observations come mainly from the Andes mountains in South America, but sightings have been reported in the European Alps, Mexico and Lapland. The light takes the form of a single flash, intermittent or regular flashes, or a beam shining above the peaks. The phenomenon is usually seen when relative humidity is low. Weather is often cloudless, but sightings occur mostly towards dawn when a strong temperature inversion often exists, a factor which may be contributory to the discharge.

Brush discharge can be dangerous in the presence of inflammable vapour, and is suspected of causing explosions during vigorous cleansing of empty tankers.

One of the worst disasters, attributed to brush discharge, happened on 6 May 1937. The German airship *Hindenburg* had crossed the Atlantic and was close to the mooring mast at Lakehurst airfield, New Jersey, with her lines already thrown out, ready for tying up. There was a sudden flash; an explosion, and in moments the airship was ablaze: 35 people were killed, or later died of burns, but 62 miraculously survived. The cause of the explosion was never proven, but St Elmo's Fire had been seen playing around the airship during its flight against strong head winds. It was suggested that the charge had jumped violently across to the mast tip, and ignited some leaking inflammable gas.

St Elmo's Fire, a brush discharge often seen at the tips of masts or spars. (Mary Evans Picture Library)

A thunderstorm is the most powerful electrical phenomenon in nature. Extremely high electrical differences build up in deep cloud and eventually discharge as lightning. Thunder is the sound made by the violent expansion of air, which is heated along the line of the flash.

Thunder rumbles because the sound waves echo from intervening obstructions. Freak reflections or bending of sound waves may cause silent zones quite near to the storm, while the noise is heard far away. Thunder is usually audible 10 miles (16 km) away but it has been heard from a distance of 40 miles (65 km).

A thunderstorm day is defined as one in which thunder is heard even if the listener does not actually suffer the storm. Statistics, therefore, do not necessarily imply that a storm has been overhead, merely in the neighbourhood.

In Britain, 9 July 1981 was particularly thundery, with many parts of England and Wales suffering their worst storms for 5 years. London had torrential rain which caused considerable flooding and the thunderstorm was probably the most ferocious since records began in central London in 1940.

The separation of electrical charge within a cloud is still not fully understood. Friction, and the processes of water transformation, play their parts. Water drops which break apart acquire positive charge on the larger fragment but negative charge on the finer spray. Supercooled water drops which freeze, often with a thin coating of rime outside, acquire negative charge while the tiny ice splinters or droplets ejected in the freezing process acquire positive charge. There is a charge transfer between ice crystals of different temperature and between ice crystals which rub together. All these processes, and probably others not yet discovered, contribute to the electrification of a cloud.

Cumulonimbus are the principal thunderstorm clouds, because they contain violent and disruptive winds as well as a plentiful supply of supercooled water drops. Glaciation triggers off large electrical charge separation. It has been proved that positive charge collects at the top of a cumulonimbus and negative charge near the base, usually in the region of the 14°F (−10°C) isotherm. There is also a small positive charge area low down in the region of heavy rain. The negatively charged base of the cloud attracts a positively charged 'shadow' on the ground, which follows the cloud along the highest contours available in an attempt to meet the attracting charge above.

Thunderstorms occur in two types of cumulonimbus clouds: those with low bases, probably less than 2000 ft (600 m) above ground, which develop in air streams which are unstable from the ground up to great heights; and those with high bases at 6000 ft (1800 m) or more, which develop from castellanus cloud in an upper layer of unstable air during heat waves. The necessary atmospheric conditions for thunderstorms to develop are therefore the same as those necessary for the formation of cumulonimbus clouds (see also Chapter 11).

Thunderstorms of short duration may occur at any time of the year when conditions are suitable for the development of low base cumulonimbus. They are most frequent in late spring and summer, but they can strike in winter and often accompany vigorous cold fronts. Winter thunderstorms are sometimes called 'freaks', but they are really quite normal occurrences. However, they usually pass quickly and therefore make less of an impression than the high level storms of summer.

Low-base thunderstorms travel with approximately the same speed and direction as the wind at 10 000 ft (3000 m), and this is usually fairly strong in an unstable air stream. There is only a germ of truth in the tradition that 'thunderstorms travel *against* the wind'. An approaching cumulonimbus affects surface wind in much the same way as a vacuum cleaner, pushed across a carpet, affects the particles of dirt lying in its path. They are sucked *towards* the cleaner in the opposite direction from that in which it is being pushed. Similarly, surface wind alters temporarily as it gets sucked towards the base of an approaching cumulonimbus which is nevertheless moving inexorably towards an observer.

Thunderstorms of long duration occur in high-base cumulonimbus, which develop after the accumulated heat of summer breaks from a lower stable layer of air into unstable air above. These clouds travel on the upper winds, which are usually light at the end of a summer anticyclone. Moreover, the idea that 'thunderstorms move in circles' is no worse than slightly inaccurate. Each storm cell probably lasts no longer than 30–40 minutes and does

Water droplets and tiny splinters of ice being repelled electrically from the rime-coated surface of a small hailstone. Each ejected ice crystal may form the nucleus on which more supercooled drops can freeze, making for rapid glaciation of a cloud with a build-up of high electrical voltage. (R.J. Cheng)

not have time to move in a circle. However, each down draught from one dying thunder cloud provides the impetus for another to form within the self-contained region of unstable air. Hence self-propagated thunderstorms may be observed in all directions during a whole night of thunder activity, giving the impression that one storm only has been moving in a circle.

The most frequent thunderstorms happen within equatorial regions.

In Uganda, Tororo suffered an annual average of 251 thunderstorm days between 1967 and 1976.

In Indonesia, on the mountainous island of Java, an average 322 thunderstorm days per annum were recorded at Bogor for the period 1916–19. Even allowing for the fact that this figure included days when thunder was heard in the distance but no stormy weather materialised, Bogor is probably the most thundery place in the world. It has at least 25 severe storms each year, when cloud-to-earth lightning occurs within a ½-mile radius at least every 30 seconds for up to half an hour or more.

Thunderstorms are virtually unknown in polar regions because cumulus clouds do not develop to any great height, and there are no intense heat waves. These regions, however, have many spectacular electrical displays, caused by friction between ice crystals in snow blizzards, or by solar discharges which appear as waving curtains of light due to the Earth's magnetic field. (See Aurora).

In middle latitudes thunderstorms are most frequent over land masses providing a strong thermal heat source. In the United States the frequency of thunderstorm days varies from three per annum along the west coast, to approximately 45 in the central states and up to 70 in Florida. In Britain, the Midlands have an average 20 thunderstorm days per annum, and the south-east of England has a relatively high number of 15 because cumulonimbus are often 'imported' from France. The remaining coastal regions of the country average only four thunderstorm days per annum, although experienced observers reported 38 at Stonyhurst, Lancashire in 1912 and at Huddersfield, West Yorkshire in 1967. Possibly other places could have equalled these records, but for the difficulty of detecting distant thunder amidst all the other noises of urban life.

Thunderstorms in progress at 6 pm, or during the previous 6 hours, on 9 July 1981. (The Daily Weather Summary, as issued by the London Weather Centre)

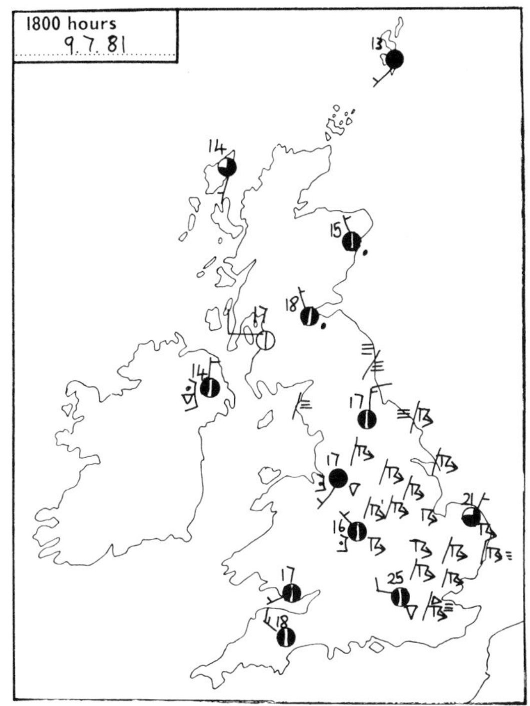

Thunder head seen from Hayling Island, looming above the haze and giving a violent storm over the mainland. (I. Holford)

Lightning is the discharge of an electric field which has developed within a cloud; the discharge may occur within the cloud, from one cloud to another or between cloud and ground. However, since air is normally non-conductive, discharge can only occur after channels of ionised air have been established.

A leader stroke is a channel of ionised air, formed when electrons are accelerated by the intense electrical field. The stroke darts downwards from the cloud base in progressive steps of about 150–300 ft (50–100 m) until it establishes an open conductive channel to the ground. The first leader strokes are normally invisible but the final stepped leader which reaches ground is visible, and looks like an illuminated river with tributaries. The speed of the leader stroke varies enormously, from as little as 100 miles/s (160 km/s) to as much as 1000 miles/s (1600 km/s).

The return stroke streaks up the channel from ground to cloud, and is the faster bright flash usually referred to as lightning. The speed of the return stroke may approach 87 000 miles/s (140 000 km/s), which is nearly half the speed of light itself. The flash, therefore, lasts a mere millionth of a second, but persistence of the image on the retina of the human eye makes it appear to last longer. There is evidence that the temperature of the air in the channel of the return stroke may reach 54 000°F (30 000°C), which is more than five times hotter than the surface of the Sun.

A typical lightning flash consists of three or four leaders each followed by a return stroke, but one flash sequence was photographed and found to have 26 strokes. The width of the channel is seldom more than 1 in (25 mm).

Lightning appears to be forked when both leader and return stroke are visible without obstruction from other clouds.

Sheet lightning is forked lightning which is obscured by other cloud, and is therefore seen only as a reflected illumination.

Volcanic lightning often accompanies the eruption of volcanoes and has been described as 'twisted' or 'serpentine'. The phenomenon is still the subject of research but is thought to be caused by the charging of steam particles as water is fragmented into droplets on contact with hot lava surfaces.

The distance of a lightning flash from an observer can be estimated by the difference between the almost instantaneous receipt of the light signal and the delayed slower noise of thunder. Sound travels at approximately 1 mile per 5 seconds (1 km per 3 seconds). So that, if T is the time in seconds between the flash seen and the thunder heard, the distance of the flash is:

$$\frac{T}{5} \text{ miles or } \frac{T}{3} \text{ km}$$

Sferics are directional fixes on lightning flashes received by aerial and registered on cathode ray tubes at observing stations some distance from each other. Thousands of electrical discharges occur in the atmosphere every second, but only relatively few reach the ground as a strike. In Britain there is an average six lightning strikes per mile^2 (4 per km^2) every year.

Fulgurites are thin tubes of glass formed when lightning enters quartz sand. Charles Darwin found many near the mouth of the river Plate, Argentina, in July 1832, and described them in detail. The fulgurites were generally vertical in the sand, though a few had side branches. Some of the heads were exposed above the shifting dunes and the longest he could piece together measured over 5 ft (nearly 2 m). The outer surfaces were of glazed rounded sand particles, some with longitudinal furrows caused by compression of the surrounding sand in the softened quartz. Internal surfaces of the tubes were completely vitrified, sometimes with a metallic lustre, the thickness of the tubes varying between 1/30 and 1/10 in (0·8–2·5 mm).

Thunderbolts do not exist in the way many people believe, ie as solid objects ejected from a thunderstorm cloud. However, lightning does make a loud noise when it strikes the ground and it throws up a plume of steam when striking water. On 14 August 1975, lightning struck ground at Hampstead, the highest area of London, and an observer nearby reported that the noise sounded like machine-gun fire.

Ball lightning may or may not exist. Many people, including some meteorologists, think it is all imagination, influenced perhaps by the fact that fireballs cannot be explained or be artificially produced in a laboratory. However, reports of ball lightning have been made throughout history, sometimes by persons who had no previous knowledge of the phenomenon and no obvious reason to concoct false evidence.

The general picture which emerges is that ball lightning is spherical or pear shaped, with a diameter of 4–8 in (100–200 mm), and often has fuzzy edges. It can be seen in daylight and has the intensity of a domestic light bulb; it is stationary or wanders with slow erratic movement. Sometimes it travels along conductors such as metal window frames, but it often enters houses by chimney or door, either explosively or silently. A few cause damage but most hardly cause alarm to the people who witness them. Few accounts make any mention of a sensation of heat. One experience from Steeple Ashton in Wiltshire, was recorded in volume 63 of the *Philosophical Transactions* (1773). Two clergymen were in the parlour of the vicarage talking together about a loud clap of thunder which had just occurred when they saw a ball of fire between them at face level. It was the size of a 'sixpenny loaf' and surrounded with a dark smoke. It burst with the sound of cannon fire, filling

Causes of damage or death by lightning

By vaporisation, so that moisture in any container expands suddenly and causes an explosion. Damp brickwork may shatter, road surfaces with underlying moisture can be ripped up and trees explode.

In Australia, eucalyptus trees commonly known as 'Darwin Woolly Butts' are particularly prone to explosion. Many trunks are channelled with termite nests, giving a moist core of honeycombed mud and humus approximately 3 in (75 mm) across which reacts like a bomb when struck by lightning.

On 12 July 1981, lightning caused an explosion, followed by fire, on *Hakuyoh Maru*, a tanker in Genoa harbour, Italy. There were seven deaths.

By melting and fusion: Nails in brickwork may melt and fall out of their holes and metal joints may fuse, sometimes in extraordinary circumstances. On 10 August 1975, a cricket umpire near Berwick-upon-Tweed was struck by lightning which welded solid an iron joint in his leg.

By burning — a hazard at the end of summer heat waves when the countryside is especially dry. The USA is particularly prone to thunderstorms in summer, and lightning starts many forest fires. On 15 August 1967, lightning started a fire in Idaho state, which spread in strong wind to encompass 90 miles^2 (240 km^2). Firebrands were carried in the wind some 10 miles (16 km) ahead of the flame front.

By conduction along wires which are not intended for discharge of lightning, so that explosions occur at the end of the conductor, for instance in television sets or electric power installations. Surge arrestors and suitably placed lightning conductors can do much to prevent such damage but complete protection is impossibly expensive.

A particularly thundery day, which interrupted the 1975 summer heat wave in Britain, was 8 August. Storms built up in Devon and Cornwall in the early morning and lightning blew out several transformers and telephone installations. Storms spread during the day to most of the country and in the evening set fire to an electricity substation at Bradford on Avon. A person can be protected against arcing from a television set, or explosion within a set, by pulling out the plug connected to the electrical circuit. This will not, however, prevent lightning from travelling via the aerial into the electrical circuit or other parts of the house — but that risk is small. Aerials projecting above houses in urban areas are relatively insignificant features of a generally rough surface contour, and it is only the lone high-rise building which suffers particular risk from a lightning strike.

By compression and decompression of air near a flash, which may blast the clothes off a person or knock him down. On 28 June 1976, lightning felled six golfers playing at Oakbrook, Illinois, but caused them no injury.

By direct lightning strike to the human body, most likely to kill when it passes close to the respiratory centre in the lower part of the brain, or when passing close to the heart. The most dangerous flash is therefore one which strikes the head and passes close to these sensitive regions, on its way to earth. However, lightning does not seek out these organs and many lucky escapes have occurred because the flash travelled from shoulder to leg, or arm to arm, bypassing the head or heart. The chances of being killed by lightning are many times less than the chances of being killed in a traffic accident.

Eleven soccer players were each struck by lightning as they left the field, during a storm at Caerleon, Gwent on 8 April 1979. One was critically burnt, while four others were detained in hospital with minor burns and shock. The remaining six were discharged after treatment.

The only man to have survived a lightning strike seven times is the American Park Ranger Roy C. Sullivan. He lost a big toe nail in 1942, his eyebrows in July 1969 and was burnt on the left shoulder in July 1970. His hair was set on fire in April 1972 and again in August 1973. In June 1976 his ankle was injured and on 26 June 1977 he suffered chest and stomach burns.

Lightning made a 'hole in one', leaving its imprint on a green at Chevy Chase Club, near Washington, DC, USA.

By a potential difference and current from one point on the ground to another, caused by temporary rearrangement of electric charge over the surface as the lightning strikes. A human may experience this current up one leg and down the other and the shock will be greater with his feet far apart. Hence it is safer for anyone caught in open country in a thunderstorm to crouch down, with feet together rather than stand upright and walk with long strides. Cattle are more prone to be killed than humans, because their legs are further apart and a strike from one leg to another necessarily passes close to the heart. On 22 July 1975 several cows were killed by lightning at Congleton, Cheshire; and another storm on 8 August 1975 near Huddersfield, Yorkshire, so frightened cattle that they stampeded and trampled a woman to death.

the room with a suffocating smoke and disagreeable smell, like 'sulphur, vitriol and other minerals in fusion.' One gentleman was not hurt, but the other was struck on the shoulder and briefly stunned. He remembered having seen the ball of fire for a few seconds *after* he was struck, and he mentioned a great quantity of fire of different colours vibrating swiftly.

On 29 July 1980, a motorist in Coventry, Warwickshire, saw a 'flashing ball of fire' pass his car, followed by an explosion. Other people nearby heard a loud noise but there were no reports of damage.

In December 1979, a retired eye surgeon in Guildford, Surrey, saw a green and orange glow filling his hall when he awoke from an afternoon nap. A fireball 1 ft (30 cm) in diameter was suspended a few inches above the ground and then faded away, leaving a strong chemical smell.

Lightning has been known to strike out of a clear sky, a phenomenon which has not yet been explained.

In the United States in September 1966, a lightning flash from an apparently clear sky felled 30 workers, who were picking peppers at Alfrida, Arizona, killing three of them.

In Australia, on 2 June 1976, a single blinding flash of lightning occurred at Myrtleford, Victoria, on a cloudless night. A fireball was seen to explode over three houses, a television set blew up and telephones were put out of order. Iron sheds fused together, wire fencing welded, and three football-sized marks were found burnt into the ground near the houses. A 66 000-volt powerline fused, blacking out a large area, and one shed had a burn hole as large as a tennis ball.

Lightning chooses the highest point available by which to discharge to earth. On a landscape with only a few prominent peaks, these will therefore be most prone to damage by lightning. Before the invention of the lightning conductor, churches with high towers or spires used to be particularly vulnerable.

Lightning can strike twice in the same place. The Church of St Mary the Virgin in Steeple Ashton, Wiltshire, was originally built in the early 13th century. It was largely rebuilt and a tower was added in the 15th century. This was surmounted by a steeple 93 ft (28 m) high which was ruptured by lightning on 25 July 1670. Repairs were set in hand at once and almost finished by 15 October, when lightning again struck the steeple, which collapsed. Two workmen were killed and the falling spire damaged the main structure of the church, which took another five years to repair. The steeple was not renewed.

Taking into consideration also the fireball incident at the vicarage in the same village it was perhaps tempting providence to live in Steeple Ashton, when bearing the name of Bolt. On 26 June 1973 an 84-year-old pensioner, Mr Bolt, was thrown across his kitchen when a flash of lightning wrecked a hay barn some few yards from his house.

A particularly disastrous lightning strike occurred at Widecombe in the Moor, Devon, on 21 October 1638. Afternoon service was in progress in the parish church when a severe thunderstorm occurred with consequences which were described by Richard Hill, the village schoolmaster. His florid verse is still displayed on boards in the church, and indicates that a huge storm cloud wielded all the powers at its disposal.

A crack of thunder suddenly, with lightning hail and fire
Fell on the Church and tower here, and ran into the Choir.
A sulphurous smell came with it, and the tower strangely rent,
The stones abroad into the air with violence were sent . . .
One man was struck dead, two wounded so they died a few hours after . . .
One man was scorched so that he lived but fourteen day and died,
Whose clothes were very little burnt. But many there were beside
Were wounded, scorched and stupified . . .
Some had their skin all over scorched, yet no harm to their clothes
One man had money in his purse which melted was in part,
A key likewise which hung thereto, and yet the purse not hurt
Save only some black holes so small as with a needle made . . .
The Church within so filled was with timber stones and fire
That scarce a vacant place was seen in church or in the choir.

It is highly likely that there was also a tornado associated with the storm. A Puritan pamphlet issued some time later, in which the tragic story was recounted as a punitive manifestation from the Lord, was illustrated with a cloud over the church from

Right: Lightning conductor placed by Benjamin Franklin on Ben West's home in Philadelphia, USA, in 1760.
(Mary Evans Picture Library)

BANK
BENIANIN WEST
LEBRETON

Two men sitting in a car were unhurt when bombarded by man-made lightning from a powerful generator at the Siemens High Tension Centre in Berlin, Germany. Some of the bolts struck the car with a force of two million volts. (Mercedes Benz, Great Britain, Ltd)

which a funnel cloud descended. There were approximately 60 casualties from the storm, including four dead.

Lightning conductors were first used in the United States, after Benjamin Franklin fixed one to his own home in Philadelphia in September 1752. The conductor consisted of a pointed iron rod to collect the charge, reaching about 9 ft (3 m) above the roof. Connected to the rod was a copper strip down the outside wall of the house, which led to a metal plate bedded 6 ft (2 m) into the ground, the whole conductor providing an easy route to earth for lightning. Franklin arranged similar protection for two of the public buildings in Philadelphia, and he published a description of his invention in November 1752, claiming no patent rights. Americans adopted lightning conductors with enthusiasm, except in some parts of New England, where the idea was deemed to be an interference with Divine Providence. Franklin's invention also met with a marked lack of enthusiasm in Europe, partly for religious reasons, and in Britain simply because it was American and political relations were somewhat strained at the time.

In Russia in 1753, the scientist Georg Wilhelm Richman was experimenting during a thunderstorm with collecting charge on an iron rod when he sat too near the rod. A flash leapt across the gap to his head, earthed down through a leg, bursting his shoe and killed him. Needless to say this did little to promote lightning conductors.

In Europe the first public building to be protected by a lightning conductor was the Church of St Jacob in Hamburg in 1769, and St Paul's Cathedral in London followed suit the next year. Dr William Watson, Vice President of the Royal Society, London, set an earlier example by fixing a conductor on his own home at Payneshill in London in 1762.

A vertical lightning conductor, well earthed, is considered to give reliable, though not certain, protection within a cone whose vertex is the top of the conductor. The base of this conical safety zone has a radius equal to the height of the conductor.

Horizontal lightning conductors are now known to be as effective as vertical rods provided they are properly bonded to roofs or chimneys and incorporated with conductive metal strips, guttering or drain pipes into an earthed protective ring around the house.

Lightning can jump a gap between its initial strike path and an alternative route close by. This may be from the outside of a roof to a water tank inside, from a tree through a person standing beneath, or from an extended car aerial to someone nearby. It is certainly safer to have the aerial retracted during a storm in case it conducts lightning into the vehicle, but this should be done at the first sign of approaching storm cloud and not during the storm itself.

One of the safest places in a thunderstorm is inside a car particularly when one is not touching the sides. The vehicle acts like a Faraday cage and any lightning flash travels over the outside surface and runs to earth through the tyres. Although these are usually made of rubber, which is an insulating material, there are enough other constituents in the fabric to make tyres excellent conductors, especially on wet roads. Nevertheless, it is a frightening experience to be inside a thin metal cage with lightning flashing all around, and heavy rain falling on the roof with a deafening noise. In order to convince people of the inherent safety of a car in lightning, intrepid volunteers from both the Ford Motor Company and Mercedes Benz sat in cars, which were bombarded by artificial lightning at two million volts generated at the Siemens High Tension Centre in Mannheim, Germany. Lightning struck the cars with a roar like thunder, but none of the occupants was hurt.

In Texas, USA, 1979 lightning struck a pick-up truck. Three people sitting in the open back were killed and one injured; but the fortunate three riding inside the cab were uninjured.

17. Whirlwinds, tornadoes and water spouts

Small but intense vortices of air assist the major weather systems in their efforts to balance the distribution of heat in the atmosphere. Some spinning cells originate on cloudless days over hot ground, and their winds rotate in either direction according to chance circumstances. Larger vortices originate within clouds and develop downwards to the ground. These usually, but not invariably, rotate anticlockwise in the northern hemisphere and clockwise in the southern hemisphere. All these air vortices develop suddenly, are too transient to appear on weather maps and have very low pressure centres.

Whirlwind is a general term, covering all rotating wind storms which originate on the ground and spiral upwards. Some have sufficient strength to cause damage. Less vigorous vortices are called land devils or water devils according to the surface over which they originate; or they have names describing the particles which are carried along in the whirling wind.

Sand pillars form over hot desert surfaces, where the temperature of the air close to the sand may be many degrees higher than air a few feet above. Air tries to obey the buoyancy rules by rising, but since the whole surface layer cannot lift at once, the desired result is achieved by small individual cells. In a wind these may be set spinning into columns of sand which rise a few feet, travel a short distance and then collapse, their temporary job of transporting heat accomplished.

Sand pillars constantly form and disperse along the sandy hills of the Namib Desert along the coast of south west Africa as cool winds from the sea blow onshore.

Dust whirls in north-west Libya have been studied closely by meteorologists. Small vortices often form during the hot months of the year on the plain between the Mediterranean and the Jebel Hills. Air temperatures close to the ground may be 16F (9C) degrees higher than that at 4 ft (1·2 m) above ground. The dust whirls are shaped like inverted cones and tilt forward by 5°–15° from the vertical along their path of movement, as if anxious to reach their destination. They often attain heights of 200 ft (60 m), but a whirl reaching 400 ft (120 m) has been observed with a tilt of nearly 40°. The dust whirls sometimes move in procession down wind of particular hot spots at an average speed of 10 mph (16 km/h), but the life span of each individual whirl is a matter of minutes only.

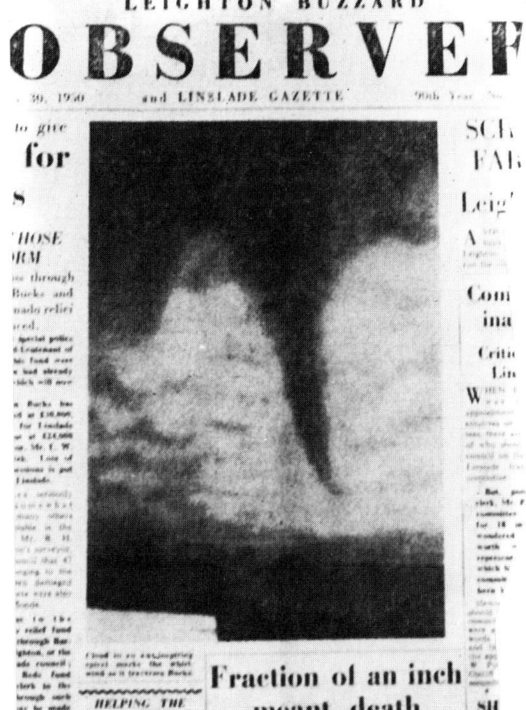
LEIGHTON BUZZARD
OBSERVE
and LINSLADE GAZETTE
Fraction of an inch meant death

Funnel cloud over Berkshire on 21 May 1950, which developed into a disastrous tornado causing much damage, particularly at Linslade. (*Beds. and Bucks. Observer*)

Spectacular land devils in the USA form over the dusty desert of south west Arizona, where on hot summer days the ground temperature may be as much as 150°–160°F (65°–70°C). This results in an extremely unstable layer of air close to the ground, in which rising air is set spinning into dust devils, which often reach heights of 300 ft (100 m). Exceptionally, they have been known to reach 3000 ft (1 km). They are visible because of the dust they collect and because of condensation in the soaring air. However, the environment air is usually too dry to sustain convection and produce cloud. The majority of Arizona dust devils last for only 3 or 4 minutes, and the slightest interruption to the rising air causes them to collapse. However, larger devils have been known to last for 30 minutes, and some can be as destructive as narrow tornadoes. On 29 May 1902, a livery stable in Phoenix, Arizona, was demolished, and on 2 June 1964 a church under construction was destroyed, both by tornado-like dust devils.

Land devils in Britain occur during summer, usually over particularly sheltered surfaces heating in the sunshine. When the pressure wind is more than 10 mph (16 km/h), turbulence alone achieves the disposal of the heated air which rises into the horizontal air stream. But when the wind is very light, the rising air over the hot spot may be set spinning. Land devils may be visible because of the dust which they suck up, but sometimes they are invisible and are detectable only by sudden bursts of wind, often accompanied by a hissing noise.

The larger land devils can be destructive. On 30 July 1975, at Warmley, Bristol, wind roared like an express train as it moved a factory shed through 30 ft (10 m) while workers stood watching. The side of the roof blew off and landed on a car 120 ft (40 m) away. The day was warm and cloudless, and the temperature of the air at 3 pm when the damage was caused, was 72°F (22°C).

Water devils are vortices of air over a water surface. They usually form over land and travel thence on to water when they quickly collapse. They occasionally form over a warm water surface which is suddenly overrun by cold air. This can happen, for instance, when a cool sea breeze penetrates inland during a summer afternoon and passes across a lake which has been steadily heating during a long heat wave. The rotating winds in water devils lift spray into the circulation and may cause undulation on the surface.

Water devils have been less often reported throughout history than have water monsters. This has prompted G. T. Meaden to suggest in an article in the *Journal of Meteorology* that water devils and monsters may be one and the same thing. In October 1979, a person watching the still water of Bala lake, in the Welsh hills, suddenly saw the surface bubble and foam and a huge hump-backed form appear only to disappear almost as quickly below the water. This description is consistent with a water devil, because of the bubbling appearance of the water.

Sea monsters are by no means the prerogative of the British, whose most famous is the Loch Ness Monster. In British Columbia a legendary water serpent called Ogopogo inhabits Lake Okanagan. The lakes of Kashmir are reputed to house mysterious monsters and both the Chinese and Arabs have many stories about sea monsters. A common factor of them all could be the physical laws governing vortices.

Fires sometimes produce whirlwinds, in which heated air escapes upwards.

In Britain, on 11 September 1978, a whirlwind formed where two fires met in a burning stubble field at Climping in Sussex. The whirlwind travelled 600 ft (200 m), carrying glowing ash which set fire to and destroyed four thatched buildings. The wind strength close to the whirlwind was such that it was difficult to shut the door of a parked car.

On 7–8 September 1940, enemy bombing produced the first firestorm of the war in Quebec Yard, Surrey Docks, London, when rapidly convecting air sucked in replacement air with the aid of whirlwinds.

In Germany, Hamburg was bombed on 27 July 1943, and violent convection and whirlwinds helped to burn down 8 miles² (20 km²) of the city. In the devastating raid on Dresden on 13–15 February 1945, whirlwinds of such intensity developed that people attempting to escape were instead carried into the fires by the spiralling winds.

Off Iceland, in 1965, vigorous whirlwinds were seen around the cloud of ash erupted from the volcano which formed the new island of Surtsey.

In Japan, over 120 vigorous vortices occurred over the fire following the Tokyo earthquake of 1923.

Tornadoes are bad-weather vortices, small but extremely powerful, embedded within large cumulonimbus or the clouds near the centres of hurricanes or intense depressions. They appear to be counterbalancing features to the central core of rapidly rising air at the centre of storms. The National Severe Storms Laboratory in the United States has been using Doppler radar to detect these separate

Whirlwind seen at 1325 hours on 18 August 1976 in a field near Braintree, Essex. At peak development it was about 100 ft (30 m) in diameter and 100 ft high. It lasted about 3 minutes. (R. Williamson)

violent parts of storm clouds. Both the central rising currents and the descending tornadoes can be detected by different sound signatures, determined by the rapidly changing winds. In 1973 a tornado at Union City, Oklahoma, was located nearly half an hour before it touched ground.

A funnel cloud signals a tornado, tapering from a broad exit at the main cloud base down to a narrow tip which sometimes reaches ground and causes damage but otherwise remains harmlessly above ground. A tornado funnel may touch ground several times during its journey across country, leaving intermittent trails of havoc to mark its leapfrog passage. It may be deflected by the wind, sometimes almost towards the horizontal, and can look like a writhing reptile hanging from the main cloud.

Several funnel clouds may extend downwards at the same time, creating an impressive sight.

The Hebrew prophet Ezekiel (*c.* 590 BC) had probably never seen such a sight before, when he recounted his experience near the river of Chebar in the land of the Chaldeans.

> 'a whirlwind to northwards, a great cloud and a fire infolding itself . . . out of the midst thereof came the likeness of four living creatures . . . and everyone had four wings . . . and their feet were straight feet and the sole of their feet was the sole of a calf's foot . . . and they went every one straight forward . . . and they turned not when they went . . . Their appearance was like burning coals of fire . . . it went up and down among the living creatures and the fire was bright and out of the fire went forth lightning.'

Ezekiel's account is embellished by further descriptions but the meaning is clear. There was a storm, four tornadoes which progressed with the main cloud, and there was lightning. 'The sole of a calf's foot' may be reference to a suction mark.

TORNADOES HISTORICAL AND MODERN

AUSTRALIA

On 21 December 1977, a tornado passed close to the Northam Research Station, 50 miles (80 km) north-east of Perth, but caused no damage to buildings. It was estimated to have circulating winds of about 185 mph (300 km/h). (See photograph on cover of this book).

BANGLADESH

On 1–2 April 1977, there were violent tornadoes particularly in the Madaripur district, 80 miles (128 km) from Dacca; 500 people were killed and more than 6000 injured, while hundreds of thousands were left homeless.

BELGIUM

On 30 November 1976, the worst tornado for many years moved across open country near Houwaart. It touched the ground three times, uprooting small trees and felling a large tree across the main road. Many roofs were damaged.

CANADA

On 30 June 1912, a tornado in Regina, Saskatchewan, killed 28 people and injured 100 more.

On 7 August 1979, tornadoes and severe thunderstorms devastated a wide area from Woodstock to Waterford, Ontario. Two people were killed, 142 injured and more than 300 homes and eight factories were damaged or destroyed.

GREAT BRITAIN

On 17 October 1091, a tornado struck London, with about TORRO force 8. The roof of the church of St Mary le Bow was lifted off killing two people, while four rafters 26 ft (8 m) long were driven into the ground with such force that barely 4 ft (1·2 m) protruded above ground. Various chroniclers, however, recount that 600 houses were demolished and other churches ruined, which suggests that there were also strong winds blowing, contributing to the widespread scale of destruction.

On 26 November 1703 there occurred the nearest to a true hurricane that the south of England has known (see Chapter 7). The storm reached a peak in the west country some hours before midnight, but already in the afternoon gale winds were blowing, and a tornado was sighted in Oxfordshire. Daniel Defoe received this report from a witness.

> 'A spout marching with wind like the trunk of an elephant snapped the body of an oak, sucked up water in cart ruts, tumbled an old barn and twisted its thatch around in the air. A quarter of a mile away it knocked down a man.'

On 15 January 1968, a deep depression crossed central Scotland during the night, and the average wind speed in Glasgow was 61 mph (98 km/h) with gusts up to 102 mph (164 km/h). Enormous damage was done in the city but, when the army started to make temporary repairs to roofs it was noticed that there were definite paths of damage. A resident in the highest part of the city reported four distinct

A row of trees uprooted by a tornado at Newmarket, Cambridgeshire, on 3 January 1978. (Syndication International)

The stump of a fruit tree from which the top was twisted by the Wisley tornado passing across the grounds of the Royal Horticultural Society on 21 July 1965. Note undamaged trees in background. (R. P. Scase)

bursts of exceptional violence during the night accompanied by noises like an express train approaching, which suggests that the depression was accompanied by tornadoes.

On 3 January 1978, a swarm of 10–14 tornadoes accompanied an active cold front crossing east England. From north Humberside to Cambridgeshire houses were damaged, caravans overturned and trees uprooted. The strongest tornado, TORRO force 5 or 6, passed through the south of Newmarket. Racing stables, a hotel and 150 homes were badly damaged and cars overturned. A railway signal box had most of its windows blown out and was so shifted from its foundations that it had to be demolished. Some 136 pink-footed geese dropped dead out of cloud along a 28-mile (45 km) track in Norfolk. Autopsies were carried out on five of them which were found to have extensive lung haemorrhages and damaged livers. This was probably due to the decompression effects of being whirled aloft in a tornado.

On 30 May 1979 there was a tornado associated with a line squall over Salisbury Plain. It was estimated at force TORRO 4–5, and destroyed 200 mature firs over a path 150 ft (50 m) wide.

ITALY

On 11 September 1970, a tornado in the Gulf of Venice lifted a steam yacht with 60 people on board and sank it near Santa Elena, killing 36. The same furious wind circulation destroyed a camping site nearby, killing eleven people and injuring hundreds.

NEW ZEALAND

On 10 May 1976, a tornado demolished a church at Arahura, near Hokitika, forcing debris 18 ft (6 m) into a cliff alongside a railway cutting. A signal box, as well as a bus shelter with occupant, were both deposited on to the railway line. A piece of sheet iron which was hurled across the power lines caused disruption of electricity supplies.

UNITED STATES

On 18 March 1925, eight separate tornadoes plagued Missouri, Illinois and Indiana. The principal one developed in the afternoon and travelled for 219 miles (352 km) at speeds between 55 and 75 mph (88 and 120 km/h). A trail of damage resulted but the worst hit town was Murphysboro in Illinois where children were still in school and adults in offices and factories. Three miles of buildings collapsed and 200 people in the town died. The tornadoes retracted from the ground occasionally, so that during a day in which there were 695 deaths and 2027 injuries, four small towns were almost totally destroyed, yet others were untouched.

On Palm Sunday, 11 April 1965, 37 tornadoes afflicted the mid-western states when 271 people were killed and more than 5000 injured.

On 3–4 April 1974, 148 authenticated tornadoes swept through the southern and mid-western states. Some small communities in Ohio and Kentucky were almost obliterated and at least half the town of Xenia, Ohio (25 000 inhabitants), was destroyed as if by bulldozer. More than 300 people were killed that day and 4000 were injured. Seven states were declared disaster areas and yet, in the usual capricious manner with which tornadoes travel, some towns were quite unharmed.

On 10 April 1979, 23 tornadoes in the Red River areas of Texas and Oklahoma caused 56 deaths and a vast amount of damage. The worst hit area was Wichita Falls where 42 people were killed and more than 3000 homes destroyed.

Hurricane *Beulah*, in September 1967, is estimated to have spawned about 115 tornadoes, and hurricane *David*, in September 1979, is known to have produced at least 34. However, it is not possible to attribute damage specifically to these small vortices when hurricane winds were already causing damage generally.

Suction marks are often left in soft ground by a funnel cloud, which has dropped down to the surface. When such a cloud is tilting forwards, and particularly when traversing an upward slope, the suction is greater at the forward edge than at the back, resulting in a semicircular impression, rather like a horse's hoofmark. The account of a tornado which occurred at Scarborough, Yorkshire in August 1165, was written by a monk who referred to it as the 'old enemy' and 'the black horse'.

> 'The footprints of this accursed horse were of a very enormous size, especially on the hill near the town of Scardeburch, from which he gave a leap into the sea; and here for a whole year afterwards they were plainly visible, the impression of each foot being deeply graven in the earth'.

Lightning accompanies tornadoes. Ezekiel saw it from a distance but Frank Lane in *The Elements Rage* quotes a Kansas farmer who lay on the ground and was able to look straight upwards into the hollow funnel of cloud:

> 'There was a hollow opening in the center of the funnel, about 50 or 100 ft in diameter, and extending straight upwards for a distance of at least one half mile, as best I could judge under the circumstances.
>
> The walls of the opening were of rotating clouds and the whole was made brilliantly visible by constant flashes of lightning which zigzagged from side to side. Had it not been for the lightning I could not have seen the opening, nor any distance up into it anyway. Around the lower rim of the great vortex small tornadoes were constantly forming and breaking away. These looked like tails as they writhed their way around the end of the funnel. It was these that made the hissing noise'.

There is still doubt as to whether lightning is a *result* of the tornado, or whether it plays some part in producing tornadoes.

Wind direction in tornadoes usually, but not invariably, obeys the rules propounded by Buys Ballot for depressions and hurricanes; anticlockwise in the northern hemisphere and clockwise in the southern. However, subsidiary vortices whirling around tornadoes may rotate in either direction, set spinning by some chance factor in the same way that land devils originating above a ground surface may spin in either direction.

Collapsed barn at Craymere, Norfolk, after passage of one of a swarm of tornadoes over East Anglia on the night of 1–2 December 1975. Only bales of straw inside the barn are supporting the ruins. (J. A. Jackson)

The TORRO tornado intensity scale (abridged)

TORRO force	*Tornado description*	*Characteristic damage*
FC	Funnel cloud, incipient tornado	No damage except to top of tallest towers. Some agitation in tree tops. Possible whistling or rushing sound.
0	Light	Light litter, hay, growing plants, spiral from ground. Temporary structures, like marquees, seriously affected. Damage to unsound roofs. Twigs snapped off.
1	Mild	Planks, corrugated iron, garden furniture levitated. Damage to sheds and outhouses. Dislodged tiles and chimney pots. Hayricks disarranged, and small trees uprooted.
2	Moderate	Mobile homes displaced or damaged. Considerable roof damage. Big branches of trees torn off and tornado track traceable through crops and hedgerows.
3	Strong	Mobile homes overturned or badly damaged. Outhouses torn from supports or foundations. Roofs stripped of tiles or thatch, serious damage to windows and doors. Strong trees uprooted or snapped.
4	Severe	Mobile homes destroyed. Entire roofs torn off, but walls left standing. Well-rooted trees torn up or twisted apart.
5	Intense	Motor vehicles over 1 ton lifted clear off ground. Small weak buildings in exposed areas collapse. Trees carried through the air.
6	Moderately devastating	Motor vehicles over 1 ton lifted and carried along in air. Some heavier roofs torn off public buildings, and many less strong buildings collapse. Every tree across tornado track in open country damaged or uprooted.
7	Strongly devastating	Steel-framed industrial buildings buckled. Railway locomotives turned over.
8	Severely devastating	Frame house levelled and most other houses collapse in part or in whole. Motor cars hurled some distance.
9	Intensely devastating	Railway locomotives hurled some distance. Many steel structures badly damaged.
10	Super tornadoes	Entire frame and wooden houses hurled from foundations. Steel-reinforced concrete buildings severely damaged.

G. T. Meaden, Tornado and Storm Research Organisation, Trowbridge, Wiltshire

Wind speed in tornado circulations is difficult to measure, because ordinary anemometers cannot withstand the onslaught. Electronic measurement, based upon radar echoes from a moving funnel cloud, can be obtained, but the problem is to have an instrument positioned in the right place at the right time. On 10 June 1958, radar recorded a wind speed of 206 mph (331 km/h) in a tornado at El Dorado, Kansas, but it is considered that wind speeds more than twice that amount can happen.

A tornado inflicts damage in various ways

By the direct impact of wind, whose force is proportional to the square of wind speed. A wind of 300 mph (480 km/h) in a tornado will exert a direct force 100 times greater than the force exerted by a wind speed of 30 mph (48 km/h), and this may amount to pressures of 200 lb/ft^2 (980 kg/m^2).

By twist due to unequal wind speeds within the very narrow band of the circulation. Winds which blow in a tornado with a small cross section are often so much greater on one side of a tree than on the other, that they screw off the tree top.

By explosion when a tornado passes overhead. A barometer close to a tornado at Newtown, Kansas, has been known to record a fall of 25·7 mb in 10 minutes, followed by a rise of 31·8 mb in 17 minutes; and another in St Louis, Missouri, once fell to 912·3 mb near a tornado. It is thought that pressure gradients of about 60 mb may exist across the narrow circulation, which would result in a momentary inequality of pressure between the outside and inside of a building equivalent to an outward thrust of several tons. Roofs are sucked off and walls explode outwards. The advice given in tornado safety rules in the United States is to open doors and windows on the opposite side of the building from that of the approaching tornado, so as to facilitate the equalisation of atmospheric pressure.

There have been many reports of chickens being deplumed by tornadoes, and this could be caused by explosion of the hollow quills from the skin. The birds often survive the ordeal.

By lift and drop in the vertical currents within the tornado. An upcurrent of 150 mph (240 km/h) was indicated by a film taken in Dallas, on 2 April 1957 but even lesser currents can fill tornadoes with light debris. Sheds, cattle and humans have often been lifted high into the air, sometimes suffering injury when falling to ground again. Often, however, they are lowered gently without harm on the outer rim of the circulation, where upcurrents only just fail to maintain the weight aloft. On 4 September 1981 a 4-month-old baby, asleep in his pram outside his parents' home in Ancona, Italy, was lifted 50 ft (15 m) into the air and then landed gently on to the road 300 ft (100 m) away. The baby was still asleep.

Tornadoes achieve prodigious feats of levitation and penetration, by using a combination of all the above mentioned powers:

In Britain, on 26 September 1971, a tornado moved a 90-ton engine 150 ft (50 m) along a railway track near Rotherham, South Yorkshire, and lifted a 40-gallon (180 l) empty metal drum 3 ft (1 m) above the ground.

In the United States, on 4 February 1842, small pieces of board with blunt ends were driven into turf to a depth of 18 in (450 mm) by a tornado in Ohio. In 1931 a tornado in Minnesota lifted an 83-ton rail coach and 117 passengers 80 ft (25 m) into the air before dropping them into a ditch. On 12 June 1957, a tornado passed over a steel airport hangar in Dallas, Texas, pulling concrete piers out of the ground.

The destructive diameter of a tornado varies from a few feet to about a mile. The wider swaths of damage often occur without elongated funnel clouds, indicating that the main cloud base is so low that the broad top of the vortex sweeps the ground. By contrast, long funnels with narrow tips often pick their way with such precision that one house may be damaged, but another next door may remain unscathed.

In Britain, on 26 June 1973, a tornado at Cranfield in Bedfordshire, ripped the roof off laboratory buildings, belonging to the Environmental Science Research Unit, while leaving untouched the houses on an adjacent estate. An anemometer and wind vane, sited 300 ft (100 m) away from the wrecked building, recorded 85 mph (136 km/h) before the pen lifted off the chart and electricity supply was disrupted. The wind direction fluctuated violently.

In the United States, the tri-state tornado of 18 March 1925 had a track of 219 miles (352 km). For nearly half that distance the width of destruction was about ¾ mile (1 km) and occasionally as much as 1 mile (1·6 km).

The distance travelled by tornadoes varies so much that average figures are meaningless.

In Britain, the longest recorded distance achieved by a single tornado was 100 miles (160 km) from Great Missenden, Buckinghamshire, to Blakeney, Norfolk, at an average speed of 25 mph (40 km/h), on 21 May 1950. The tornado did not touch ground all the time, but its path was minutely tracked by H. H. Lamb of the Meteorological Office through its erratic trail of scattered trees, burst sheds and crumpled roofs.

A short-lived, but intense, tornado occurred on 21 July 1965 in Surrey, travelling 2 miles (3 km) in 10 minutes across the grounds of the Royal Horticultural Society at Wisley to the main road. Fruit trees were tilted or torn out of the ground and some had their tops twisted off. A few larger trees had their trunks split.

In the United States the flat plains of the mid-west provide minimum interruption to the progress of tornadoes. On 26 May 1917 a single tornado sped a verified 293 miles (471 km) across Texas with only occasional leaps off the ground. It travelled at 55–75 mph (88–120 km/h) for 7 hours 20 minutes.

By contrast, a tornado in Wyoming in 1954 had a track of only 45 ft (15 m), and another in Dakota was once observed to remain stationary in a field for 45 minutes.

The greatest frequency of tornadoes occurs in the United States, particularly in the mid-west states between central Texas and the Dakotas. Hundreds form each year but many go unnoticed in remote areas. In 1965, a total of 899 was recorded as compared to only 64 in 1919. More than 50 per cent happen in the spring and about 25 per cent in summer, while 60 per cent occur during the hottest part of the day, between noon and dusk. Typical conditions are when cool air from the north-west or north conflicts with warm moist air from the Gulf of Mexico, resulting in vigorous cumulonimbus and cold fronts. Most tornadoes travel towards the north-east, some towards the south-east and only a few to the west.

DESCRIPTIONS OF WATER SPOUTS

AUSTRALIA

On 16 June 1974, a water spout was seen only 300 ft (100 m) away from HMAS *Melbourne*, off the coast of Queensland. Lieutenant Commander H. L. Daw reported that the spout was transparent, rotating in a clockwise direction and was about 30 ft (10 m) in diameter, with a rather broader diameter top and bottom. The column was 2500 ft (750 m) high and upright at first, but after 5 minutes it wavered, bent, divided and disappeared. Three other spouts were sighted in the distance. All appeared to be forming beneath the leading edges of cumulus clouds whose bases were estimated to be 2500 ft (650 m) above the sea and tops 9000ft (3000 m), though still developing upwards.

BRITAIN

On 18 August 1974, numerous spouts were sighted in the English Channel, between the Isle of Wight and Hastings, Sussex. The weather was overcast but warm, with a light NE wind, which shifted considerably in direction. Various descriptions were published in *Weather*, the journal of the Royal Meteorological Society.

Water spout near San Felin de Guixol, Spain, in September 1965. It lasted for about 20 minutes.
(Syndication International)

Near the base of the three spouts there seemed to be a boiling mist, and the sea was agitated.

The spout, half a mile away, gave a terrific disturbance on the water, brilliant white.

The two spouts, side by side, seemed quite thick. They were dark grey in colour, and alternately faded and became clearer.

Six spouts in a U-shape curved round the yacht, distance 2½–4 miles. There was a solid fountain of spray, 300 ft high and 150 ft wide, with nil visibility. The spouts lasted 10–20 minutes and then dissipated. Lightning and thunder were occurring at the time.

In November 1975, a column of water 150 ft (50 m) high and 100 ft (30 m) wide was seen in the Moray Firth, Scotland. It was spinning at terrific speed with the base on the sea like a boiling cauldron, and it travelled towards Lossiemouth for 2 miles (3 km) before suddenly disappearing. The wind was fresh north-easterly.

In May 1979, two spouts were sighted off Mablethorpe, Lincolnshire, within 3 weeks. On 7 May, a 10 ft (3 m) high spout appeared suddenly after a flash of lightning, 'like steam rising off a boiling sea'. It travelled parallel to the coast before veering out to sea and disappearing. On 25 May, a bigger spout was seen about 1000 ft (300 m) high and 300 ft (100 m) in diameter where it emerged from the base of the storm cloud. It was dark grey, rotating and pulsating rapidly, and remained in view for 15 minutes.

UNITED STATES

On 2 September 1967, four students of meteorology on a flight from Miami witnessed six separate water spouts.

The diameters varied from 40 to 80 ft (12 to 24 m). The parent clouds had a base of 2200 ft (670 m) above the sea, measured by altimeter, but the tops of the clouds were estimated to be no more than 20 000 ft (6000 m), though still growing. None of the parent clouds were precipitating. A spray vortex on the surface of the sea, with well-defined wake trailing behind, gave prior indication of the spout a few seconds before the ropelike funnels became fully visible. The nearest spout was rotating anticlockwise and the spray near the sea surface was being whirled outwards with a speed of about 115 mph (185 km/h). One spout exhibited a strange pulsating outer sheath of condensation, which rotated around the better defined inner funnel and then moved upward into the base of the cloud. The largest spout was later discovered to have caused considerable damage after crossing the shore, uprooting bushes and trees, lifting a 2-ton car a few feet above ground, and causing cupboards to pop open because of reduced pressure. The wind that day was light SW at ground level, but upper air soundings revealed that wind veered with height although remaining less than 16 mph (25 km/h) up to 20 000 ft (6000 m).

WHIRLWINDS, TORNADOES AND WATER SPOUTS

Swarms of tornadoes may occur on one day or on consecutive days, and many are associated with hurricanes.

In Britain, tornadoes occur more frequently than was at one time thought, usually within an area stretching from the north Midlands south-eastwards to Kent. In the 1970s, the numbers in England and Wales reported to the Tornado and Storm Research Organisation in Trowbridge varied between 77 in 1974 and ten in 1977; there were 16 in 1980. No more than two per annum were reported from Scotland and Northern Ireland, and in 5 years there were none. On 1 December 1966, 26 tornadoes were noted in Britain.

Tornadoes are most likely to occur in July and August in thunderstorm conditions but they may also accompany intense depressions at any time of the year. The vortices may be unnoticed in the general hubbub of a strong gale or under cover of darkness, but the swaths of destruction provide evidence afterwards of their passage.

The intensity of a tornado can be described by the wind speed in the circulation, measured or estimated. Alternatively, and more suitable for people wishing to report tornadoes, intensity can be described according to the damage done. Dr G. T. Meaden of the Tornado and Storm Research Organisation has devised such a scale and welcomes notifications.

Water spouts are similar to tornadoes, but they form over the sea. A funnel lowers from the main cloud, and even before it reaches the surface of the sea the spiralling winds start a vortex agitation on the water. Spray rises towards the narrow funnel cloud and both join together to form a continuous column of water drops with a broad base. Water spouts have a short life, usually no more than 20 minutes and, although they can cause damage, they are not as violent as tornadoes. They occur with deep cumulonimbus clouds and vigorous cold fronts, but also with relatively shallow cumulus when there is an abundance of warm moisture to feed the unstable air.

Water spouts which cross land have been known to cause damage before collapsing. On 22 August 1975, one of several which formed off East Anglia ripped tiles and guttering off houses in Kessingland, Suffolk; another which struck the harbour at West Mersea in Essex, hurled a dinghy into the air and carried it 450 ft (150 m) before dashing it to ground.

Water spouts are seen frequently in the summer over the coastal waters around Florida. In Britain most sightings are made from the south and south-east coasts, but water spouts do occur also in northern coastal waters.

18. Optical phenomena

Optical phenomena, the silent and weird results of the passage of light through the atmosphere, have been as much feared or revered throughout history as noisy and violent manifestations of weather.

The sudden loss of light during an eclipse of the Sun is terrifying to primitive tribes. But even educated people who know that there are perfectly natural explanations for displays of light in the atmosphere, find something uncanny about the precise geometric designs.

The laws governing the path of light in the atmosphere are somewhat contradictory.

Light travels in straight lines — but only within a homogeneous medium, and when there are no obstructing small particles. The 'straight' lines of light are really wave motions of very small length and amplitude. Light bends when encountering small particles or when passing through a medium, such as air, which changes density gradually. Light bends abruptly when entering and leaving a boundary between air and another transparent medium such as water or ice.

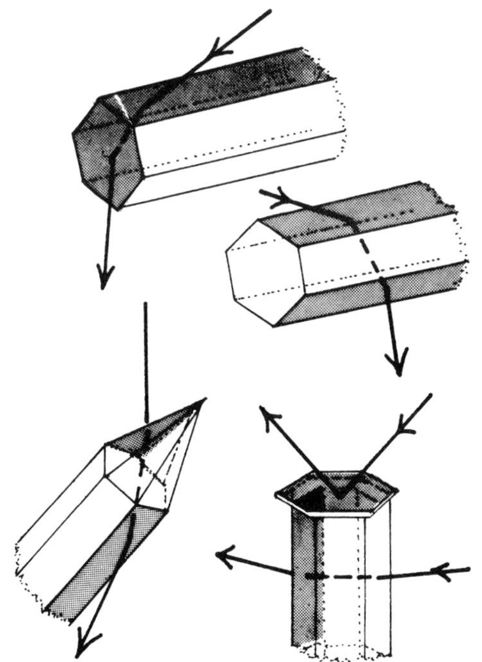

The manner in which light rays bend when passing through ice crystals, forming optical phenomena. (D. Davies)

Light rays are partly reflected and partly absorbed by materials on which they fall. The smoother the surface, the more the light is reflected, but all substances, however rough, reflect some light. In this way sunshine is diffused, (ie spread about) to provide illumination outside the vicinity of direct sunbeams.

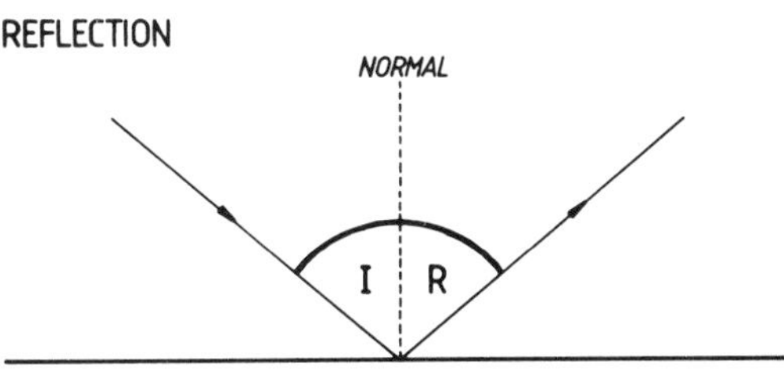

The laws of reflection are straightforward. The *normal* is defined as a line perpendicular to a surface on which light impinges. The angles of *incidence* and *reflection*, respectively, are those which light makes with the normal when striking a surface and when reflected back again.

Transparent materials permit absorbed light rays to pass right through. If the light strikes the surface at an oblique angle, more is reflected than transmitted. If the light strikes vertically, more is transmitted than reflected. On entering or leaving a boundary surface between transparent media of different density, light rays bend — a process known as *refraction*.

The laws of refraction were postulated in 1621 by Willebrord Snell (1591–1626), professor of Mathematics at Leyden University, Holland. The *angle of incidence* is that which the light ray makes with the normal *before* entering the new medium, and the *angle of refraction* that which it makes *after* entering.

REFRACTION

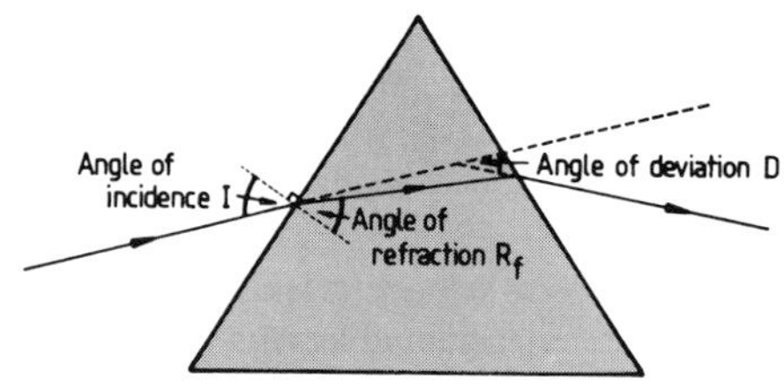

Light entering a denser medium (eg from air into water), bends *towards* the normal, so that the angle of refraction is less than the angle of incidence. On emerging from the denser medium the light bends *away* from the normal so that the angle of refraction is greater than the angle of incidence. The angle of refraction can therefore sometimes be greater than 90° when light reaches a less dense medium.

Total internal reflection occurs when light tries to escape from a dense to a less dense medium, but impinges on the boundary at such a large angle of incidence that the angle of refraction is more than 90°. The light then *reflects* from the surface instead of passing through it.

The angle of deviation is the angle which light makes with its original track, when it emerges after having passed right through a transparent substance. If the light passes through parallel boundaries (eg a rectangular block of ice or glass), the ray emerges displaced, but parallel to its original track, and without change in appearance. When light passes through transparent boundaries which are set at an angle to each other, then the whole appearance of the emerging light may be transformed.

Differences of air density cause light to bend as if it were passing through another medium. It can distort the appearance of simple objects so that they appear to be 'monsters', even rippling in life-like fashion because of density variations and small differences of viewing position.

Sir Isaac Newton (1642–1727), English physicist and mathematician, was the first to demonstrate the coloured nature of light. He concentrated a beam of white sunlight on to one face of a 60° prism of glass, and placed the prism so that the light which emerged on the far side fell on to a white wall. The result was a display of colours which ranged from red on the top to violet at the bottom. He concluded that white light consists of many superimposed colours, which bend by different amounts on entering a transparent medium.

The spectrum of light is the name given to all the colours which make up white light. These are violet, indigo, blue, green, yellow, orange and red, and their wave-lengths range from 0·4 microns (violet) to 0·7 microns (red) — (1 micron is a millionth of a metre). When entering another transparent medium, the shorter wave-lengths bend more than the longer ones but the colours are only separated enough to be recognisable when refracted more than once in the same direction on passing through a transparent medium.

Diffraction is the bending of light rays around particles or water drops which have approximately the same size as the wave-length of light. The longer wave-lengths (red) are liable to greater diffraction than the shorter (violet).

Scattering is the change in direction of light rays produced by the molecules of air itself and is most pronounced for the shorter wave-lengths (violet).

The sky appears blue and the Sun yellow when light from the Sun travels through an atmosphere which is clean and dry. Then the shortest wave-band of the visible spectrum (blue) is scattered by the molecules of the atmosphere, and the remaining light reaches the eye. Scattering only affects a very small proportion of light emitted from the Sun, which therefore appears pale yellow or whitish in the blue sky. The bluest skies in Britain occur when the Sun shines through a vigorous air stream from the north, in which thermal activity and showers have cleansed the lower atmosphere of dirt.

The sky appears white and the Sun red when sunshine travels through air which contains water droplets or dirt, scattering light in all the wave-bands. Residual rays reaching the eye are then all in the higher wave-length: red. These conditions are most frequent towards sunset in quiet high-pressure weather, when a fine cloudless day is starting to degenerate into a misty or foggy night.

The Sun glowed weirdly red through the pall of smoke which enveloped London during the Great Fire in the first week of September 1666, just as it does when shining through the ash erupted by volcanoes.

A blue Moon may be seen when particles of critical size scatter red light more than blue. It occurred in Britain on 26 September 1950, when smoke particles from forest fires in Alberta, Canada reached the country on winds at 6–8 miles (10–13 km) altitude. However, the phenomenon does not happen often, hence the expression 'once in a blue moon'.

A green flash sometimes accompanies the last or first glimpse of the setting or rising Sun. This is caused by the greater refraction of the green wave-band, the shortest after the blue and violet which are scattered by the molecules of the air. The flash is momentary only but a prolonged green flash was seen on 6 December 1970 in special circumstances: a Boeing 707 was descending towards a sheet of cloud just as the Sun was starting to rise above it. The navigator saw a green flash for about 5 seconds and then, after a 2-second return to normal coloration, he saw the flash again for a further 3 seconds. The aircraft was descending at a rate balanced by the rate of rise of the Sun.

A red flash from the wave-length with least refraction angle has occasionally been seen as the lower segment of the Sun appears below a cloud bank on the horizon.

Visibility is the distance of the furthest objects on the ground which can be seen, gauged by known landmarks of predetermined distance. Obstructions on the horizon are limiting factors so that good visibility often cannot be expressed more accurately than, for instance, 'greater than 30 miles' (50 km). However, there are always close landmarks by which to gauge poor visibility. 'A hand's length' indicates impenetrable fog, though meteorologists measure it more prosaically in metres.

Visibility depends on the quantity of obscuring particles of dirt or moisture in the air and on the relative densities of different layers of the atmosphere.

Visibility in middle latitudes is best when wind blows from high latitudes to low. These are occasions of brisk thermal activity to carry dirt upwards from polluted areas near the ground, or wash it down to ground in showers. In Britain the best visibility is usually about 130 miles (210 km); the Antrim Hills, Northern Ireland, whose highest point is 1817 ft (553 m), can frequently be seen from Ben Nevis, Scotland 4406 ft (1343 m).

Occasionally, refraction may extend visibility further. In 1965, the Wicklow Hills, Republic of Ireland (3039 ft (926 m)) were seen from Coniston Old Man in Cumbria (2633 ft (803 m)), a distance of 160 miles (257 km). The late Professor Gordon Manley thought this figure consistent with the prevailing atmospheric conditions — a ridge of high pressure, bringing cold air across warmer sea.

The poorest visibility, excluding water drop fog which may be totally obscuring, occurs in high pressure weather when a temperature inversion keeps pollution and moisture droplets trapped near the ground. The sky may then appear ominously dark, as if there were a storm cloud approaching. The oblique visibility from an aircraft on approach to a runway may be very bad, even though an observer standing vertically below can see the aircraft plainly through the shorter distance of polluted air.

Visibility in polar regions is often extremely good because of lack of pollution in the air. On cloudless days and nights shadows cast by the light of the Moon or Sun bring into relief every undulation of the white landscape. There are, however, particular visibility problems on cloudy days because of multiple reflections between white cloud and snow.

Whiteout is the confusion of normal optical senses, which occurs when light is diffused through thin cloud and reflected back again from a uniformly white snow surface. All the normal standards by which the eye judges distance and perspective — shadows, colour, horizon — disappear into a universal whiteness. Even the sense of balance is affected and it becomes quite dangerous to walk because hummocks of ice or snow drifts are unrecognisable.

However, cloud sheets are often thick enough to serve better as reflectors than transmitters of light, and the intensity of light reflected from large areas in polar regions is not always the same. In these conditions clouds become valuable mirrors.

Ice blink is a whitish glare on the horizon reflected from ice on to the underside of cloud. It has subtle tints of yellow or grey which can even indicate to experienced travellers the type of ice over which the blink is seen.

Water sky is the grey reflection cast on the underside of cloud by open water below.

A cloud map, or land sky, is the white and grey image reflected on to the underside of cloud from the surfaces below, which may be snow, ice, water, or even bare rock. The tints in a sky picture serve as an excellent aid to navigation, enabling travellers to detect geographical landmarks as well as open leads of water through the ice.

The images of very distant objects, like the stars, are always slightly displaced from their real position, because light bends gradually on travelling through progressive layers of air of different density.

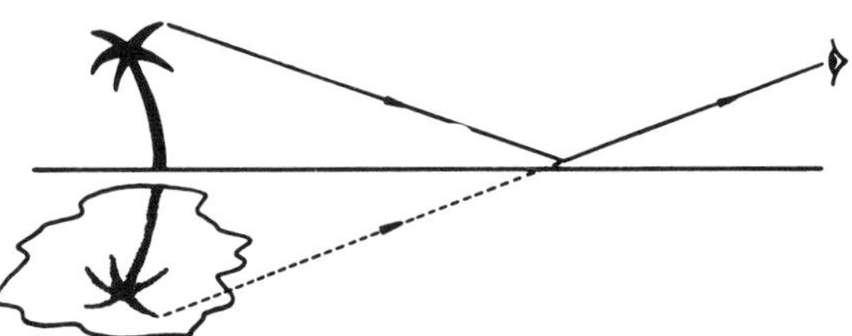

An inferior mirage is seen below the real object, when light enters an intensely hot layer of low density air, such as exists over the desert or over a tarmac road in summer. The image seen is always in the direction along which light enters the eye, irrespective of previous distortion, so the reflection of the sky appears on the ground. It shimmers, because of convection activity near the ground, and the brain reacts by thinking that the reflection of the sky must be the more usual phenomenon of water. The message has often proved tantalising and disappointing for people wandering thirsty in the desert. Since internal reflections only occur when the angle of incidence is oblique, mirages are usually seen in the distance or along an inclined surface.

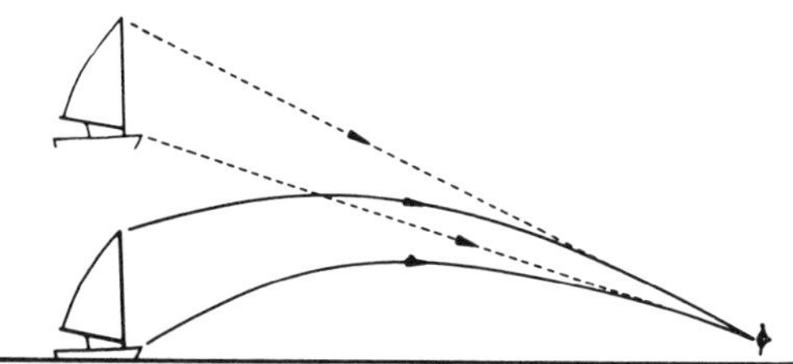

A superior mirage is an image seen above the real object. The light from the object bends downwards when travelling through layers of very cold dense air before reaching the eye. This can bring into view objects which are normally below the horizon, or it can project images into the sky.

In Antarctica a common form of superior mirage is the repeat sunset. On 15 April 1915, Sir Ernest Shackleton wrote in his diary

> 'The sun set amid a glow of prismatic colour on a line just above the horizon. A minute later Worsley saw a golden glow which expanded as he watched it, and presently the sun appeared and rose in a semi diameter clear of the horizon. A quarter of an hour later, the sun set a second time.'

In Great Britain, on 26 May 1978, Hull docks in North Humberside, were seen on the skyline from Bridlington 25 miles (40 km) away. Later the same day the tower at the entrance to Grimsby fish dock was clearly visible from a distance of 38 miles (60 km). The mirages were so sharp that even cranes could be seen working.

In Mexico ghostly mountains often appear in the sky over the Gulf of California, an hour or so before sunset. The 10 000-ft (3078 m) peak of Cerro La Encantada, on the peninsula of Baja California is not normally visible from Puerto Penasco, 116 miles (186 km) away on the other side of the Gulf. About an hour or so before sunset, the sea breeze

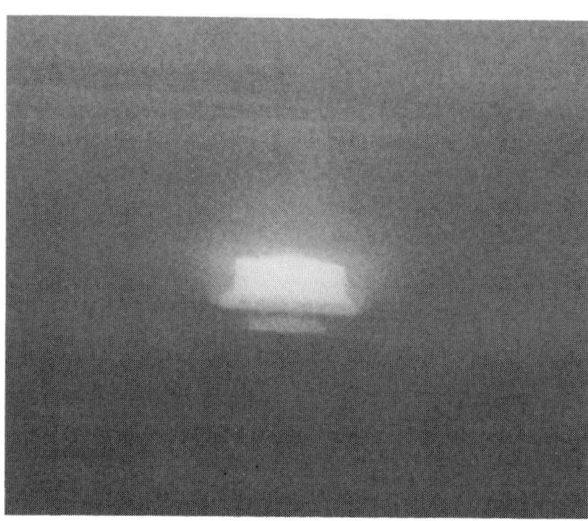

A square sun seen at Resolute, Canada, on 12 March 1978. The sky was clear, air temperature − 35°F (− 37°C) and there was no wind. Photographs were taken between 6.45 and 7.15 pm, local time. (Yasuhiko Shimazaki, Sima Creative House)

ceases, and cold air settles over the bay. Then about 45 minutes before sunset, a mirage of La Encantada looms high into the sky. The contours are quite recognisable, and it is as if the real mountain had grown to four times its true height.

Fata morgana is a complicated superior mirage caused by distortion of light, both vertically and horizontally, when passing through several layers of air of different densities. The resulting mirage bears

Superior mirage seen during the 'Germania' expedition to the North Pole in 1869, as shown by Camille Flammarion in his book 'L'Atmosphère', published in 1888. (Fortean Picture Library)

little resemblance to the viewed object and is more like a fairy landscape. Fata morgana usually occurs over water, and the name originated in Italy where the mirage is often seen over the Strait of Messina.

A square Sun has sometimes been reported by Eskimos and explorers in the Arctic. It can probably be seen elsewhere when layers of adjacent air have very different density. The first known photographs of this phenomenon were taken by Japanese cameramen accompanying Kenichi Horie's North Polar expedition in 1978. The appearance of the Sun was probably caused by both horizontal and vertical distortions of light, together with reflection from the sea.

Looming is the impression of huge size, or close distance, associated with superior mirages, or with the Sun or Moon when low on the horizon. Opinion is divided about whether this is a genuine magnification process or not. It could be caused by varying densities of atmosphere acting like a lens, or it may be a psychological reaction to what the mind knows is impossible: the setting Sun is not *really* sitting on the horizon, or nestling between houses, and mountains do not *really* stand in the sky. The only certain thing is that most observers are conscious of magnification or looming closely. Ptolemy, too, commented in the 2nd century that any object viewed across land looked larger than the same object viewed across empty space.

Circular displays of light form when particles of dust, ice crystals or water drops change the paths of light by diffraction, refraction or reflection. The Sun and Moon are so far away that all their light rays entering our atmosphere can be considered parallel to each other. After their paths have been altered by some fixed angle of deviation, they continue to be parallel but only a few can reach the eye. These are light rays which have emerged from water drops or crystals lying on a circle.

Optical displays are unique to each observer because they are determined by light reaching his eyes only. People standing alongside each other only think they are seeing the same phenomena, like rainbow or halo, because it is impossible to discern the tiny differences.

A halo is a ring of coloured light around a light source, caused by the refraction of light when passing through ice crystals which are randomly organised. Red is on the inside with yellow and blue on the outside. Sometimes the colour is faint and then the halo appears whitish.

Halo displays are often seen around street lamps near the power plants at Fairbanks in Alaska, where ejected water vapour crystallises immediately in outside air, often colder than −22°F (−30°C).

The most familiar haloes, however, are those seen around the Sun or the Moon, when they are obscured by a thin sheet of ice crystal cloud. Moonlight is not usually strong enough to produce a halo, except near the time of full-moon.

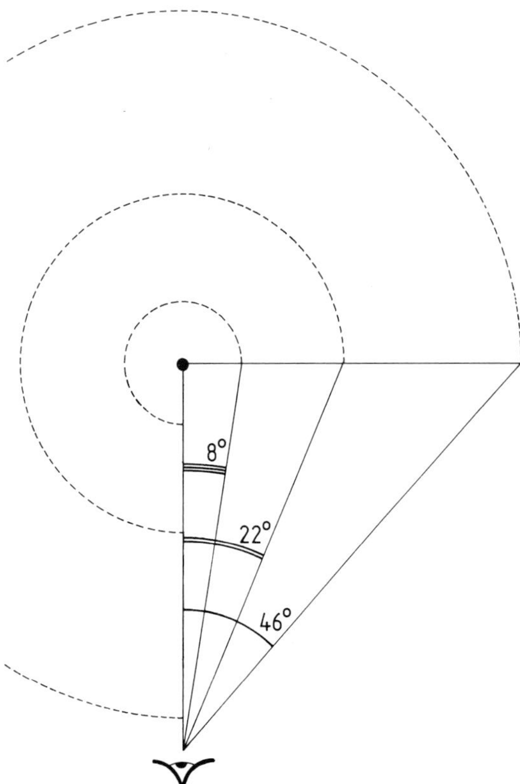

Haloes are measured by the angle subtended by the eye between the light source and the rim of the halo. An approximate measurement can be made by opening a pair of dividers with the hinge close to the eye. In practice this gives an accurate answer because the three possible sizes are so different from each other.

The 22° halo is the most common, and is formed when light passes through two alternate longitudinal faces of ice crystals.

The 46° halo occurs occasionally, when light passes through one longitudinal face of an ice crystal and the end section at right angles to it.

The 8° halo is seldom seen, and occurs when light passes through one longitudinal face of a crystal and its prism end. This halo may be more common than supposed but it is so close to the Sun that it is difficult to detect.

A halo round the Sun should *never* be measured by naked eye, even through a cloud of ice crystals. It should be viewed by reflection in a piece of dark glass, or alongside an obstruction which masks the Sun's centre.

Haloes are traditionally signs of approaching rain, and feature in a variety of rhymes. For instance:

Last night the sun went pale to bed
The moon in haloes hid her head.
T'will surely rain — I see with sorrow
Our jaunt must be put off to-morrow

There is some truth in the rhyme, because cirrostratus, producing haloes, precedes frontal rain. However, parts of haloes can sometimes be seen in patches of cirrus which are unconnected with approaching rain, and frontal belts often die out without reaching the rain stage.

An observer interested in the correlation between haloes and rain carried out an investigation near Bristol, between 1 January 1960 and 2 March 1971. Haloes were observed on 80 occasions during 66 days. Of these, 71 formed around the Sun and nine round the Moon; 39 lasted less than 5 minutes, eleven more than an hour. Twenty complete haloes were seen and 15 upper semicircles, but no lower semicircles. Twenty upper tips were noted and one lower tip.

On only 45 occasions out of 80 did rain follow within 48 hours.

Parhelia, (mock suns, or sun dogs) are images of the Sun formed by refraction of light through ice crystals aligned with their axes being vertical. Such crystals are usually surmounted by hexagonal plate crystals, which act rather like parachutes to keep the crystals suspended vertically. Parhelia are at the same elevation as the Sun and on either side of it. They are positioned on the halo when the Sun is near the horizon, but a little way outside the halo when the Sun is high in the sky. Parhelia are whitish with a red tinge on the side nearest the Sun.

Parry arcs were first reported by Sir William Parry during his expedition to the Arctic in 1819. They

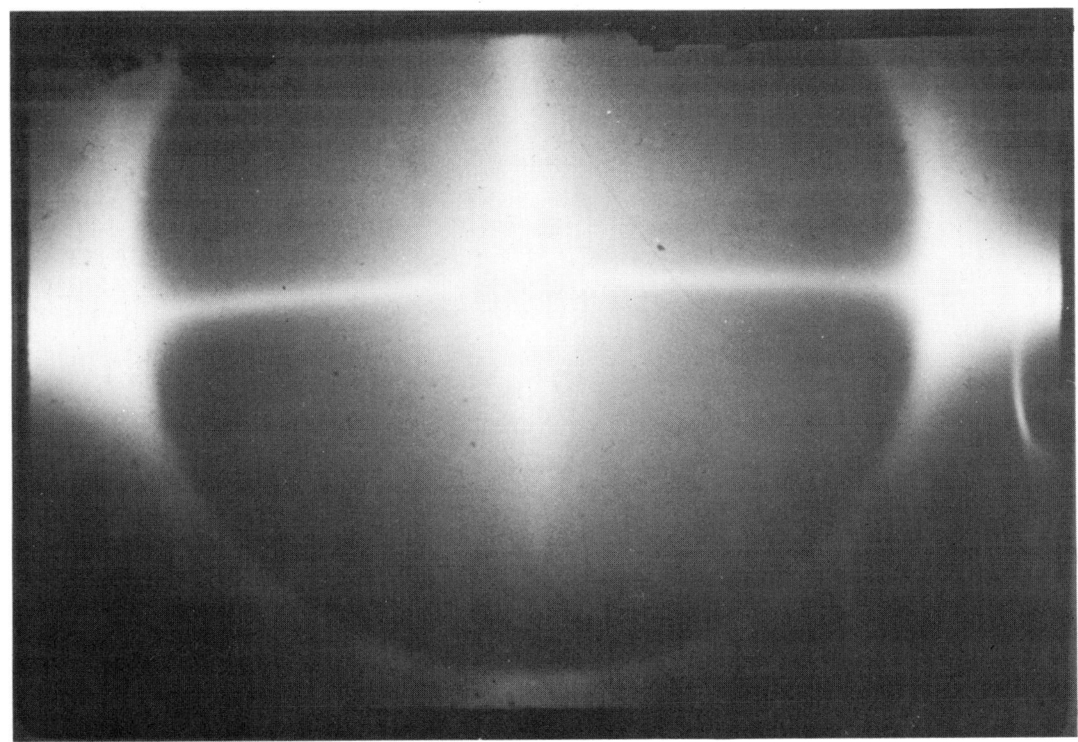

Part of the halo display seen at Saskatoon, Canada, on 3 December 1970. (W. J. Evans)

form above and below a halo when hexagonal crystals lie with their main axis and two opposite sides horizontal.

Circumzenithal arcs form by refraction through the 90° edges of vertically aligned crystals. They are vividly coloured, red towards the Sun, and are seen alone or above the 46° halo, convex to the Sun.

The parhelic circle is a whitish bright circle around the Sun, parallel to the horizon, caused by reflection from the top surfaces of ice crystals whose axes are vertical.

A sun pillar is a column of light above or below a low elevation Sun, and is caused by reflection in ice crystals which are inclined slightly to the horizontal. Being reflected light, a sun pillar has the same colour as the Sun. It is often best observed when an obstruction blocks out the view of the Sun itself, but the sun pillar may remain visible for a short time after the Sun has sunk below the horizon.

Sun crosses are seen when sun pillars intersect with an incomplete parhelic circle.

A sub sun is a reflection of the Sun seen from a mountain or aircraft, and projected on to a cloud of systematically aligned ice crystal surfaces.

The Arc of Lowitz was named after the astronomer who first saw and described it in a halo display over St Petersburg, Russia on 29 June 1790.

The Arc is a downward extension of the mock sun, caused by oscillation about the vertical of ice crystals whose axes are arranged symmetrically. It is a very rare phenomenon.

A rainbow is formed by refraction and internal reflection in raindrops, so that light emerges from the drops along a back-tracking angle of deviation. A rainbow can therefore only be seen by a person standing with his back to the Sun. The bow is measured from the imaginary shadow of the eye in the distance known as the 'anti solar point'. Only an arc of the circle is visible to an observer on the ground, because the anti solar point is on or below the ground, and the curtain of raindrops is above ground.

The lower the altitude of the Sun, the greater the arc of rainbow visible. A semi-circular bow would occur as the Sun sets, except that the light is not then strong enough. A complete circular rainbow is sometimes seen by pilots of aircraft, approaching a curtain of raindrops at a height midway between cloud base and ground.

The best coloration in rainbows appears with large water drops. When drops are smaller than 0·01 in (0·3 mm) colour separation is poor.

A primary rainbow is formed when light is refracted twice and internally reflected once, emerging with an angle of deviation between 138° at the violet end of the spectrum, and 139½° at the red end. The angular measurement of the primary rainbow from the anti solar point is 40½° for the violet colour (inside), and 42° for the red (outside).

A secondary bow occurs when there are two internal reflections within the water drops before the light emerges at angles between 233½° (violet) and 230° (red) from the original direction. The angular measurement of the bow from the anti solar point is 50½° (red) to 53½° (violet), and the colours are seen in reverse order from those of the primary bow — red inside and violet outside. The secondary bow is less bright than the primary.

Supernumerary rainbows sometimes appear just inside the primary bow, caused by more than two internal reflections. Their colours are poor and the intensity of light is weak.

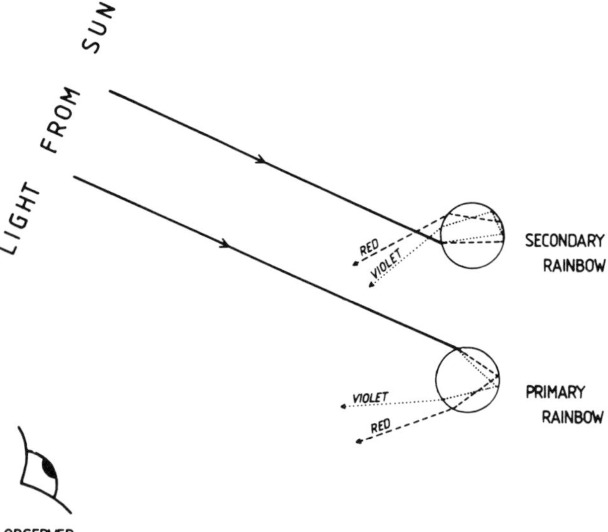

Aurora Borealis, curtain type, from Camille Flammarion's book 'L'Atmosphère'. (Fortean Picture Library)

Left: Tracks of sunlight which produce a rainbow. (S. Burt)

The distance of a rainbow from an observer may be anything from a few yards (when seen in spray thrown up on a wet road, or in the spray from a waterfall) to several miles when seen in rain.

The most usual time to see rainbows is in the afternoon on days of strong thermal activity. Cumulonimbus are then producing showers; bright periods which intervene permit the Sun to shine on a departing shower and the intensity of light is still strong. Rainbows cannot be seen when the Sun's altitude is higher than approximately 53°, because then the refracted light passes above the head of an observer on the ground.

Rainbow duration is usually short, because the relative positions of rain, sunshine, and observer are constantly changing in showery weather. However, an exceptional rainbow was seen for nearly 3 hours by Mrs Kathleen Mills of Manchester when she was on holiday between Colwyn Bay and Llandudno, Wales, on 14 August 1979. The notorious Fastnet Storm (see Chapter 8) was moving up the Irish Sea.

Aurora Borealis, sketched by A. Tissandier, as seen during the expedition of the 'Vega' in March 1879. (Mary Evans Picture Library)

The cloud bands were broken and over north Wales there was clear sky. The rainbelt was moving north-east, the Sun behind the observer was moving towards the south-east, so that she herself remained in an intermediate position until 10.15 am, when the rainbow disappeared.

'The Rainbow's End' is a phrase meaning 'the unattainable', because as soon as one tries to move towards the 'end', the original rainbow seen is displaced by another having a slightly different anti solar point as centre.

Ulloa's bow or fog bow is formed in the same way as a rainbow, except that the Sun shining behind the observer falls on to fog instead of raindrops. The diameter of fog drops is usually less than 0·002 in (0·5 mm), which ensures that the refracted coloured rays overlap to form a white bow. Only the faintest tinge of colour appears at either end of the white band, red outside and blue inside for a primary fog bow, and vice versa for a secondary bow.

A corona is a series of rings around the Sun or Moon, caused by diffraction of light close to very small water drops. The red light is diffracted more than the violet, and the inner ring of light, the aureole, is bluish on the inside and reddish brown on the outside. Sometimes the aureole is all that is seen, but on other occasions a whole series of rings extends outward beyond the aureole, again with blue on the inside and red on the outside. The smaller the water drops the larger the corona, and colour separation is best when droplets are of uniform size. The most spectacular coronae therefore often occur with newly formed sheets of stratus or stratocumulus.

Iridescence is colouring seen in the thin edges of patches of water-drop cloud, and is part of a corona.

Heiligenschein (German, meaning holy aureole) is a whitish ring of light surrounding the shadow of an observer's head on dewy grass. It is most frequently seen in early morning, while the Sun's altitude is still low and the grass wet with dew. Benvenuto Cellini (1500–71), Italian goldsmith and sculptor, was one of the first to describe the phenomenon, ascribing the aureole of light around his head to a mark of religious favour. The mundane modern explanation is that the 'schein' is caused by diffraction of light, in a similar manner to that causing a corona.

A Brocken Spectre is a shadow cast upon fog or low cloud when the Sun is shining from behind. The spectre appears enlarged because the shadow falls through a depth of water droplets. The most usual situation for viewing a Brocken Spectre is when standing on high ground and looking down on valley fog. The name comes from the Brocken summit in the Harz mountains of Germany. The area was one of the last strongholds of heathen faiths, engendering many superstitions about the devil. The uncanny ring of light which often forms around a Brocken Spectre possibly contributed to the superstitions.

A glory is a ring of light like a corona, seen around a Brocken Spectre. The reason for its formation is not certain, but it probably results from multiple reflection within tiny drops of water, and then diffraction on the return of light to the eye. A glory can only be seen around one's own shadow, but people standing alongside each other can all see each other's shadows. This is therefore one of the few occasions when it becomes obvious that circular optical phenomena are uniquely positioned for each observer.

The Bishop's Ring is a reddish brown ring round the Sun, caused by bending of light around fine dust in the atmosphere. When the Sun is high, the inside of the ring is about 10° and the outside 20°, but the ring enlarges to 30° as the Sun lowers.

The Bishop's Ring was first observed by a Mr Bishop at Honolulu, on 5 September 1883, after the volcanic eruption of Krakatoa. The heavier particles ejected into the atmosphere sifted out by gravitation, leaving a residue of tiny particles capable of producing coloured diffraction. The Bishop's Ring reached its greatest brilliance in the spring of 1884, and gradually declined until June 1886 when it disappeared.

The aurora borealis (northern lights) and **aurora australis** (southern lights) are spectacular displays of light seen in the northern and southern hemispheres respectively. In latitudes higher than 70° they are seen frequently. In lower latitudes they usually occur during periods of intense solar activity, but displays are often masked by cloud. The lights are caused by electrical solar discharges which are deflected by the Earth's magnetic field and are sometimes organised to appear like waving curtains of light. The colours vary according to the gases present in the atmosphere, and vivid displays may contain all the colours of the spectrum. Many displays, however, are less dramatic, being greyish-white.

People in northern Scotland would be able to see aurorae about 150 times per annum, if it were not for intervening cloud in the troposphere. In fact, Edinburgh may expect to see about 25 displays a year while London is lucky if it witnesses one in a year and Malta if it sees one in 10 years.

Aurorae were seen from the Shetland Isles on 203 occasions in 1957, but only 58 times during 1965, these being the record high and low number of displays since reliable observations were started in 1952. In north-west Europe spectacular displays happened on 4–5 September 1958.

Aurorae were observed in particularly low latitudes on 2 August 1744, at Cuzco in Peru and on 1 September 1859, over Honolulu, Hawaii.

19. Microclimate

Microclimate is the climate of a small environment, such as garden, room, refrigerator or even the human body. It can be created artificially in order to be different from the surrounding climate.

Outdoor microclimates cannot be controlled entirely but can be ameliorated.

□ Rainfall can be supplemented by watering, preferably lightly and persistently, so that rain has time to penetrate the soil without running off.

□ Drought can be made less harmful by covering soil, after it has been watered, with a mulch such as peat or polythene, in order to prevent evaporation.

□ Excessive rainfall can only be offset by ensuring good drainage. Water-shy plants can be given a suitable microclimate close to a wall which protects them against prevailing rain-bearing winds.

□ Sunshine benefits can be increased or decreased by building or planting strategically. A sun-facing brick wall acts as storage heater, which usefully re-radiates heat for the ripening of fruit. A south-facing slope of 10° angle in latitude 50°N has been shown to receive 50 per cent extra heat at the beginning of January, compared with level ground. The advantage of a sloping aspect decreases as the season advances, and may be no more than 15 per cent by April. Conversely, sunshine can be offset by the shade of trees or buildings.

Protected garden, whose outer brick wall serves both as a heat store and first barrier against the wind. Inner hedge completes protection against wind. (I. Holford)

□ Frost risk can be minimised by ensuring good drainage of cold air from sloping ground, eg through gaps beneath fences or hedges at the lower edge of gardens, or by planting fruit trees some way up a hill and not at the bottom. Quite modest coverings on cloudless still nights can reduce radiation heat loss and delay frost. Cars remain warmer when parked beneath trees or close to high walls. Opaque blinds or sacking over greenhouses may give some protection against short-term frost.

□ Wind barriers give protection down wind for up to ten times the height of the barrier. The most effective are semi-permeable, because they filter and break the force of the wind. Wattle or woven fences require maintenance but do not compete with plants for water in the soil; trees and hedges on the other hand make demands upon soil moisture and may cut out light. Solid wind barriers, like brick walls, may cause wind speed to accelerate over the top or round the sides, and create damaging lee eddies. A ratio of 50 per cent air space to material is ideal, but even an open wire mesh gives some protection.

Enclosed microclimates can be completely manipulated. Atmospheric pressure can be controlled, for instance in high-flying aircraft or deep sea diving capsules, but the most usual factors for manipulation are temperature, humidity and draught (wind).

Architecture often mirrors climatic conditions.

□ Walls of impermeable material, like granite, are traditionally thickest where the climate is particularly hot or cold or windy. Building materials incorporating air pockets (brick, dried mud, wood, snow) are quite good insulators on their own. They are better when used for double walls with an air cavity between and better still when the cavity is packed with insulation such as plastic granules, rock wool or quick-setting foam. Then, the need for exceptionally thick walls disappears. Lofts require 3–5 in (80–130 mm) insulation to prevent heat loss from the rest of the house.

□ Windows in hot climates are usually protected from the direct entry of sunshine by overhanging balconies or shutters on the outside. Sometimes windows are omitted altogether from sun-facing walls.

In cold climates, too, windows may be limited in size and number to minimise radiation heat loss through the glass and to reduce draughts from the outside. The more sophisticated policy is to double or even treble-glaze the windows. Sealed units have sheets of glass sandwiched with dry air and set into one frame, which must therefore fit tightly into the surround so that draughts do not penetrate the edges. Alternatively a secondary window can be fitted on the inside of the primary window. This deters radiation heat loss through the insulating barrier of air, and also provides a physical barrier against draughts.

In cool climates, windows are often designed to allow the full entry of sparse sunshine. Rare heat waves can be accommodated with temporary shades like blinds, drawn curtains over windows or whitewash over greenhouses.

□ Outer doors need protective porches to deter heavier cold air rushing to replace indoor warmth when they are opened. Entrances to temporary snow shelters or igloos should be as small and as low to the ground as possible, perhaps with an outer well to serve as a cold air trap.

The temperature of air indoors can be manipulated by the same principles of radiation, conduction and convection that the Sun uses outdoors. Solid fuel fires radiate efficiently into a room but also conduct heat away through the fire-back and waste much by convection up the flue. Electric reflector fires concentrate radiation in one direction but convector fires have

The ingredients of a comfortable indoor microclimate in winter are double glazing, floor length curtains, radiator, humidifier and insulated cavity walls. (I. Holford)

their radiant element hidden and project heated air into the room, often with the aid of fans.

The best way to obtain consistent temperature throughout all rooms in a building is again to copy nature. This means importing heat from a remote source into every area, either directly by duct from a boiler room or indirectly as hot water into radiators.

Relative humidity decreases when the temperature of air is raised. For instance,

If air at 41°F (5°C) and RH 80 per cent is warmed to 68°F (20°C), RH falls to 30 per cent.

If air at −50°F (−46°C) and RH 100 per cent is warmed to 75°F (24°C), RH falls as low as 5 per cent.

Very low relative humidity encourages evaporation from any source of water available — the human body, plants or fibrous materials like wood and cloth, and this may cause discomfort or damage. Dry air, below 50 per cent RH, also encourages the accumulation of static electricity which discharges painfully at finger tip (see Chapter 16). The remedy is to increase the vapour content of the air with humidifiers, though even they cannot overcome the problems of extreme dryness indoors in a very cold climate.

A medium size room of 2000 ft³ (57 m³), having an air temperature of 70°F (21°C) and an RH of only 20 per cent, contains about ½ pt (2·8 dl) of water vapour. To raise the RH to a comfortable 50 per cent requires a further ¾ pt (4 dl) or about 1 pint (5·6 dl) each hour to allow for air change.

Humidifiers work on three different principles.

☐ Evaporator pads, saturated with water and in perforated metal containers, are hung on radiators. Evaporation is slow and inadequate to achieve significant rises in RH. Efficiency is increased when air is pumped continually across a pad kept moist with water, as in some air conditioning systems.

☐ Evaporation humidifiers are containers of water which are heated electrically until vapour steams into the air and is immediately absorbed. Water kept at a temperature of about 140°F (60°C) is adequate for small rooms, but in large premises, where apparatus can be sited safely away from risk of scalding, boiling water can inject large quantities of vapour very quickly.

☐ Fine sprays can eject water droplets into the air, a suitable method for greenhouses, where the slight cooling effect of the spray does not matter. It is not appropriate for living rooms, because minerals remain to stain furniture after the water evaporates.

Shutters prevent ingress of sunshine during summer.
(I. Holford)

Cooling a microclimate is more complicated than warming it because *cold* is not a phenomenon in its own right — it is merely absence of heat. Modern refrigerating surfaces are obtained by using adiabatic principles (see Chapter 11). Gas is compressed in an outside chamber and its temperature then allowed to fall to that of the environment. Then, the compressed gas is released into the connecting circuit of pipe or flat container inside the closed environment. The expansion of the gas causes the temperature of the container to fall and air cools upon its surface. Because this method of cooling warms the outside environment, a refrigerator should not be kept in a larder which also needs to remain cool.

Most air conditioning systems duct cooled air direct into each room from a remote source. However, experiments are being made to cool ceilings in individual rooms, on which air may cool and sink into the room.

Evaporation of water was the only possible way to cool small microclimates before refrigerating principles were understood. Enclosed courtyards featured pools and fountains, whose evaporation extracted heat from the environment and lowered air temperature. Butter stood in water inside a porous dish, from whose outer surface evaporation took place, thus cooling the contents. Similarly, drinking water stood in porous jars.

The most precious commodity in hot weather was ice which was collected during winter (see Chapter 9) and stored until needed.

Ice storage houses were designed on sound meteorological principles and were so successful that the ice was available throughout summer.

A pit with drainage holes for melt water was dug and covered with a roof insulated according to local method. An outer door led to an inner door by means of a passage, and always positioned on the shaded side. Ice was packed into the pit and layered with straw, while the cold air remained at low level, in the same way that it stays in a top-opening freezer, even with the lid open.

Persian ice houses were made of mud and many have consequently crumbled. They were sometimes as much as 50 ft (15 m) high, where the warm air syphoned off from a vent hole at the top. In India, ice houses were often thatched, made of mud and shaded from the sun by a bamboo framework covered with straw. In Britain ice houses were usually built into the sides of hills, with soil and turf covering the tops.

Above: Interior of the ice house at Tong Castle, Shropshire which is being demolished to make way for a major road. The ice house will eventually be re-built at the Avoncroft Museum of Buildings, Bromsgrove, Worcestershire. (Derek Millward)

Left: The exterior of the Tong ice house, showing part of the passage leading to the doorway and the double skin construction of the outer wall. (A. Wharton)

Right: Ice house near Sirjar, Iran. The outer wall shaded a pool from which water was taken to make ice on cold winter nights. The outer wall also served to protect against any wind turbulence which might deter radiation cooling. Most Iranian ice houses were made of dried mud and consequently many have crumbled, lacking maintenance. (E. Beazley and M. Harvenson, 'Living with the desert')

The human body can control its own microclimate within certain narrow limits.

☐ It produces heat from food and physical exertion.

☐ Blood conducts heat from the centre of the body, known as the core, to the skin surface.

☐ Skin radiates heat and one person can raise the temperature of an unventilated room measuring 1000 ft³ (28 m³) by 15F (8C) degrees in an hour. Large assemblies of people in confined surroundings create uncomfortably hot conditions for themselves without any other heat source.

☐ Insensible perspiration moistens the skin all the time, and sweat glands provide additional water for evaporation when the need arises, causing body temperature to fall.

☐ Exhalation of water vapour increases the relative humidity of the immediate surroundings, enough to cause misting problems in a confined space such as a car.

☐ The respiratory system is a natural air conditioner. Inhaled air is warmed to core temperature, and moisture is added by mucus in the bronchial tubes, so that air is almost saturated by the time it reaches the lungs. Oxygen then liquefies for use in the blood circulation and waste carbon dioxide is exhaled. The nose needs to humidify about 17 600 pt (10 000 l) of air per day and the daily volume of nasal excretion is about 2½ pt (1½ l). In the case of bronchial diseases, or when inhaled air is too dry, the respiratory system finds its task too difficult and headache or sinusitis may result.

☐ The body has only limited success in retaining body heat without the aid of clothes. Animals raise their fur to improve the insulating barrier of air pockets around them in cold weather. The miserable array of hairs standing upright from 'goose pimples' on the human skin does little more than show that we are cold.

Thermal equilibrium is the comfortable balance of internal heat production and dissipation. It is achieved by an unclothed person at rest, in still air with temperature of 86°F (30°C). When lightly clothed, the same person maintains thermal equilibrium in still air of temperature 70°–75°F (21°–24°C).

At air temperatures above 90°F (32°C) even bare skin cannot radiate enough heat to maintain normal body temperature and the sweat glands take over the task. When air is very moist, evaporation may not take place fast enough, and a temperature of 90°F and 75% RH taxes the body to the limit and sweat pours. Air temperature of 100°F (38°C) and 40% RH is equally uncomfortable.

A marathon runner cannot dissipate all the heat necessary even by radiation and sweating, and his body temperature may rise to over 105°F (41°C).

The 'apparent' air temperature is a measure of what hot weather feels like to the average person, taking into account the relative humidity. The more moist the air, the hotter it feels.

Very low air temperature can be endured, provided the body is adequately insulated against heat loss. This is a much greater problem in windy weather than in calm conditions. Several layers of cellular clothing are better than one thick garment of non-cellular material, but the final outer garment should

be an impervious 'wind cheater'. In Arctic weather one needs five times as much insulation when at rest than when working.

The equivalent air temperature is the actual air temperature corrected for the effect of wind chill. When the wind blows at 20 mph (32 km/h) and air temperature is 34°F (1°C) skin cools at the same rate as it would in calm conditions with an air temperature as low as −38°F (−39°C).

Americans have a 30-30-30 Rule of Survival for those sojourning at bases in the Arctic or Antarctic. The grim message is that when human flesh is exposed to a wind of 30 mph in air temperature of −30°F, it freezes in 30 seconds.

The British Transglobe Expedition on the Antarctic ice cap in July 1980 experienced an equivalent temperature of −116°F (−82°C).

Normal temperature of a healthy person is 98·6°F (37°C) in the core of the body, and 91·4°F (33°C) at the skin surface. The difference ensures that heat is conducted from the core to the radiating surface of the skin. Shivering starts when skin temperature falls to 86°F (30°C).

Hypoaesthesia is the loss of sense of pain or touch which occurs when skin temperature falls to about 50°F (10°C).

Hypothermia is a condition of abnormally low core temperature and is often fatal. The body loses thermal control when core temperature falls below 90°F (32°C) and coma follows. Death occurs any time after core temperature falls to 79°F (26°C) but two casualties have been known to survive temperatures of

Below right: Oliver Shepard, Charles Burton and Ranulph Fiennes, of the Trans Globe Expedition, suitably dressed for the weather at the Geographic South Pole in January 1981. (Taylor Woodrow Group)

Apparent temperatures due to relative humidity

Air temperature °F \ Relative humidity %	0	5	10	15	20	25	30	35	40	45	50	55	60	65	70	75	80	85	90	95	100
140	125																				
135	120	128																			
130	117	122	131																		
125	111	116	123	131	141																
120	107	111	116	123	130	139	148														
115	103	107	111	115	120	127	135	143	151												
110	99	102	105	108	112	117	123	130	137	143	150										
105	95	97	100	102	105	109	113	118	123	129	135	142	149								
100	91	93	95	97	99	101	104	107	110	115	120	126	132	138	144						
95	87	88	90	91	93	94	96	98	101	104	107	110	114	119	124	130	136				
90	83	84	85	86	87	88	90	91	93	95	96	98	100	102	106	109	113	117	122		
85	78	79	80	81	82	83	84	85	86	87	88	89	90	91	93	95	97	99	102	105	108
80	73	74	75	76	77	77	78	79	79	80	81	81	82	83	85	86	86	87	88	89	91
75	69	69	70	71	72	72	73	73	74	74	75	75	76	76	77	77	78	78	79	79	80
70	64	64	65	65	66	66	67	67	68	68	69	69	70	70	70	70	71	71	71	71	72

Heat Stress Category	*Apparent temperature*
Caution	80°–90°F
Extreme caution	90°–105°F
Danger	105°–130°F
Extreme danger	130°F or more

R. G. Steadman and R. Quayle, National Climatic Center, Asheville, USA

Equivalent and apparent temperatures are not real, measurable values. They are subjective impressions of temperature, exaggerated either because of wind or relative humidity. There are other formulae which give different results.

Equivalent temperatures due to wind chill

Estimated wind speed	Actual thermometer reading °F 50	40	30	20	10	0	−10	−20	−30	−40	−50	−60
	Equivalent temperature °F											
Calm	50	40	30	20	10	0	−10	−20	−30	−40	−50	−60
5 mph	48	37	27	16	6	−5	−15	−26	−36	−47	−57	−68
10 mph	40	28	16	4	−9	−21	−33	−46	−58	−70	−83	−95
15 mph	36	22	9	−5	−18	−36	−45	−58	−72	−85	−99	−112
20 mph	32	18	4	−10	−25	−39	−53	−67	−82	−96	−110	−124
25 mph	30	16	0	−15	−29	−44	−59	−74	−88	−104	−118	−133
30 mph	28	13	−2	−18	−33	−48	−63	−79	−94	−109	−125	−140
35 mph	27	11	−4	−20	−35	−49	−67	−82	−98	−113	−129	−145
40 mph	26	10	−6	−21	−37	−53	−69	−85	−100	−116	−132	−148

Wind speeds greater than 40 mph have little additional effect	*Little danger for properly clothed person*	*Increasing danger*	*Great danger*
		Danger from freezing of exposed flesh	

National Science Foundation, Washington DC

60°F (16°C). Core temperature of some survivors of the Fastnet race in August 1979 fell to 91·4°F (33°C) and they were treated by immersion in water at a temperature of 106°F (41°C).

Immersion in water allows heat to be conducted away from the body 23 times faster than in air. If one can keep still, some of this heat may provide a thin cocoon of warmed water close to the body. Therefore lifejackets, which lessen the need to swim, may delay the onset of hypothermia.

When water is as warm as 61°F (16°C) a person can survive in it for about 2 hours. Immersion in water at temperatures less than 35°F (2°C) causes death in about 15 minutes.

The sea temperature, 180 miles from Madeira, was 64°F (18°C) on 24 December 1963 when the cruise ship *Lakonia* caught fire; 128 deaths resulted, mostly from prolonged immersion in the sea.

Frostbite is the injury caused to body tissue at sub-freezing air temperatures, due to formation of ice crystals within the tissue and to constriction of the blood vessels and impaired circulation. The skin then appears white and, if noticed on an uncovered face, serves as visual warning that treatment is urgently required. Gloved hands and booted feet, however, cannot be seen and may be numb with cold until it is too late to remedy frostbite. Hence, these extremities suffer permanent damage more often than other parts of the body.

Heat stroke is the breakdown in thermal control of excessive body temperature, and can be fatal. Irreversible damage to the body is liable to occur when core temperature rises above 106°F (41°C) though two patients have been known to survive temperatures of more than 110°F (43°C).

In the British Isles, most heat waves cause some deaths, and often these could be avoided if people appreciated the need to drink enough liquid to replace sweat.

In the United States, an average summer results in about 175 deaths from heat stroke. During the heat waves of 1930–36, which created the drought areas of the Dust Bowl, an estimated 15 000 people died from heat stroke, 4768 of these during 1936. The 1980 heat wave caused at least 1265 deaths.

In Saudi Arabia, during 1980, 174 heat stroke cases amongst pilgrims to Mecca were cured by using equipment designed at the London School of Hygiene and Tropical Medicine. Patients whose body temperature needs to be lowered urgently are lain in stainless steel hammocks over which play jets of cold air.

All living species create suitable microenvironments for their embryos to develop, either inside the body, in outer pouches or in eggs laid in suitable situations.

The Mallee fowl, which takes its name from the dwarf mallee eucalyptus tree in south-east Australia, buries its eggs in a sand depression, lined with fermenting leaves, and covered with sand till the mound measures about 12 ft (4 m) across. During incubation the bird shifts about one ton of sand a day in order to keep the egg chamber at a steady 94°F (35°C) assessing the temperature with its beak. It scratches sand *over* the mound in the afternoon in order to minimise heat loss at night, and then takes some *off* again next morning to allow sunshine to penetrate the mound.

Bees fan their wings vigorously at the entrance to a hive in order to create a through draught when the

Young strawberry plants growing under black polythene, which retains heat and prevents evaporation from the soil. (I. Holford)

Some examples of optimum man-made microclimates

	Temperature °F	°C	*Relative humidity* per cent
Living room or office	70–75	21–24	50
Operating theatre	75–80	24–27	50–65
Incubator for unclothed baby, 2 lb (1 kg) birth weight	95	35	50
Respiratory tent for bronchial patients	70	21	100
Tropical plant house	90	32	90
Fruit and vegetable store	40	5	75–80
Florists shop	55	13	50–65
Chrysanthemum growing house	59	15	55
Museums, art galleries	65	18	50–55
Cotton weaving	68–75	20–24	70–80
Paper store	60–80	16–27	35–45
Storage of furs	28–40	−2 to +5	25–40

inside microclimate becomes too hot. Thus they maintain a uniform temperature of about 93°F (34°C) in the brood nests, even when the outside air temperature rises to 120°F (49°C), so long as water is available to air condition the cluster. When outside air temperature falls below 57°F (14°C) the bees stop flying and form a tight cluster to conserve heat.

Plants adapt to their native climate. Much plant tissue is about 90 per cent water, obtained by capillary action, through root fibres and stems, from the soil. If the water supply cannot replenish the amount transpired from the pores on leaves, wilting occurs. Leaves curl to preserve transpired vapour within a tiny favourable microclimate. Indoor plants benefit from being grouped together, so that they trap transpired vapour between them. A bottle garden maintains a continually moist atmosphere for its contents by allowing water vapour to condense on the sides of the glass and run back again into the soil.

Fibrous materials used in manufacture — paper, wood, cotton, leather etc — are critically sensitive to relative humidity. Too much moisture causes them to swell, too little makes them shrink and become brittle. Wood, dried naturally and from which most antique furniture is made, retains about 12 per cent of its weight in moisture content. Modest fluctuations in relative humidity in homes without central heating do not cause damage to furniture. But in heated buildings where the relative humidity is continually very low and no humidifiers supply additional moisture, much damage can be done to furniture, books, paintings and textiles. Wood shrinks by different amounts according to the direction of the grain.

20. Forecasting

Weather lore is the accumulation of rules and rhymes for predicting the weather, often formulated before instruments were invented and before the causes of weather were understood. Many of the dicta are based on false premises and even the best can do little more than predict for a few hours ahead.

Precipitation advice features in many sayings.

Rain before seven
Fine before eleven

is valid in so far as rain belts accompanying depressions usually last about 4 hours. However, there is no significance in the hours of seven and eleven, except that they rhyme, because depressions can arrive at any time of day or night.

Rules incorporating wind direction may have only local validity. All the following refer to the temperature latitudes of the northern hemisphere only. In the southern hemisphere, the cold winds come from the south and the veering wind is the one to beware.

The north wind doth blow
And we shall have snow.

Backing is a bad sign with any wind
A nor'wester is not long in debt to a sou'wester

The following references to the dry winds of the eastern Mediterranean and to those in Britain are interchangeable by coincidence only.

'An east wind shall come up from the wilderness and his spring shall become dry and his fountain shall be dried' *Hosea 13*

When the wind is in the east,
'tis neither good for man nor beast

The Moon is an excellent aid to observation at night because its light and appearance help detect the presence of cloud. *The Moon in haloes hides her head* when seen through ice crystal cloud, so the old weather sages were able to predict rain. Virgil was probably describing the next stage of an advancing front, thin water drop cloud, when he wrote in *The Georgics* on the 'Art of Husbandry'

If she should clasp a dark mist within her unclear crescent
Heavy rain is in store for farmer and fisherman.

A sharply outlined Moon, on the other hand, denotes an absence of cloud cover, heat loss at night, and hence frost. But

full moon, frost soon

would have been more reliable as

clear moon frost soon

because the risk is every bit as great when the moon is new as when it is full. The most reliable rhyme concerning the Moon is

The Moon and the weather
May *change together,*
But a change of the Moon
Does not change the weather.

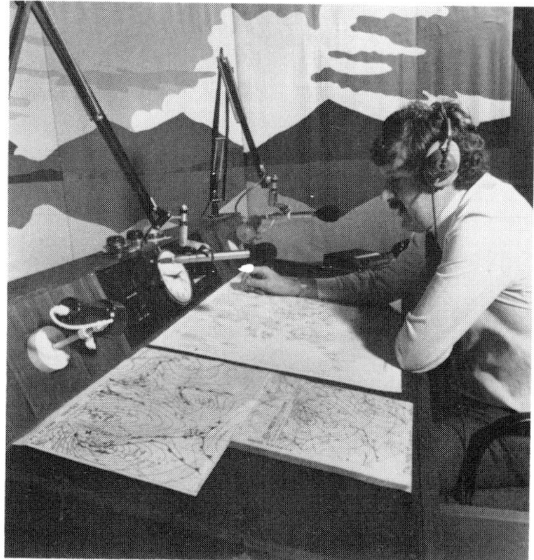

Radio forecast in progress from the London Weather Centre. (Crown Copyright, Meteorological Office)

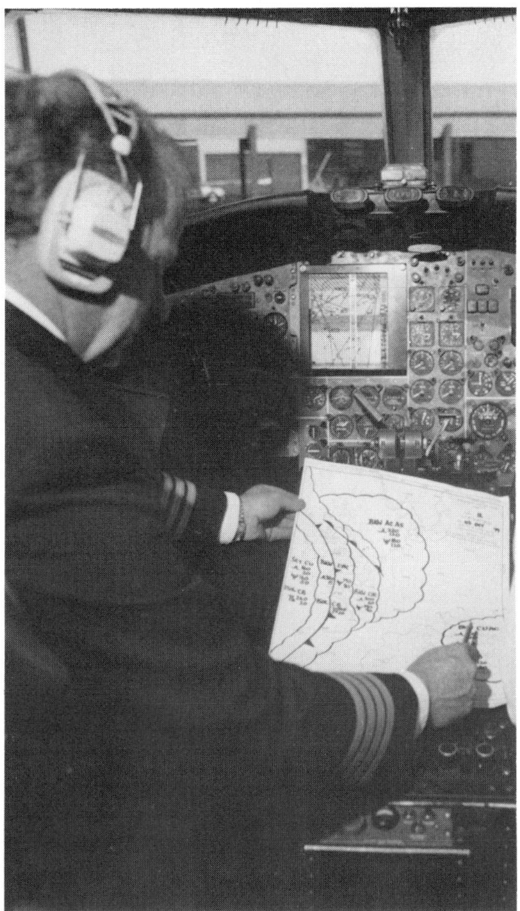

Route forecast, with clouds to be expected, prepared for aircraft pilots. (Crown Copyright, Meteorological Office)

The Moon's phases do affect ocean tides, and if high tide coincides with strong winds the combination can be disastrous; but the Moon does not cause the winds.

Sky colour is often quoted.

Red sky in morning,
shepherds are warning

refers to the unobscured Sun in the east shining on the underside of advancing frontal cloud from the west, in which case rain may be on the way. But red sky can occur with other clouds and it is far more reliable to observe their shapes rather than their colour when lit by the Sun.

Animal behaviour is usually a reaction to current weather conditions, though research may prove that some animals, insects and birds can react in advance to humidity and wind. The human body, too, reacts to current weather conditions. Neuritis pains accompany wind changes and rheumatic joints stiffen in damp weather, but that does not make the body a predictive instrument.

Long range weather lore is mostly useless. The St Swithin's legend of 40 days rain after July 15, if that day should be wet, was based upon one episode only. The story arose in the year AD 971 when the body of Swithin, Bishop of Winchester, was due to be removed to a new resting place within the Cathedral. Since his death in AD 862 he had been buried, at his own request, in the churchyard where the rain might fall from the eaves on to his grave. The rain fell so heavily on 15 July 971 that the re-burial was postponed and when the wet spell continued (perhaps for 40 days) it was taken as a sign that the Saint's last wishes should be respected, and that he be left in the churchyard. Statistical analysis has shown that the continuing superstition does not 'hold water'.

Abundant berries in autumn are often quoted as a portent of a hard winter. There is no evidence, however, that the berry crop is anything more than a reflection of the weather conditions which prevailed during its formative season — it is *hind* casting rather than *fore* casting.

Many remarks about barometric tendency are reasonably sound, if incomplete, advice.

Sharp rise after low
Oft foretells a stronger blow

A greying sky and falling glass
Soundly sleeps the careless ass.

The word 'forecast' was first used by Admiral Fitzroy, Chief Meteorologist to the Board of Trade in Britain in the 1850s. The study of weather had been dignified with the name 'meteorology' (after Aristotle's *Meteorologica*, a discourse on atmospheric phenomena) and it was a sensible corollary to create a new image for the more scientific methods of predicting the weather.

In Britain the first forecasts for the public were issued to the press in July 1861. These were based upon 22 reports received each morning (except Sunday) and ten reports each afternoon from various parts of the country with a further five from the continent. Forecasters had little information from the Atlantic, from which direction most of the weather came, and they had none about the upper air which was as up-to-date as the surface observations. Nevertheless, the early forecasts were the best available and were welcomed by the public. When Fitzroy died in 1865, gale warnings and forecasts for the public were stopped on the recommendation of the Royal Society because they thought that current scientific knowledge was inadequate. The public, however, insisted that inadequate forecasts were better than none and storm warnings to seaports were soon resumed.

Forecasts for the public were resumed in 1876 and relayed by notice board, telephone, telegram and press.

In the United States forecasting services developed along similar lines to those in Britain. The Post Offices Department worked closely with the Weather Bureau to try to improve the dissemination of forecasts. In 1895 a post card service was inaugurated, which proved highly successful for 30 years. The forecast was handstamped on to the back of cards and mailed to subscribers. At its peak 90 000 cards were being sent each day but the number dropped substantially in the 1920s with the expansion of radio and telephone and more local newspapers.

Some post offices also experimented with backstamping all mail with the current weather forecast, but this proved too labour intensive and was soon stopped.

In Britain the first radio forecasts were gale warnings to ships in the eastern North Atlantic, in 1911. Shipping bulletins began in 1919.

The first weather forecast for the London area was included in the evening news bulletin on 14 November 1922, and district forecasts were sent to local radio stations at Birmingham, Manchester, Newcastle, Cardiff and Glasgow. General forecasts replaced district forecasts in 1924.

In 1932, the Automobile Association in conjunction with the Meteorological Office started a service of weather reports from Heston aerodrome and, in July 1935, this was transferred to special studios at Borough Hill, Northampton, under the direction of the Meteorological Office. Continental reports were included from September 1935, reflecting the growth of private flying.

Airmet broadcasts started from Borough Hill, in conjunction with the Meteorological Office at Dunstable, on 7 January 1947. Continuous weather information was broadcast from 7.10 am until 6.10 pm and included reports from 40 aerodromes, forecasts and warnings in continual succession. The service was closed a few years later.

London Volmet is a service for aircraft started by the Civil Aviation Authority in the early 1960s. Statements of weather at selected airports are broadcast at half hourly intervals from four transmitters. Aircraft in flight can receive these observations up to 200 miles (320 km) from a transmitter but the range is only about 50 miles (80 km) when listening from the ground.

Professional meteorologists began live radio forecasting on the national network in 1959, and the practice has spread to local and commercial stations.

The first television weather chart was shown in Britain on 1 November 1936 from Alexandra Palace, but the 1939–45 World War rendered weather information secret, and the public was deprived of all forecasting services.

Forecasts on television were resumed again on 29 June 1949 with weather maps and captions being shown. In 1954, the first live presentations of forecasts were made by professional meteorologists.

Increasing use is being made today of computer-bank methods to present weather data, on demand, on television sets adapted for the purpose.

There were few spectacular developments in weather forecasting until the late 1930s. Analysis techniques were greatly improved when Bjerknes's theories of air masses and fronts were adopted, but there was still too little information available about the upper air. Three-dimensional weather was virtually being forecast on the basis of two-dimensional information. This was all the more frustrating for meteorologists because one man had devised a mathematical method of forecasting.

Lewis Fry Richardson (1881–1953), English physicist and meteorologist, worked out a scheme by which weather could be predicted by differential calculus using reports from 2000 regularly spaced weather stations over sea and land. His *Weather Prediction by Numerical Process* was published in 1922 although he himself admitted that it provided a dream for the future and was not a practical proposition at that time. The calculations would have required an army of 64 000 mathematicians working every hour of the day all the year, and still the weather itself would progress faster than the answers designed to forecast it! Fortunately, Richardson lived long enough to be reasonably sure that his particular 'science fiction' was going to come true.

John von Neumann (1903–57), the Hungarian-American mathematician, had built during the mid 1940s an electronic computer at Princeton University, USA. It was known as MANIAC, short for

Satellite view, from METEOSAT 2, of Europe at 1155 GMT on 17 August 1981. Cloud systems progress but also develop or decay, so that forecasting ahead is not simply a matter of moving the clouds forward according to wind speed. (European Space Agency)

Mathematical Analyser, Numerical Integrator and Computer, and in the first few years during which von Neumann and his team of meteorologists experimented, the computer often lived up to its mad name.

After 10 years, however, they were able to use the formulae governing the physical processes of the atmosphere in such a way as to get acceptable forecasts of pressure patterns from the computer. These early efforts improved steadily, and as soon as they proved to be consistently better than prognostic charts made by forecasters, the task was left entirely to the computer.

The present state of the atmosphere is a necessary starting point for computer calculations for forecasts up to about a fortnight ahead. Five thousand observing stations, mainly on land, report regularly from all over the world to data collecting centres; 1000 stations make regular soundings of the upper atmosphere with radio sonde. Satellites orbit with sophisticated instruments to determine temperature and humidity in the vertical atmosphere and to monitor cloud systems on both visible and infra-red wave-lengths. Commercial shipping and aviation add their contributions and the assembled data are transmitted to central weather offices by a communications system dedicated solely to that purpose. And yet it is still not enough. There are vast unobserved spaces, and what information is available is clustered unevenly over the populated areas of the world. The computer requires a regularly spaced diet of information on which to base its calculations.

Pseudo weather data can be compiled from the discontinuous real data, by using formulae which acknowledge the interdependence of various weather factors and geographical features. Temperature, wind and humidity can be calculated for evenly spaced intervals, so that instead of a real, discontinuous and incomplete picture of the present atmosphere, one gets a pseudo, regular *model* of the atmosphere, though still incomplete.

A model atmosphere for the computer is created for several horizontal levels, each divided into square grids. The complexity of the model depends upon the capacity of the computer, which must be able to do its arithmetic in short enough time to be of practical use to forecasters.

At the UK Meteorological Office in Bracknell, an IBM 360 computer has worked, since 1972, on a model with ten horizontal levels of the atmosphere, each divided into grids of 186 miles (300 km) square, for the hemisphere north of 17°N. A finer mesh 'window' with a grid length 62 miles (100 km) covers north-west Europe, Greenland and the North Atlantic as far as Canada. The computer is programmed to advance data, step by step, according to thermodynamic equations until it arrives at the required forecast time. It can project 36 hours ahead for the fine mesh area in a matter of 12 minutes, but a prognosis for 6 days takes only 3 minutes longer.

In August 1981, a new CYBER 205 computer was installed which is about ten times faster than the older IBM, and can carry out 400 million operations

Cloud systems over the Atlantic and Europe, after satellite information has been processed for the computer. Such information can then be projected ahead by mathematical formulae, to give reasonably accurate results for up to 7 days ahead. (European Centre for Medium Range Weather Forecasts, Shinfield, Berks.)

per second. This will be used not only for operational forecasting for up to 5 days ahead, but also for more complicated research into climatological forecasts — up to 3 years ahead. The new computer will be able to calculate for more levels and for both hemispheres, as well as include more types of information.

At the European Centre for Medium Range Weather Forecasts at Shinfield, Berkshire, a CRAY 1 computer forecasts data for 10 days ahead, for dissemination to the 17 European states which established the Centre. That computer works a 15 level model with a grid length of 108 miles (175 km) covering both hemispheres. The computer can deal with 50 million instructions per second and produces 10-day forecasts for various weather parameters in 8 hours from the start of its 15-minute step calculations.

The accuracy of computer forecasts depends upon the reliability of the material fed in and the quality of the formulae projecting it. Meteorologists are continually striving to improve the models, but even the real data which arrive on the international communications system are sometimes wrong. Perhaps someone's finger slipped on the teleprinter keyboard, or an instrument is not working properly. Every slight error in initial data multiplies with every step it is projected ahead. Computer programmes sort out the obviously incorrect values, which are then altered or rejected before being used in the computer.

Computer forecasts sometimes have a bias towards certain types of weather — fronts may be advanced too quickly or temperature may be underestimated. Sometimes a meteorologist can introduce an extra observation in order to counteract such bias but it needs considerable human skill to judge whether or not to interfere with the computer processes.

A computer produces forecasts in numerical form, which cannot be assimilated by the human brain. However, the figures can be processed into charts or diagrams for easy study and for transmission direct to outstations by facsimile machine. It is from these prognostic charts, upper air graphs and computer drawn current weather charts, that the meteorologist prepares his forecasts. There are no mathematically correct answers to what weather will develop and the clues are continually changing.

A forecaster's task is like that of a detective:

☐ First he locates centres of high or low pressure on the current weather map.

☐ Next, he draws the fronts which are detectable by

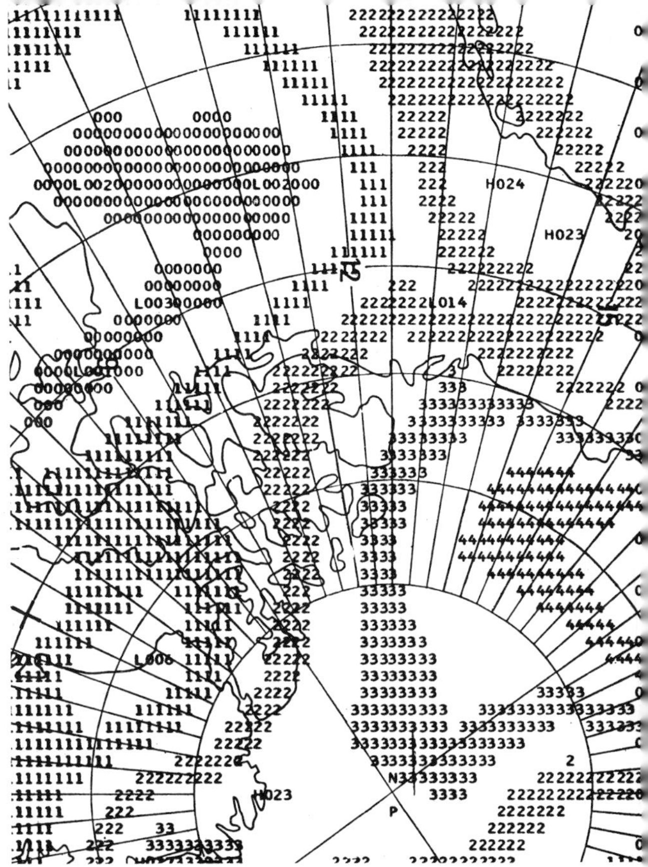

Machines can 'draw' isobars by alternating use of digits and no-digits for ranges of pressure. On this sample chart 1 = 1008–1012 mb, 2 = 1016–1020 mb etc. The intervening blank spaces represent 1012–1016 mb, 1020–1040 mb etc.

pressure tendencies over the past 3 hours, wind direction changes, dewpoint variations, sky type, precipitation etc. Active fronts are often easy to position, but those which have been in existence for some time may be diffuse and slow moving. Some die out while others are rejuvenated around secondary depressions. The satellite pictures are scrutinised and the present weather chart compared with the prognostic chart for the next 24–72 hours.

☐ Isobars are drawn on the chart, determining wind speed and direction at 2000 ft above the ground. Wind at higher levels is checked from upper air ascents, satellite observation and contour maps for the 500 and 200 mb levels of the atmosphere. Again the forecaster checks with the forecast charts, to see how they align with reality.

☐ Upper air ascents are scrutinised to detect the advance of warm air ahead of a front or the existence of inversions of temperature which might inhibit cloud development or the clearance of fog. If convection clouds are possible the height of their tops can be gauged with considerable accuracy from these temperature profiles. However, their location is random within the showery area and cannot be pin-pointed in advance.

☐ When clear skies and light winds are expected at night there are a variety of formulae for assessing minimum temperatures and the risk of fog or frost. By adapting a particular formula for local topography or nearness to the sea, quite accurate forecasts can be made.

Forecasts for the public are issued at regular intervals of the day via all the media. Many newspapers publish isobaric charts, necessarily slightly out of date because of the time lag due to printing, but nevertheless extremely helpful to anyone who scans them with a practised eye. Detailed 5-minute shipping bulletins, from which local up-to-date isobaric charts can be quickly constructed, are broadcast four times daily in Britain. Radio broadcasts are interrupted with warnings of gales or weather hazardous to motoring; and during the summer particularly, local stations give generous time to weather information for yachtsmen. In addition, general forecasts for local areas are tape recorded and available by telephone.

Specialised forecasts are now issued for all manner of public interests. Frost, snow and fog warnings go to motoring organisations, forecasts of rainy or wet spells concern farmers, and even pigeon racing enthusiasts can get wind forecasts tailored for their requirements. Personal briefings about the weather are given to all aircraft navigators and many commercial ships avail themselves of a ship routeing service. In Britain, a team of Master Mariners works closely with forecasters at the Central Forecasting Office at Bracknell to route ships according to their performance characteristics and the weather which they may encounter. The shortest distance does not necessarily mean the shortest journey time.

Broad outlines of weather type — wet or dry, warm or cold, windy or calm — for 10 days or a fortnight ahead are much appreciated by industry and commerce. They enable manufacturers to plan their switch from one seasonal product to another and give power stations advance warning of possible surges in demand.

Long-term forecasts, for several months or even years ahead, are not yet attainable by proven scientific methods. Nevertheless, because they are so much desired every year sees a crop of 'infallible' predictions for the coming seasons. Most have only a 50/50 chance of being right.

The efficiency of any forecasting system depends ultimately on the ability of the recipient to understand the information given. Time is always the scarce commodity, and a forecaster cannot supply every locality with the tiny details which make weather slightly different from one place to another. The only viable alternative is for everyone to add such detail himself, just as has always been done by farmers and sailors. This has earned them the enviable reputation of forecasting 'better than the professionals', but the skill is no more difficult to achieve by anyone else. Machines may continue to provide increasing information but nothing is ever likely to replace the eyes and logical reasoning of human beings.

BIBLIOGRAPHY

The following books or articles refer to topics mentioned briefly in the various chapters of this book. The subject is added in parentheses wherever it is not obvious from the title.

Journal of Meteorology, Cockhill House, Trowbridge, BA 14 9 BG

Weather, Journal of the Royal Meteorological Society, James Glaisher House, Grenville Place, Bracknell, Berks. RG 12 1 BX

Weatherwise, Heldref Publications, 4000 Albemarle St., NW, Washington DC 20016

Chapter One

Blackwell, M. J., The bicentenary of Kew Observatory. *Weather* June 1969

Hatch, D. J., Sunshine at Kew Observatory 1881–1980. *Journal of Meteorology* Apr. 1981

Chapter Two

Knowles Middleton, W. E., Invention of thermometers. Johns Hopkins, Baltimore

Landsberg, H. E., A note on the history of thermometer scales. *Weather* Jan. 1964

Negretti and Zambra, A story of temperature measurement.

Chapter Three

Booth, R. E., Winter of 1963. *Weather* Nov. 1968

Brinkman, W. A. R., What is a foehn? *Weather* June 1971

Diaz, H. F., Extreme temperature anomalies, March 1843 and Feb. 1936. *Monthly Weather Review*, USA

Diaz, H. F., and Quayle, R. G., Three extraordinary winters. *Weatherwise* Feb. 1980

Douglas, K. S., Lamb, H. H., Loader, C., The Spanish Armada storms July–October 1588. University of East Anglia

Lamb, H. H., The English Climate. English Universities Press

Lawrence, E. N., The earliest known journal of the weather (W. Merle). *Weather* Dec. 1972

Manley, G., The coldest winter in the English instrumental record, 1684. *Weather* Dec. 1975

Meaden, G. T., Britain's extreme temperatures by month of the year. *Journal of Meteorology* Oct. 1975 and Dec. 1975

Phillips, D. W. and Aston, D., A record cold month in North America (Eureka). *Weatherwise* Feb. 1980

Virgo, S. E., Hazards of the Föhn wind in Switzerland. *Weather* Sept. 1966

Chapter Four

Glaisher, R., Travels in the air

Fotheringham, R. R., The Earth's atmosphere viewed from space. University of Dundee

Paton, J., Ben Nevis Observatory 1883–1904. *Weather* Sept. 1954

Pettifer, R. E. W., Introduction to the UK mark 3 radiosonde system. *Weather* Mar. 1979

Smith, A. A., The Mount Washington Observatory. *Weather* Dec. 1964

Chapter Five

Förchgott, J., Evidence for mountain-sized lee eddies. *Weather* July 1969

D'Allenger, P., Parachuting and the weather. *Weather* May 1970

King-Hele, D., Erasmus Darwin, grandfather of meteorology? *Weather* June 1973

Loewe, F., Land of storms (Antarctica). *Weather* Mar. 1972

Neumark, O. U., The flight of Daedalus. *Weather* May 1966

Wallington, C. E., Forecasting for gliding. *Weather* June 1968

Chapter Six

Bader, M., Douglas, H. A. and Kerley, M. J., The UK National Data Buoy. *Weather* Sept. 1978

Kington, J. A., The Societas Meteorologica Palatina. *Weather* Nov. 1974

Ratcliffe, R. A. S., The story of the Royal Meteorological Society. *Weather* July 1978

Sutton, Sir G., Admiral Fitzroy and the storm glass. *Weather* Sept. 1965

Chapter Seven

Aanensen, C. J. M., Gales in Yorkshire Feb. 16, 1962. *Geophysical Memoir, UK Met. Office* 108

Booth, B. J., The Royal Charter storm. *Weather* Dec. 1970

de Angelis, Hurricanes David and Frederic. *Weatherwise* Oct. 1979

Defoe, D., The Great Storm 1703.

Fitzroy, R., The Weather Book (Royal Charter Storm).

Hamilton, M. G., Indian cyclones of November 1977. *Journal of Meteorology* Jan. 1978

Hughes, P., The Great Galvestone hurricane. *Weatherwise* Aug. 1979

Shellard, H. C., Collapse of cooling towers in a gale at Ferrybridge. *Weather* June 1967

Shields, A. J. and Gourlay, R. G., Queensland meteorologist the first to name cyclones. *Science News* May 1975 (Australia)

Chapter Eight

Alcock, R. K. and Morgan, D. G., Investigation of wind and sea state with respect to the Beaufort Scale. *Weather* July 1978

George, K. J. and Thomas, D. K., The Morning Cloud storm surge in the English Channel. *Weather* June 1978

Grieve, H., The Great Tide (definitive history of 1953 storm). *Essex Record*, 1959

Chapter Nine

Andrews, W., Famous frosts and frost fairs.

Houghton, D., Acapulco 65. *Weather* Jan. 1969

Knowles Middleton, W. E., Invention of meteorological instruments. Johns Hopkins, Baltimore

National Science Foundation, Washington, Survival in Antarctica.

Chapter Ten

Benson, C. A., Ice fog. *Weather* Jan. 1970

Dubois, E., Fog dispersal on runway approaches. *Weather* Oct 1965

Kunkel, B. A., Controlling fog. *Weatherwise* June 1980

Ohtake, T. and Jayaweera, K., Ice crystal displays from power plants (Fairbanks, Alaska). *Weather* July 1972

Chapter Eleven

Blench, B., Luke Howard and his contribution to meteorology. *Weather* March 1963

Fogle, B., Noctilucent clouds in the southern hemisphere. *Weather* Dec. 1965

George, D. J., Mother of pearl clouds in Antarctica. *Weather* Jan. 1971

McIntosh, D. H., Mother of pearl clouds over Scotland. *Weather* Jan. 1972

Smith, R. K. and Goodfield, J., The 1979 Morning Glory expedition. *Weather* May 1981

Walker, J. M., After Bjerknes (convergence cloud). *Weather* Apr. 1970

Chapter Twelve

Brooks and Douglas, Glazed frost of January 1940. *Geophysical Memoir, UK Met. Office* 98

Folland, C. K. and Wales-Smith, B. G., Richard Townley and 300 years of regular rainfall measurement. *Weather* Dec. 1977

Jackson, M. C., Largest two-hour falls of rain in the British Isles. *Weather* Feb. 1974

Jackson, M. C., The largest fall of rain possible in a few hours in Great Britain. *Weather* May 1979

Kessler, E., On the artificial increase of precipitation (cloud seeding). *Weather* May 1973

Moody, P. J., The Yorkshire Television storm; instantaneous rainfall measured by amateur observers. *Weather* Nov. 1980

Pedgley, D. E., Cyclones along the Arabian coast. *Weather* Nov. 1969

Chapter Thirteen

Bell, W. G., The Great Fire of London.

Delderfield, E. R., The Lynmouth Flood Disaster. E.R.D. Publications Exmouth

Fisher, S. H., Weather in history (Drought in Egypt). *Journal of Meteorology* Sept. 1976

Foggitt, W., Extracts from a North Yorkshire weather diary (Solway Moss flood). *Weather* Dec. 1971

Keers, J. F. and Wescott, P., The Hampstead storms 14 Aug. 1975. *Weather* Jan. 1976

Lansford, H., Tree rings; predictors of drought? *Weather* Oct. 1979

Meaden, G. T., Late summer weather in Kent 55 BC. *Weather* Aug. 1976

Schove, D. J., Fire and drought 1600–1700. *Weather* Sept. 1966

Chapter Fourteen

Carter, C., The Blizzard of 91. David and Charles, Newton Abbot

Fraser, C., The Avalanche Enigma. Murray, London

Jackson, M. C., A classification of snowiness in 100 winters. *Weather* Mar. 1977

Manley, G., Snowfall in Britain over the past 300 years. *Weather* Nov. 1969

Manley, G., Mountain snow of Britain. *Weather* May 1971

Schaeffer, V. J., The preparation of snow crystal replicas. *Weatherwise* June 1980

Walker, J. M., Utilisation of icebergs; conference report. *Weather* Nov. 1980

Chapter Fifteen

Gourlay, R. J., Clement Wragge and the Stiger. *Weather* Dec. 1973

Long, I. F., Fossil hail prints. *Weather* Apr. 1963

Meaden, G. T., The giant ice meteor mystery. *Journal of Meteorology* Mar. 1977

Mossop, S. C., Some hailstones of unusual shape. *Weather* May 1971

Chapter Sixteen

Meaden, G. T., Four storm stories from Steeple Ashton. *Weather* Dec. 1973

Pounder, C., Volcanic lightning. *Weather* Dec. 1980

Stow, C. D., The voyage of the Beagle, meteorological notes and curiosities. *Weather* Sept. 1978

Chapter Seventeen

Golden, J. H., Waterspouts at Lower Matecumbe Key, Florida 2 September. 1967. *Weather* Mar. 1968

Lane, F., The Elements Rage. Sphere Books, London

Meaden, G. T., Meteorological explanation for mysterious sightings on Loch Ness and other lakes. *Journal of Meteorology* Jan. 1976

Meaden, G. T., Tornadoes in Britain; intensities and distribution. *Journal of Meteorology* May 1976

Meaden, G. T., Tornado on a wild goose chase. *Journal of Meteorology* Oct. 1978 and Mar. 1979

Meaden, G. T., Tornadoes at Scarborough AD 1975 and AD 1165. *Weather* Sept. 1975

McGinnigle, J. B., Dust whirls in north west Libya. *Weather* Aug. 1966

Ray, P. S., Brown, R. A. and Ziegler, C. L., Doppler radar (storm detection). *Weatherwise* Apr. 1979

Radford, J. A., Formation of the Wisley tornado. *Weather* June 1966

Peterson, R. E., Minor, J. E., Golden, J. H. and Scott, A., An Australian tornado (Northam). *Weatherwise* Oct. 1979

Staff members National Severe Storm Forecast Center, US. Tornadoes — when, where and how often. *Weatherwise* Apr. 1980

Stevens, L. P., Waterspouts in the English Channel (1974). *Weather* Mar. 1976

Chapter Eighteen

Catchpole, A. and Moodie, D., Multiple reflections in Antarctica. *Weather* Apr. 1971

Evans, W. and Tricker, R., Unusual arcs in the Saskatoon halo display. *Weather* June 1972
Floor, C., The Omega shape of the low sun. *Weather* Mar. 1981
Goldie, E. and Heighes J., The Berkshire halo display 11 May 1965. *Weather* Feb. 1968
Ives, R., The mirages of La Encantada. *Weather* Feb. 1968
Slingo, A., Fogbows and glories. *Weather* Aug. 1981

Chapter Nineteen
Bainbridge, J. W., Stocking Northumbrian ice houses. *Weather* Feb. 1973
Beazley, E. and Harverson M., Living with the desert (ice houses). Aris and Phillips Ltd, Warminster.
Millington, R. A., Physiological responses to cold. *Weather* Nov. 1964
Quayle, R. and Doehring, F., Heat stress. *Weatherwise* June 1981
Turner, A. E., Discomfort in Bahrain. *Weather* Sept. 1978

Chapter Twenty
Hughes, P., American weather services. *Weatherwise* June 1980
Kawamoto, T. M., Via US Mail — early weather forecasts. *Weatherwise* June 1981
McAllen, P. F., A brief history of weather forecasting (UK). *Weather* Nov. 1979
Meads, D., A simple method of frost forecasting for growers. *Weather* Nov. 1963

WEATHER EXTREMES

SUNSHINE
1 **Highest percentage of possible Sahara**

TEMPERATURE
2 **Hottest** (mean annual) **Dallol**
3 **Highest** (maximum) **Al Aziziyah**
4 **Coldest** (mean annual and lowest minima) **Vostok**

WIND
5 **Windiest** (annual mean) **Eastern Adelie Land**
6 **Highest gust and twenty-four hour mean Mt Washington**

WAVE
7 **Highest recorded North Atlantic**

PRESSURE
8 **Highest Agata**
9 **Lowest West Pacific**

FOG
10 **Most persistent sea fog Grand Banks**
11 **Worst photochemical Los Angeles**

RAIN
12 **Wettest** (annual mean and most rainy days) **Mt Wai-ale-ale**
Highest point rainfalls
13 Fifteen-days—two year period **Cherrapungi**
14 Nine hours—eight days period **La Reunion**
15 Twenty minute period **Curtea-de-Arges**
16 Fifteen minute period **Plumb Point**
17 Eight minute period **Fussen**
18 One minute period **Unionville**
19 **Longest absolute drought Calama**

SNOW
20 **Highest annual total Paradise Ranger Station**
21 **Greatest five day fall Thomson Pass**
22 **Greatest one day fall Silver Lake**

HAIL
23 **Heaviest stone Coffeyville**

THUNDER
24 **Most thunder days Bogor**

TORNADOES
25 **Most frequent Central plains**

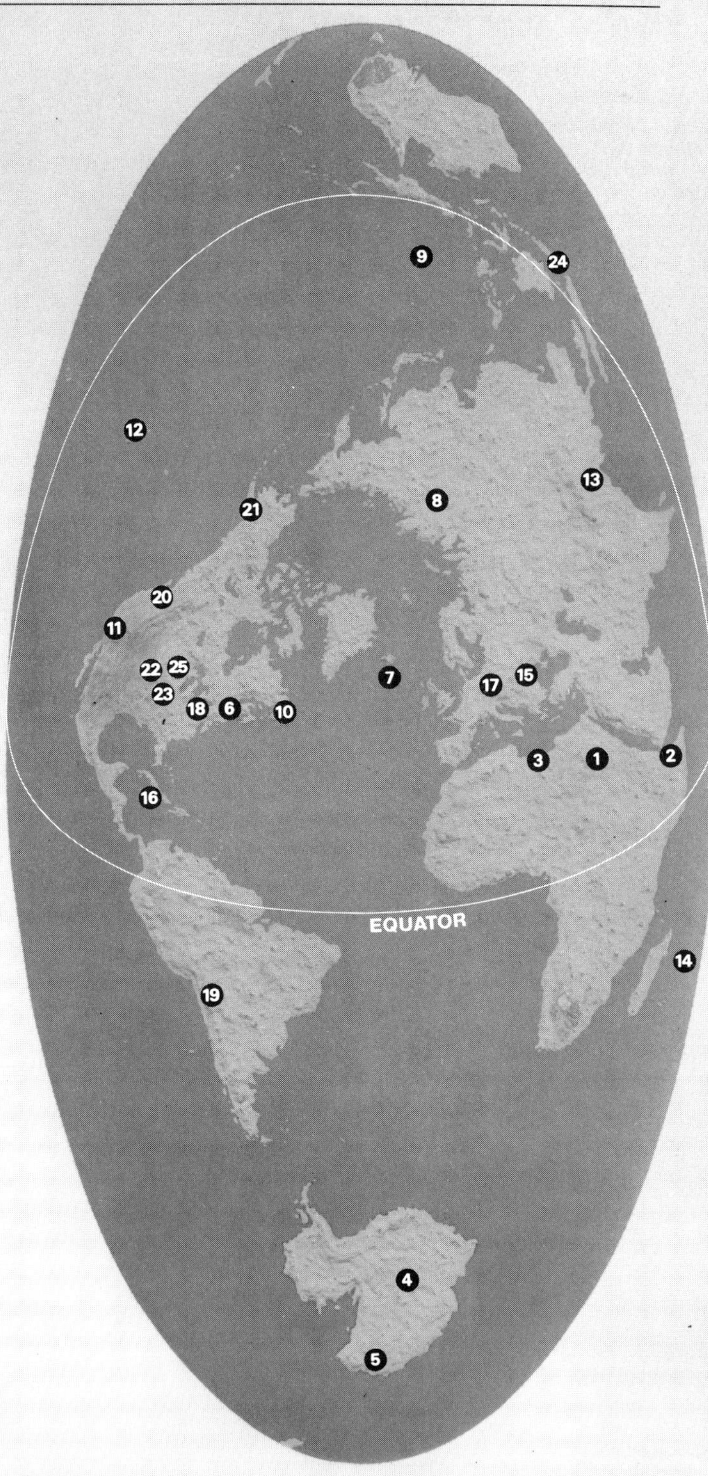

INDEX

Page numbers in italics refer to black and white illustrations.
Bold numbers refer to colour pictures on pages 145–160.